Writing

INSIDE

LANGUAGE · LITERACY · CONTENT

PROGRAM AUTHOR

Gretchen Bernabei

Acknowledgments

Grateful acknowledgment is given to the authors, artists, photographers, museums, publishers, and agents for permission to reprint copyrighted material. Every effort has been made to secure the appropriate permission. If any omissions have been made or if corrections are required, please contact the Publisher.

Photographic Credits

Cover (front): Squirrel Treefrog in Hibiscus Flower, JH Pete Carmichael. Photograph © JH Pete Carmichael/Riser/Getty Images. **Cover (back):** Hibiscus Flower, Bali, Indonesia, Loeiza Jacq. Photograph © Loeiza Jacq/Gamma-Rapho via Getty Images.

Acknowledgments continue on page 538W.

For product information and technology assistance, contact us at **Cengage Learning Customer & Sales Support, 888-915-3276**

For permission to use material from this text or product, submit all requests online at **www.cengage.com/permissions** Further permissions questions can be emailed to **permissionrequest@cengage.com**

National Geographic Learning | Cengage Learning
1 Lower Ragsdale Drive
Building 1, Suite 200
Monterey, CA 93940

Cengage Learning is a leading provider of customized learning solutions with office locations around the globe, including Singapore, the United Kingdom, Australia, Mexico, Brazil, and Japan. Locate your local office at **www.cengage.com/global**.

Visit National Geographic Learning online at **ngl.cengage.com**
Visit our corporate website at **www.cengage.com**

Printer:Quad/Graphics, Versailles, KY

ISBN: 978-12854-37163

Printed in the United States of America
18 19 20 21 22
10 9 8 7 6 5 4

Contents

THE
Building
Blocks
OF WRITING

Project 1 Paragraph Structure:
Ways to Organize ▪ INFORMATIVE/EXPLANATORY

THE Writing Process

Project 2 Use the Writing Process · NARRATIVE

At Each Stage of the Writing Process—

THE Many Writers
YOU ARE

Project 3 Write to Summarize · INFORMATIVE/EXPLANATORY

Chapter 3, continued

Chapter 3, continued

Chapter 3, continued

THE
Building
Blocks
OF WRITING

Paragraph Structure:
Ways to Organize

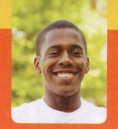

Model Study

Sentences and Paragraphs

One great way to express your ideas is through writing. When you write, your reader can understand your ideas more easily if they are presented clearly and in an organized way.

Start with Sentences

You start with writing a group of words that relate a complete thought. There are four types of sentences:

Type of Sentence	Example
A **statement** tells something.	I grew up in Tallahassee, Florida.
A **question** asks something.	What elementary school did you go to?
An **exclamation** shows strong emotion.	That's a really cool name!
A **command** tells you to do something.	Tell Mom I'm staying over at Gary's house tonight. Look at that car!

Build to Paragraphs

When you write, you put sentences together in an organized way to create **paragraphs**. Make sure that each paragraph has a clear **main idea** stated in a **topic sentence**. The other details in the paragraph should support the main idea with **details** and **examples**.

The Move

by Jim Kozlowski

This is the **topic sentence.** It tells the main idea of the paragraph.

Sometimes moving to a new neighborhood can be difficult, but it is a good way to meet new people and see new places. For example, I met my best friend when my family moved two years ago. At first, I didn't think I would be happy leaving my old school. However, I ended up liking my new school even better.

This **detail** supports the main idea.

An **example** clarifies the main idea.

Student Model

PARAGRAPH

A good paragraph

✓ has a topic sentence that states the main idea

✓ contains details that tell more about the main idea.

Feature Checklist

Organize Your Paragraphs

 **What's It Like** ?

What do you think of when someone talks to you about his or her "best friend"? You may not know all of the details of the friendship, but you have a good sense of what to expect. A topic sentence works that way, too. It doesn't give away all of the details, but it tells the reader what to expect.

Getting to a Topic Sentence

First, you need to decide what to write about. That will be your **topic**. Then think about what you want to say in general about your topic—that will be your **main idea**. Next, follow these steps to get to a topic sentence:

- Write as many details as you can that support your main idea.

- Look to see how the details are related to each other and to the main idea.

- Write a full statement that expresses your main idea as it relates to the details you plan to cover in your paragraph.

Here's how one student got to her topic sentence.

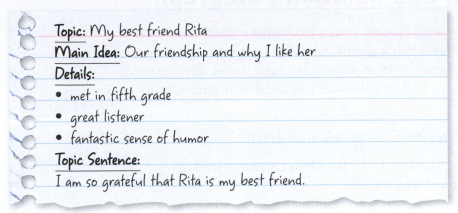

Topic: My best friend Rita

Main Idea: Our friendship and why I like her

Details:
- met in fifth grade
- great listener
- fantastic sense of humor

Topic Sentence:
I am so grateful that Rita is my best friend.

Paragraph Organization

Your topic sentence and supporting details will determine how your paragraph is organized. Below are four common types of paragraph organization. We'll go through each type in more detail on pages 6W–13W.

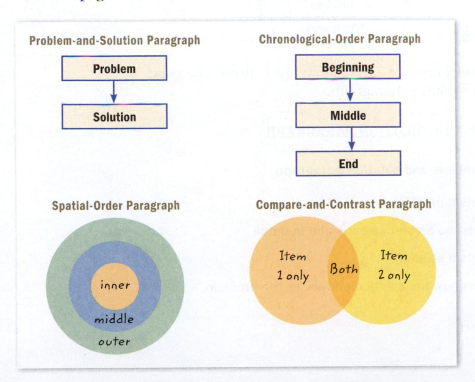

Problem-and-Solution Paragraph

Problem → Solution

Chronological-Order Paragraph

Beginning → Middle → End

Spatial-Order Paragraph

inner
middle
outer

Compare-and-Contrast Paragraph

Item 1 only | Both | Item 2 only

Problem-and-Solution Paragraph

Everyone comes up against tough problems sometimes. People face problems and think about solutions every day. How do you solve problems in your day-to-day life? If you want to write about a problem and its solution, you need to organize your ideas clearly:

- Begin by describing the problem in detail.

- Explain how you think the problem can be solved, or describe how it was solved.

Before you start writing, you can use a problem-and-solution chart to help organize your thoughts.

Problem-and-Solution Chart

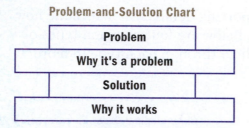

| Problem |
| Why it's a problem |
| Solution |
| Why it works |

Read the model on page 7W. It shows the features of a good problem-and-solution paragraph.

PROBLEM-AND-SOLUTION PARAGRAPH

A good problem-and-solution paragraph

☑ presents a problem

☑ explains the problem clearly and in detail

☑ presents a solution

☑ explains how the solution addresses the problem.

Feature Checklist

The Surprise Party

by Serena Jones

The writer describes the **problem** Belinda encountered.

Belinda decided to throw a surprise birthday party for her friend Alicia. After she had already sent the invitations, she discovered that Alicia's family was leaving town to visit relatives that same weekend. Belinda used her phone and e-mail to contact everyone on her list. Luckily, she was able to change the party date to the following weekend.

Then, the writer shows the **solution** Belinda found.

Student Model

Problem
Alicia's family is going out of town.

Why it's a problem
Belinda has already sent out invitations for a suprise birthday party.

Solution
Belinda contacts everyone by phone and e-mail.

Why it works
She is able to change the party for the following weekend.

Chronological-Order Paragraph

You often tell about things that happen to you. When you retell events, you usually tell them in the order they happened. If you mix present and past events, your listener will have a hard time following what you are saying.

When you want to write about a series of events, retell the events in the sequence in which they occurred. This sequence is called **chronological order.** Start with what happened first, and lead the reader to the final event. When you write events in chronological order, use words such as *first, then, after,* and *finally.*

Read the student model on page 9W. It shows the features of a good chronological-order paragraph.

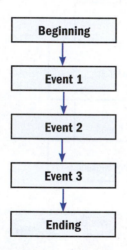

CHRONOLOGICAL-ORDER PARAGRAPH

A good chronological-order paragraph

✓ tells events in the order they happened

✓ uses words like *first, next, then, after,* and *finally* to show the sequence of events.

Feature Checklist

Cooking with Katrina

by Priya Mehtani

These two events are in **chronological order**.

Once a month, my best friend Katrina and I use the Internet to find a recipe we've never tried before, and then we walk to the grocery store to buy the ingredients. After we purchase what we need, we go home and start on our new creation. Then we read the recipe's directions carefully. Next, we decide how to divide the labor so the process goes smoothly. Finally, we get to work, measuring and pouring and slicing and dicing. Soon we have an interesting new dish to try.

Signal words help the reader understand when something happened.

Student Model

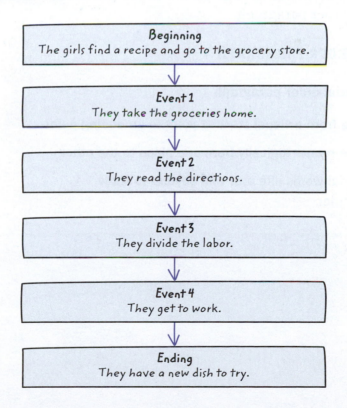

Beginning
The girls find a recipe and go to the grocery store.

Event 1
They take the groceries home.

Event 2
They read the directions.

Event 3
They divide the labor.

Event 4
They get to work.

Ending
They have a new dish to try.

Spatial-Order Paragraph

How would you describe the way someone was dressed on a special occasion? You might start by describing the person's hairstyle or hat. Then you'd move down, describing each item of clothing until you got to the person's shoes. To do this a different way, you could start with the shoes and then move up.

When you write to describe something you see, choose a starting point and then move in a clear direction. Use **spatial order** to describe something so your reader can picture what it's like. Proceed from inside to outside, left to right, or top to bottom.

You might want to begin by drawing and labeling a picture. This will help you organize the details of your description.

Read the student model on page 11W. It shows the features of a good spatial-order paragraph.

SPATIAL-ORDER PARAGRAPH

A good spatial-order paragraph

✓ proceeds from a visual starting point to an ending point

✓ takes the reader logically from one place to the other

✓ uses signal words like *over* and *beyond* to show spatial order.

Feature Checklist

My Neighborhood

by José Torres

The writer describes his neighborhood from the nearest area to the farthest area.

As you approach the main street of my neighborhood, the first thing you see is the cars—lots of them, lining the wide street. Light poles on the other side of the street tower over the trees. There are houses and shops all along the busy street. Farther back, in the distance, you can see the bay, with sailboats cruising in the breeze. Beyond the bay are high, grassy hills.

Student Model

Hills

Houses

Light Poles

Trees

Cars

Compare-and-Contrast Paragraph

When you want to bring attention to the similarities or differences between two things, you write a paragraph that compares and contrasts.

When you **compare,** you write about how two things are similar. When you **contrast,** you write to show how two things are different.

You can use a **Venn diagram** to show the similarities and differences between two things. A Venn diagram uses overlapping circles to organize these details.

How they are alike

Old Neighborhood
lively and noisy

houses close together

people call out to each other

Both
people are friendly

made some good friends

New Neighborhood
quiet, a little dull

houses farther apart

people don't talk as much

How they are different

Read the student model on page 13W. It shows the features of a good compare-and-contrast paragraph.

COMPARE-AND-CONTRAST PARAGRAPH

A good compare-and-contrast paragraph

☑ names the items being compared

☑ describes ways the items are similar

☑ describes ways the items are different

☑ includes signal words like *both, same, different,* and *however* to show similarities and differences.

Feature Checklist

A New Place

by Cassie Edwards

The writer **names the things** being compared.

The writer tells how the neighborhoods are different.

The writer tells what the neighborhoods have in common.

My new neighborhood is very different from my old neighborhood in some ways, but also similar. My old neighborhood was always lively and noisy, while my new neighborhood is quiet and a little dull. In my old neighborhood, the houses are close together, and people call out to each other whenever they're working outside. Here, however, the houses are farther apart, and people don't talk to each other. People in both places are friendly, though. I've made some good friends here, just as I did in my old neighborhood.

These **signal words** cue the contrasts.

These **signal words** cue the similarities.

Student Model

Write a Paragraph

WRITING PROMPT   There are more things to write about than there are people in the world! Now that you have learned about different ways of organizing paragraphs, pick a topic related to your life and write a paragraph. You can choose any of the four structures you have learned about.

Be sure you include

- a topic sentence
- a clear text structure
- interesting details that support your topic sentence.

Plan and Write

Here are some ideas for how you can plan and then get started on your writing.

1 Choose a Topic

Decide what to write about. You can't tell everything about your favorite animal in one paragraph, so what is it that you want readers to understand? This will be your main idea.

My Life
—grew up in Austin, Texas
—love playing the piano
—have lots of great friends

2 Get Some Details Down on Paper

After you choose your topic and decide what you want to say about it, list some details and examples that support your main idea.

—started taking lessons
  when I was five
—had my first solo recital
  when I was nine
—want to go to music school
  when I'm older

3 Choose an Organization and Write a Topic Sentence

Think about how your details relate to one another and to the main idea. Your main idea and details will usually suggest a specific organization. Write a topic sentence that expresses your main idea fully and reflects your organization.

Topic Sentence for Chronological-Order Paragraph

> Playing the piano has always been an important part of my life.

4

Turn each detail on your list into a supporting sentence to flesh out your paragraph. Each sentence should explain the main idea or give an example of it. A graphic organizer might help you arrange the sentences effectively.

> Playing the piano has always been an important part of my life. I was only five years old when I started taking lessons from old Mr. Aiello down the block.

started lessons at five

↓

first solo recital at nine

↓

plan to go to music school

Reflect

- Is your main idea clear in your topic sentence?

- Are all of your details connected?

THE Writing Process

Writing Strategy

The Writing Process

Learning to write well is like learning to play the guitar. It takes a lot of time and practice to become really good at it. And there's a process. You figure out the basics first—what you'll write about and how you'll organize it. Then you put your ideas together in a creative way and fine-tune them until they sing.

What Are the Steps of the Writing Process?

Writers follow a process to make their writing the best it can be. The writing process usually involves five stages—**prewriting, drafting, revising, editing and proofreading,** and **publishing**.

1 Prewrite—Get Ready to Write

Prewriting is what you do before you write. You choose a topic, think about what to say, and develop a plan. What is the plan that works best for you? You can write notes, make an outline, or even sketch drawings.

2 Draft—Get It Down on Paper

Drafting is the next step. Writing down that first draft is sometimes the hardest part. But it can also be the most exciting. Remember, your first draft doesn't have to be perfect. You can make changes later, so relax and enjoy the work.

3 Revise—Get It to Sing

After you finish your draft, put it aside for a while. Then you can come back to it with fresh eyes. You might end up making major changes! You might move sentences around or add new ideas.

4 **Edit and Proofread—Get It Right**

Once you've made the big changes, work on getting the details right. This is when you correct your sentences and fix any mistakes in grammar, spelling, or punctuation.

5 **Publish, Share, and Reflect—Get It Out There**

Do you want other people to read your work? Then publish it! Writers share their work in newspapers, magazines, and books. More and more writers publish on the Internet, too. Sharing your writing with your family, friends, and classmates is another form of publishing. Don't forget to reflect on your writing yourself—think about what you have worked so hard to create!

Your Job as a Writer

Good writers have many trade secrets. One of them is using the writing process. Try it on this project.

Write a Personal Narrative

WRITING PROMPT   Everyone has stories to tell about his or her life. What are the most important events of your own life? How have they influenced or changed you, and what have you learned from them?

Think about an important event from your own life. Then write two or three paragraphs about it. Your paragraphs should

- tell a true story with a beginning, middle, and end
- present events in chronological order
- use specific details, including sensory details, to help readers imagine the event
- express your thoughts and feelings about the event.

Prewrite: Collect Ideas

Where can you get ideas for your writing? Look around you.
What you see, hear, and read will give you ideas. You can get
ideas from inside, too—from your feelings and imagination.
Once you start looking for inspiration, you'll find it everywhere.

Ways to Come Up with Ideas

Rev up your idea engine. Think about:

- funny, strange, or confusing situations in your life

- the music you love

- places, objects, or events that mean a lot to you

- your top ten favorite memories

- your favorite people

- your favorite fictional or historical characters

- an imagined or overheard line of dialogue

- times when you felt really sad, nervous, or thrilled

- why you've kept things like tickets, letters, photographs, or souvenirs

- quotations you feel strongly about

> "To love someone deeply gives you strength. Being deeply loved by someone gives you courage."
> —Lao Tzu

Top Ten Memories

1. The day my baby sister was born
2. My fishing trip with Uncle Julio
3. Going to the prom with Emily
4. Passing my driver's test

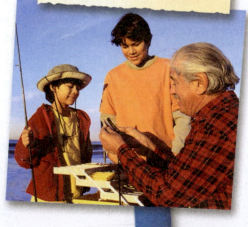

Where to Keep Your Ideas

Start an idea file to keep your ideas together in one place. Just about any kind of container will do.

- Put your ideas inside a cereal box or in a basket.
- Keep a journal of your thoughts and feelings.
- Fill a file folder with interesting articles, stories, and photos.

- Make a section in your Writer's Notebook just for collecting your ideas.
- Keep a special Writing Ideas file on your computer.
- Send voice-mail idea messages to yourself.

On-the-Go Inspiration

When you don't have your idea collection with you, try asking yourself questions like these:

- What would a perfect day be like for me?
- What would my best friend's perfect day be like?
- What would a perfect day be like for Tom Sawyer?
- What's the most important value I want to teach my children?

- If I could travel anywhere in the world, where would I go?
- Where would my sister like to travel?
- What's one action I would go back and undo if I could?
- What action would Scout from *To Kill a Mockingbird* undo?

Prewrite: Collect Ideas, continued

Some things, like science or spelling, you know in your head.
Other things, about people or the world, you know in your
heart. That's your truth. When you write about one thing you
believe in your heart, your writing will sing.

Speak Your Truth

What do you believe is true about people or the world? You may
already have an idea in your head, but sometimes looking at a
photograph can help you discover your truth. What truth would
you add to this list?

<u>Truths</u>

1. Everyone needs help to learn new things.

2. Families spend time together.

3. Not everyone can get things right without some help.

4. People change as they get older.

5. There are many ways to define a family.

Something that is true for one person is not necessarily true for others. When you look at these photographs, does a different truth come to mind?

Working together is so much better than working alone.

Communication mistakes can cause serious problems.

Sometimes you have to look from a distance to see something clearly.

Shopping is like searching for treasure; you never know what you're going to bring home.

Prewrite: Choose Your Topic

You can use your idea collection to come up with a topic—the subject you want to write about. Make sure you narrow your topic so that it is not too general, or broad, for the kind of writing you'll do.

A specific, or smaller, topic is easier to write about and is much more interesting for your readers. Take a look at how one writer narrowed the topic "Friendship" for a three-paragraph essay.

Friendship
This topic would take pages and pages to cover. Why?

Broad

My best friend
This is better, but still too broad. How many things are there to say about a best friend?

The day I almost lost my friendship with Carlos
This topic is interesting because it's specific. Would it be easy to tell what happened in three paragraphs?

Narrow

> **Your Topic is Too Broad When . . .**
>
> • you type key words into a search engine and get thousands of hits
>
> • you search a library database and find hundreds of books
>
> • there are so many main ideas, you don't know where to start

Choose Your Audience

After choosing a good topic, you need to think about your audience—the people who will read your writing. That will help you choose the appropriate style and tone for your writing.

Audience	Tone	Language
your best friend or someone your own age	very informal	Hey, Karen— What's up? You ready for Frank's party on Thursday?
an older relative	somewhat informal	Hi, Uncle Terry, Do you have any Hawaiian shirts I could borrow? I need one for a party Thursday. Thanks.
your teacher	somewhat formal	Dear Mrs. Smith, I wonder if it might be possible for me to turn my paper in on Monday instead of Friday. I have an important after-school event on Thursday night.
someone you don't know	very formal	Dear Tropical Paradise Staff: Do you carry Hawaiian shirts in size Large? I'm looking for something under $25.00. I'd appreciate any information you could give me. Thank you.

Who is the audience for each of these e-mails?

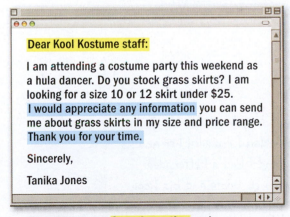

The writer uses a **formal greeting** and language that gives her message **a polite, businesslike tone.**

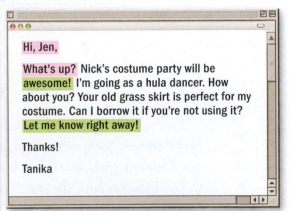

The writer uses an **informal greeting** and **casual, friendly language.** Her words show **strong emotion or feelings.**

Prewrite: Choose Your Purpose

What do you want your audience to know or do? That'll be your **purpose**, or reason, for writing. When you write, choose a tone that fits your purpose.

What is the writer's purpose in the e-mail below? What is the writer's purpose in the journal entry?

E-mail

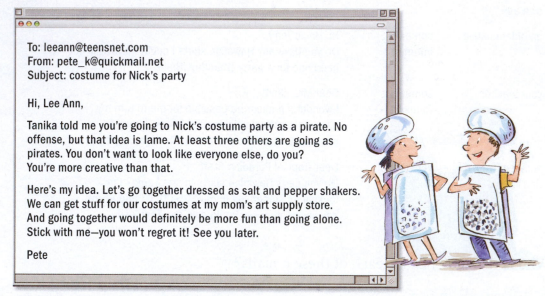

To: leeann@teensnet.com
From: pete_k@quickmail.net
Subject: costume for Nick's party

Hi, Lee Ann,

Tanika told me you're going to Nick's costume party as a pirate. No offense, but that idea is lame. At least three others are going as pirates. You don't want to look like everyone else, do you? You're more creative than that.

Here's my idea. Let's go together dressed as salt and pepper shakers. We can get stuff for our costumes at my mom's art supply store. And going together would definitely be more fun than going alone. Stick with me—you won't regret it! See you later.

Pete

Journal Entry

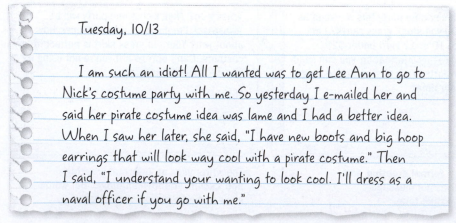

Tuesday, 10/13

I am such an idiot! All I wanted was to get Lee Ann to go to Nick's costume party with me. So yesterday I e-mailed her and said her pirate costume idea was lame and I had a better idea. When I saw her later, she said, "I have new boots and big hoop earrings that will look way cool with a pirate costume." Then I said, "I understand your wanting to look cool. I'll dress as a naval officer if you go with me."

Pete wrote the e-mail to argue why Lee Ann should change her costume and go with him to the party. He wrote in his journal to narrate what happened as a result of what he had done. What is his purpose for writing this letter to his friend Gabe?

Letter

October 16, 2008

Dear Gabe,

You know that girl Lee Ann who came to the beach with us last summer? She's been one of my best friends ever since we met in third grade. Well, I almost blew it!

You see, I asked Lee Ann to go with me to Nick's costume party. She wanted to be a pirate, but I I told her pirate costumes were lame and unoriginal. She was so mad. But we talked later, and Lee Ann explained why she wanted to dress as a pirate. When I said that was cool, she agreed to go to the party with me.

Are Your Audience and Purpose Connected?

Yes. Your audience and purpose are related to each other. One way to get clear about your purpose is to consider how you want your audience to react to what you have to say.

If You Want Your Audience to . . .	Your Purpose Is . . .	For Quick Topic Ideas, List . . .
• learn something new • understand something better	to inform or explain	• ten things people can learn from you • ten things you can do really well
• laugh • feel a deep emotion • enjoy reading your work	to narrate	• ten funny situations • five opening sentences that would get a reader hooked on a book
• believe something • do something • take action on an important issue	to argue	• ten claims about things you'd like to change • five clear reasons and relevant evidence to support one of your claims

Prewrite: Choose Your Purpose, continued

Does Your Form Connect to Your Purpose?

You can change how and what you write to fit your purpose.
Look at the examples on these pages.

To Inform or Explain

Write to tell readers something they need to know or to explain how to do something.

Directions to My House
(from School)
1. When you leave the parking lot, turn right onto Hurffville Road.
2. Go through two traffic lights.
3. Make a right onto Greentree Road.
4. Make a left onto Haines Drive.
5. My house is number 20, on the right.

Directions

My house is all the way at the end of the street. It's a red house with a brown roof and brown trim. There's a big vacant lot right before my house. A brown station wagon and a black pickup truck are parked in the driveway.

Paragraph

Healthy Birthday Snacks

With so many overweight kids, it's important to provide healthy choices when planning the menu for your birthday party. No, you don't have to feed your guests celery and carrot sticks. Making a few healthy substitutions can go a long way. Instead of fried potato chips, serve baked sweet-potato chips. Put out low-fat cheese and hummus with broccoli, snow peas, baby corn, and whole-grain crackers. With all these healthy choices, your guests won't feel guilty about treating themselves to some of your cake.

Informative Paragraph

Why Choose Healthy Snacks?

Astonishingly, over 50 percent of Americans' calories come from processed and refined foods, which contain no fiber and tiny amounts of vitamins and minerals. By replacing them with whole foods—which are loaded with fiber, vitamins, and minerals—you will feel better right away. You won't have any of those yo-yo spikes in your blood sugar and insulin levels. Once your energy levels have straightened out, your body won't store as much fat, and the pounds will drop off.

Explanatory Paragraph

Write to make a claim. Support the claim with reasons and evidence.

THE PRICE OF A GOOD PARTY

The amount of money people spend on parties is totally out of control. One child's celebrity parents spent $100,000 on her second birthday. A non-celebrity mother spent over $10,000 for a princess-themed party for her daughter's birthday. People don't need to buy expensive presents, flashy clothes, and fancy decorations. After all, the purpose of a party is to have fun with your friends, not to try to impress them.

Editorial

Dear Parents:

It is time to curb the skyrocketing costs of hosting birthday parties for our children. According to Minnesota Department of Family Social Science, splurging on parties sets a bad example for our kids. They become very materialistic, wanting more than they need. Not getting everything they want also generates feelings of disappointment and envy because someone always gets more.

To reverse this trend, I suggest that we have "presence without presents" parties.

Formal Letter

To Narrate

Write to tell about your experiences by using descriptive details and logical sequence.

The Worst Party Ever

The birthday cake lay on the ground where I had dropped it. Then the doorbell rang, and I stepped right in the cake on my way to answer it. Now my foot was covered with chocolate icing! I greeted my friend anyway, but my foot slipped and kicked her in the shin. When we both looked down to see if she was OK, we bumped heads—ouch!

"Welcome to my party," I said. And that was only the beginning!

Essay

An Uninvited Guest

Kendra and Damon stared wide-eyed at the movie on TV. Something terrible was about to happen to the main character. Right at that moment, they heard a loud, insistent knocking. Their hearts beating wildly, they both jumped up from their seats. "Did you invite someone over?" asked Kendra.

"Nope," said Damon. "I don't know who that could be so late at night." Then they heard the doorbell chime loudly, again and again.

Short Story

Prewrite: Organize Your Ideas

You know your topic, your purpose, and the form. You know who your audience will be. Sum them up in an FATP chart.

FATP Chart

Form: _personal narrative_

Audience: _classmates_

Topic: _my friendship with Carlos_

Purpose: _to tell how friendships can change_

You can organize the same information in different ways, depending on what you want your readers to understand.

1. Maybe you want to explain a central idea by discussing related ideas. You could use **logical order** to organize your ideas.

Carlos and Me

Carlos has always been more outgoing than I am. Whenever there is a new kid at school, Carlos is the first one to say hello. The other day in gym class, Carlos invited the new kid, Eliot, to join our basketball team. I envy Carlos's ability to make friends so easily.

The **topic sentence** shows the main idea.

The writer discusses a **related idea**.

2. Maybe you want to describe how an event or problem developed over time. Then you would use **chronological order.**

Carlos and Me

Last year, I sensed that the friendship between Carlos and me was changing. At first, I thought it was just because we were both busy with school and sports. By the end of the year, Carlos and I hardly ever hung out.

Time words and phrases help to show chronological order.

3. Maybe you want to describe a scene, so that readers can picture it in their minds. Then you would use **spatial order.**

Carlos and Me

One thing that Carlos and I used to do is build skate ramps. We used cement blocks to build the base of each ramp. Then we would lay down flat pieces of plywood, slanting upward from the ground to the top of the cement blocks. We bolstered up the sides with more cement blocks. The ramps were various heights and widths depending on the size of the wood scraps we found.

The writer describes the ramps from **bottom to top.**

4. You might want to describe how two people, places, or things are alike or different. In that case, you would use a **comparison-and-contrast** structure.

Carlos and Me

We may be best friends, but Carlos and I are nothing alike. Carlos never cracks open a book but somehow manages to get straight A's. As for me, I struggle just to scrape by with B's and C's. Carlos is cool and confident—always the life of the party. I'm quiet and kind of shy.

The writer describes **ways he and his friend are different.**

Check out the graphic organizers in the Writer's File at the back of the book. They'll give you some tools for organizing your writing.

Reflect

• What do you want your audience to understand about your narrative?

• How can you explain events clearly?

Draft

When you look at just the framework of a house, you can't tell exactly what it will look like when it's built. You can see it start to take shape, slowly, as each new piece is added. Drafting is like that. Once you have a framework, you start building! Get your ideas down on paper and, over time, the "shape" of your draft will become clearer.

How Do You Face a Blank Page?

Now that you have a plan, it's time to start the first draft of your personal narrative. Sometimes, the hardest part of writing a paper is getting started! As you will see, there is no one right way to write a first draft.

All drafts start with a blank piece of paper—or a blank computer screen. Here are some ideas to help you get started:

- Gather all the tools you need. Get pencils and paper. Collect the notes and graphic organizers that you made during prewriting. If you are using a computer, create a folder for your files.

- Find a good place to write. It doesn't have to be a desk, but make sure there are no distractions.

- Start writing! Remember, a draft does not have to be perfect. Just get your ideas down on paper!

Look at Jeff's draft on page 33W. What makes it a good start? How much does it matter if there are spelling mistakes in the first draft?

> Jeff wrote without worrying about little mistakes. Now he has a draft to work with.

A Good Friend

Jeff Kominsky

All friendships have their ups and downs. Relationships can be complickated even between the best of friends. Sometimes its hard to tell who you're real friends are.

Carlos asked me to go to an ice-hockey game with him. I was really exsited. I even bought a jersey with the goalies number to where. Well, Carlos let me down. He asked the new kid Eliot to go with him instead. I showed up at Carlos's house. There were three of us and only two tickets. I was pretty annoied. I just left.

Carlos and I have been best friends since fifth grade. He helped me meet new people when I moved. He invited me to play in the neighborhood football games. He is the guy I can always count on.

It turned out I totaly missunderstood the situation. Carlos wanted to invite Eliot since he's new at school. He doesn't really know anyone yet. And Carlos is kind of scatterbrained. He didn't plan ahead.

Drafting Checklist

In a good draft:

- ☑ the title shows the main idea
- ☑ the writing includes the main points from beginning to end
- ☑ the message is clear, and the writing sticks to the topic
- ☑ writers set down ideas quickly, without worrying about spelling or grammar mistakes.

Draft, continued

Writing is like playing sports. You don't have to be perfect. You just need to do your best. On the next few pages are some ideas about writing a first draft. Which ideas sound familiar? Which ideas seem like they would work for you?

Getting Started

Q: What do I need to get started?

A: Find a quiet place where you can work. Make sure you have enough pencils and paper, or a computer. You should also have your notes and your graphic organizers. These materials will help you when you are unsure about how to organize your writing.

Q: What's the right way to start a draft?

A: Writers are like snowflakes. No two are exactly alike. While there's no "right" way to start, here are some ideas:

- Draw pictures to get yourself thinking. You can also write whatever comes into your head to get your ideas flowing. It's like doodling with words.

- Write your ideas down quickly. Don't worry about finding exactly the right word.

- Spend some time working on the first paragraph. This will help you find a direction for the body of the paper.

- Work out of order if you need to. Write the parts you feel more comfortable with. Then move to the other paragraphs.

How Do You Start Writing a Draft?

“I write down every idea I have about my topic, even if it seems silly. If I get a whole bunch of ideas on paper, I know some of them will be good ones.”

—Katya

“I make a storyboard to plot out the events of my narrative. That helps me picture what happens.”

—Darrell

“I talk to my friends about my ideas. If I'm writing about something that happened to us, I ask them what they remember about it. It helps to get other people's perspectives!”

—Ricardo

“I write my ideas on sticky notes and post them on my wall. That way I can move them around and figure out the best way to organize my thoughts.”

—Meg

Draft, continued

Staying on Track

Q: Sometimes while I'm writing I get distracted or lose my train of thought. How can I stay on track?

A: You can try working with a writing partner first—someone you trust. You can ask your partner to read your work, or you can read your work aloud and ask for feedback.

Another approach is to write a "kernel essay" first, before you begin your real essay. A kernel essay shows just the main points of your essay, without any details. See how this writer used the ideas from her kernel essay in her composition.

Susan's Kernel Essay

From Susan's Essay

I was tired of always being broke. Then my friend Mark told me his aunt was looking for someone to babysit for his four-year-old cousin, Anita. The next day, I went to meet Mark's aunt, Mrs. Rodriguez, and her daughter. Anita was a little shy with me at first, but after I was there for a little while, she started talking to me. Actually, she started babbling to me about her books, her dolls, and her drawings.

Q: Sometimes I run out of things to say right away. How can I keep myself going?

A: Don't stop even when your writing seems to be flowing very slowly. Write about not having anything to say, if you have to!

How Do You Stay on Track?

" I need quiet when I write. I look for a private space where I can put all my notes up on the wall. I keep them all in front of me and look at them when I need to. **"**

—Eva

" I usually write for five or ten minutes and then reread what I've written. If I like it, I go back and write for ten more minutes. If not, I take a short break. Then I decide how I want to fix it. Maybe I need to add more details. Maybe I need to cut out a chunk. **"**

—Marcus

" I just let myself get distracted sometimes—but I try to control my distractions so that I will finish. Sometimes I just need to empty my head of my writing so that I can go back to it feeling fresh. **"**

—Carmen

" I focus on getting my draft out of my head and onto the page as quickly as possible. That way I have something there to work with and polish. **"**

—Bassam

Draft, continued

Knowing When You're Done

Q: How do I know when I'm done with the draft and I can move on to the next step?

A: You know you are finished when your ideas are all down on paper (or on your computer). Reread your essay and ask yourself some questions:

- Is my opening paragraph interesting? Will it make a reader want to know more?

- Does my writing say what I want it to say? Do I need to add any details? Is there something I should cut?

- Does the ending flow smoothly? Does it seem tacked on?

The Truth About Drafting

FICTION: **You should write your entire draft at once.**
FACT: Sometimes you can write a draft all at once. But most drafts will take more time. Take a break if you need to!

FICTION: **You should use a pencil and lined notebook paper for a draft.**
FACT: Use whatever works best for you. Some writers take notes on lots of scraps of paper. Others write on plain paper with colored pens. Some people use a computer to write. The important thing is to keep writing.

FICTION: **You should never, ever write a draft without doing prewriting first.**
FACT: Prewriting is a good way to organize your ideas. But sometimes the best way to figure out what you want to say is to just start writing! That way, you have some ideas down on paper. You can always go back and reorganize your ideas later.

FICTION: **You should always stick to your plan when you're writing.**
FACT: It's a good idea to stick to your writing plan. But that doesn't mean you can't change your mind. As you write, you might come up with new and better ideas. Don't be afraid to be flexible and change your plan if you need to.

What's One Truth You Want to Share About Drafting?

"Don't keep writing just to fill up space. As long as you've communicated your thoughts clearly, you've done your job as a writer."

—Shawn

"Always be on the lookout for fresh ideas. Keep thinking about your draft even when you're not sitting at your computer. You never know when inspiration will strike!"

—Alissa

"Go with the flow when you're drafting. If you have a new idea that wasn't in your plan, that's OK—you can change your plan if you need to."

—Robert

"Don't feel like you have to use regular notebook paper for drafting. Some writers draft in brown journals or on flower-scented paper. Others type on their laptops. It doesn't matter how or where you write, just that you do!"

—Desiree

Reflect

- What helps you get started with writing?

- Which idea from other writers will be most helpful to you?

Write Effective Sentences

Combine Sentences

Good writing has a certain rhythm to it. The sentences are varied and interesting to read. If your writing sounds choppy, with too many short sentences, try to combine some sentences.

Short, Choppy Sentences

The first day of school is always scary. I'm a new kid from one coast. I'm going to a new school on the opposite coast. It's even scarier. My new school is huge. It has almost 1,000 students. The kids look friendly, though. They dress like me.

One Way to Combine Sentences

The first day of school is always scary. ~~Since~~ I'm a new kid from one coast. I'm going to a new school on the opposite coast, It's even scarier. My new school is huge. It has ~~with~~ almost 1,000 students. The kids look friendly, though. ~~and~~ They dress like me.

This writer combined sentences 2–4, sentences 5 and 6, and sentences 7 and 8.

Another Way to Combine Sentences

The first day of school is always scary. ~~For~~ I'm a new kid from one coast. I'm going to a new school on the opposite coast, It's even scarier. My new school is huge. It has almost 1,000 students. ~~who~~ The kids look friendly though. ~~and even~~ They dress like me.

This writer combined sentences 2–4, and sentences 6–8.

Vary Your Sentences

Your writing will be livelier if you make some sentences short and others long. That way you can create a nice rhythm and flow. Use different kinds of sentences, too—simple, complex, and compound.

Hi, all!

My new school is great. It is so big. The students come from lots of different places. Some of my classes have too many students in them. The number of after-school activities makes up for class size. We have science clubs, student boosters, and football and basketball teams, just like at home. This big school also has lots of different clubs, like language and drama. It also has more sports, like soccer, hockey, and swimming. I don't even know how many others there are.

Write back soon.

: -)

Sheri

All the sentences are simple statements and are about the same length.

Hi, all!

Despite being huge and a little scary, my new school is great. The students are so diversified; they come from countries I've never even heard of. Although some of my classes are overcrowded, the variety of courses and the number of after-school activities make up for class size. Just like at home, there are science clubs, student boosters, and football and basketball teams. But, in addition to those, this school has language clubs, a drama club, art workshops, soccer, hockey, and swimming. I can't even count how many others there are. How awesome is that?

Write back soon and let me know what's up with you guys.

: -)

Sheri

The writer mixes short and long sentences and uses compound and complex sentences.

Revise: Gather Ideas

You are going to a party and you know what you're going to wear. But before you leave, you take time to make sure you truly look your best. You ask yourself: *Should I wear a different pair of jeans? Would my red sweater match this?* Revising is like that. Before you share your writing, make sure that everything looks just fine.

What Is Revising?

When you revise your draft, you are making your writing better. Here are some tips for revising:

- Develop your main idea by adding details and support or including more about your thoughts and feelings.

- Add signal words—or even rearrange sentences—to make your ideas flow better.

- Remove information that you don't really need.

How do you know what's good about your draft and what needs more work? Getting feedback from other people will help you improve your writing. Ask someone you trust if there are parts of your writing that are confusing. Gather ideas about how to make your writing better.

You can choose to get help during the revising process in different ways. Pages 43W–45W show some techniques you might want to try.

*Tech*TIP

Save your work often! You can use different file names to save new versions of your draft. That way, if you try an idea and it doesn't work, you can go back to what you had before.

Read Your Paper Out Loud

Perhaps the most important person who can help you is . . . *you!* Try reading your paper aloud to yourself. Listen to it as if someone else wrote the paper. Do you hear anything confusing? Is the paper easy to follow? Is the writing clumsy? Can you think of ways to make the writing better?

A Good Friend

Jeff Kominsky

All friendships have their ups and downs. Relationships can be complickated even between the best of friends. Sometimes its hard to tell who you're real friends are.

Carlos asked me to go to an ice-hockey game with him. I was really exsited. I even bought a jersey with the goalies number to where. Well, Carlos let me down. He asked the new kid Eliot to go with him instead. I showed up at Carlos's house. There were three of us and only two tickets. I was pretty annoied. I just left.

Carlos and I have been best friends since fifth grade. He helped me meet new people when I moved. He invited me to play in the neighborhood football games. He is the guy I can always count on.

It turned out I totaly missunderstood the situation. Carlos wanted to invite Eliot since he's new at school. He doesn't really know anyone yet. And Carlos is kind of scatterbrained. He didn't plan ahead.

Jeff thinks:

" My sentences sound kind of choppy and disconnected. I need to make my writing flow better. "

Revise: Gather Ideas, continued

Read Your Paper to a Friend

Ask a friend to draw a sketch of your work. If your friend can "see" your ideas, it means you're on the right track.

Next, ask your partner to write three questions about your draft. This will show what you need to change. It will also help you understand how to revise your paper.

> All friendships have their ups and downs. Relationships can be complickated even between the best of friends. Sometimes its hard to tell who you're real friends are.

- Why is it hard to tell who your real friends are?

- What's the main point of your narrative? I don't get it.

Jeff thinks:

❝ I'm not making my main idea clear enough. I need to get to the point faster.❞

Read Your Paper to Different People

Share your personal narrative with at least one adult and one classmate. When you read, ask your listeners for feedback using some of these ideas.

8 Good Ways to Ask for Feedback

1. What's the most important thing you learned from my essay?

2. What part do you remember best?

3. Did any words confuse you?

4. What's one truth you learned from my story?

5. Which part could you see most clearly in your mind?

6. What parts do you wish you could picture more clearly?

7. Does this story remind you of anything that's happened to you?

8. Are there parts where the essay doesn't "flow" quite right?

Share Your Draft

Let some other people read your draft. They can tell you what they think about it.

- Have your friends and family read your draft. What did they like most? What didn't they understand?

- Post your paper on your school's Web site or on a bulletin board. Ask for comments.

- Share your writing with your classmates. Write down what they tell you. Think about what your readers want you to change, and why.

How to Conduct a Peer Conference

GETTING FEEDBACK

- Don't explain your ideas before your classmates read your paper. Let it speak for itself.

- Ask how your reader reacted to the whole paper. What were the strongest and weakest parts? Were any parts confusing?

- Ask for ideas about what to change. What parts could be cut out or explained more fully? Do the ideas flow smoothly and make sense?

GIVING FEEDBACK

- Look for the main idea and supporting details. Does the flow of ideas make sense?

- How did you feel about the whole paper? Did you understand it? What parts did you like the most or least? Why?

- Give specific suggestions. What parts need more information? What parts could be deleted? Does the paper need to be reorganized?

- Don't focus just on problems. Explain what the writer does well.

Revision in Action

Keep your audience and purpose in mind as you revise your work. Follow these steps.

1 Evaluate Your Work

Choose one of the techniques you have read about to gather ideas for your revision. Then ask yourself questions.

- **About the Form** Am I giving enough information? Are the events in my narrative clear and organized?

- **About the Organization** Do the sentences flow together? Do events flow in a logical order?

> ## Revision in Action

From Jeff's Draft

Carlos asked me to go to an ice hockey game with him. I was really exsited. I even bought a jersey with the goalies number to where. Well, Carlos let me down. He asked the new kid Eliot to go with him instead. I showed up at Carlos's house. There were three of us and only two tickets. I was pretty annoied. I just left for home.

Carlos and I have been best friends since fifth grade. He helped me meet new people when I moved. He invited me to play in the neighborhood football games. He is the guy I can always count on.

It turned out I totaly missunderstood the situation. Carlos wanted to invite Eliot since he's new at school. He doesn't really know anyone yet. And Carlos is kind of scaterbrained. He didn't plan ahead.

Jeff thinks:

"**I need to add signal words to show the order of events.**"

"**I should move this paragraph so it comes earlier in the narrative.**"

"**I could combine some sentences to make my writing flow better.**"

② Mark Your Changes

Add Text To make your ideas clearer, sometimes you need to add details. Use this mark: ∧ .

Delete Text Sometimes you have given information that really isn't necessary. Use this mark: ⌒℘ to take out words and sentences that you don't need.

Rearrange Text You might need to move sentences or paragraphs that are out of order. Circle the text you want to move, and draw an arrow to the place where you want to move it: ↶⟲ .

Reflect

- Do you tell your story clearly, presenting events in order?

- Do you need to add, delete, or rearrange information?

Revising Marks

MARK	∧	↶⟲	⌒℘
WHAT IT MEANS	Insert something.	Move to here.	Take out.

Revised Draft

> ⟍ Last month,
> ∧Carlos asked me to go to an ice hockey game with him. I was really exsited. I even bought a jersey with the goalies number to where. Well, Carlos let me down. He asked the new kid Eliot to go with him instead. When∧ I showed up at Carlos's house. ∧There were three of us and only two tickets. I was pretty annoied, so∧ I just left ~~for home.~~
>
> (Carlos and I have been best friends since fifth grade. He helped me meet new people when I moved. He invited me to play in the neighborhood football games. He is the guy I can always count on.)
>
> It turned out I totaly missunderstood the situation. Carlos wanted to invite Eliot since he's new at school.℘ and∧ ~~He~~ doesn't really know anyone yet. And Carlos is kind of scaterbrained. so∧ He didn't plan ahead.

Jeff added signal words to make the order of events clearer.

Jeff moved this paragraph, since it discusses events that happened earlier.

Jeff combined sentences so his writing would flow more smoothly.

Edit and Proofread

You played with your puppy before the party, and now you have dog hair all over your shirt. You want to look as nice as you can, so you clean it off. Editing and proofreading is like that. You take time to fix the little mistakes so they won't take attention away from your paper.

Make Your Paper Ready for Your Readers

You have revised your paper to make sure your ideas are clear. Now it's time to fix any mistakes in spelling and grammar.

- Look for errors in grammar, spelling, and mechanics. Reading your paper out loud may help you catch these errors.

- Sometimes something looks wrong, but you're not sure why. Check a dictionary, or get help from your teacher.

- Reread your paper many times, looking for different mistakes each time.

- After you fix any mistakes, be sure to make a clean copy of your paper.

Look at the edited paper on page 49W. What kind of changes is the writer making?

A Good Friend

Jeff Kominsky

All friendships have their ups and downs. Relationships can be complicated even between the best of friends. Sometimes its hard to tell who you're real friends are.

Carlos and I have been best friends since fifth grade. He helped me meet new people when I moved. He invited me to play in neighborhood games. I can always count on him.

Last month, Carlos asked me to go to an ice hockey game with him. I was really exsited. I even bought a jersey with the goalies number to where. Then, he asked the new kid Eliot to go with him instead. When I showed up at Carlos's house, there were three of us and only two tickets. I was pretty annoyed, so I just left.

It turned out I totaly missunderstood the situation. Carlos wanted to invite Eliot since he's new at school and he doesn't really know anyone yet. And Carlos is kind of scaterbrained, so he didn't plan ahead.

Editing and Proofreading Marks

MARK	WHAT IT MEANS	MARK	WHAT IT MEANS
∧	Insert something.	/	Make lowercase.
∧	Add a comma.	ℒ	Delete, take something out.
∧	Add a semicolon.	¶	Make new paragraph.
⊙	Add a period.	◯	Spell out.
⊙	Add a colon.	⌐	Replace with this.
⌄⌄	Add quotation marks.	∼	Change order of letters or words.
⌄	Add an apostrophe.	#	Insert space.
≡	Capitalize.	◡	Close up, no space here.

Edit and Proofread, continued

Tools: The Dictionary

The right tool makes any job easier. The dictionary is a tool you can use for editing and proofreading. It can help you check the spelling of a word, of course. But it can also tell you how to use words the right way.

Guide words: first and last entries on the page

Pronunciation **Part of speech**

345

farrier • fastball

far·ri·er \'far-ē-ər\ *n* : a blacksmith who shoes horses [Medieval French *ferrour*, derived from Latin *ferrum* iron]

¹**far·row** \'far-ō\ *vb* : to give birth to pigs [Middle English *farwen*, derived from Old English *fearh* "young pig"]

²**farrow** *n* : a litter of pigs

far·see·ing \'fär-'sē-ing\ *adj* : FARSIGHTED 1

Far·si \'fär-sē\ *n* : PERSIAN 2b

far·sight·ed \-'sīt-əd\ *adj* **1 a** : seeing or able to see to a great distance **b** : able to judge how something will work out in the future **2** : affected with hyperopia — **far·sight·ed·ly** *adv* — **far·sight·ed·ness** *n*

¹**far·ther** \'fär-thər\ *adv* **1** : at or to a greater distance or more advanced point **2** : more completely [Middle English *ferther*, alteration of *further*]

usage *Farther* and *further* have been used more or less interchangeably throughout most of their history, but currently they are showing signs of going in different directions. As adverbs, they continue to be used interchangeably whenever distance in space or time is involved, or when the distance is metaphorical. But when there is no notion of distance, *further* is used ⟨our techniques can be *further* refined⟩. *Further* is also used as a sentence modifier ⟨*further*, the new students were highly motivated⟩, but *farther* is not. A difference is also appearing in their adjective use. *Farther* is taking over the meaning of distance ⟨the *farther* shore⟩ and *further* the meaning of addition ⟨needs no *further* improvement⟩.

²**farther** *adj* **1** : more distant : REMOTER **2** : ³FURTHER 2, ADDITIONAL

far·ther·most \-,mōst\ *adj* : most distant : FARTHEST

¹**far·thest** \'fär-thəst\ *adj* : most distant in space or time

²**farthest** *adv* **1** : to or at the greatest distance in space or time : REMOTEST **2** : to the most advanced point **3** : by the greatest degree or extent : MOST

far·thing \'fär-thing\ *n* : a former British monetary unit equal to ¼ of a penny; *also* : a coin representing this unit [Old English *fēorthung*]

far·thin·gale \'fär-thən-,gāl, -thing-\ *n* : a support (as of hoops) worn especially in the 16th century to swell out a skirt [Middle French *verdugale*, from Spanish *verdugado*, from *verdugo*

Word History The English words *fascism* and *fascist* are borrowings from Italian *fascismo* and *fascista*, derivatives of *fascio* (plural *fasci*), "bundle, fasces, group." *Fascista* was first used in 1914 to refer to members of a *fascio*, or political group. In 1919 *fascista* was applied to the black-shirted members of Benito Mussolini's organization, the *Fasci di combattimento* ("combat groups"), who seized power in Italy in 1922. Playing on the word *fascista*, Mussolini's party adopted the fasces, a bundle of rods with an ax among them, as a symbol of the Italian people united and obedient to the single authority of the state. The English word *fascist* was first used for members of Mussolini's *fascisti*, but it has since been generalized to those of similar beliefs.

Fa·sci·sta \fä-'shē-stä\ *n, pl* -**sti** \-stē\ : a member of the Italian Fascist movement [Italian]

¹**fash·ion** \'fash-ən\ *n* **1** : the make or form of something **2** : MANNER, WAY ⟨behaving in a strange *fashion*⟩ **3 a** : a prevailing custom, usage, or style **b** : the prevailing style (as in dress) during a particular time or among a particular group ⟨*fashions* in women's hats⟩ [Medieval French *façun, fauschoun*, "shape, manner," from Latin *factio* "act of making, faction"] — **after a fashion** : in a rough or approximate way ⟨did the job *after a fashion*⟩

synonyms FASHION, STYLE, MODE, VOGUE mean the usage accepted by those who want to be up-to-date. FASHION may apply to any way of dressing, behaving, writing, or performing that is favored at any one time or place ⟨the current *fashion*⟩. STYLE often implies the fashion approved by the wealthy or socially prominent ⟨a superstar used to traveling in *style*⟩. MODE suggests the fashion among those anxious to appear elegant and sophisticated ⟨muscled bodies are the *mode* at this resort⟩. VOGUE applies to a temporary widespread style ⟨long skirts are back in *vogue*⟩.

²**fashion** *vt* **fash·ioned**; **fash·ion·ing** \-ning, -ə-ning\ : to give shape or form to : MOLD, CONSTRUCT — **fash·ion·er** \'fash-nər, -ə-nər\ *n*

fash·ion·able \'fash-nə-bəl, -ə-nə-\ *adj* **1** : following the fashion or established style : STYLISH ⟨*fashionable* clothes⟩ **2** : of or relating to the world of fashion : popular among those who

Synonyms and shades of meaning

Different forms of the word

fascis bundle]

fas·cism \'fash-,iz-əm\ *n, often cap* : a political philosophy, movement, or regime that promotes nation and often race above individual worth and that supports a centralized autocratic government headed by a dictator, severe economic and social regimentation, and forcible suppression of opposition [Italian *fascismo*, from *fascio* "bundle, fasces, group," from Latin *fascis* "bundle" and *fasces* "fasces"] — **fas·cist** \'fash-əst\ *n or adj, often cap* — **fas·cis·tic** \fa-'shis-tik\ *adj, often cap*

curving downward slope to the rear; *also* : an automobile with such a roof

fast·ball *n* : a baseball pitch thrown at full speed

\ə\ **abut**	\aú\ **out**	\i\ **tip**	\ò\ **saw**	\ú\ **foot**
\ər\ **further**	\ch\ **chin**	\ī\ **life**	\òi\ **coin**	\y\ **yet**
\a\ **mat**	\e\ **pet**	\j\ **job**	\th\ **thin**	\yü\ **few**
\ā\ **take**	\ē\ **easy**	\ng\ **sing**	\th\ **this**	\yü\ **cure**
\ä\ **cot, cart**	\g\ **go**	\ō\ **bone**	\ü\ **food**	\zh\ **vision**

Pronunciation key: helps you say the word

Tools: Spell-Check

If you write on a computer, the program you use can check your spelling. If you misspell a word, that word will appear underlined. The program then gives you a choice of possible words you might want to use.

Look at the words the spell-check program shows you. Then choose the one that fits.

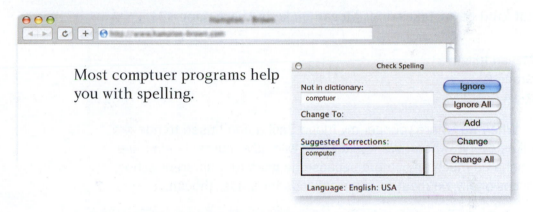

Don't trust spell-check completely, though! The program only looks at spelling, not word meanings. So if you used the wrong word, the spell-check program might not find it.

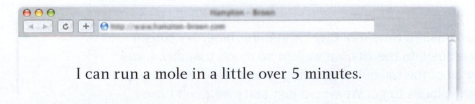

Even if you use a spell-check program, you still need to proofread your paper carefully.

Edit and Proofread, continued

Tools: Your Own Checklist

The English language can be tricky! It seems like there are a million different mistakes you could make. In fact, most people make the same mistakes over and over.

Look at your old papers to see which mistakes you make again and again. You could also ask your teacher about mistakes to look out for.

What kind of mistakes does Megan make in these papers?

Megan Knight
Grade 8
2/14

When we ~~where~~ *were* younger my friend Sasha and I used to ride ~~are~~ *our* bikes every where. We would go on wild adventures. I didn't *don't* see Sasha as much any more because he goes to a different school, occasionally we meet on the weekends for a ride, though.

Megan Knight
Grade 8
4/10

Last year I visited New York City for the first time. My cousin and I took a bus into the city we walked so much that day. I was amazed by all of the tall buildings every where. New York City has so many places to go. We ~~where~~ *were* just sorry we ~~don't~~ *didn't* have more time to spend there. I think if we went more often, it could become ~~are~~ *our* favorite place. I'm happy to go there any time.

A view of New York City across the Brooklyn Bridge ▶

Make a list of the mistakes you make in your papers. Use this list to look out for those mistakes when you write. When you no longer make a mistake, take it off the list. Be sure to add new errors to look for!

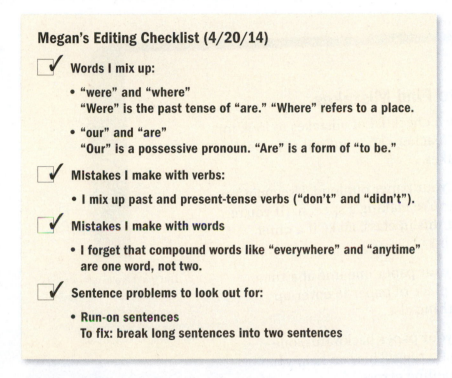

Megan's Editing Checklist (4/20/14)

☑ **Words I mix up:**

- "were" and "where"
  "Were" is the past tense of "are." "Where" refers to a place.

- "our" and "are"
  "Our" is a possessive pronoun. "Are" is a form of "to be."

☑ **Mistakes I make with verbs:**

- I mix up past and present-tense verbs ("don't" and "didn't").

☑ **Mistakes I make with words**

- I forget that compound words like "everywhere" and "anytime" are one word, not two.

☑ **Sentence problems to look out for:**

- Run-on sentences
  To fix: break long sentences into two sentences

TechTIP

Create a computer file for your checklist. That way, you can add to it as you learn more.

If you are writing your paper by hand, be sure to use good handwriting. After you fix your mistakes, rewrite your paper using your best handwriting.

Edit and Proofread, continued

Catch and Correct Your Mistakes

When you proofread, it can be hard to find your mistakes. Errors in spelling, grammar, and punctuation are small details. They are easy to miss. Here are some tips to help you find your mistakes.

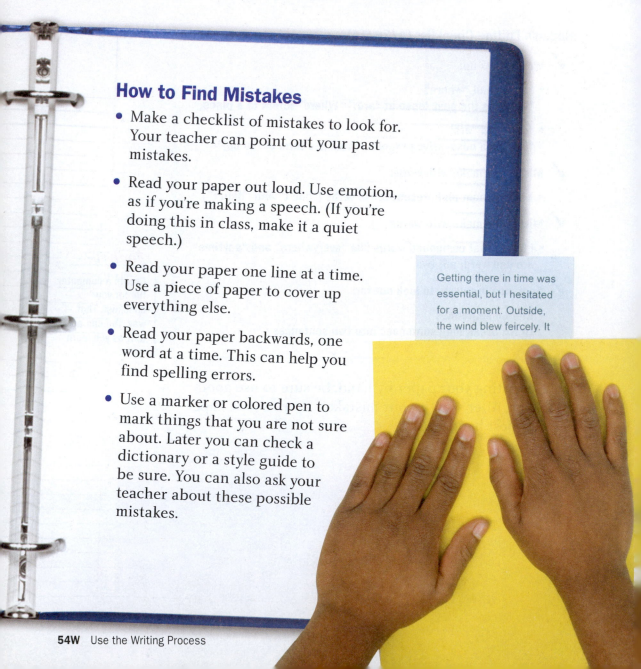

How to Find Mistakes

- Make a checklist of mistakes to look for. Your teacher can point out your past mistakes.

- Read your paper out loud. Use emotion, as if you're making a speech. (If you're doing this in class, make it a quiet speech.)

- Read your paper one line at a time. Use a piece of paper to cover up everything else.

- Read your paper backwards, one word at a time. This can help you find spelling errors.

- Use a marker or colored pen to mark things that you are not sure about. Later you can check a dictionary or a style guide to be sure. You can also ask your teacher about these possible mistakes.

Getting there in time was essential, but I hesitated for a moment. Outside, the wind blew feircely. It

Proofreading Marks in Action

This paper is edited using some common proofreading marks. Look at the model to see how these marks are used.

How I Learned to Prooofread

I used to think that editing my essay just meant running the computer's spell-check program and accepting whatever changes it suggested. Now I no better. A computer will not catch mistakes like correctly spelled words that our used incorrectly. In english class my teacher taught us how to use proofreader's marks to correct mistakes like words that need to be capitalized or made Lowercase. You can use a caret to insert any words that you forgot to put.

My english teacher said Different kinds of carets are used to insert quotation marks apostrophes commas and semicolons however, dont use a caret to insert a colon. Here's how to insert a period or colon use a circle with one or two dots inside

Also, if you accidentally type a word twice, use the delete mark to remove the extra extra word. You can use a similar mark to cross out words or phrases.

Finally, know what marks to use to insert a space, close up a space, and fix letters or words that are in the order wrong. Practice your proofreading skills, and soon your writing will be letter-perfect

Editing and Proofreading in Action

Read your paper again to fix language errors. This is what you do when you edit and proofread your work:

- **Check the Grammar** Make sure that you have used correct and conventional grammar throughout. In particular, make sure you used complete sentences, and check your subject-verb agreement. (See page 57W.)

- **Check the Spelling** Spell-check can help, but it isn't always enough. For errors in forming the plurals of nouns, you'll have to read your work carefully, and perhaps use a dictionary. (See page 58W.)

- **Check the Mechanics** Errors in punctuation and capitalization can make your work hard to understand. In particular, check that your sentences begin with a capital letter and end with a period, a question mark, or an exclamation point. (See page 59W.)

Use these marks to edit and proofread your narrative.

Editing and Proofreading Marks

MARK	WHAT IT MEANS	MARK	WHAT IT MEANS
∧	Insert something.	/	Make lowercase.
∧	Add a comma.	℘	Delete, take something out.
∧	Add a semicolon.	¶	Make new paragraph.
⊙	Add a period.	◯	Spell out.
⊙	Add a colon.	⌐	Replace with this.
∨ ∨	Add quotation marks.	∼	Change order of letters or words.
∨	Add an apostrophe.	#	Insert space.
≡	Capitalize.	◡	Close up, no space here.

Reflect

- What kinds of errors did you find? What can you do to keep from making them?

Grammar Workout

Check for Correct Sentences

A complete sentence has a **subject** and a **predicate**.

EXAMPLE   My friend Leo played basketball.
           Subject   Predicate

- The subject of a sentence is the person or thing the sentence is about.

- The **complete subject** includes all the words that tell about the subject. The most important word in the complete subject is usually a **noun**.

    EXAMPLE   My friend Leo played basketball.

- The **complete predicate** often tells what the subject does. The **verb** shows the action.

    EXAMPLE   My friend Leo played basketball.

- When a verb in the present tense tells about a singular third-person subject (like **he, she,** or **it**), it must have –**s** at the end.

    EXAMPLE   I **play** pretty well.
               My friend Leo **plays** like a pro.

Find the Trouble Spots

Carlos's cousin Leo. ⟨is⟩ An awesome basketball player. He want⟨wants⟩ to play in college when he get older. Practiced almost every day as a little kid. Not any more, because he's so good. Need to stay in shape, though, if he want to get better.

Find and fix the other problem verbs and sentences.

Editing and Proofreading in Action, continued

Spelling Workout

Check Plural Nouns

A plural noun names more than one person, place, or thing.

- To make most nouns plural, just add -*s*.

    EXAMPLES   invention + s = inventions   problem + s = problems
    librarian + s = librarians   judge + s = judges

- If the noun ends in *s, z, sh, ch,* or *x*, add -*es*.

    EXAMPLES   coach + es = coaches   flash + es = flashes
    gas + es = gases   box + es = boxes

- If the noun ends in a vowel plus *y*, just add –*s*.

    EXAMPLES   day + s = days   way + s = ways
    boy + s = boys   decoy + s = decoys

- If the noun ends in a consonant plus *y*, change the *y* to an *i* and then add -*es*.

    EXAMPLES   lady + es = ladies   country + es = countries
    baby + es = babies   try + es = tries

Find the Trouble Spots

Recently Carlos and I joined a pen-pal program. Our teacher matched us up with two ~~boyz~~ **boys** from Russia. We write e-mail ~~messagies~~ **messages** to each other about once a week. Although we come from different countrys, we're totally buddys now. We all like soccer, and we talk about different plaies we learn.

Find and fix three more errors with plural nouns.

Mechanics Workout

Check Sentence Punctuation

- Make sure every sentence ends with the right punctuation mark.

Sentence Type	End Punctuation	Mark
statement	period	.
question	question mark	?
exclamation	exclamation point	!
command	period or exclamation point	. or !

EXAMPLES   Carlos wanted to throw a party. **(statement)**
Is Carlos going to throw a party? **(question)**
Carlos is throwing a great party! **(exclamation)**
Come to the party at 6:00. **(command)**

Find the Trouble Spots

Carlos is throwing a party for all of the kids in our class○ At first, I was excited. Then I found out it was a costume party⌄What was I going to wear. My friend Mike said I could go as a clown. What a boring idea. So instead I went to my computer in hopes of finding some good costume ideas online

Find two more errors in punctuation or capitalization to fix.

Publish, Share, and Reflect

You just finished decorating your bedroom in your new house. The walls are your favorite color and they're covered with cool posters. You won't just sit in there by yourself—you'll invite your friends over to show it off! Of course, you'll arrange everything just so before they arrive. This is what publishing is like. You invite other people to read your writing, and you make sure it looks great.

Now you are ready to publish your personal narrative. The ideas that follow will help you with the finishing touches.

How Should You Share Your Writing?

Once you're done with your paper, what happens next?

- Collect your writing in a portfolio.

- Decide how to publish your writing. Decide who your audience will be. Do you want to share your writing with just a few people you're close to or with a wider audience?

- Keep thinking about your writing. This will help you improve over time.

You can share your writing with just a few people or with the whole world.

Sharing It with Friends

If you want to keep your writing private, here are some personal ways to share it:

- Write a letter to a friend or family member asking him or her to read your writing. Include a copy of your paper.

- Send your writing attached to an e-mail to someone you trust.

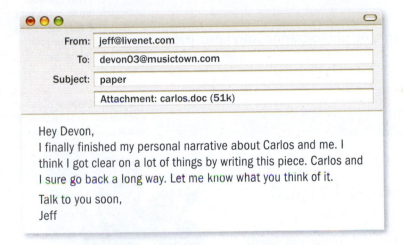

From: jeff@livenet.com
To: devon03@musictown.com
Subject: paper
Attachment: carlos.doc (51k)

Hey Devon,
I finally finished my personal narrative about Carlos and me. I think I got clear on a lot of things by writing this piece. Carlos and I sure go back a long way. Let me know what you think of it.

Talk to you soon,
Jeff

TechTIP
Keep safety in mind when publishing your work—especially when publishing online. Review the Acceptable Use Policy for your school before posting online.

- Another cool way to share your writing is to give it to someone as a gift. Suppose you've written a paper about your best friend. You could give him or her a copy of your paper, typed or carefully handwritten on nice paper. You could even frame it.

Making It Public

Sharing your writing with other people feels good! The feedback you get from them will help you become a better writer. Are you ready to share your writing with people you do not know as well? Here are some ways to make your writing public.

- Submit your work to your school newspaper or literary magazine.

- Look for writing contests in your local paper or online.

- Read your work out loud to another class in your school.

Publish, Share, and Reflect, continued

Adding Pictures to Your Work

Adding pictures to your paper can help people understand your ideas better. If you're using a computer, it's easy to add illustrations to your paper.

- Make copies of interesting photos to tape or glue to your paper.

- Scan drawings, charts, or photographs into your paper.

Reflect

- How will you choose to share your personal narrative?

- What can you do to make your essay especially right for your audience?

Ready for Publishing

The writer added a photograph so his narrative would seem more personal.

A Good Friend

Jeff Kominsky

All friendships have their ups and downs. Relationships can be complicated even between the best of friends. Sometimes it's hard to tell who your real friends are.

Carlos and me in 2012

Carlos and I have been best friends since fifth grade. He helped me meet new people when I moved. He invited me to play in the neighborhood football games. He is the guy I can always count on.

Last month, Carlos asked me to go to an ice hockey game with him. I was really excited. I even bought a jersey with the goalie's number to wear. Then, he asked the new kid Eliot to go with him instead. When I showed up at Carlos's house, there were three of us

Keep Thinking About Your Writing

Finishing a paper doesn't mean you stop thinking about it. Looking back on your work can help you improve your writing. Ask yourself what worked in this paper and how you can improve your writing. Reflect on your writing by asking yourself questions.

Questions to Think About

1. What do I like most about my writing?

2. Did I get any unexpected questions or comments from readers?

3. How did this paper make me a better writer?

4. What was the hardest part about writing this paper?

5. What did I learn by working on this paper?

6. How can I improve my writing?

7. What other topics would I like to write about?

8. What other kinds of writing would I like to try?

Build Your Portfolio

Making a portfolio is a good way to store and organize your best work. You can use a file folder or binder to save your papers. You may also include drafts in your portfolio. This will help you see how your writing has improved.

You can make your portfolio public or keep it private. Many writers use portfolios to show off their work. If you do this, you should keep more personal papers, such as journal entries, in another place.

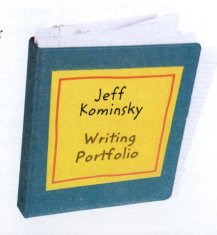

Use Multimedia

If you are making a presentation to a large group, make it more impactful with visuals, sound, and computer technology.

Enhance Your Presentation with Visuals

There's an old saying that goes, "A picture is worth a thousand words." You can integrate pictures and other visuals into your presentation to clarify information, strengthen claims and evidence, and add interest.

- Show or project photographs that relate to your topic. Make sure they are eye-catching and large enough to be seen easily.

Campground

- Show illustrations that will clarify information to help your audience understand the claims you make.

Choose My Plate

- Use charts or graphs to present a lot of data at one time. Graphics help your audience see the relationships among data, and they strengthen your evidence.

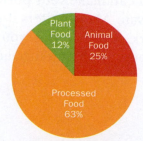

U.S. Food Consumption

- Does your presentation include historical or geographical information? Consider displaying a map to help your audience visualize the location.

- Present a short clip from a video, using a DVD player.

Enhance Your Presentation with Sounds

Consider using sound recordings to make your presentation really "sing." Use your imagination, and think of different sounds to help your audience relate to your subject or to identify your arguments and claims.

- Play a patriotic song from the country that is the topic of your presentation. Or, play a recording by a musician from the time period described in your presentation.

Music in My Life
by Myra Poe

- Share parts of a recorded interview or comments by experts whom you quoted to provide evidence in support of claims you make in your presentation.

- Present clips from a speech by a famous personality, researcher, or politician.

> "Let us all hope that the dark clouds of racial prejudice will soon pass away and the deep fog of misunderstanding will be lifted from our fear-drenched communities. . . ."
>
> —*Martin Luther King, Jr.*

- Ring a bell or play a ring tone between major parts of your presentation to help your audience tell when one point ends and another begins.

Remember: The goal of using media is to make your presentation "sing"—not to replace its content. Use photos, charts, and graphics to convey only information that relates directly to your topic. Videos and sound recordings should also be used sparingly. Short clips are enough to keep your audience's attention.

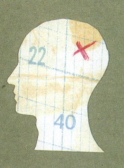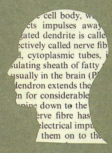

e cell body, w
cts impulses away
gated dendrite is calle
ectively called nerve fib
, cytoplasmic tubes, i
sulating sheath of fatty
usually in the brain (P
endron extends the
n for considerable
pine down to the
erve fibre has
electrical impu
them on to the

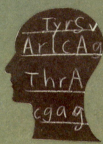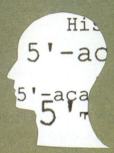

TyrSv
ArtcAg
ThrA
cgag

HiS
5'-ac
5'-aca
5'

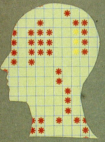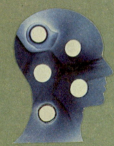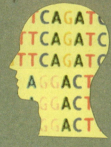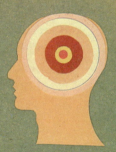

TCAGATC
TTCAGATC
TTCAGATC
AGGACT
GGACT
GGACT

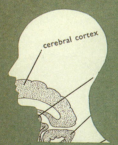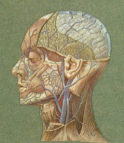

cerebral cortex

MOTHER

THE Many Writers YOU ARE

Model Study

Summary Paragraph

What was the last movie or book you told a friend about?
Did you describe the events word for word? Probably not.
You probably gave your friend a **summary** of the events, or a
shortened version of the story—a version that included only the
most important parts.

In the same way, when you do research for a project or study
for an exam you often need to summarize what you read. You
need to read closely and evaluate which ideas are important and
which are not.

To summarize a paragraph or a short passage, you might write a
one-sentence **summary statement**. To summarize an article or a
book, you might write a **summary paragraph**.

Read the student model on page 69W. It shows the features of a
good summary.

SUMMARY PARAGRAPH

A good summary

☑ gives the title and the author of the work

☑ restates the writer's ideas in your own words

☑ includes all the main ideas and important details

☑ leaves out details that are not important.

Feature Checklist

The Cuttlefish
by Carol Robinson

What squirts ink, has a beak, and flashes colors like a neon sign? It's a cuttlefish, one of nature's most fascinating creatures.

A cuttlefish isn't really a fish at all. In fact, these creatures have more in common with garden snails than with true fish. That's because cuttlefish are mollusks, like octopuses and squid.

A cuttlefish is a master of disguise. It can change its color and the texture of its skin easily. Its skin is covered with special cells that reflect light in many different colors. This way, the cuttlefish is able to blend in with its surroundings. Some people call the cuttlefish "the chameleon of the sea."

When a cuttlefish senses danger, it can shoot out a cloud of dark brown ink. Like a smokescreen on land, the cloud of ink hides the cuttlefish from its attacker. The ink also tastes bad and may get into the attacker's nostrils.

A cuttlefish has eight sucker-covered tentacles in the front part of its body. The tentacles are used for grasping crabs, fish, and other prey. A cuttlefish has a sharp beak that looks like a parrot's. It can use this beak to defend itself and to crush prey.

Cuttlefish are fascinating creatures of the deep. Fish experts aren't sure, but a cuttlefish's brain may be larger than an octopus's.

> Some people call the cuttlefish "the chameleon of the sea."

Good Summary

Carol Robinson's "The Cuttlefish" tells about the unique qualities of this mollusk, which has many ways of protecting itself. The cuttlefish can change its color at will. It can protect itself by shooting out jets of ink. It uses its eight arms and its beak to grab and eat prey. Its beak is also used for self-defense.

> The writer retells all of the main ideas.

Student Model

Write a Summary Paragraph

WRITING PROMPT When you read, summarizing the main ideas can help you better understand and remember what you read. When you write a summary, include the most important parts and leave out the rest.

Read the article "Pufferfish" on page 71W. Then, write a summary paragraph that

- restates the main ideas in your own words
- includes only the most important details
- leaves out unimportant details.

Prewrite

Here are some tips for planning your summary paragraph.

1 Keep Track of Important Ideas

Read carefully. Think about the title and any headings. They usually name the key ideas. Underline or highlight the main idea of each paragraph. (Often the main idea is stated in the first or last sentence.)

Pufferfish

by Matt Galeano

Most species of pufferfish are poisonous. Their internal organs contain tetrodotoxin, a bad-tasting and highly toxic chemical. This poison can kill predators—

▲ In some cultures, pufferfish is a delicacy.

2 Take Notes

As you read, jot down key ideas from each paragraph. Use paper, type notes into a computer file, or add sticky notes.

Pufferfish

by Matt Galeano

Pufferfish are strange-looking fish with long bodies and bulbous heads. They are found in warm water in a number of places around the globe.

Most species of pufferfish are poisonous. Their internal organs contain tetrodotoxin, a bad-tasting and highly toxic chemical. This poison can kill predators—including human beings. One pufferfish can have enough tetrodotoxin to kill 30 people! Ingesting it can also cause paralysis.

However, some think pufferfish is a delicious delicacy. In Japan, for example, the fish is known as fugu. Even though specially trained chefs know how to remove the dangerous parts, anyone who eats fugu is taking a huge risk. Even tiny amounts of tetrodotoxin can be fatal.

The lethal poison is not the only unusual feature of the pufferfish. Some species also have a strange way of defending themselves from predators. When threatened, they gulp water until they swell to three times their size. That, along with stiff spines some have on their skin, make pufferfish very unpopular prey!

Pufferfish, weird-looking

—poisonous
—tetrodotoxin in organs kills and paralyzes

—eat pufferfish in Japan
—chefs careful, but still risky

—unusual defense
—puff up to 3X size
—can have stiff spines

③ Use a Graphic Organizer

Now try organizing all your notes in a web or a diagram.

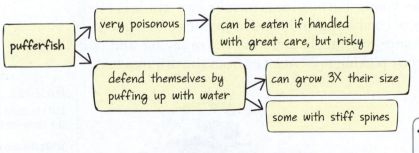

Reflect

- Did I identify the main idea of each paragraph?
- Did I note only the key ideas?

Draft

Now that you've made some notes, use them to draft your summary paragraph.

- **Start with a One-Sentence Summary** Try summing up the main idea of what you read in just one sentence. That will get you to focus on the most important ideas. Then develop and expand the sentence into a paragraph.

Sally's One-Sentence Summary

> In "Pufferfish," Matt Galeano explains how the pufferfish can be deadly and how they "puff up" to protect themselves.

- **Add the Most Important Ideas** Your notes probably show the key ideas you'll include in your summary. As you turn those ideas into sentences, try to express each idea with as few words as possible. Leave out unimportant details.

Sally's Notes

—poisonous
—tetrodotoxin in organs kills and paralyzes

From Sally's Draft

Pufferfish can be dangerous because their organs carry tetrodotoxin, a powerful poison.

- **Use Your Own Words** Putting ideas in your own words is often the best way of combining and condensing. It's also a good way to make sure you understand what you're saying, and that you are not just picking up sentences from the original text.

Spines on a pufferfish make it even less attractive to its prey. ▶

Reflect

- Did I include all the main ideas?

- What details can I leave out?

- Did I use my own words?

DRAFTING TIPS

Trait: **Style**

Combining Sentences

Since your draft just gets your ideas down on paper, it's easy to forget about style. Good writing has a rhythm to it. The sentences are varied in length and structure.

If Your Writing Sounds Choppy. . .

> Pufferfish are weird-looking fish. They have long bodies, stiff spines, and bulbous eyes. When threatened, most pufferfish gulp air or water. This enables them to blow up to three times their normal size.

Try Combining Sentences

This writer combined sentences 1 and 2.

> Pufferfish are weird-looking fish. ~~They have~~ **with** long bodies, stiff spines, and bulbous eyes. When threatened, most pufferfish gulp air or water. This enables them to blow up to three times their normal size.

This writer combined sentences 1 and 2 and sentences 3 and 4.

> Pufferfish are weird-looking ~~fish.~~ **because** They have long bodies, stiff spines, and bulbous eyes. When threatened, most pufferfish gulp air or water. **which** ~~This~~ enables them to blow up to three times their normal size.

Revise

When you revise, think about your audience and remember the purpose of your summary—to state in your own words all the important ideas in something you've read.

1 **Evaluate Your Work**

Read your draft aloud slowly, one sentence at a time, to see how it can be made more concise. As you read, ask yourself:

- **About the Form** Did I include all the main ideas? Did I include only the important details?

- **About the Sentences** Are my sentences concise? Are there any wordy sentences I could cut down?

▲ Despite the risks of consuming pufferfish, some people consider it a delicacy.

Revision in Action

Sally's Draft

In "Pufferfish," Matt Galeano explains how the pufferfish can be deadly and how they "puff up" to protect themselves. Pufferfish can be dangerous because their organs carry tetrodotoxin, a powerful poison. This powerful poison tastes bad. It can kill. It can also paralyze predators. But, some people still risk eating pufferfish. It must be carefully prepared. Chefs must be carefully trained in how to prepare it so it is safe to eat. In addition to being poisonous, a pufferfish has an unusual way to stay safe from all kinds of predators it encounters in the water. It can quickly swallow enough water to grow three times bigger. Not many of its enemies can eat it then.

Sally thinks:

❝It's not important to know the poison tastes bad. I'll take it out.❞

❝These ideas can be collapsed into one sentence.❞

❝I can take out several unnecessary words here.❞

2 Mark Your Changes

Delete Text Does your summary have unnecessary or unimportant details? If so, use ✐ to take them out.

Consolidate Text You might need to make your writing shorter and more concise. You can consolidate text by

- using fewer words to say the same thing

- taking out repetitive words or phrases

- combining sentences.

Reflect

- Does every sentence tell about something important?

- Can you make any sentences shorter?

Revising Marks

MARK	∧	↶	↰	✐	¶
WHAT IT MEANS	Insert something.	Move to here.	Replace with this.	Take out.	Make a new paragraph.

Revised Draft

In "Pufferfish," Matt Galeano explains how the pufferfish can be deadly and how they "puff up" to protect themselves. Pufferfish can be dangerous because their organs carry tetradotoxin, a powerful poison. ~~This powerful poison tastes bad.~~ **Tetrodotoxin** It can kill. It **or** ~~can also~~ paralyze predators. But, some people still risk eating pufferfish. **when it is** ~~It must be~~ carefully prepared. **by trained** Chefs ~~Must be carefully trained in how to prepare it so it is safe to eat.~~ In addition to being poisonous, **Another unusual trait of a** a pufferfish ~~have an unusual way to stay safe from all kinds of predators it encounters in the water.~~ **is how** It can quickly swallow enough water to grow three times bigger. Not many of its enemies can eat it then.

Sally took out an unimportant detail.

Sally consolidated ideas by combining sentences and using fewer words.

Sally took out repetitive and unnecessary details.

Edit and Proofread

After you're satisfied with the content of your summary paragraph, read your paper again to fix language errors. This is what you do when you edit and proofread your work:

- **Check the Grammar** Make sure that you have used correct and conventional grammar throughout. In particular, check for correct use of subject pronouns. (See page 77W.)

- **Check the Spelling** Spell-check can help, but it isn't always enough. Pay special attention when spelling compound words. (See page 78W.)

- **Check the Mechanics** Errors in using capital letters can make your work look careless. Be sure to capitalize all proper nouns. (See page 79W.)

Use these marks to edit and proofread your summary paragraph.

Editing and Proofreading Marks

MARK	WHAT IT MEANS	MARK	WHAT IT MEANS
∧	Insert something.	/	Make lowercase.
∧	Add a comma.	ℰ	Delete, take something out.
∧	Add a semicolon.	¶	Make new paragraph.
⊙	Add a period.	◯	Spell out.
⊙	Add a colon.	⌒	Replace with this.
⌄ ⌄	Add quotation marks.	∼	Change order of letters or words.
⌄	Add an apostrophe.	#	Insert space.
≡	Capitalize.	◡	Close up, no space here.

TechTIP

After you've checked your spelling, use the spell-check feature on the computer as a double-check.

Reflect

- What kinds of errors did you find? What can you do to keep from making them?

GrammarWorkout

Check Subject Pronouns

- Use *he* to refer to a man or a boy. Use *she* to refer to a woman or a girl. Use *it* to refer to a thing.

    EXAMPLE   My friend Tom was happy. He won first prize at

    the science fair. It ended today.

- Use *he, she*, or *it* when referring to only one person. Use *they* when referring to more than one person or thing.

    EXAMPLE   Tom and Sara both won prizes. They did projects about fish.

- Be sure the pronoun is not confusing.

    CONFUSING   Sara and Velma usually win, but she did not do a project ?
    this year

    CLEAR   Sara and Velma usually win, but Velma did not do a project
    this year.

Find the Trouble Spots

Matt Galeano knows a lot about pufferfish. ~~They~~ He
is an expert. Matt describes the danger of the
tetrodotoxin in pufferfish. ~~They~~ It can be lethal. Some
researchers, though, think the poison can be useful.
She think tetrodotoxin can be used in medicine.
They might be a good painkiller.

Find two more
pronoun errors
to fix.

Edit and Proofread, continued

> **Spelling Workout**

Check Compound Words

A compound word is made up of two smaller words. Most of the time, you just put the two short words together without changing their spellings.

EXAMPLES				
armchair	=	arm	+	chair
bedtime	=	bed	+	time
desktop	=	desk	+	top
teabag	=	tea	+	bag
flagpole	=	flag	+	pole

Sometimes people mistakenly write compound words as two separate words, or as two words joined with a hyphen. If you are unsure of how to write a compound word, look it up in the dictionary.

Find the Trouble Spots

Pufferfish are sometimes called ~~blow fish~~ *blowfish*. Most species are ~~salt water~~ *saltwater* fish, but some can be found in rivers. Their teeth are fused together to form a beak like structure that can crush prey. The poison in pufferfish can cause a reaction similar to the reaction caused by some shell fish poisoning. Despite the fish's dangerous qualities, some people keep pufferfish as pets in fish bowls.

Find three more misspelled compound words to fix.

Mechanics Workout

Check Capitalization of Proper Nouns

Proper nouns name a specific person, place, or thing. When you use proper nouns, always capitalize them. Here are a few examples:

- Capitalize people's names.

  EXAMPLES   **D**r. **G**arrison   **L**aura **C**aldwell   **K**endra

- Capitalize months, days of the week, and holidays.

  EXAMPLES   **M**arch   **S**unday   **A**rbor **D**ay

- Capitalize the names of countries and continents. Also capitalize names from geography, including geographic regions.

  EXAMPLES   **C**anada   **S**outh **A**merica
  　　　　　　 Bangladesh   **C**aspian **S**ea
  　　　　　　 Brazil   **G**reat **B**arrier **R**eef

Find the Trouble Spots

I recently read "Pufferfish" by matt Galeano. The article explains how pufferfish abound in the waters near japan. Despite being extremely poisonous, pufferfish is served as a delicacy there. According to galeano, pufferfish is also popular in other countries in asia, such as korea.

Find three more capitalization errors to fix.

Model Study

Modern Fairy Tale

What is your favorite folktale, fable, or fairy tale? *Cinderella? Jack and the Beanstalk? Stone Soup?* Imagine your favorite tale taking place in a modern setting. How would that change the story?

No matter how much you change a traditional tale, it will always have the same key elements of a story. It'll have a **setting**, a problem or **conflict** that the **main character** needs to solve, a **plot**, and a satisfying **resolution**.

To write a modern fairy tale, you can use one of your favorites as inspiration. Just place your characters in a new setting and give your plot some modern twists!

Read the student model on page 81W. It shows the features of a good modern fairy tale.

MODERN FAIRY TALE

A good modern fairy tale includes

- ✓ interesting **characters**
- ✓ details for a modern **setting**
- ✓ recognizable **elements from an existing tale**
- ✓ a **conflict** a character has to solve
- ✓ a **plot** that makes the conflict worse until it comes to a turning point
- ✓ a satisfying **resolution**, or ending.

Feature Checklist

Jorge and Gabriela

by Michael Vasquez

The beginning introduces the characters and the setting.

One day, Gabriela and Jorge passed the new bakery, entranced by the delicious smells. "Let's sweet-talk that lady into free treats," said Gabriela. They entered and asked.

"Sure, dearies," the shopkeeper replied. "I have special goodies in the back." Jorge and Gabriela followed her into a storeroom full of baked goods and a giant bowl of dough.

The middle develops the conflict and the plot.

As they bent over the muffins, they heard a key turning in a lock. The heavy door shut behind them.

"I hate inventory," sneered the shopkeeper. "Now you two can do it. Count each item. Write the numbers on the yellow pad. Be finished by midnight or else!"

Jorge groaned, but his sister had a plan. "Count out loud," she whispered. For the next few hours, they pretended to count, pausing only to gobble a few muffins. Then Gabriela called loudly, "Nine hundred and ninety-nine million, nine hundred and ninety-nine thousand, nine hundred and ninety-nine ... Hey lady! What comes next?"

The resolution shows how the problem was solved; it gives a modern twist to the usual fairy-tale ending.

"One billion," muttered the shopkeeper crossly.

"Huh? How do you write it?" asked Jorge, playing along.

"It'll be faster to show you." The shopkeeper stormed in. Jorge and Gabriela grabbed her and plunged her feet-first into the bowl of dough and made their escape. They lived happily ever after, knowing now that nothing in life is free.

This story is based on the fairy tale "Hansel and Gretel."

The dialogue keeps the plot moving and gives the story a modern feel.

Student Model

Organization

 **What's It Like?**

How does this painting make you feel? The artist carefully arranged the images so you could appreciate having a relaxing, delicious lunch as you gaze out over the water. Writers work in much the same way, arranging their ideas purposely so their writing flows and readers can appreciate the masterpiece!

Why Does Organization Matter?

When a story is well organized, readers can easily tell what's happening to the characters, when it's happening, and why.

Writers organize their ideas in a way that fits their purpose for writing. Below the writer structures her story so it's easy to follow how a character tries to solve a problem.

> Marcie had to meet Grandma at the other end of the mall by 10 p.m., so she had to hurry. The mall was ablaze with light, but suddenly the lights went out!
>
> Her heart pounding, she felt her way through the dark. Finally, she stumbled into a dark, but very quiet figure. "It must be Grandma," she thought. "It's as tall as Grandma, smells sweet like her, and has on that soft, fuzzy sweater she always wears." But how could she be sure?

Transition words link one plot event to the next.

Study the rubric on page 83W. What is the difference between writing with a score of 2 and writing with a score of 4?

Organization

	Does the writing have a clear structure, and is it appropriate for the writer's audience, purpose, and type of writing?	How smoothly do the ideas flow together?
4 Wow!	The writing has a structure that is <u>clear</u> and appropriate for the writer's audience, purpose, and type of writing.	The ideas progress in a smooth and orderly way. • The introduction is strong. • The **ideas** flow well from **paragraph** to **paragraph**. • The ideas in each paragraph flow well from one **sentence** to the next. • Effective **transitions** connect ideas. • The conclusion is strong.
3 Ahh.	The writing has a structure that is <u>generally</u> clear and appropriate for the writer's audience, purpose, and type of writing.	<u>Most</u> of the ideas progress in a smooth and orderly way. • The introduction is adequate. • Most of the **ideas** flow well from **paragraph** to **paragraph.** • Most ideas in each paragraph flow from one **sentence** to the next. • Effective **transitions** connect most of the ideas. • The conclusion is adequate.
2 Hmm.	The structure of the writing is <u>not</u> clear or <u>not</u> appropriate for the writer's audience, purpose, and type of writing.	<u>Some</u> of the ideas progress in a smooth and orderly way. • The introduction is weak. • Some of the **ideas** flow well from **paragraph** to **paragraph.** • Some ideas in each paragraph flow from one **sentence** to the next. • **Transitions** connect some of the ideas. • The conclusion is weak.
1 Huh?	The writing is not clear or organized.	<u>Few or none</u> of the ideas progress in a smooth and orderly way.

Organization, continued

Compare Writing Samples

A well organized story presents events that lead logically to a **resolution** of a conflict. It also includes **transitions** between events. Study the two examples of modern fairy tales on this page.

Well Organized

Kate and the Magic Slippers

In the Jones household, fourteen-year-old Kate and her four-year-old twin sisters, Jennifer and Jessica, were treated very differently. Kate was the oldest, so she did all the work. Jennifer and Jessica had no chores. Kate ran herself ragged to meet their demands.

Kate decided to teach them a lesson. So she bought a pair of red ballet shoes and showed them to her sisters. "See?" she said. "My fairy godmother gave me these magic slippers as a reward. Maybe someday, if you start helping out, she'll give you each a pair, too." Since they were only four, the twins fell for this story. Soon they were begging to help Kate.

The writer introduces a **conflict** and describes plot events that lead to the **resolution**.

Transitions show the order of events.

Not So Well Organized

Kate and the Magic Slippers

In the Jones household, fourteen-year-old Kate and her four-year-old twin sisters, Jennifer and Jessica, were treated very differently. Kate was the oldest. She did all the work. Jennifer and Jessica had no chores.

Kate decided to teach them a lesson. She bought a pair of red ballet shoes. She showed them to her sisters. "See?" she said. "My fairy godmother gave me these magic slippers as a reward. Maybe if you start helping out, she'll give you each a pair, too."

The writer introduces a **conflict,** but the story's plot events and resolution aren't clear.

The story lacks transitions, so the events don't flow smoothly.

Evaluate for Organization

Now read carefully the story below. Use the rubric on page 83W to score it.

Sleeping Beauty
by Trina Simons

Aurora Anderson was sweet and beautiful. She was her wealthy father's pride and joy. He was so devoted to her that he was overprotective. Aurora's aunt mentioned a dream in which Aurora was hurt by a sewing machine. Her father insisted that Aurora avoid any house with a sewing machine.

Aurora was visiting her friend Tricia, and they decided to explore the dusty old attic. They got a ladder and climbed up. Aurora pried open the heavy door. She had no idea that right next to it was an enormous sewing machine. It slid across the warped floor and conked her in the head. She lay at the foot of the ladder, unconscious. Tricia called an ambulance.

Aurora was in a coma. Tricia tried to see the bright side of things. At least Aurora didn't have to worry about algebra tests or cheerleading tryouts. Of course, her family was devastated and longed for her to wake up.

Dr. Ginelli, the doctor in charge of Aurora's case, suggested a radical treatment. "If this were a fairy tale," she explained, "a kiss from Prince Charming would wake your daughter up. But how is anyone going to make a profit from that? I suggest we administer *puekaw,* a medicine developed from a tropical Hawaiian flower. Each injection costs only $99.95. Of course, it's new. It may not be covered by insurance."

Mr. Anderson stared at her blankly.

Is the conflict clear?

Is the order of events clear? Does Trina need to add transitions?

Do the events keep the story's plot moving? Is the resolution of the story clear?

Raise the Score

These papers have been scored using the Organization Rubric on page 83W. Study each paper to see why it got the score it did.

Overall Score: 4

The Lonely Prince

Julia Moriarti

The **beginning** introduces the setting and the characters.

Prince Solitario had one problem—he couldn't find true love. The women he met liked him for silly, shallow reasons. They enjoyed being chased by reporters and seeing their photographs all over the Web.

One day, Prince Solitario hurt his ankle so he couldn't walk. A passerby named Isabel wrapped his ankle in a cloth bandage. Grateful, Prince Solitario asked her out. "I am sorry," she replied, "but my schoolwork keeps me too busy to date anyone." Then she walked off.

The **middle** develops the **conflict. Plot events** build to a turning point.

Two days later, the prince had his assistant find Isabel's address. But when he knocked, Isabel refused to open the door. "Go away!" cried Isabel. "Ever since I helped you, I have gossip hounds bugging me 24-7."

As soon as Prince Solitario heard those words, he knew he had found his true love. He raced back to his castle and had his cooks make a fancy dinner for two. Then he sent his driver in a beat-up old pickup truck to fetch Isabel and fool the newshounds.

The **ending** provides a clear **resolution** to the conflict.

When Isabel realized what he'd done, she laughed. "This is more like it!" she said. "I'd love to have dinner with the prince." Soon they fell in love.

The **conflict** is clear. The prince cannot find true love.

Transitions make the story flow smoothly.

The Lonely Prince

Prince Solitario had never been in love. The women he met liked him for silly, shallow reasons. They enjoyed being chased by the press and seeing their photographs all over.

One day, Prince Solitario hurt his ankle. A passerby named Isabel wrapped his ankle in a cloth bandage. Grateful, Prince Solitario asked her out. "I am sorry," she replied, "but my schoolwork keeps me too busy to date anyone." She walked off.

The prince had his assistant find Isabel's address. He knocked on Isabel's door. But she refused to open it. "Go away!" cried Isabel. "Ever since I helped you, I have gossip hounds bugging me 24-7."

As soon as Prince Solitario heard those words, he knew he had found his true love. He raced back to his castle and had his cooks make a fancy dinner for two. He sent his driver in a beat-up old pickup truck to fetch Isabel and fool the newshounds.

Isabel realized what he'd done. She laughed. "This is more like it!" she said.

RAISING *THE SCORE*

What details could the writer add to make the conflict and resolution clearer? Where could transitions be added to improve the flow of ideas?

Raise the Score, continued

Overall Score: 2

The Lonely Prince

Prince Solitario didn't really like the women he went out with. They enjoyed being chased by the press. They dated him for silly reasons.

One day, Prince Solitario ran into a tree. He couldn't walk. A woman named Isabel wrapped his ankle in a bandage. Prince Solitario asked her out. "I'm sorry, but I'm in college and schoolwork keeps me really busy," she replied. She walked off.

The prince bought Isabel a bunch of flowers. But she refused to open the door when his assistant found her address.

As soon as Prince Solitario heard those words, he knew he had found his true love. He sent his driver in an old pickup truck to fetch Isabel and fool the press. He had his cooks make dinner for two.

Isabel realized what he'd done. She laughed.

The writer could make the **conflict** clearer.

The **structure** of the story is not always clear.

Some of the **plot events** are jumbled.

The **resolution** is weak.

The writer uses only a few **transitions** and should add more to make the story flow smoothly.

RAISING *THE SCORE*

The writer needs to be clearer about what occurs and when. Which sentences should be rearranged so the paragraphs flow better?

The Lonely Prince

Women dated Prince Solitario for silly reasons. The press chased them all the time.

Prince Solitario ran into a tree. He couldn't walk. A woman named Isabel helped him. Prince Solitario asked her out. She replied, "No offense, but I'm busy." She walked off.

He bought Isabel a bunch of flowers. Isabel refused to open the door. The prince had his assistant find Isabel's address.

Prince Solitario sent his driver in an old truck to fetch Isabel. He went back to his castle and had his chefs prepare dinner for two.

The **conflict** is not explained.

The **structure** of the story is unclear.

Events are out of order, and the sentences don't flow well.

There is no resolution because there is no apparent conflict.

RAISING *THE SCORE*

The writer needs add details to make the conflict and resolution clear. What could she add?

How to Make Your Ideas Flow

What's It Like ?

Finding your way to your destination can be tricky sometimes. In the fairy tale "Hansel and Gretel," the children marked their trail with breadcrumbs so they wouldn't get lost. As a writer, you can use transitions to set up the path you want readers to follow. They're like signposts that guide your reader through your story.

Use Transitions

A **transition** is any word or phrase that serves to connect ideas. When you add transitions, the sentences work together as a team to get your story across.

Which of the examples is easier to follow?

Without Transitions

Marianna was the most charming girl in school. Everyone wanted to sit next to her. Kian was impressed by her on his very first day at Newbury Junior High. He was sure Marianna never noticed him. He was quiet and shy.

The short, choppy sentences make the writing hard to follow. Ideas are not well connected.

With Transitions

Marianna was the most charming girl in school, so everyone wanted to sit next to her. Kian was impressed by her on his very first day at Newbury Junior High but was sure Marianna never noticed him because he was quiet and shy.

With **transitions**, the writing flows smoothly from one idea to the next.

Choose the Right Transitions

Transition words and phrases show how ideas are connected.

Causes	Time	Order	Emphasis
because	one day	first	in fact
since	earlier	then	more important
as a result	before	finally	amazingly
Examples	**Contrast**	**Comparison**	**Summary**
for instance	although	also	all in all
for example	but	likewise	finally
as you can see	however	similarly	in the end

Another way to connect your ideas is to repeat a key word or phrase.

Marianna and Kian didn't seem to be much **alike** from the outside. However, once they started talking to each other, they realized they were more **alike** than different.

A **repeated** word links the sentences and ideas.

How to Connect Your Paragraphs

Just as transition words help you connect your sentences, they can also help you tie your paragraphs together. Effective transitions between paragraphs tell your reader what to expect next.

In this story excerpt, the writer explains the events in the story, but she does not use transitions.

Without Transitions

The Rich Kid's New Footwear

Darren always had the coolest sneakers. He was rich. He loved to brag about how he could buy new shoes any time.

Darren saw a street vendor selling Zoom 222-VIPs sneakers. He confronted the vendor and rudely insisted, "I have every pair of Zoom. I've never heard of 222-VIPs. Show them to me right away!"

"They are special," explained the vendor. "They are made of a magical material that's visible only to very important people. *You* see them sitting right here on this table."

"Oh, yes, they're awesome," Darren replied. He couldn't see anything. He opened his wallet.

Darren couldn't wait to show the new sneakers off. He walked into school and all of the students gathered around, asking why he wasn't wearing any shoes. "These are the new Zoom 222-VIPs. Everybody who's anybody can see them," Darren boasted. His friends exchanged confused looks.

Principal Miller walked by. "Darren, what are you doing walking around school barefoot?" he scoffed. "Put on some shoes right away." Darren's face turned red.

Now look at how a few transitions connect the whole story, making it easier for the reader to follow.

The Rich Kid's New Footwear

Darren always had the coolest sneakers. Because he was rich, he loved to brag about how he could buy new shoes any time.

One day, Darren saw a street vendor selling Zoom 222-VIPs sneakers. He confronted the vendor and rudely insisted, "I have every pair of Zoom sneakers, but I've never heard of 222-VIPs. Show them to me immediately!"

"They are special," explained the vendor, "because they are made of a magical material that's visible only to very important people. *You*, for instance, must see them sitting right here on this table."

"Oh, yes, they're awesome," Darren replied. Although he couldn't see anything, he opened his overstuffed wallet.

The next morning, Darren couldn't wait to show the new sneakers off. As soon as he walked into school, all of the students gathered around, asking why he wasn't wearing any shoes. "These are the new Zoom 222-VIPs. Everybody who's anybody can see them," Darren boasted. His friends exchanged confused looks.

Just then, Principal Miller walked by. "Darren, what are you doing walking around school barefoot?" he scoffed. "Put on some shoes right away." Immediately Darren's face turned red.

These **transitions** show how one idea relates to another.

These **transitions** show when events occurred.

Write a Modern Fairy Tale

WRITING PROMPT All cultures have passed down fairy tales and fables that introduce readers to larger-than-life characters—kings and queens, talking animals, and beings with magical powers. And those story characters face larger-than-life problems.

Think about what kinds of problems a character might try to solve in a modern fairy tale. Write a modern fairy tale that includes

- a main character who must solve a problem
- details about the setting and other interesting characters
- recognizable elements from a classic tale
- a clear conflict and turning point
- plot events that lead to a resolution.

Prewrite

Here are some tips for planning your story.

1 Think About Your Characters and Setting

Decide who the characters of your story are, and where and when your story takes place. Don't worry about planning all the details right away. Just get some ideas down.

Here's how Kendall began planning his story:

List of Characters

Setting: the city of Nairobi, Kenya, in modern times	
Characters:	
Anansi	clever, kind, confident
Mr. Nyame	powerful, arrogant, wealthy

② Plan Your Plot—What's the Problem?

One way or another, good stories are *always* about problems. Think about who your characters are and where they live. What kinds of problems might they face? Choose a problem on which you can base your plot.

> Mr. Nyame has bought the copyright to all the words in the city. Anansi wants to get them back so he can help people talk to one another again.

③ Plan Your Plot from Beginning to End

Next, think about what will happen in the beginning, middle, and end of your story. You might not have your whole plot figured out yet. That's OK—just make sure you have some rough ideas. Use a **plot diagram** like the one below to plan.

Plot Diagram

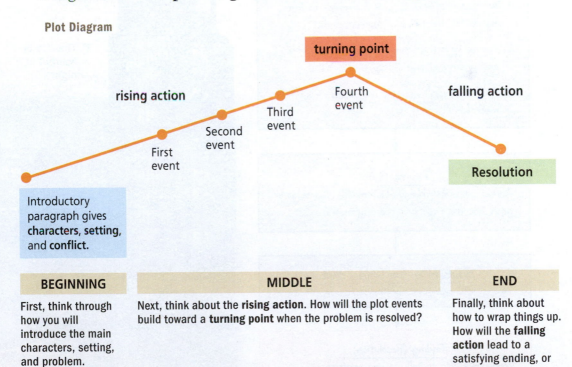

turning point

rising action

Fourth event

Third event

Second event

First event

falling action

Resolution

Introductory paragraph gives **characters, setting,** and **conflict.**

BEGINNING	MIDDLE	END
First, think through how you will introduce the main characters, setting, and problem.	Next, think about the **rising action.** How will the plot events build toward a **turning point** when the problem is resolved?	Finally, think about how to wrap things up. How will the **falling action** lead to a satisfying ending, or **resolution?**

Prewrite, continued

4 Flesh Out Your Plot

Now that you've planned the overall structure of your story, flesh it out with details. You might like to use an organizer like the one Kendall used for his story about Anansi's problem.

Kendall's Plot Diagram for His Story

> <u>Beginning</u>
> A wealthy tyrant, Mr. Nyame, owns the rights to all of the words in Nairobi. Anansi wants to get them back so people can talk again.

> <u>Before the Turning Point</u>
> 1. Mr. Nyame agrees to give the words back to Anansi for the price of three sounds.
> 2. Anansi gets the sound of a child's laughter and a woman's joyful cry.
> 3. Anansi struggles to get the sound of an old man's whistle.

> <u>Turning Point</u>
> Anansi presents the sounds to Mr. Nyame, who gives him the rights to the city's words.

> <u>Events After the Turning Point</u>
> Anansi lets everyone use the words for free.

> <u>Ending (Resolution)</u>
> People are able to talk to one another freely again.

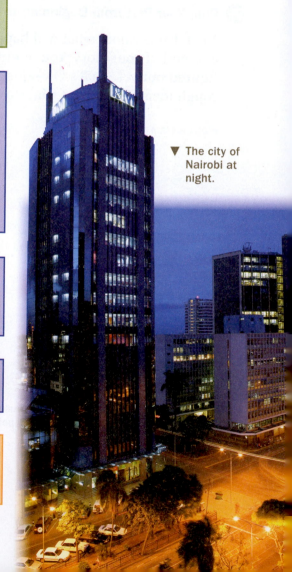

▼ The city of Nairobi at night.

5 **Plan to <u>Show</u>, Not Tell**

When you write a story, try to show, not tell, what happens. Instead of writing, "It was a hot day," include vivid details that *show* the day was hot. Instead of writing, "Tania was smart," *show* it with dialogue and actions.

Sensory details are one way to show what happens. Kendall used a Five-Senses Diagram to plan:

Five-Senses Diagram

Anansi saw . . .	• people ignoring each other • Mr. Nyame's massive office
Anansi heard . . .	• silence in Nairobi • Mr. Nyame's harsh voice • laughter, crying, and whistling
Anansi smelled . . .	• cleaning supplies • baked goods
Anansi tasted . . .	• the sweetness of the bread
Anansi felt . . .	• a strong hug • hard pavement

You don't need to tell readers everything about your characters. A few key details, along with dialogue, can pack a lot of meaning. Use a chart like Kendall's to plan.

Character Chart

Detail	What It Means
Anansi wants to help people talk to one another again.	Anansi is kind and thoughtful.
Anansi is able to achieve his goal.	He is clever and persistent.
Mr. Nyame charges people money for each word they say.	Mr. Nyame is mean and greedy.

Reflect

• Do you know your character's problem and how he or she solves it?

• Have you thought of what obstacles stand in the character's way?

Draft

Now that you have it all planned out, it's time to draft your story. Don't worry about getting it perfect on the first try, but do follow your plan.

- **Use Your Organizer** Follow your writing plan. That way, the events of your story will flow smoothly, and the ending will be clear.

> The city of Nairobi was a very quiet place. However, it had not always been that way. In 2013, a wealthy company executive named Mr. Nyame started buying the rights to different words. He charged people heavy fees whenever they used one of *his* words. Eventually, people could not talk to each other without getting a big bill, so they rarely spoke. A young man named Anansi was saddened by this silence.

Kendall followed the beginning of his plan to introduce the setting, characters, and conflict.

- **Add Details and Dialogue** Details and dialogue work to show your reader what's happening. Add sensory details, key details about characters, and dialogue to liven up your story.

From Kendall's Draft

> Anansi walked into Mr. Nyame's big office nervously.
> "I'm working on purchasing that sound you just made," Mr. Nyame said in his deep, harsh voice. "You'd better use it as much as you can while it's still free." He chuckled.
> "Mr. Nyame, I have come to make you a business proposal," Anansi said stiffly. "I … I would like to buy the rights to the words of Nairobi."

TechTIP

List details as phrases or sentences. Then use cut and paste from the **Edit** menu to move details around as you need to.

Reflect

- Read your draft. What details show how you've modernized the story?

- Does your story have a strong ending?

DRAFTING TIPS

Trait: **Organization**

If You Need More Details . . .

Sometimes, your writing and your characters seem boring. You've followed your plan, but somehow your writing seems lifeless.

Try Adding Snapshots and Thoughtshots

Read your writing to yourself. Pick one important moment. Picture it in your mind.

- What does the character see, hear, smell, and taste? Write down these details to create a **snapshot** of that moment.

- Now ask: what does the character think? Write down your character's thoughts. This description is called a **thoughtshot**.

Kendall used the answers to his questions to add details to his story.

Snapshots	Thoughtshots:
Where was Anansi? What was happening?	How did Anansi feel after Mr. Nyame's request? Did Anansi think the task was possible?

From Kendall's Draft

Anansi paced back and forth on the street in front of Mr. Nyame's office. He was worried that he might have been tricked. He wondered if it was even possible to get the sound of a child's laugh, a woman's joyful cry, and an old man's whistle. Also, he could only get those sounds by using three words lent by Mr. Nyame.

Revise

As you revise your work, keep your audience and purpose in mind. Will your audience be entertained?

1 Evaluate Your Work

Read your story aloud to a partner. Have the partner sketch the scenes. Look at the sketches and ask yourself:

- **About the Form** Do the sketches show the setting? Do they reflect my character's problem and what the character does about it?

- **About the Organization** Do the sketches show events in order? Are there any gaps? Does one show how the story ends?

Revision in Action

From Kendall's Draft

Anansi needed to achieve the difficult task of recording the sound of a woman's joyful cry. An idea flashed in his head like lightning, but to carry it out he would need to use his three words. He looked up and saw Ms. Abula sadly slumped over the counter of her bakery stand.

Anansi ran over to Ms. Abula's stand and purchased one of her homemade loaves of bread. Right there, he bit into it enthusiastically.

"This is *delicious*," he said in a friendly voice. Ms. Abula stood up. Her big dark eyes were shiny with tears. It had been so long since anyone had complimented her baking, she couldn't help but cry.

Kendall thinks:

" **The events are confusing. What gives Anansi his idea?** "

" **I think I need some transitions to tell when things happen.** "

" **I should *show* Ms. Abula's reaction. That'll make it clearer.** "

2 Mark Your Changes

Add Text To help your reader understand your story, you may need to add

- sensory details to help readers picture the events of your story

- transitions to show how events are connected.

Rearrange Text To keep the order of events clear and improve the flow of your story, you may need to change the order of sentences and paragraphs. Use this mark: ↷ to show the new order.

You may also want to break your paragraphs up differently. Use the ¶ symbol to show the start of a new paragraph.

Reflect

- Are the events of your story clear to the reader?

- Do you need to add more details?

Revising Marks

MARK	∧	↷	⌐	ꝗ	¶
WHAT IT MEANS	Insert something.	Move to here.	Replace with this.	Take out.	Make a new paragraph.

Revised Draft

Anansi needed to achieve the difficult task of recording the sound of a woman's joyful cry. ~~An idea flashed in his head like lightning, but to carry it out he would need to use his three words.~~ He looked up and saw Ms. Abula sadly slumped over the counter of her bakery stand. ∧

Immediately
Anansi ran over to Ms. Abula's stand and purchased one of her homemade loaves of bread
warm and sweet and golden.
Right there, he bit into it enthusiastically.
and let the crunchiness and softness fill his mouth. ∧

"This is *delicious*," he said in a friendly voice.

Suddenly
Ms. Abula stood up. Her big dark eyes were shiny with tears. ¶Because It had been so long since anyone had complimented her baking, she couldn't help but cry.
"Oh, Anansi!" she cried happily. "Thank you!" ∧

Kendall fixed the order of events.

Kendall added sensory details to "show" what the scene was like.

Kendall added transitions and started a new paragraph to fix the flow.

Edit and Proofread

Are you happy with the way your modern fairy tale turned out? Now it's time to read it again to fix language errors. This is what you do when you edit and proofread your work:

- **Check the Grammar** Make sure that you have used correct and conventional grammar throughout. In particular, check for subject-verb agreement with forms of *be* and *have*. (See page 103W.)

- **Check the Spelling** Spell-check can help, but it isn't always enough. For errors with two-syllable words, you'll have to read your work carefully and perhaps use a dictionary. (See page 104W.)

- **Check the Mechanics** Errors in punctuation and capitalization can make your work hard to understand. In particular, check that you have used correct punctuation and capitalization in dialogue. (See page 105W.)

Use these marks to edit and proofread your modern fairy tale.

Editing and Proofreading Marks

MARK	WHAT IT MEANS	MARK	WHAT IT MEANS
∧	Insert something.	/	Make lowercase.
∧	Add a comma.	ℒ	Delete, take something out.
∧	Add a semicolon.	¶	Make new paragraph.
⊙	Add a period.	◯	Spell out.
⊙	Add a colon.	⌐	Replace with this.
∨ ∨	Add quotation marks.	∼	Change order of letters or words.
∨	Add an apostrophe.	#	Insert space.
≡	Capitalize.	◡	Close up, no space here.

Reflect

- What kinds of errors did you find? What can you do to keep from making them?

GrammarWorkout

Check Subject-Verb Agreement

- Use a form of the verb **be** to tell what a subject is like.

  EXAMPLES   I **am** a banker.

  Anansi **is** clever.

  "Now, we **are** free to talk!" say the townspeople.

  They **are** excited.

  "You **are** our hero, Anansi," they exclaim.

- Use a form of the verb **have** to tell what a subject owns or possesses.

  EXAMPLES   I **have** bread to sell.

  Mr. Nyame **has** the copyright.

  Ms. Abula **has** bread and muffins.

  The townspeople say, "We **have** our words back!"

  "You **have** a clever brain, Anansi," they say.

  Now they **have** all the words they need.

- The forms of **be** and **have** you use depend on your subject. Make sure the forms of **be** and **have** you use in your sentences agree with the subject.

Find the Trouble Spots

> Anansi must record the sound of a child's laughter. Luckily, he ~~have~~ _has_ bubbly neighbors named Kayla and Lucas. "I ~~is~~ _am_ going to wear the funniest costume I can," he thought. "Both Kayla and Lucas has wonderful laughs! If I wear a funny costume, at least one child are likely to fall over laughing."

Find and fix two more errors in subject-verb agreement.

Edit and Proofread, continued

> ## SpellingWorkout

Check Two-Syllable Words

Many English words follow a pattern, or a regular form. Learning these patterns can help you spell words correctly. Learn the following patterns for **two-syllable words.**

- When the first syllable contains a short vowel, it is often followed by a double consonant. This pattern is referred to as **VCCV** (vowel, consonant, consonant, vowel).

EXAMPLE	**suggest** ⟶	sug | gest
	connect ⟶	con | nect
	batter ⟶	bat | ter

- When the first syllable contains a long vowel, it is often followed by a single consonant. This pattern is referred to as **VCV** (vowel, consonant, vowel).

EXAMPLE	**rudest** ⟶	ru | dest
	shaken ⟶	sha | ken
	rotate ⟶	ro | tate

Find the Trouble Spots

Anansi remembered an old teacher that worked at his formmer school. He had a favor to ask of her.

Anansi asked Ms. Abula, "Can I borow your bicycle?"

"I supose so," answered Ms. Abula as Anansi rode away. Time was about to run out, and Anansi needed the bicycle so he could get the harddest sound.

Find and fix two other spelling errors.

Mechanics Workout

Check Capitalization and Punctuation

Help your readers follow your characters' dialogue:

- Capitalize the first word of a quotation. Use quotation marks to show where a quotation begins and ends.

  EXAMPLE   Anansi said, "This will make her laugh."

- Use commas before or after dialogue tags, such as *James asked* or *Carla replied*. When a dialogue tag comes before a quote, include a comma between the tag and the opening quotation marks.

  EXAMPLE   Anansi exclaimed, "Wow! These are truly delicious!"

- When a dialogue tag comes after a quote, use a comma inside the ending quotation mark, unless the quote ends in a question mark or exclamation point.

  EXAMPLE   "It's a deal," he said.

Find the Trouble Spots

"Silence has plagued our city for too long, but that is all going to change" Anansi shouted to the crowd. The crowd stood silent. Then one person yelled, "what do you mean?"

"I mean you are free to speak. I bought the rights to our words back from Mr. Nyame" Anansi said.

The crowd collectively yelled, "hooray! Our words are ours again!"

Find and fix two more errors in punctuation or capitalization.

Publish, Share, and Reflect

You've written a modern fairy tale that is well organized and full of vivid details and that tells an engaging story. It's time now to share it.

1 **Publish and Share Your Work**

One way to share your modern fairy tale is to read it aloud. This way, you can dramatize parts of your story. You can also give emphasis to key lines of dialogue. Here are a few ways to share it aloud:

- Organize a reading with other people you know who have written stories.

- Read it to your classmates or teacher.

- Read it to a children's group at a library or daycare center.

Here are some ways to make sure that everyone will find your reading exciting:

- Use sound effects, like music, to create atmosphere.

- Use visual aids, like posters or maps, to *show* your audience what happened instead of just telling them about it.

- Practice, practice, practice! Once you are familiar with your story, you will be confident and ready to speak in front of an audience.

2 **Reflect on Your Work**

Publishing and sharing a piece of writing doesn't mean you can't alter or add to your story. Think back on what you have written. Ask yourself if there is anything you might change.

Reflect

- What did I learn about developing a plot?

- What was the hardest part of creating characters?

How to Do a Dramatic Reading

Entertain a group with your modern fairy tale. Reading it aloud will bring the characters and events to life! Don't tell your listeners what parts are sad or frightening or funny—show them:

1. Give a brief introduction to your story. You might explain how it is similar to and different from the original fairy tale and give any background information your listeners will need to understand the events, setting, and characters.

2. Practice speaking with **diction**. Pronounce each word clearly. Practice saying difficult words until you can say them fluently and clearly.

3. Vary the **tone** and **pitch** of your voice to fit different parts of your story. Create one "voice" for each character and use it every time that character speaks.

4. Plan and rehearse your **tempo**. Which parts will you read quickly? Slowly? Highlight those in different colors. Where will you pause to give your audience time to think or laugh? Mark those points with a large dot, and write *pause* in the margin.

" See? My fairy godmother gave me these magic slippers as a reward. "

5. Be an actor! Ham it up by using **gestures** and facial **expressions** to communicate as you read. Practice your gestures in front of a mirror or a friend, or record yourself and watch your performance.

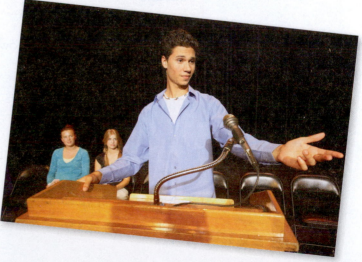

Write to
Solve a Problem

Model Study

Problem-and-Solution Paragraph

When you write a **problem-and-solution paragraph**, you present a **problem** and discuss a **solution**. A typical problem-and-solution paragraph follows a "road map" like the one below.

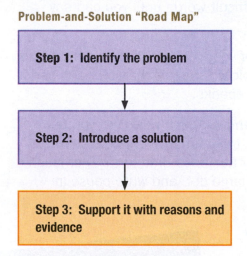

Problem-and-Solution "Road Map"

Step 1: Identify the problem

Step 2: Introduce a solution

Step 3: Support it with reasons and evidence

Read the student model on page 109W. It shows the features of a good problem-and-solution paragraph.

PROBLEM-AND-SOLUTION PARAGRAPH

A good problem-and-solution paragraph

✓ presents a problem

✓ offers and supports an effective solution.

Feature Checklist

Ramp It Up

by Brandy Jones

The writer presents a **solution** to a problem.

Lendale Middle School would benefit from having wheelchair ramps at more than one entrance. Right now, it has only one ramp for wheelchair access to the building. According to the American Disabilities Act, all buildings are required to have "adequate" wheelchair access. Having only one ramp at a school like Lendale is not adequate, and this creates problems for wheelchair users like me. Although there are several entrances to the school, I can use only the side entrance with the ramp. At the beginning and end of the day, when many students crowd around the entrance, this is a problem. I am sometimes late to class or school activities. Occasionally I miss my bus. Other Lendale students who use wheelchairs face the same problems. Although additional ramps may be expensive, the school district could set aside money from the budget for their construction. With more ramps, it would no longer be a struggle for students like me to enter and leave school.

She supports her solution with fact-based **evidence** and uses a credible source.

She further supports her solution with **reasons**.

She anticipates **objections** and provides a **counterclaim**.

Her **conclusion** supports her argument.

Student Model

Write a Problem-and-Solution Paragraph

WRITING PROMPT You face problems every day at home, at school, and in your community. Figuring out how to solve problems is a skill that you use all the time. What's a problem in your life that you've recently solved—or that you're trying to solve now?

Think about a problem that you have recently faced or are currently facing. Write a problem-and-solution paragraph that

- presents a problem
- offers a solution
- provides evidence and reasons to support the claim.

Prewrite

Here are some tips for planning your paragraph.

1 Identify a Problem as the Topic

Brainstorm a list of problems that you have faced or are currently facing. Try to think of problems that you care a lot about and that you have solved or have some idea about how to solve.

Write down a few possibilities, and then choose the best one. Sung made a list like this one.

> **Ideas**
> - I'm having a hard time getting up on time.
> - I lose stuff in my locker because it's messy.
> - Eighth graders at my school are treated unfairly.
> - There's too much trash in my neighborhood.

② Narrow Your Topic

Make sure that your topic is specific. A large problem may actually consist of three or four smaller ones. A smaller, more specific problem will be easier to write about in a paragraph, and easier for your readers to understand.

Take a look at how Sung narrowed down his problem.

How Sung Narrowed His Problem

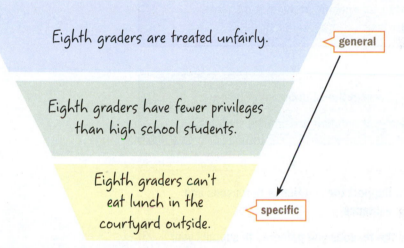

Eighth graders are treated unfairly. — general

Eighth graders have fewer privileges than high school students.

Eighth graders can't eat lunch in the courtyard outside. — specific

③ State and Support a Solution

Next, gather all the logical reasons and relevant evidence to support your solution. This will help you see your problem and solution more clearly. Take notes in a chart like this to help you later as you draft. Here is what Sung wrote.

Problem and Solution	Reasons and Evidence
—The school policy that prevents eighth graders from eating lunch in the courtyard with the older students is unfair. —We should sign and send a petition to Mrs. Angeles, the principal, asking her to change the policy.	—The school nurse, Mr. Beasley, says students are better able to concentrate after spending time outdoors. —The policy is unfair and makes eighth graders feel disrespected. —If older students object, eighth graders can go outdoors at an earlier or later time.

Prewrite, continued

4 Organize Ideas

Once you've chosen your problem and solution and gathered all the details, plan your paragraph with a "road map."

Problem-and-Solution "Road Map"

> **Step 1: Identify the problem**
>
> - **State your specific problem in a simple, clear way.**

↓

> **Step 2: Present the solution**
>
> - **State your solution in a simple, clear way.**

↓

> **Step 3: Support the solution with reasons and evidence**
>
> - **Use the reasons you gathered to support your solution.**
>
> - **Provide evidence from a reliable source to support your solution.**

Here's Sung's developed plan for his problem-and-solution paragraph.

Sung's Plan

Step 1: Identify the problem

- Eighth graders are not allowed to eat lunch in the courtyard as high school students do.

↓

Step 2: Present the solution

- Eighth graders should sign and send a petition to the principal, asking her to let us have lunch in the courtyard once a week.

↓

Step 3: Support your solution with reason and evidence

- It's not fair.
- It makes eighth graders feel disrespected.
- According to Mr.Beasley, the school nurse, students can concentrate better after spending time outdoors.

Problem-and-Solution Map

Reflect

- Is your problem focused and specific enough?

- Is your solution clearly explained and supported with reasons and evidence?

113W

Draft

Now that you have some great ideas to work with, it's time to draft! Use your map to make your draft go smoothly.

- **Identify the Problem** Refer to the top box of your map to draft your topic sentence. State the problem clearly.

> The school policy that bans eighth graders from eating lunch in the courtyard with the older students is unfair.

- **State Your Proposed Solution** Refer to the second box of your map again. Be sure to state your solution clearly so that it directly relates to the problem.

> We should sign and send a petition to Mrs. Angeles, the principal, requesting that this policy be changed.

- **Give Reasons and Evidence to Support Your Solution** Look at your map again. Number the reasons and evidence you listed there in order of importance. Try to anticipate objections to your solution and provide counterclaims to them.

> According to Mr. Beasley, the school nurse, students can concentrate better after spending time outdoors. The policy is unfair. It makes eighth graders feel disrespected. If the older students object, our courtyard time can be scheduled earlier or later than theirs.

From Sung's Draft

> The school policy that bans eighth graders from eating lunch in the courtyard with the older students is unfair. Eighth graders should sign and send a petition to the principal, requesting that she change this policy.

Reflect

- Do you clearly state the problem?
- Does your solution flow from the problem?
- Are your reasons logical?
- Is your evidence from a reliable source?
- Do you have a counterclaim for any objections?

Sung used the first two steps of his plan to draft the beginning of his paragraph.

DRAFTING TIPS

Trait: **Organization**

If Your Writing Is Vague. . .

If you don't support your solution with clear reasons and relevant evidence from reliable sources, your readers won't understand what you're trying to say.

Try Drawing a Target Diagram First

You want readers to understand what the problem is and why your solution will work. To develop your ideas, answer these questions on a **target diagram**.

1. What problem is the topic of your paragraph?

2. What solution do you propose to solve the problem?

3. What relevant reasons support your solution?

4. What evidence from a reliable source can you provide?

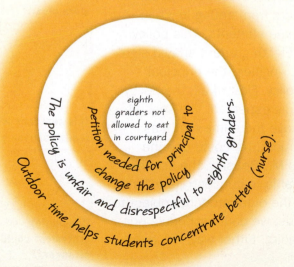

Sung's Target Diagram

Revise

As you revise your work, think about your audience and your purpose for writing. Consider whether your work does what you intend it to do.

1 **Evaluate Your Work**

Read your paragraph aloud to yourself. As you read, pretend that you're listening to someone else's paper. Ask yourself:

- **About the Form** Will my readers really understand the problem? Does my solution seem reasonable?

- **About the Organization** Do I include clear reasons and relavent evidence ? Do I anticipate objections and provide a counterclaim?

Revision in Action

Sung's Draft

At our school, eighth graders have classes in the same building as the high school students, but school policy prevents eighth graders from eating lunch in the courtyard with those same students. This policy is unfair on several levels. Eighth graders should sign and send a petition to Mrs. Angeles, the principal, asking her to change the policy. First of all, the policy makes eighth graders feel disrespected, like second-class citizens. We should have the same rights as the older students. Furthermore, we could use the time outdoors. According to Mr. Beasley, the school nurse, students are better able to concentrate after spending time outdoors. If the older students object to sharing the courtyard with us, we could schedule our lunchtime before or after theirs. Either way, the policy needs to be changed.

Sung thinks:

" **The problem could be stated a little more clearly.** "

" **This sentence isn't really necessary.** "

" **Concluding statement could be stronger.** "

2 **Mark Your Changes**

Add Text If you want to give more information and details, you will need to add text. Use this mark: ∧.

Delete Text When you're making your changes, you may find that you need to take out something. Use this mark to delete text: ⟿.

Rearrange Text Sometimes, a sentence fits better in another place. To move text, circle it and draw an arrow to where you want it to go: ↶.

Reflect

• What could you add to make your writing clearer?

• Do you need to move or delete any text?

Revising Marks	**MARK**	∧	↶	↖	⟿	⨍
	WHAT IT MEANS	Insert something.	Move to here.	Replace with this.	Take out.	Make a new paragraph.

Revised Draft

At our school, eighth graders have classes in the same building as the high school students, but school policy prevents eighth graders from eating lunch in ∧outdoors the courtyard with those same students. ~~This policy is unfair on several levels.~~ *an unfair* Eighth graders should sign and send a petition to Mrs. Angeles, the principal, asking her to change the policy. First of all, the policy makes eighth graders feel disrespected, like second-class citizens. ~~We should have the same rights as the older students.~~ Furthermore, we could use the time outdoors. *According to Mr. Beasley, the school nurse,* ∧Students are better able to concentrate after spending time outdoors. If the older students object to sharing the courtyard with us, we could schedule our lunchtime before or after theirs. Either way, the policy needs to be changed.

Sung stated the problem more precisely.

Sung rearranged text to clarify his ideas.

Sung took out unnecessary text.

Edit and Proofread

After you're happy with the content of your paragraph, read it again to fix language errors. This is what you do when you edit and proofread your work:

- **Check the Grammar** Make sure that you have used correct grammar throughout. In particular, check for correct use of past tense verbs. (See page 119W.)

- **Check the Spelling** Spell-check can be helpful, but it won't catch all your spelling mistakes. It is important to read your work carefully and use a dictionary to double-check words ending in -*ed* and -*ing*. (See page 120W.)

- **Check the Mechanics** Mistakes in punctuation and capitalization can make your work hard to understand. In particular, check to be sure that proper nouns are correctly capitalized. (See page 121W.)

Use these marks to edit and proofread your paragraph.

Editing and Proofreading Marks

MARK	WHAT IT MEANS	MARK	WHAT IT MEANS
∧	Insert something.	/	Make lowercase.
⋏	Add a comma.	℘	Delete, take something out.
⋏	Add a semicolon.	¶	Make new paragraph.
⊙	Add a period.	◯	Spell out.
⊙	Add a colon.	⌐	Replace with this.
ᵛ ᵛ	Add quotation marks.	∼	Change order of letters or words.
ᵛ	Add an apostrophe.	#	Insert space.
≡	Capitalize.	◡	Close up, no space here.

Reflect

- What kinds of errors did you find? What can you do to keep from making them?

Grammar Workout

Check Verbs in the Past Tense

- Use the **past tense** of a verb to tell about an action that has already happened.

EXAMPLES   Thurgood Marshall **finished** law school in 1933.
He **helped** African Americans win legal rights.

- For most verbs, add **-ed** to show past tense.

EXAMPLES   march + -ed = marched
talk + -ed = talked
succeed + -ed = succeeded

Find the Trouble Spots

Last week in class, we ~~discuss~~ *discussed* the life of Thurgood Marshall. His actions showed me that it's important to fight for a cause. A few days ago, we ~~sign~~ *signed* a petition and mail it to our principal. In the petition, we asked our principal to let eighth graders eat lunch in the courtyard. Marshall work for much bigger causes, of course, but this situation is important to us!

Find and fix two other errors with past tense verbs.

Edit and Proofread, continued

> ## Spelling Workout
>
> # Check Verbs with -*ed* and -*ing*
>
> Follow these rules when you add -**ed** or -**ing** to a verb.
>
> - Add the ending directly to words that end with one vowel and two consonants.
>
>   EXAMPLES   fill + -ed = filled
>   turn + -ing = turning
>
> - Add the ending directly to words that end with two vowels and one consonant.
>
>   EXAMPLES   need + -ed = needed
>   explain + -ing = explaining
>
> - When a word ends in silent *e*, drop the *e*. Then add the ending.
>
>   EXAMPLES   live + -ed = lived
>   smile + -ing = smiling
>
> - When a word ends in one vowel and one consonant, double the consonant before adding the ending.
>
>   EXAMPLES   jog + g + -ed = jogged
>   tap + p + -ing = tapping
>
> ### Find the Trouble Spots
>
> >   Our social studies teacher, Mr. Tollson, ~~stoped~~ **stopped** to talk about our problem yesterday. He understands why we want to have lunch **sitting** ~~siting~~ outside in the courtyard. He wishd us good luck with our petition. We said that we are hopeing to hear from the principal soon.
>
> Find and fix two other spelling errors.

Mechanics Workout

Check Capitalization of Proper Nouns

The names of specific people, places, and organizations are called **proper nouns**. Proper nouns always start with a capital letter.

Common Nouns (general)	Proper Nouns (specific)
writer	Herman Melville
ocean	the Atlantic Ocean
restaurant	Spice Heaven

Capitalize each important word in each of the following:

- Proper names of people

  EXAMPLES   Sarah Jones   Henry Blanco

- Proper names of places

  EXAMPLES   the Rocky Mountains   New York City

- Proper names of organizations

  EXAMPLES   the Little Rock School District
  the National Aeronautics and Space Administration

Find the Trouble Spots

After reading our petition, Mrs. angeles allowed eighth graders to use the courtyard. This is a real victory for eighth-grade kids at brookside school! Because of this success, the authors of the petition joined the brookside student government association. In fact, Lori carpenter might run for president!

Find and fix two more capitalization errors.

6 | *Write as a* Community Member

Model Study

> "I don't like to just complain about problems. I like to find solutions."
>
> —Keenan

Problem-and-Solution Essay

You can say more about a problem and solution in an essay.

Structure of Problem-and-Solution Essay

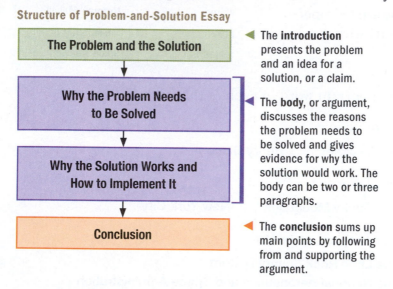

◄ The **introduction** presents the problem and an idea for a solution, or a claim.

◄ The **body**, or argument, discusses the reasons the problem needs to be solved and gives evidence for why the solution would work. The body can be two or three paragraphs.

◄ The **conclusion** sums up main points by following from and supporting the argument.

See the features of the model essay on page 123W.

PROBLEM-AND-SOLUTION ESSAY

A good problem-and-solution essay

☑ presents a problem and a solution

☑ discusses the reasons for needing to solve the problem

☑ gives evidence for why the solution works and how to make it happen

☑ summarizes important points.

Feature Checklist

Study Hall for Everyone

by Shira Nagaraj

The introduction states the problem and solution.

Many students at Fellsburg Middle School have trouble completing their homework at night. Right now, study hall periods are just for students with special needs. However, extra study halls with help from teachers would benefit all students.

Fellsburg is a challenging school, and students get a lot of homework. Many students don't have time to finish their assignments, especially if they have after-school activities. They stay up late at night doing homework and come to school tired the next day. Also, many classes are too crowded, so teachers don't have time to help with homework.

Shira gives reasons the problem needs to be solved.

Shira supports her claim with evidence from a reliable source.

A 45-minute study hall period would give students extra time to complete their homework. The school could build this period into students' daily schedules. According to Principal Paul Wardinski, adding study halls to the regular school day "helped all kids. Our 'F' ratio dropped by about a third." Teachers from different subject areas could monitor students in study halls. Some teachers might think monitoring a study hall is extra work, but they would be providing help only with old material and they wouldn't have to prepare new lessons.

Shira provides a counterclaim for those who might object.

The conclusion sums up the important points.

School-wide study halls would benefit all students. We would no longer be overwhelmed by homework after school, and we could come to class better prepared.

Student Model

Focus and Unity

What's It Like?

If you want to go to a new place in your town, you find it on a map and then connect the streets to get you there. Writing needs the same focus. Zero in on a central idea, then connect other ideas to get it across. That way, your writing will be headed in the right direction!

Why Do Focus and Unity Matter?

When a paper has focus and unity, the problem and solution are clear. All the ideas support the solution and go together.

Staying focused helps writers achieve their purpose. For instance, if you're writing to argue, you'll be more convincing if every idea in your paper supports the point you want to prove. If you're writing to inform, readers will follow your ideas more easily if the ideas relate to your topic.

To make your writing focused, start off with a brief, clear statement of what your essay is about. Then, as you write, keep asking yourself: Do these points relate to my problem and solution, or am I writing off-topic?

Study the rubric on page 125W. What is the difference between a paper with a score of 2 and one with a score of 4?

Focus and Unity

	How clearly does the writing present a central idea or claim?	How well does everything go together?
4 Wow!	The writing expresses a **clear** central idea or claim about the topic.	**Everything** in the writing goes together. • The main idea of each paragraph goes with the central idea or claim of the paper. • The main idea and details within each paragraph are related. • The conclusion is about the central idea or claim.
3 Aaah.	The writing expresses a **generally** clear central idea or claim about the topic.	**Most** parts of the writing go together. • The main idea of most paragraphs goes with the central idea or claim of the paper. • In most paragraphs, the main idea and details are related. • Most of the conclusion is about the central idea or claim.
2 Hmmm.	The writing includes a topic, but the central idea or claim is **not** clear.	**Some** parts of the writing go together. • The main idea of some paragraphs goes with the central idea or claim of the paper. • In some paragraphs, the main idea and details are related. • Some of the conclusion is about the central idea or claim.
1 Huh?	The writing includes many topics and **does not** express one central idea or claim.	The parts of the writing **do not** go together. • Few paragraphs have a main idea, or the main idea does not go with the central idea or claim of the paper. • Few paragraphs contain a main idea and related details. • None of the conclusion is about the central idea or claim.

Focus and Unity, continued

Compare Writing Samples

In a focused and unified essay, the problem and solution in each paragraph go with each other and with the claim. Read the excerpts from a problem-and-solution essay on this page.

Focused and Unified

Keep Kids Awake

If you walk into a middle-school classroom during first period, you'll probably see a few sleeping students. They're not bored or lazy; they're just exhausted. School starts too early in the day, usually between 7:30 and 7:45 a.m. Schools can help keep students awake by starting an hour later.

Schools should start later because teens need more than nine hours of sleep at night according to the American Sleep Disorders Association. Having to get up for early classes deprives students of the sleep they need to stay awake in class and to concentrate. Furthermore, most of the school's curriculum can be taught in four hours, so there's no need for students to start school so early.

The writer presents a **problem** and a **solution**, or **claim**.

Evidence from reliable sources and **relevant reasons** support the claim.

Not Well Focused and Unified

Middle School Hours

Students often sleep through their first class of the day. They're exhausted because middle school starts too early, usually between 7:30 and 7:45 a.m. If school started an hour later, kids wouldn't be tired during class.

Vending machines don't help, either. Tired students have trouble retaining the information they learn. As many as 28 percent of students fall asleep in the first class of the average school day, according to a study by the National Sleep Foundation. It is also disruptive to teachers when they have to interrupt class to wake a student. Starting school an hour later would help kids pay attention in class.

The writer states a **problem** and **solution**.

This sentence does not relate to either.

This **detail** relates to the problem, but does not support the claim.

Evaluate for Focus and Unity

Now read carefully the problem-and-solution essay below. Use the rubric on page 125W to score it.

How to Fix Overcrowded Classrooms
by Uma Marks

Overcrowded classrooms are a major problem facing Springfield Middle School. Some teachers have even been forced to teach in the library or the gymnasium.

Overcrowded classrooms make it harder for students to learn. Rooms designed for twenty-five students are forced to cram in almost forty. With so many people in the classroom, it is difficult to concentrate on what the teacher is saying. It isn't fair to the teacher, either. He or she ends up spending more time controlling the crowd than teaching the class.

Extending the school day one hour is the best solution. This allows time for one additional class during the day. That, in turn, would make smaller class sizes possible. The district should think about hiring more teachers, too. We particularly need teachers in math and science.

A longer school day would put an end to crammed classrooms. Teachers and students would be much more comfortable and better able to concentrate on their work.

Does the introduction identify a problem and a solution?

Does the body of the essay include any unrelated details?

Does the conclusion clearly summarize the important points?

127W

Raise the Score

These papers have been scored using the **Focus and Unity Rubric** on page 125W. Study each paper to see why it got the score it did.

Overall Score: 4

Extending the Media Center's Hours

Leroy Nadal

The first paragraph presents a **problem** and a **solution** as the claim.

Hill Valley Middle School's media center is a valuable resource. Unfortunately, it closes its doors as soon as the final bell rings. This is a problem for students who want to use the library during after-school hours. It would benefit students if the center stayed open for 90 minutes after the last bell.

The second paragraph tells more about the problem.

These paragraphs tell more about the problem and solution.

Having the media center close so early prevents students from getting the most out of this resource. Students often don't have enough time during the day to use the computers or check out a book. Also, many students have after-school activities. If they want a quiet place to study before their activity starts, they don't have many options.

The third paragraph argues to support the solution with evidence and reasons.

Extending the media center's open hours is a simple solution that would be easy to implement. Student volunteers could help out at the center during the extra hours. Many kids like the media center, so they would probably be happy to help.

The **conclusion** sums up the problem and its solution.

Because of the media center's limited hours, students miss out on all it has to offer. Extending the hours would help everyone take advantage of this resource.

Extending the Media Center's Hours

At Hill Valley Middle School, the media center closes at the end of the school day. What happens to students who want to use it after school? It would be good for students if the center stayed open for a while after the last bell rings.

Having the media center close right away makes it harder for students to use this resource. Students don't really have enough time to use the computers or check out a book during the day. Also, several students might want a quiet place to stay and study after school is out.

Keeping the media center open after hours is a simple solution that would be easy to do. Students could volunteer to work at the center during the extra hours. Some reports say that volunteering is increasing in America. Lots of kids like the media center, so they would probably like working there, too.

Having the media center stay open after school is in everyone's best interests. Students can study after school and better appreciate their school library.

The writer presents a **problem** and **solution** but could state them more clearly.

The second paragraph tells more about the problem.

The third paragraph argues to support the claim with evidence.

This **detail** doesn't help support the claim.

The **conclusion** sums up the important ideas.

RAISING *THE SCORE*

The claim should be more specific and unrelated details should be cut. Where should the writer make changes?

Raise the Score, continued

The writer's claim is vague because the **problem** and **solution** aren't stated clearly.

The details in the third paragraph do not argue to support the claim with evidence or reasons.

Overall Score: 2

Extending the Media Center's Hours

Hill Valley Middle School's media center has been a part of the school for many years. It has up-to-date computers and a huge selection of books. Its hours are from 8 o'clock in the morning to 3 o'clock in the afternoon. That isn't enough time for some people. Students enjoy using this library and would like to use it more often.

The media center closes around the same time the school day ends. Its busiest time is during lunch. At that time many students stop by to read a magazine or newspaper. The media center is right across the hall from the cafeteria. It is also very busy in the morning. Some teachers regularly take their classes to the library.

The library is the busiest when research papers are due. There are always several classes in here during that time. Even then, some students don't get all their research done. Teachers should assign fewer research papers.

The media center is important to the school. Students really want to use it more often.

The details in the second paragraph do not tell more about the problem.

The **conclusion** revisits the problem and solution, but the ideas are still vague.

RAISING THE SCORE

How could the writer state the claim more clearly and support it? How should he revise the conclusion?

Extending the Media Center's Hours

Hill Valley Middle School's media center closes pretty early. It closes right after the last bell of the day. I usually use the media center's computers when I get the chance. Their Internet connection is really fast!

A lot of students complain about this closing time. Some of them might have a book to return, but they can't because the library's already closed.

For example, I checked out a book last semester. I had forgotten about it until my teacher gave me an overdue slip. The slip said that I owed the library money for not returning a book! I don't even remember what the book was about.

Sometimes, I have to leave notes and reminders for myself. When I check out a book, I have to make sure I don't misplace it because I don't want to owe money again. I need to remember to return books during school hours. It's too bad the media center isn't open after school.

RAISING *THE SCORE*

The writer needs to focus on one topic. If his claim focused only on the center's limited hours, which ideas and details could he keep?

State a Claim

Have you ever had something exciting or interesting to tell someone, but then got distracted talking about the details and didn't get to the main point? When you write, it's very important that you get to the main point. Do it by clearly and briefly expressing the important thing you want to say early on in your essay.

Introduce a Claim

When you write a problem-and-solution essay, you tell what the problem is and then present a solution. By telling how you would solve the problem, you are introducing a **claim**. You then need to present a good argument to support your claim by providing clear reasons and relevant evidence from a reliable source.

Here's what one writer did for a problem-and-solution essay.

Topic or Problem

I am writing about the problem of irresponsible students.

Sample Claims or Solutions

The school can help make sure students don't do irresponsible things. ⟩ **Too broad**

Jeb Hannah, Luz Garcia, and some other kids created false fire alarms this year. So the school should install special security cameras. ⟩ **Too narrow**

To prevent students from pulling fire alarms as a prank, the school could install more security cameras. ⟩ **Just right**

Focus Your Paragraphs

All your paragraphs have to go with your claim, or solution. To keep your paragraphs focused and unified, follow these steps.

1 Use a Topic Sentence to State the Problem

Although the topic sentence can be in the beginning, middle, or end of a paragraph, it is usually at the beginning or the end. Depending upon where you place the topic sentence, you may need to change the supporting reasons and evidence you use or how you organize them.

- If you want your readers to know right away what your paragraph is about, place the topic sentence at the very beginning. Then add the supporting reasons and evidence.

- If you want to emphasize your point a little more, give the supporting reasons and evidence first and put the topic sentence at the end.

2 Be Sure Each Detail Relates to the Problem

Ask yourself: Does each detail say something more about the problem or solution? Are all the details important?

Now, look at the topic sentence in each paragraph. Then notice how the details flow.

To prevent students from pulling fire alarms as a prank, the school could install more security cameras. Westlake Middle School has security cameras, but none of them face the alarms. False alarms have become a problem over the past two years. Students may think it's funny, but false alarms take fire trucks away from real emergencies. The alarm also disrupts class. If students knew they were on camera, they might think twice before pulling the alarm.

False fire alarms have become a problem at Westlake Middle School over the past two years. Students may think it's funny, but false alarms take fire trucks away from real emergencies. The alarm also disrupts class. Westlake has security cameras. However, none of them face the fire alarms. To prevent students from pulling fire alarms as a prank, the school could install more security cameras.

Writing Strategy

Stay in Control from Start to Finish

Have you ever seen a really great diver soar off a diving board? The diver controls his or her body from the beginning of the dive to the end. Writing works the same way. To make your essay effective, focus on your central idea from the start to the finish.

Organize Ideas and Details

In a problem-and-solution essay with four or five paragraphs, you can maintain your focus by using a graphic like this one.

Essay Diagram

Introduction: The problem is described, and an idea for a solution, or a claim, is presented.

Body: Paragraphs discuss the reasons the problem needs to be solved and give evidence for why the solution would work.

Conclusion: Revisits and summarizes the important points by following from and supporting the argument.

Read the claim below and the paragraphs that follow. How could you fix each paragraph to go better with the claim of the essay?

Claim

Soda isn't good for kids, so we should replace it in school vending machines with healthy alternatives.

This **transition word** helps connect the ideas.

Paragraph

Studies show that drinking too much soda causes health problems in children. It can cause tooth decay and weight problems. However, I like drinking soda. Like a lot of kids at school, every morning I stop and get a soda from one of the vending machines. Ms. Carcetti won't let us drink soda in class, though.

These **details** do not support the claim.

Paragraph

Water and fruit juices are excellent replacements for vending-machine sodas. Water not only tastes good, but it also helps the body function properly. It cleanses the body and adds moisture to the skin. When you buy fruit juice, you should check the sugar content. Fruit juice isn't very healthy if you're mostly drinking sugar water!

Does this entire paragraph maintain the focus of the claim?

Write a
Problem-and-Solution Essay

WRITING PROMPT Often a small group or even a single person can help solve a problem in a school or neighborhood. What problems do you know about in your school, neighborhood, or community?

Choose a problem that you know about and think about how it could be solved. Then write a problem-and-solution essay that

- identifies the problem and a solution, or a claim
- discusses the reasons for needing to solve the problem
- tells why the solution is good and how to make it happen
- sums up the important ideas.

Prewrite

Here are some tips for planning your essay.

1 **Choose a Topic**

Talk to a teacher or a family member to help you identify a problem in your school or community. Or, look in a newspaper or school newsletter for articles about current problems.

Kathy used a chart like this one to record her ideas.

Problem	Solution
The animal shelter doesn't have enough workers.	The shelter could train volunteer students to help.
There's a lot of litter in my neighborhood.	I could try to start a litter-prevention club.
Foreign exchange students usually have a rough time when they first come to our school.	Some students might want to create a group to help foreign exchange students.

❷ Write Your Introduction

The introduction briefly and clearly presents the problem and an idea for a solution, or claim. It's best to state your problem and solution in the first paragraph of, or introduction to, your essay.

To get started, Kathy wrote her problem and solution at the top of an **essay diagram**.

Kathy's Problem and Solution

Foreign exchange students feel isolated and confused when they come to our school. So a group of us should create an organization to help them.

❸ Focus Your Ideas

Next, map out the reasons and the evidence that support your solution, or claim.

Here is how Kathy mapped out a reason her problem needs to be solved and gave evidence to support it.

How Kathy Mapped Out Her Second Paragraph

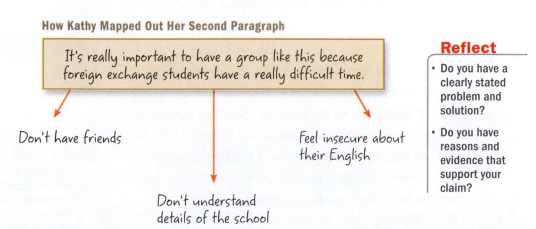

It's really important to have a group like this because foreign exchange students have a really difficult time.

Don't have friends

Don't understand details of the school

Feel insecure about their English

Reflect

- Do you have a clearly stated problem and solution?
- Do you have reasons and evidence that support your claim?

Draft

Once you know what you want to say in the introduction, body, and conclusion of your essay, start writing your draft. Keep your prewriting materials in front of you as you work. That way, you can refer to them as you write.

- **Focus on One Section at a Time** If you try to write about everything at once, you might become confused and lose your focus. Focus on each section of your essay in the proper order.

> Foreign exchange students feel isolated and confused when they come to our school, so we should create a group to help them. We could call it The Welcome! Group.

Kathy used the top part of her diagram to draft the introduction to her essay.

- **Expand Each Section** Expand each section in your essay into a paragraph. If you completed an **essay diagram** as Kathy did, you have the problem and its supporting reasons and the solution, or claim, with its evidence right at your fingertips!

Write a clear sentence that identifies what each paragraph is about. Then add reasons that support your problem and evidence that argues to support your solution, or claim. Here's how Kathy drafted her second paragraph.

From Kathy's Draft of Her Second Paragraph

> I think it's really important to form a group to support foreign exchange students. They are far from home without a friend. All the details of the school—like class schedules, cafeteria rules, and teachers' names—can be overwhelming. On top of all that, they have to speak a foreign language all day long. I know that many foreign exchange students feel insecure and shy about speaking English.

Reflect

- Read the draft of your second paragraph. Do all the details provide logical reasons related to the problem?

DRAFTING TIPS
Trait: **Focus and Unity**

If Your Writing Sounds Like a List...

Listy writing goes from one thing to the next too quickly, without developing anything or connecting the ideas. It is like a skeleton—bare bones.

Try Zeroing In on One Part

If you are writing about your solution, or claim, for example, be sure that it is stated clearly at the beginning of the paragraph.

> Creating a group to welcome and help foreign exchange students is a great solution to helping them adjust to their new surroundings.

Examine the evidence that supports your claim. Arrange those details in a logical order. Add words and phrases that help tie the ideas together.

> The Welcome! Group can greet new students as soon as they arrive at school. Having kids their own age to guide them around school will help the new students feel at ease. In addition, their guides can introduce them to other students and answer any questions. The student guides can even help the foreign exchange students with their English, reassuring them that they are doing really great!

Think about people who might object to your solution, or claim. Present a counterclaim.

> The Welcome! Group will have enough members so that no one student guide needs to miss class in order to help a foreign exchange student.

Revise

As you revise your work, ask yourself: Does my writing do what I want it to do? Will it connect with my audience?

1 Evaluate Your Work

Survey several friends and see if they can identify the problem and solution in your paper. What other questions do they have? As you work with your friends, ask:

- **About the Form** Do I have an introduction, two or three paragraphs in the body, and a conclusion?

- **About the Focus and Unity** Is my claim clear? Does everything in my paper go together?

Revision in Action

From Kathy's Draft of Her Third Paragraph

> From the moment new students arrive at school, kids their own age will be available to guide and support them. Creating a group to welcome and help foreign exchange students is a great solution. The Welcome! Group can make sure they meet other students. Group members can personally guide them around the school and answer all their questions. They can even help foreign exchange students with their English—and reassure them that they are doing really well! I'm trying to learn Japanese, and I know how important it is to have someone help and support you.

Kathy's friends think:

❝ This is confusing. Your topic sentence should go first. ❞

❝ You could add more evidence here to show how and why the solution would work. ❞

❝ This detail doesn't relate to the problem or to the solution. ❞

2 **Mark Your Change**

Add Text To show where you will add text, use a caret ∧.
You can use this mark to

- add text to clarify your claim

- add reasons to clarify the problem and evidence to support your solution, or claim.

Delete Text You can use a delete mark to take out words and sentences: ___ᵒ. Use this mark to take out details that don't go with your problem or solution.

Rearrange Text Sometimes, you can clarify your ideas by moving a sentence or a phrase to a different place. To move text, circle the text and draw an arrow to where you want to move it: ↶⟲.

Reflect

- Is your claim clear?

- Do you need to add, delete, or rearrange text?

- Did you add a conclusion?

MARK	∧	↶⟲	↖	___ᵒ	¶
WHAT IT MEANS	Insert something.	Move to here.	Replace with this.	Take out.	Make a new paragraph.

Revising Marks

Revised Draft

From the moment new students arrive at school, kids their own age will be available to guide and support them. Creating a group to welcome and help foreign exchange students is a great solution. The Welcome! Group can make sure they meet other students. *as well as people in the community* Group members can personally guide them around the school and answer all their questions. They can even help foreign exchange students with their English—and reassure them that they are doing really well! ~~I'm trying to learn Japanese, and I know how important it is to have someone help and support you.~~

Kathy clarified her claim by moving the topic sentence.

Kathy added a detail that provides additional evidence to support her claim.

Kathy took out an unnecessary detail.

Edit and Proofread

After you're satisfied with the content of your problem-and-solution essay, read your paper again to fix language errors. This is what you do when you edit and proofread your work.

- **Check the Grammar** Make sure that you have used correct and conventional grammar throughout. In particular, check for use of irregular past tense verbs. (See page 143W.)

- **Check the Spelling** Spell-check can help, but it isn't always enough. Double-check your work carefully, especially words with prefixes and suffixes. You can use a dictionary to find the correct spelling. (See page 144W.)

- **Check the Mechanics** Errors in punctuation and capitalization can make your work hard to understand. In particular, check that your abbreviations are correctly capitalized and punctuated. (See page 145W.)

Use these marks to edit and proofread your essay.

Editing and Proofreading Marks

MARK	WHAT IT MEANS	MARK	WHAT IT MEANS
∧	Insert something.	/	Make lowercase.
∧	Add a comma.	ℰ	Delete, take something out.
∧	Add a semicolon.	¶	Make new paragraph.
⊙	Add a period.	◯	Spell out.
⊙	Add a colon.	⟋	Replace with this.
⩗ ⩗	Add quotation marks.	∼	Change order of letters or words.
⩗	Add an apostrophe.	#	Insert space.
≡	Capitalize.	⌣	Close up, no space here.

Reflect

- What kinds of errors did you find? What can you do to keep from making them?

GrammarWorkout

Check Irregular Past Tense Verbs

- Regular verbs add **-ed** to form the past tense. Irregular verbs do not follow this rule to change forms.

    EXAMPLES   Yesterday, we **talked** about solving the problem at school. (regular verb)

    Yesterday, we **spoke** about solving the problem at school. (irregular verb)

- Each past tense form of an irregular verb must be memorized.

Present Tense	Past Tense
feel	felt
get	got
give	gave
know	knew
see	saw
speak	spoke
tell	told
think	thought

Find the Trouble Spots

Last year, a friend of mine ~~thinked~~ *thought* of the idea of starting an organization to help foreign exchange students. He ~~gived~~ *gave* it the name The Welcome! Group. He getted the idea because he knew a student from Morocco who was having trouble adjusting to his new life in the United States. When my friend told me about his idea, I really liked it.

Find and fix two more irregular past tense verbs.

Edit and Proofread, continued

Spelling Workout

Prefixes and Suffixes	Meaning
-able	able, likely, or fit to be
dis-	not, opposite of
-ly	in a certain way
-ness	state of
re-	again, back
un-	not, opposite of
under-	below, inferior
-y	having the quality of

Check Prefixes and Suffixes

Many words are made up of a base word with prefixes and suffixes added.

Adding a prefix does not change the spelling of a base word. Sometimes, the spelling of the base word changes when you add a suffix.

- If the base word ends in *e* and the suffix starts with a vowel, you usually drop the final *e* before adding the suffix.

  EXAMPLE   believe ⟶ believable

- If the base word ends in *y* with a consonant before it, you usually change the *y* to an *i* before adding the suffix.

  EXAMPLE   pretty ⟶ prettiness

- If the base word ends in a short vowel and a consonant, double the consonant before adding the suffix **-y** or another suffix starting with a vowel.

  EXAMPLES   fun ⟶ funny

  win ⟶ winnable

Find the Trouble Spots

You can't ~~underrestimate~~ *underestimate* how great The Welcome! Group is. I learned a ~~valueable~~ *valuable* lesson through the group. I learned that foreign and American students have a higher level of happyness when they share experiences. Some may dissagree, but I think The Welcome! Group is the best!

Find and fix two more spelling errors.

Mechanics Workout

Check Abbreviations

When you talk to adults, you often use titles—such as *Mister* or *Doctor*—before their names.

In writing, titles are usually abbreviated, or shortened. Always capitalize an abbreviation and add a period at the end. But watch out! Do not capitalize titles when they are used without a name.

EXAMPLE Only one **senator** opposed the bill.

Mr.	Mister, for a man
Mrs.	Mistress, for a married woman, but pronounced *missus*
Ms.	for any woman
Dr.	for a doctor
Pres.	for the president of a country, a company, a club, or an organization
Sen.	for a member of the U.S. Senate
Rep.	for a member of the U.S. House of Representatives
Capt.	for a captain

Study the list of commonly abbreviated titles. Check a dictionary if you are unsure about an abbreviation.

Find the Trouble Spots

My teacher, mrs Bennington, suggested I speak with ^Mr. Mister Ennio Morales, who is president of a support group for immigrants. It was a great idea. President Morales gave many tips for The Welcome! Group. For example, some foreign students are not familiar with the American healthcare system. So I asked my neighbor, doctor Lee, to speak to the students and give them information.

Find and fix two more abbreviation errors.

Publish, Share, and Reflect

You've written a problem-and-solution essay that is unified, focused, and clear. Maybe you even wrote about being part of the solution. It's time to share your work.

1 **Publish and Share Your Work**

There's more than one way to share your problem-and-solution essay. If the problem is of special interest to just a few people, you might share it with a small audience of family or friends. You might

- give a final copy of your essay to a friend
- read your essay aloud to a club or group that's concerned with the problem.

If you want to reach a wider audience, you might

- post it on a blog or Web site
- send it to your school or town newspaper
- publish it in your school or class newsletter
- read it on a local radio show.

No matter how you publish your essay, you can use the word-processing software on your computer to add finishing touches like these:

- headers
- footers
- page numbers
- breaks between pages.

2 **Reflect on Your Work**

Even after you've published your work, you'll probably still keep thinking about it. Ask yourself questions to decide what went well for this assignment and what areas you want to keep working on as a writer.

Reflect

- Did my writing identify a problem and provide a solution that could solve it effectively?

- What other problems and solutions could I write about?

Emphasize Your Points

Read your Problem-and-Solution Essay to your classmates to get their reactions to your argument.

To give a successful oral presentation:

1. **Plan** Read your essay aloud on your own. Make notes in the margins about how you would like each part to sound. Underline or highlight the important points that you want to emphasize.

2. **Practice** Focus on using a clear voice that can be heard by your audience. Also be sure to pronounce your words distinctly so that salient, or important, points don't get lost. Use natural-looking gestures to help emphasize important points. Practice your delivery in front of a mirror or record yourself on a video.

3. **Present** Briefly introduce your essay before you read. You might explain why you wrote it or why the issue is important to you. Then read your essay to the audience, clearly and expressively. Remember:

- Make eye contact with your listeners while you read so that you can monitor their reactions and confirm their understanding.

- If you used formal English in your essay, use a formal tone for your presentation. Slow down and speed up as needed to get your argument across.

- Don't be afraid to "ham up" your presentation a little. It will help keep your audience's attention.

" When I first started school, I didn't know how to speak English, so I know how important it is to help foreign exchange students when they first arrive at school. "

Model Study

Research Report

Writing a research report involves three key steps:

1 **Gather Information**

Choose a specific, focused topic. After deciding what questions you want to explore, gather information from a variety of reliable sources and take notes to record important facts.

2 **Organize and Digest the Information**

Now get organized. Be sure that you understand all your notes. Use them to create an outline—a plan for how to present your ideas.

3 **Present the Information**

The last step is the most exciting—writing about your findings and presenting the facts in your own unique way.

Study the student model on pages 149W–151W. It shows the features of a good research report.

RESEARCH REPORT

A good research report

☑ is focused on a specific topic

☑ gives information from a variety of sources

☑ is well organized with an introduction, body, and conclusion.

Feature Checklist

How the Moon Formed
by Keisha Robbins

When did the Moon lose its magical appeal? Probably in 1609 when Italian astronomer Galileo Galilei looked at the Moon through a telescope he invented. Scientists have studied the Moon ever since. In the centuries that followed, astronomers explained how the Moon orbits the Earth, how old it is, and why it looks the way it does. One question remains. How did the Moon form? No one knows for sure, but there are several possibilities.

Some Proposed Explanations

From the 1600s through the 1800s, astronomers presented different theories. One explanation was the co-accretion theory. *Accrete* means "grow together." It suggests that the Moon and all of the planets in the solar system formed out of dust and gas that accreted, or grew together (Lewis 145).

After learning more about what the Moon is made of, scientists questioned this theory. The Moon is nowhere near as dense as the Earth. This is most likely because, unlike the Earth, the Moon does not have a large iron core (Jefferson 78). Geologist Abigail Richards asks, "If Earth and Moon formed out of the same dust and gas, shouldn't they have a similar core?"

Introduction
The writer uses a question to introduce the topic.

The writer presents the **central idea** for her report.

Body
The writer uses **headings** to organize the paper.

Meteorites smashing into the Moon's surface created its distinctive craters.

149W

Research Report, continued

The fission theory is another idea. *Fission* refers to "splitting apart." This theory says the Moon and Earth were once one molten globe. Because Earth spun so fast, a glob flew off and formed the Moon (Lewis 148).

But fission theory doesn't explain why rocks on the Moon are so different from those on Earth (Pacheco 12). Also, scientists do not know of anything else in our solar system that was created that way (Pacheco 21).

The capture theory suggests that the Moon formed elsewhere in the solar system. When it drifted close, it was "captured" by Earth's gravity (Lewis 156). However, many scientists think it's more likely that the Moon would have smashed into the Earth (Taft 56–58).

Each theory has its supporters. Another theory has recently become most popular: the giant impact theory.

The Big Whack

The giant impact theory says that the body that became our Moon formed about 4.5 billion years ago (Taft 40). The solar system at that time contained rocky bodies, forming a lot of debris (Taft 45).

When a huge asteroid or meteorite smacked into Earth at high speed, the impact knocked off parts of both bodies. The parts formed a ring around Earth and then came together to form the Moon. (Lewis 160-161).

Some experts think this theory is unlikely. However, it's the best explanation scientists have so far, based on what they know about the Moon's orbit and

Each **main idea** is supported by facts and details from the writer's research.

The writer gives **source information** for each fact.

Each section relates to the writer's **central idea**.

composition (Vanbrugh 288). Astronomer Eric Woo explains, "A good theory gives a reasonable explanation based on available facts."

Direct quotes help make the report lively and interesting.

Evolution of the Moon

Scientists have learned more about the Moon since 1969. They've studied rocks collected by the Apollo mission of that year (Eban 14). The Moon has a great deal of anorthosite, a rock that only forms in molten magma (Eban 15).

A photo makes the report more interesting.

The maria are vast, flat regions on the Moon.

Astronomers think the Moon was covered in hot magma when it formed (Guterres 69). As the magma cooled over millions of years, minerals formed and hardened (Eban 16-17). Asteroids continually hit the Moon, creating craters (Lewis 200). The lava cooled and hardened to form huge, dark regions called *maria* (Burke 41). As volcanic activity slowed, the surface stabilized.

The Future of the Moon

The volcanic activity has almost stopped. The lack of atmosphere, winds, and storms means the Moon's surface will change little over time (Guterres 69).

Future explorations will help us discover more about the Moon. Will astronomers come up with a better explanation for how the Moon formed? Time will tell.

Conclusion relates ideas to the **central idea**. It ends with a question to wonder about.

Write a Research Report

RESEARCH PROMPT Is there something about the universe you wish you knew more about? Maybe you'd like to learn about the formation of celestial bodies, or research a particular planet or star.

Think of a specific topic you'd like to research. Then collect all your sources and write a report. Your report should

- be about something that truly interests you
- be well organized, with a central topic idea and a lot of evidence to support it
- present information from at least five reliable sources. (Only one of your sources should be an encyclopedia.)

Develop a Game Plan

For some school assignments, you may not be entirely free to choose your topic. Your teacher will have an area in mind: the Civil War, let's say, or adaptation of organisms to their surroundings. Still, use what choice you have to suit your research to your interests:

- Focus and narrow your topic to a specific aspect of the general area you have been assigned.

- Write research questions to pinpoint what you want to know about the topic.

Once you have research questions down, check out a variety of different sources to answer them, and keep detailed notes of the information you find. Remember that not all information is found in books.

Look at the photo on the next page. Choose a research question. Name at least three places you could look for answers. Include at least one person who could serve as a source.

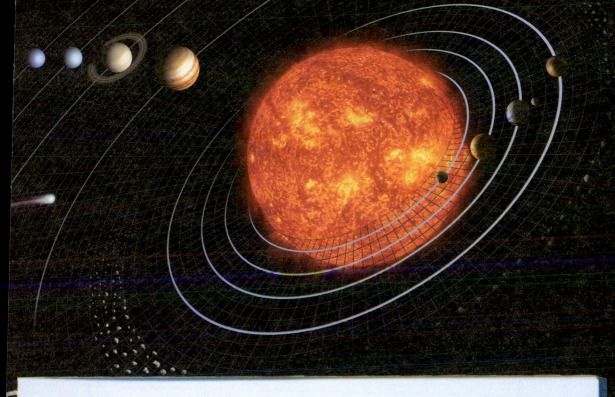

Research Questions

- Is there life on other planets?

- How come Pluto's not considered a planet anymore?

- What makes the large "gas giants" different from other planets?

- How do stars form?

- What do scientists know about black holes?

Develop a Game Plan, continued

How to Get from A to B

As you investigate your topic, you take notes, put together your ideas, develop an outline, and use it to write your finished report. This diagram summarizes the path from "raw research" to finished report.

1 **Conduct Research and Take Notes**

Note Cards

Moon Formation: Co-accretion Theory
— The Moon and the Earth formed
   at the same time.
— The Moon's core is different
   from the Earth's.
                    Students' Encyclopedia

Moon Formation—Fission Theory
— The Moon detached from the
   Earth.
— Scientists don't know of any
   similar events.
                    Pacheco, 21

2 **Synthesize Your Ideas**

Inquiry Chart

Research Questions	Source Information	Synthesis
What does the co-accretion theory suggest?	The Moon and the Earth formed from the same dust and gases. (Students' Enc.) The Moon and the Earth formed at the same time. (Lewis 145) The Moon and Earth were equally distant from the Sun. (Jefferson 148)	The Moon and the Earth formed simultaneously out of the same material, about the same distance from the Sun.

3 **Develop an Outline**

Outline

Scentists studied rocks to learn about the Moon's composition and core. ▼

II. Some Proposed Explanations
    A. Co-accretion theory
       1. Explanation
       2. Problems
    B. Fission

4 **Use the Outline to Write the Research Report**

Research Report

Some Proposed Explanations

From the 1600s through the 1800s, astronomers presented different theories. One explanation was the co-accretion theory. *Accrete* means "grow together." It suggests that the Moon and all of the planets in the solar system formed out of dust and gas that accreted, or grew together (Lewis 145).

After learning more about what the Moon is made of, scientists questioned this theory. The Moon is nowhere near as dense as the Earth. This is most likely because, unlike the Earth, the Moon does not have a large iron core (Jefferson 78). Geologist Abigail Richards asks, "If Earth and Moon formed out of the same dust and gas, shouldn't they have a similar core?"

Develop a Game Plan, continued

Choose and Focus Your Topic

You've made the right choice for a research topic if you can answer "yes" to each of these questions:

- Does the topic interest you?

- Will you be able to find enough information about the topic?

- Is your topic focused and specific?

Look at the planning chart that Keisha prepared below. How did she narrow her topic?

▲ The Moon is just one of the celestial bodies in our solar system.

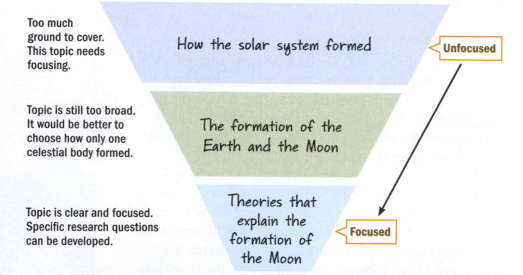

Too much ground to cover. This topic needs focusing.

How the solar system formed — **Unfocused**

Topic is still too broad. It would be better to choose how only one celestial body formed.

The formation of the Earth and the Moon

Topic is clear and focused. Specific research questions can be developed.

Theories that explain the formation of the Moon — **Focused**

Presearch and Put Together an FATP Chart

To really nail down your topic, and before diving into in-depth research, it helps to do a little *presearch*—you don't know what's out there until you look around a bit.

The Web is great for presearch. A little time spent Web-surfing at the beginning can help you choose a topic that is interesting, specific, and about which there is enough information.

Through her Internet research, Keisha learned about the different theories about how the Moon formed. Now the research project came together in her head and she was able to write her FATP Chart.

FATP Chart

Form: research report

Audience: my teacher and classmates

Topic: theories about how the Moon formed

Purpose: to inform readers how the Moon formed and developed

List Research Questions

Next, put together some research questions you want your report to "answer." Start out with a main research question, and then break it into more specific sub-questions.

Reflect

- Is your research topic specific and interesting enough?
- Do you need to write more questions to guide your research?

Vague

Main Question:
How did the Moon form?

Sub-Question:
1. What theories explain this?
2. Are these theories believable?
3. Which theory is popular today?

Specific

Main Question:
What are the theories for how the Moon formed?

Sub-Question:
1. What does each theory suggest?
2. What problem does each present?
3. Which theory is now the most popular? Why?

Locate Information Sources

A **source** is a place where you go to get something. Three kinds of sources are:

- the world around you—all you have to do is make a direct observation. This is not always possible (and, if you're researching rattlesnakes, may not be a good idea). But if you're researching the behavior of, say, butterflies in your backyard, open your eyes and look at your backyard!

- experts—people who know a lot about a topic, through study or through experience

- published materials which may be printed, transmitted electronically over the Internet, or captured in media such as films or sound recordings.

Getting Info from Experts

For Keisha's report on the formation of the Moon, an expert might be an astronomy professor who studies our solar system, or a science teacher who has studied the properties of the Moon. Interviews are a great way to get first-hand information and eyewitness accounts of an event. You can interview experts in person, by phone, or through e-mail.

How to Conduct an Interview

1. Explain the purpose of the interview when you contact the person to set up an appointment.

2. Plan your questions in advance. Ask questions that will get more than just a "yes" or "no" response.

3. Always be respectful and courteous to the person you are interviewing.

4. Follow your plan, but be flexible. Your subject might bring up important issues you hadn't thought of before. Ask follow-up questions if you need to know more.

5. Tape-record your subject's responses or take detailed notes.

Getting Info from Published Sources

Most published research resources are available both in print and over the Internet. Different types of sources contain different types of information.

Type of Source	Print	Web	Description and Uses
almanac	√	√	An almanac offers a compact summary of information, such as facts and statistics. Use it to find facts about history, geography, and politics.
encyclopedia	√	√	The most important general information about a topic is in an encyclopedia. Use it to get a broad overview of a topic and verify facts.
magazines and newspapers	√	√	These periodicals contain current news and trends. Use them when you want to learn about recent local, national, and world events.
nonfiction books	√		Books include in-depth information on a topic. Use them to get deep knowledge of a narrow topic.
online database		√	Databases give access to regularly updated facts, statistics, or a bibliography on a topic. Use them to check facts or to locate sources of information on a topic.
primary sources, such as a historical document, diary, letter, speech, etc.	√	√	Primary sources document past events as they were happening. Use them to gain first-hand information about historical or geographically distant people and events.
reference books	√		These books give detailed information on specialized topics. They are useful for gathering and checking facts.
Web sites		√	The Web offers a wide range of information, from general to quite specific. Locate sites that give an overview of your topic and link to other sites with more sources of information.

Locate Information Sources, continued

Libraries have Internet access and tons of print materials. They also have reference librarians—they may not be expert in the topic you are researching, but they are all-around information experts.

Finding Printed Materials on the Shelves

Knowing where and how to find materials in the library is key to spending your research time wisely. Here's how research materials are arranged in most libraries:

- **Nonfiction books**—by subject area using call numbers based on the Dewey Decimal System:

000–099	General Interest	500–599	Pure Sciences
100–199	Philosophy	600–699	Technology
200–299	Religion	700–799	The Arts
300–399	Social Sciences	800–899	Literature
400–499	Language	900–999	History and Geography

- **Biographies**—usually grouped with other nonfiction by the last name of the person the book is about

- **Periodicals**—alphabetically by title

- **Reference books**—in their own section or grouped with other nonfiction.

Searching on the Online Catalog

You can use the online catalog to search for print and multimedia resources by title, author, subject, or keyword. With so many sources available, be sure to focus your search to avoid "information overload"!

1 A subject search shows you how many sources are available about your topic. Type in your subject to see what's available, and then choose the ones you want.

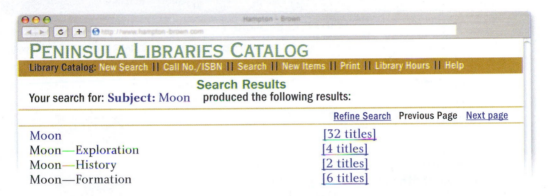

2 Once you've decided which specific subjects to look at, read the titles and locations of sources to find the best ones. The location and call number help to tell you whether the source was written for adults, for teens, or for children.

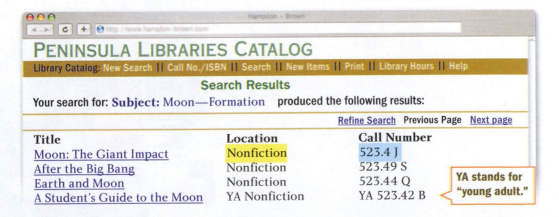

Locate Information Sources, continued

3 Read the <mark>catalog summary</mark> for an overview of the contents. If the source looks promising, check the <mark>status</mark> to see if it's available. Then write down or print out the information.

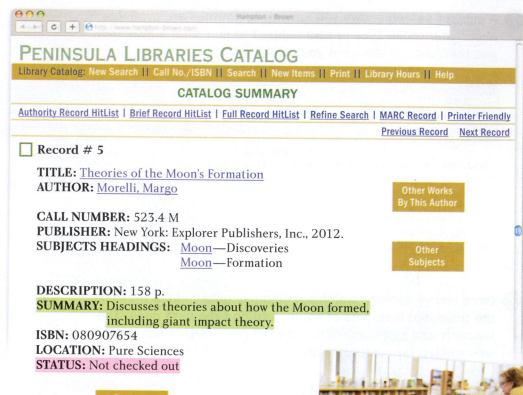

PENINSULA LIBRARIES CATALOG

Library Catalog: New Search || Call No./ISBN || Search || New Items || Print || Library Hours || Help

CATALOG SUMMARY

Authority Record HitList | Brief Record HitList | Full Record HitList | Refine Search | MARC Record | Printer Friendly

Previous Record   Next Record

☐ **Record # 5**

TITLE: Theories of the Moon's Formation
AUTHOR: Morelli, Margo

[Other Works By This Author]

CALL NUMBER: 523.4 M
PUBLISHER: New York: Explorer Publishers, Inc., 2012.
SUBJECTS HEADINGS: Moon—Discoveries
Moon—Formation

[Other Subjects]

DESCRIPTION: 158 p.
<mark>**SUMMARY:** Discusses theories about how the Moon formed, including giant impact theory.</mark>
ISBN: 080907654
LOCATION: Pure Sciences
<mark>**STATUS:** Not checked out</mark>

[Request Title]

Beyond Paper: Electronic Sources

Books and periodicals are important in research, but you can get a lot of information without ever opening a book! Just use electronic sources, which store vast amounts of information and include search tools to help you locate information quickly. Electronic sources often include audiovisual information as well.

Some electronic sources are:

- **DVDs** Look for documentaries or educational programs that relate to your topic. Often programs originally on TV are available later on DVDs.

- **CDs** Listen to music, lectures, or books on tape.

- **CD-ROMs** Compact discs aren't just for music and video games. They can also contain information in text or audio format. Because they store a lot of data in one place, CD-ROMs often contain lengthy works, such as encyclopedias.

At the library, the reference librarian can show you how to use these specialized sources.

Locate Information Sources, continued

The Web: Time Saver or Time Waster?

The World Wide Web is your connection to virtually unlimited information on every topic imaginable. And it's not all words, words, words on the Web. Many Web sites feature images, sound files, or video clips.

You can get onto this "information superhighway" from anywhere there is a computer with Internet access—the library, your classroom, or your home.

As with any highway, though, it will only be useful to you if you know how to drive safely in very heavy traffic.

The advantage of the World Wide Web is that it has more information than any library could possibly hold. A 10-minute visit to the World Wide Web can let you know what books are available at the public library in the next town, or what research is being conducted halfway across the world.

If you know how to use it, the Web can be a big time saver. Unfortunately, doing research on the Web can also be difficult because there's so much information out there. Finding good sites can be like looking for a needle in a haystack.

If you waste hours online without finding anything useful, you'll end up feeling frustrated. That's why it's important to be a smart searcher.

Keeping Safe While You Search

The Internet makes it easy for people to find and exchange information—and information on the Web is available to anyone, anywhere. That's mostly a good thing, but it's important to be extra careful about protecting your personal information online. Here are some basics:

- **NEVER** give out your personal information to strangers online. Period. People can easily misrepresent themselves on the Internet, so don't take any chances.

- What if you want to make an online purchase or subscribe to a publication? Before you give out contact information and credit card numbers, check with an older relative. Also, check the site's security features.

- Don't give out personal information in chat rooms or on discussion boards, or when posting comments on a blog. These types of sites aren't reliable resources anyway.

- If you do stumble onto a Web site that looks fishy, just click the back button on your Web browser or, if necessary, close the browser window.

Get Information from the Web

If you know how, you can get information quickly from the Web.

Accessing a Database

A database is a huge computer file of information. Databases usually have search tools. You may find information of two types:

1. specific information about a particular topic

This site contains many types of information about the Moon's formation.

2. references to other materials with information about a topic

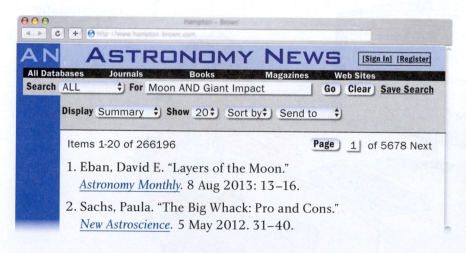

Search results show a bibliography of books and magazine articles about the Moon and the giant impact theory.

Here are some tips for smart searching with databases:

- Before you start, invest a little time in reading the guidelines for using the database.

- Do specific subject and keyword searches.

- If a bibliography-type database includes summaries, read the summaries carefully to see if the article looks promising. Check icons or other indicators to see if the full article is available on the database.

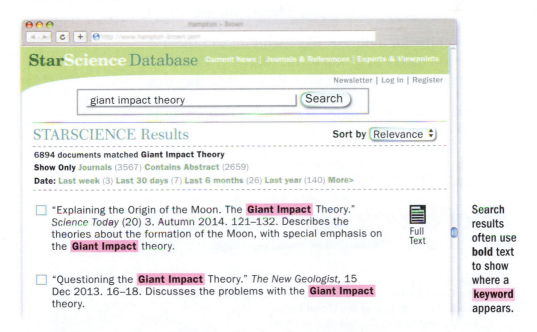

- Save your searches to a separate document on your computer, so you know which subjects or keywords you have looked for.

- Finally, be sure to save any leads that look promising. You can save them within the database, print out articles or summaries, or e-mail search results to yourself.

Get Information from the Web, continued

Using a Search Engine

A search engine is a powerful computer program capable of "reading" *very* fast through the entire World Wide Web, looking for anything you tell it to.

Usually, the problem with these searches is that they return more information than you know what to do with. To focus your search, try these techniques:

- Make keywords as specific as possible to limit your results.

- When searching for a phrase, like "giant impact theory," use quotation marks to group words together. That way you won't get results for Web sites about other theories.

- Don't type in questions. Type in the answer you want to find, such as "how the moon formed."

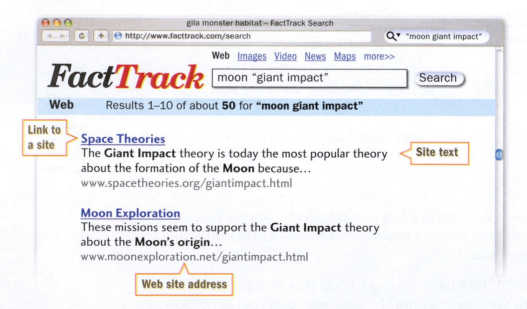

Scan the results and click on a link to go directly to the site.

Saving Search Results

When you find a good Web site, you'll probably want to access it again. Keep track of useful sites using these techniques:

- Use your browser's "Bookmark" or "Favorites" feature to save good links. Organize your links in folders so you can find them easily.

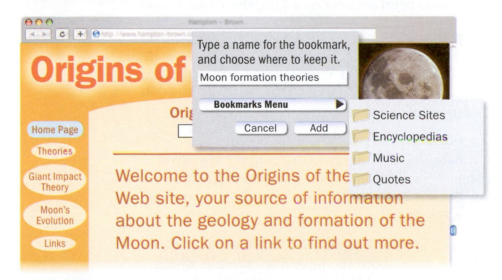

- Copy useful links into a separate document to use as your own handy personal "directory."

- Print out Web pages so you can refer to the paper copies when you're not at your computer.

Sort Through the Information

Part of being a smart searcher is recognizing that not all sources are trustworthy. And also, that not all reliable information is useful. You have to sort through your sources to end up with good stuff you can use.

Evaluating Print Sources

Carefully evaluate print sources by asking these questions:

1. **Is it up-to-date?**

   In many fields, such as science and medicine, information becomes quickly outdated as new discoveries are made. Check the publication date and use the most up-to-date sources to keep your facts accurate.

2. **Who wrote it?**

   Have you ever heard the saying "Consider the source"? Sometimes an author may slant the facts to fit a personal bias or prejudice. Choose sources that are objective and don't have an axe to grind.

   You also need to think about whether or not the author is qualified to write about the topic. For example, which would be a more reliable source for an article about a space flight to Mars: an aerospace engineer or a heart surgeon?

3. **What's the purpose of the publication?**

   Was the publication written to entertain or to inform? If you are researching facts about desert reptiles, an entertaining feature about pet lizards is probably not as useful as an encyclopedia article about how lizards survive in the desert.

Evaluating Web Sites

While many Web sites are carefully researched and checked, many others are put up by people without any special knowledge or expertise and contain incorrect information.

When you look at online sources, ask the same questions you ask for print sources, plus a few more:

1. **Does it look and sound professional?**
   Look for content that is well-written, organized, and free of obvious errors.

2. **When was it last updated?**
   Many sites include this information on the home page.

3. **What kind of site is it?**
   The last letters of a site's URL, or Web address, tell what kind of site it is.

If the URL ends in . . .	The site is maintained by . . .
.gov	a federal government organization
.mil	the U.S. military
.edu	a school, college, or university
.org	a professional organization
a state abbreviation (such as CA or TX) followed by .us	a state government
.biz	a business
.com or .net	a business or an individual

Generally, sites maintained by the government, colleges and universities, and professional organizations are more accurate than commercial or personal sites.

4. **Is the information confirmed by other Web sites?**
   Even when you're using a source that seems very reliable, it's still a good idea to double-check your facts with other sources.

Sort Through the Information, continued

Recognize Relevant Information

Once you've found a source that seems reliable, you can skim and scan to decide which information will be most useful.

When you skim and scan, you quickly read titles, headings, and key words in **bold** or *italics* to give you an idea of what the text is about. If the text seems to have useful information, you'll need to read it more carefully.

Some of the information you find will be interesting and related to your topic, but just not relevant or important enough to include in your report. Just as you sort through sources, you'll need to sort through information. To help you decide what's important:

1 Think About Your Research Questions as You Read

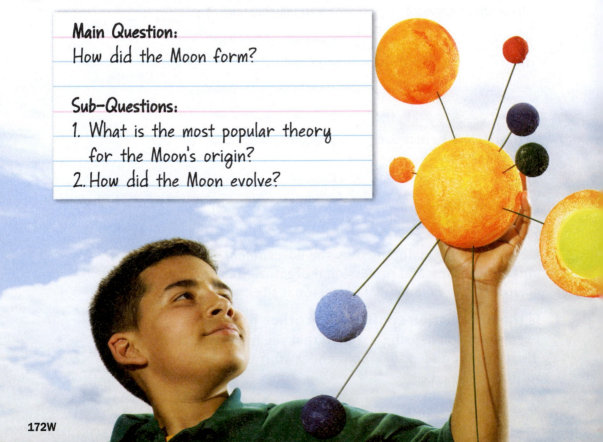

Main Question:
How did the Moon form?

Sub-Questions:
1. What is the most popular theory
   for the Moon's origin?
2. How did the Moon evolve?

2 Read the Source Carefully

☽ THE BIRTH OF A MOON

The Moon is a rocky celestial body which orbits Earth. It is slightly more than one-fourth the size of Earth. Because it appears to lack organic compounds, it is very unlikely there has ever been life on the Moon.

Most scientists currently embrace one idea for the Moon's origin: the giant impact theory. It states that Earth was struck by a massive celestial object. The impact ejected crust matter into orbit. This matter slowly combined to form the Moon.

During its evolution, the Moon was constantly struck by meteorites, which created craters. Many of the craters are named for philosophers and scientists.

3 Ask Yourself Questions About the Information

Which facts or details answer my questions? Do they support the main points I want to explain in my report?

☽ THE BIRTH OF A MOON

The Moon is a rocky celestial body which orbits Earth. It is slightly more than one-fourth the size of Earth. Because it appears to lack organic compounds, it is very unlikely there has ever been life on the Moon.

Most scientists currently embrace one idea for the Moon's origin: the giant impact theory. It states that Earth was struck by a massive celestial object. The impact ejected crust matter into orbit. This matter slowly combined to form the Moon.

During its evolution, the Moon was constantly struck by meteorites, which created craters. Many of the craters are named for philosophers and scientists.

> " This is interesting, but it doesn't answer either of my questions. It's not relevant for my report."

> " This detail doesn't explain how the Moon evolved."

Take Good Notes

As you gather information from a variety of sources, you're not going to be able to keep it all in your head! So, you'll need a system for recording and organizing what you learn:

- As you come across important facts and ideas in your sources, write them on index cards or in a computer file.

- Keep your notes organized by using a heading for each card or for each group of related notes.

- On each card, or at the end of each note, identify the source (by title or author) and the page where you got the information.

- Separately, also record complete publishing information (title, author, publisher, etc.) for every source you use. You'll need this information for the Works Cited section of your report. (See pages 194W–197W for more details.)

Effective note-taking involves a mixture of **paraphrasing**, **summarizing**, and **direct quotation**.

*Tech*TIP

Save your research ideas, notes, and source information in a single file folder on your computer. That will make it easier to find everything when you need it.

Paraphrasing

When you paraphrase, you use your own words to restate what an author has written. Using your own words is a good way to make sure you understand the ideas. To paraphrase:

1 **Read the Source Carefully**

The Giant Impact Theory

The giant impact theory is today considered the most reasonable explanation for the Moon formation. When the Earth was formed 4.6 billion years ago, it was a globe of hot, molten lava. The solar system was then full of rocks moving around. At some point, an "impactor" as big as Mars hit the Earth, detaching a piece of it. The meteorite and the Earth's piece joined together to form the Moon.

2 **Record the Important Information in Your Own Words**

Use a heading on the card to help you keep the notes organized. Make sure each entry relates to the heading. Use separate cards or headings as needed.

Disorganized

> —A meteorite hit the Earth.
> —It took off a piece of the Earth.
>
> The Giant Impact Theory, 8

Organized

> Giant Impact — Theory
> The Earth was hit by a Mars-sized meteorite and lost a piece.
>
> The Giant Impact Theory, 8

> Heading

> Source: book title and page number

Use your own sentence patterns and vocabulary. Do not use language that is too close to that of the source unless you think it's necessary to use a direct quote (see page 181W).

Too close to the source

> Giant Impact — Theory
> An "impactor" as big as Mars hit the Earth, and detached a piece of it.
> The Giant Impact Theory, 8

The researcher's own words

> Giant Impact — Theory
> A Mars-sized "impactor" hit the Earth and knocked off a piece.
> The Giant Impact Theory, 8

Try to keep your paraphrase about the same length as the original text or a bit shorter.

About the right length

> Giant Impact — Theory
> When the Earth was a large globe of molten magma, it was hit by a Mars-sized meteorite. The meteorite took off a large piece of the Earth.
> The Giant Impact Theory, 8

A geologist suggested that the piece that broke off from the Earth once floated over the Pacific Ocean. ▼

Take Good Notes, continued

Summarizing

When you summarize you find and condense the most important ideas, leaving out many details. To summarize:

1 **Read Your Source Carefully**

To locate the most important ideas, look at titles, headings, and key words in *italics* or **bold** type. In an article or a longer passage, determine the main idea of each paragraph.

2 **Keep Track of Important Ideas and Details**

You can make notes in a graphic organizer to hold your thinking and then use it as a guide for your summary.

> Main Idea: Over time, the Moon cooled down and stabilized into the satellite we know today.
>
> > Detail: The Moon's surface progressively cooled down, although it was still affected by volcanic activity.

If you have your own copy of the source, you can highlight ideas. Or, use sticky notes to mark key points.

The Moon's Development
Mark McCullough

After the Moon formed, it was still a large mass of molten lava. Over millions of years, the surface of the Moon began to cool down. Its core remained hot for a long time. Occasionally, there were outbursts of lava from the core. The lava that poured on the surface created vast dark regions called maria. During the cooling-down period, rocks floating around the solar system kept on smashing against the Moon's surface. Those meteorites are responsible for the craters that now are a characteristic feature of the Moon's surface.

3 Restate the Main Idea in Your Own Words

Try to get it all into one sentence, if at all possible.

> As the Moon's surface cooled, some lava
> still kept coming up from the hot core and
> meteorites crashed down into it.

4 Condense the Important Details and Examples

In your summary, you will not include every detail that is in the original—just the most important points. The length of your summary will vary depending on how long your source is.

▲ A meteorite is a rock that has traveled through space and landed on the surface of a planet or moon.

> The Evolution of the Moon
> As the Moon's surface cooled, some lava
> still kept coming up from the hot core and
> meteorites crashed down into it. The lava
> spread out over the surface and formed
> large dark areas. When the meteorites hit,
> they formed craters.
>
> McCullough, 99

Source: author's name and page number

Don't forget to add a heading telling what the summary is about, and to identify the source and page number(s).

5 Check for Accuracy

Once you've written your summary, read it over and compare it to the source material. Does your summary represent the source accurately? Are you sure you've captured the most important ideas? If necessary, revise your summary.

Avoid Plagiarism

Plagiarism is the act of passing off someone else's words or ideas as your own. Some writers do this on purpose. At 2 a.m. the night before a paper is due, it can be very tempting to copy something from the Internet and hand it in.

More often, writers plagiarize accidentally. If you haven't taken careful notes, it's easy to forget that you did not in fact come up with that great sentence yourself, but copied it straight out of a book and should have used quotation marks!

Either way, consequences can be harsh. Student writers might fail an assignment or get kicked out of school. Professionals can lose their jobs. Any writer who plagiarizes risks his or her reputation. The bottom line: never plagiarize intentionally, and keep careful notes to avoid doing it accidentally.

The Facts About Plagiarism

FICTION: It's easy to plagiarize without getting caught.
FACT: Teachers get to know different students' writing styles, so they can recognize unoriginal work. They can also use search engines to find writing that's plagiarized from the Internet.

FICTION: It's not plagiarism if you change the author's wording a little bit.
FACT: Any time you use an author's basic wording or ideas, you must credit the author by citing the source.

FICTION: Listing sources on your note cards is a waste of time. You can figure out that stuff later when you're writing your paper.
FACT: Sloppy, incomplete notes can lead to accidental plagiarism. **Always** keep track of sources, use quotation marks when necessary, and separate your own thoughts from the author's.

FICTION: Plagiarism is a great way to cheat the system.
FACT: If you plagiarize, you're cheating yourself. You miss out on the satisfaction that comes from tackling a challenging assignment and doing the best you can.

What Does Plagiarism Look Like?

Compare the source article below with the student report based on that article. Notice the too-similar words and phrases.

Source

Earth has other neighbors in our solar system. Asteroids are chunks of rock and metal. Asteroids move around our sun and most asteroids are found between Mars and Jupiter. Some asteroids are as small as a house while others are as big as a city. One asteroid is the size of Texas!

Meteoroids are chunks of debris in space. Meteoroids are smaller than asteroids and some meteoroids are even smaller than an ant. Still, others are as big as a bus.

Artist's rendition of a meteoroid approaching Earth ▼

Student Report

Our other neighbors in the solar system include asteroids, which are chunks of rock and metal, and meteoroids. Asteroids can be as small as a house or as big as a city. The chunks of debris in space called meteoroids can be smaller than an ant. Sometimes, they're as big as a bus.

How Can You Avoid Plagiarism?

First be sure to use quotation marks when you take word-for-word notes from a source.

Note Card

Asteroids are "chunks of rock and metal" that vary in size. Experts say they range from "as small as a house" to "as big as a city" or larger. Meteoroids are pieces of outer space debris. They are much smaller. Meteoroids can be little specks or "as big as a bus."

Avoid Plagiarism, continued

When you write your report, you can credit the source and show the writer's exact words in quotations.

> Asteroids are pieces of rock and metal. Experts say they range from "as small as a house" to "as big as a city" or larger (Phelan 258). Meteoroids are pieces of outer space debris. They are much smaller. Meteoroids can be tiny specks or "as big as a bus" (Phelan 258).

The original writer's words are in **quotations** and the **source** is named.

Or, you can combine the information from the source with other notes and your thoughts to put the information in your own words.

> As Glen Phelan points out, both asteroids and meteoroids vary in size. The largest asteroids can be as big as an entire town. The smallest meteoroids are just little specks.

This large asteroid travels around the sun. ▶

Using Direct Quotes

Usually it's best to paraphrase or summarize source material. However, including a few direct quotes can spice up your report, especially if a writer's words are vivid or memorable.

The Giant Impact Theory
Robert Carruthers

One popular theory to explain the Moon's formation is the giant impact theory. According to this theory, billions of years ago the solar system was made up of a random assortment of asteroids, planets, and debris. These objects were constantly moving at high speeds. One of them hit the Earth. It knocked off a large chunk.

Keep these points in mind when you write down quotes:

- Record the exact words used in your source. If you need to add or change a word, either to make the meaning clear or to shorten or condense the quote, use square brackets [ ] to show where you made a change.

> Giant Impact Theory
> "According to this theory, billions of years ago the solar system was made up of [various] asteroids, planets, and debris. These objects were constantly moving at high speeds."

- If you need to leave out part of a quotation, use an ellipsis [...] to show the omission. Make sure you don't alter the meaning!

> Giant Impact Theory
> "According to this theory, billions of years ago the solar system was made up of a random assortment of asteroids, planets, and debris . . . constantly moving at high speeds."

Organize Your Notes

What's It Like?

When you create a playlist of your favorite tunes, you probably organize the songs by artist or style. That makes it easier to find the one you want to hear. Organizing your research notes is like that, too. Once you get your notes in order, it's easier to find the facts you want to include in your research paper.

Why Organize?

If your notes are organized, your research paper will be, too. Organizing your notes will also help you discover if anything vital is missing:

After you've taken a lot of notes about your topic, you should

- put together, or synthesize, ideas from different sources

- decide if you have enough information on your topic or need to do more research

- use your notes to create an outline for your paper.

▼ Surface of the Moon

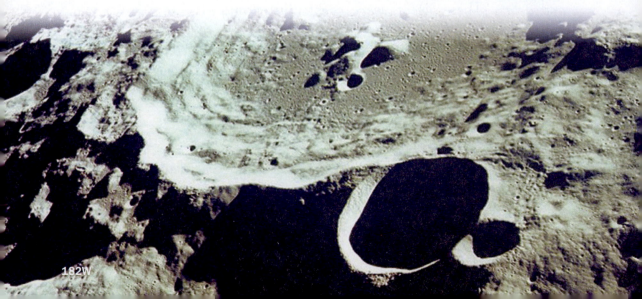

Look at the outline below. How did the writer organize the information she gathered?

Title ▷

How the Moon Formed

I. Introduction
   A. Moon studied by scientists since 1609
   B. How the Moon formed isn't known, but there are theories

Main topic, with roman numeral ▷

II. Some Proposed Explanations
   A. Co-accretion
      1. Explanation
      2. Problems
   B. Fission
      1. Explanation
      2. Problems
   C. Capture Theory
      1. Explanation
      2. Problems
   D. Giant Impact Theory

Subtopic, with capital *A, B, C*, etc. ▷

Supporting detail, with numeral 1, 2, 3, etc. ▷

III. The Big Whack (Giant Impact Theory)
   A. Explanation
   B. Why it's the most popular theory

IV. Evolution of the Moon
   A. The Moon cools down
   B. Outbursts of lava and creation of maria
   C. Formation of craters

V. Conclusion
   A. Moon unlikely to change much
   B. Future explorations will reveal more

Organize Your Notes, continued

Synthesizing Ideas

Your research notes may have come from many different sources, but now you have to somehow **synthesize** them, or pull them together, into the paper you're going to write. To synthesize ideas, you can build an **Inquiry Chart**:

1 **Start with a Chart**

Set up a chart to determine how all the information you've gathered fits together and whether you've answered your research questions. Start by filling in the questions.

Inquiry Chart

Research Questions	Source Information	Synthesis
Can the fission theory explain how the Moon formed?		

2 **Group Note Cards by Related Ideas**

Use the headings and keywords on your note cards to decide which cards should be grouped together.

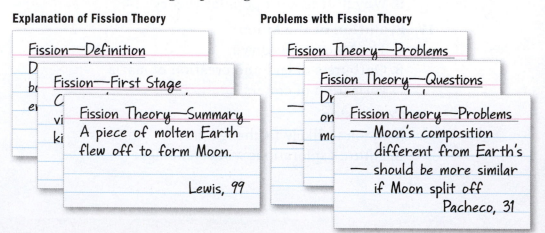

Explanation of Fission Theory

Fission—Definition
D
b
e
vi
ki

Fission—First Stage
C

Fission Theory—Summary
A piece of molten Earth
flew off to form Moon.

Lewis, 99

Problems with Fission Theory

Fission Theory—Problems
—

Fission Theory—Questions
Dr
on
mc

Fission Theory—Problems
— Moon's composition
    different from Earth's
— should be more similar
    if Moon split off
              Pacheco, 31

3 Fill In the Chart

Using your grouped note cards, fill in the Inquiry Chart to get an organized overview of what you've learned.

To fill in the Synthesis column, review all the notes for a particular research question. What can you conclude from the information? Use your own words to write a statement that synthesizes the ideas.

Inquiry Chart

Research Questions	Source Information	Synthesis
Can the fission theory explain how the Moon formed?	The fission theory proposed that a piece of molten Earth split off to form the Moon. (Lewis 99) The Moon's composition is different from the Earth's. (Pacheco 31) No other moons were created this way. (Eban 45)	The fission theory, which says the Moon is a piece of the Earth that split off, leaves too many unanswered questions.

If you have trouble synthesizing the ideas, try rereading your notes, or go back to your original sources. Still stumped? You may have to do additional research to get more information about the question that's puzzling you.

Organize Your Notes, continued

Checking for Completeness and Focus

Before you move on to creating a formal outline for your report, take some time to check for

- completeness: Do you have all the information you need?

- focus: Is the information focused on your topic?

Take a hard look at your Inquiry Chart. Does it seem complete? Maybe you need to do additional research to answer some of your research questions more fully. Maybe, now that you know more about the topic, you can think of other interesting questions you want to research.

Inquiry Chart

Research Questions	Source Information	Synthesis
What is the "capture theory"?	According to the capture theory, the Moon originally formed far away from the Earth. (Lewis 100) *Where did it form? What was it made of?*	
	It drifted close to Earth and was captured by Earth's gravity. (Eban 48)	
	Most astronomers question this theory. (Milano 34) *Find articles by scientists who disagree with capture theory.*	

Interviewing an expert on your topic is a valuable source of information. ▶

Too Much Information

Well, you can never really have too much information, but you want all the information you present to have a focus. Remember that not every note you take has to show up in your paper. Leave out information that

- doesn't relate to your research questions

- is contradicted by several other sources.

Inquiry Chart

Research Questions	Source Information	Synthesis
What have we learned from missions to the Moon?	Scientists have studied moon rocks to understand how the Moon developed. (Lewis 100)	
	~~The first man to walk on the Moon said "That's one small step for man, one giant leap for mankind." (Fitzgerald 88)~~	"This is interesting, but it's not about what we learned from Moon missions. I'll leave it out."
	The Moon was covered by molten rock when it first formed. (Pacheco 34)	
	~~The Moon formed about 5 billion years ago. (Austen 91)~~	"This is the only source that says the Moon is that old. I can't find this information anywhere else, so I'd better leave it out."

Good researchers follow their "gut" as they pursue their research. So if you don't have enough information, or if the information isn't focused enough, think of additional questions, and head back to the library or into the field.

Develop an Outline

Now you're ready to develop your outline—a final plan for your report. Here's how:

1 **Start with a Title**

Use a title that tells readers what your report will be about. Use key words from your research questions or ask a question.

Outline Title

> ## How the Moon Formed

2 **Decide On Your Introduction**

Your opening paragraphs should introduce your topic. Plan a central-idea statement that summarizes your answer to your main research question.

Outline for Part I

> ## How the Moon Formed
>
> **I. Introduction**
>   A. Moon studied by scientists since 1609
>   B. How the Moon formed isn't known, but there are theories
>
> **Central idea**

Main Research Question
What are the theories for how the Moon formed?

3 **List Your Main Topics**

List them in order, using roman numerals, and see if you like the flow of your ideas.

Main Topics in the Outline

> **I. Introduction**
> **II. Some Proposed Explanations**
> **III. The Big Whack (Giant Impact Theory)**
> **IV. Evolution of the Moon**
> **V. Conclusion**

These will become the subheads or section heads once you write your report. Plan on a conclusion, too.

4 **Complete Your Outline**

Fill in subtopics and supporting details under each main topic, following the model on page 183W. Use the information in your completed Inquiry Chart:

- Draw <mark>subtopics</mark> for your outline from key words in your research questions.

- Your synthesis statements will give you a clue as to which <mark>supporting details</mark> go under each subtopic.

Inquiry Chart

Research Questions	Source Information	Synthesis
Can the fission theory explain how the Moon formed?	The fission theory proposed that a piece of molten Earth split off to form the Moon. (Lewis 99)	The fission theory, which says the Moon is a piece of the Earth that split off, leaves too many unanswered questions.
	The Moon's composition is different from the Earth's. (Pacheco 31)	
	No other moons were created this way. (Eban 45)	

Outline for Part III

II. **Some Proposed Explanations**
   A. Co-accretion
      1. Explanation
      2. Problems
   B. <mark>Fission</mark>
      1. Explanation
      2. Problems

Now you're ready to turn your research and thinking into sentences and paragraphs for your research report.

Draft

Work from Your Outline

Your outline provides the skeleton for your report. As you draft your report, you'll put some meat on those bare bones. (And, of course, you can change your "skeleton" as you write.) Use your outline to:

1 Draft the Introduction

Get your readers interested from the beginning. Try one or more of these techniques:

- Show how your topic relates to your readers' experiences.

- Ask the question you will answer in your paper.

- Present an attention-getting fact, quotation, or anecdote.

Be sure your introduction also includes some background about your topic and a central idea that gives the main point of your paper.

2 Draft the Body of Your Report

Look at the sections with roman numerals in your outline. Turn each of those main points into one or more paragraphs.

3 Sum Up Your Ideas in the Conclusion

In the final paragraph, relate your ideas to your central idea. Leave your reader with something to remember, such as a solution for a problem, a new question, or an interesting quote.

> **Tech**TIP
>
> On the computer, you can save different versions of your writing. Use the **Save As** command from the file menu and add a number to the document name. Then you can look back and choose the version you like best.

Scientists used to believe the Moon's craters formed because of volcanic explosions. ▶

Outline

How the Moon Formed

I. Introduction
   A. Moon studied by scientists since 1609
   B. How the Moon formed isn't known, but there are theories

Question

How the Moon Formed

How did the Moon form? Astronomers have explained how the Moon orbits the Earth, how old it is, and why it looks the way it does. But no one knows for sure how it formed. There are a few theories about the Moon's origin, however.

Central Idea

Draft of the Introduction

Outline

II. Some Proposed Explanations
   A. Co-accretion
     1. Explanation
     2. Problems

The co-accretion theory says that the Moon and the planets formed out of dust and gas that came together. After learning more about the Moon's composition, scientists questioned this idea.

Draft of Paragraph in the Body

Outline

V. Conclusion
   A. Moon unlikely to change much
   B. Future explorations will reveal more

In the future, the Moon probably won't change much. It has little volcanic activity, and no atmosphere, wind, or storms to affect the surface. Future explorations will tell us more about its formation. For now, the giant impact theory is still the most popular.

Draft of the Conclusion

Integrate Ideas from Your Research

One of the trickiest things to do when you write a report is to make sure your ideas and the information from your research flow together smoothly. As you write and revise your paper, try these techniques for integrating facts and ideas:

1 **Support General Statements with Facts from Your Research**

Unsupported

There are many different theories to explain how the Moon formed. Supposedly a meteorite banged into the Earth and knocked pieces off, which then joined to form the Moon. It sounds bizarre, but it's the best theory yet.

Supported

There are several theories to explain how the Moon formed. The most accepted one is the giant impact theory (Lewis 98). This theory suggests that after a meteorite banged into the Earth and knocked pieces off, the fragments joined to form the Moon (Eban 88).

The writer supports a statement with a **fact**.

2 **Stay Focused**

Any quoted or paraphrased material within a paragraph should clearly connect to the main idea.

Unfocused

At first the Moon's surface was covered by hot magma. Now there's a lot of anorthosite on the Moon (Pacheco 50). Eventually crystals formed on the surface (Carruthers 76). There are large, smooth, dark places called maria (Lewis 98).

Focused

At first the Moon's surface was covered by hot magma. Scientists know this because the Moon now has lots of anorthosite, a rock that forms only in magma (Pacheco 50). Crystals formed on the surface as the magma cooled (Carruthers 76). Lava eruptions from the core formed large, smooth, dark places called maria. (Lewis 98).

3 **Use Your Own Ideas as the Backbone of Your Paper**

As you decide what details to include from your research, think about how you'll "connect the dots" for your readers.

Disconnected Facts/Too Many Citations

One theory to explain the Moon's formation was the co-accretion theory (Lewis 97). It says the Moon formed from dust and gas (Lewis 99). All the other planets formed in this way, too (Lewis 105). Scientists now reject this idea (Lewis 100). Unlike the Earth, the Moon does not have a large iron core (Carruthers 69). This makes no sense, because supposedly the Earth, Moon, and planets all formed from the same dust and gas (Tanaka 75). They should have the same iron core (Tanaka 71).

Integrated Ideas and Citations

Scientists considered but rejected the co-accretion theory. The theory suggests that the Moon and all of the planets in the solar system formed from the same dust and gas (Lewis 99). Scientists reject this idea because, unlike Earth, the Moon does not have a large iron core (Carruthers 69). If co-accretion theory were true, the Moon's core would resemble the Earth's (Tanaka 21).

4 **Cue the Quotations**

It's usually best not to leave a quotation standing alone; the mix of "voices" can make the writing sound awkward. The addition of transitional words (in red below) makes for a smooth connection

Awkward Quotation, Fixed

So far, the Giant Impact theory is the most likely explanation for the Moon's existence. Yet this explanation is by no means final. Astronomer Eric Woods has his doubts. *He explains,* "It's just a theory, and no one can really prove or disprove it. In time, I think science will come up with a better explanation."

Reflect

- Do your introduction and conclusion give a good idea of what your report is about?

- Have you included enough details to support your central idea?

How to Cite Sources

You should briefly identify your source any time you refer to someone else's words or ideas in your paper. That way, you give other writers credit for their work and provide your readers with a way to learn more about your topic. At the end of your paper, provide a full list of your sources.

Keeping Track of Your Sources

If you record your sources right from the start, you won't have to spend hours figuring out where you found each fact.

- As you do research, create a card with bibliographic information for every source, or keep a list of all of your sources. Page 196W tells what information you should record.

- As you take notes, always write down the source's author or title (or both) and the page where you found the information.

Source Card

> Source #1
> Title: After the Big Bang
> Author: Adrian Pacheco
> Publisher: Canton Press
> City: Baltimore
> Year: 2014

Note Card

> Capture Theory
> According to capture theory, the Moon formed far away from the Earth. It was captured by Earth's gravitational pull.
>
> Pacheco, 40

- Include information about sources in your draft. You don't have to worry about using the perfect format, but do add a note about where you found each fact or idea.

> Yet another explanation for the formation of the Moon is the capture theory. This theory suggests that the Moon originally formed far away from the Earth. At some point, drifting close to our planet, it was "captured" by the Earth's gravitational pull. (PACHECO, PAGE 40.)

How to Cite Sources in Your Final Draft

The point of including references in the body of your report is to help your reader find the full bibliographic information that appears at the end (see pages 196W–197W). The FAQ chart below outlines a system that most teachers will accept.

FAQ	Answer	Example
How do I cite a book or an article?	Give the author's last name and the page number where the information is found.	Fission theory suggests the Moon was part of the Earth (Lewis 14).
What if the authors of two or more of my sources have the same last name?	Add an initial or a full first name to the reference.	Fission theory suggests the Moon was part of the Earth (S. Lewis 14).
What if my source has more than one author?	If there are two or three authors, list them all. If there are more than three, use the first author's name followed by the abbreviation et al., which means "and others."	Galileo was the first to look at the Moon through a telescope (Marini and Hausman 44). The Moon's maria were formed by lava (Taft et al. 107).
What if I used two different sources by the same author?	Mention the title also, in full or abbreviated.	Fission theory does not explain the composition of the Moon (Pacheco, *Into the Solar System* 76).
What if my source has an organization as its author?	Give the name of the organization, in full or abbreviated, just as you would with a person.	The *Apollo 11* missions of 1969 provided many answers (Astroscientist Network 13).
How do I cite a Web site?	Use the author's name, if known, or the name of the Web site.	The asteroid must have been the size of Mars (Solar System Origin Site).

How to Create a List of Works Cited

You won't be finished with your research paper until you create your list of works cited. This is where you give your reader complete bibliographic information for each of the sources mentioned in the body of your report. The rules for putting together this list are many and complicated, so listen up:

1 **List all the publication details about each source you used.**

- For books:

  Pacheco, Adrian. *After the Big Bang*. Baltimore: Canton Press, 2007.

  Author with last name first | **Title, in italics** | **City of publication** | **Publisher** | **Year of publication**

- For magazine articles:

  Eban, David E. "Layers of the Moon." *Astronomy Monthly*. 8 August 2007: 13–16.

  Article title | **Magazine title, in italics** | **Issue date** | **Page numbers**

- For newspaper articles:

  Taft, Milo J. "How Did the Moon Form? No One Is Sure." *Youngstown Times*. 18 July 2007: B13.

  Section and page number

- For articles from academic or professional journals:

  Tanaka, Takeshi. "Questioning the Giant Impact Theory." *Science Today*. 12.6 (2007): 131–132.

  Volume number **Issue number**

- For an article in an online magazine:

  Cassar, Mario. "The Giant Impact Theory." *Moon Exploration*. 5 Oct. 2005. 8 May 2008. <http://www.moonexploration.net/giantimpact.html>.

  Page URL, underscored | **Issue date** | **Date of access**

Head spinning yet? And these are only some of the rules! If you need to know more, you can link to more-complete guidelines through hbgoodwriters.com.

2 Then list all sources alphabetically. The finished monster should look something like this:

Works Cited

Carruthers, Robert. *The Moon.* Sewanee: Craven Press, 2012. Book

Cassar, Mario. "The Giant Impact Theory."
   Moon Exploration. 5 Oct. 2005. 8 May 2014.
   <http://www.moonexploration.net/giantimpact.html>. Article from a Web site

Eban, David E. "Layers of the Moon." *Astronomy Monthly.*
   8 August 2013: 13–16. Magazine article

Lewis, Sylvia. *The Mysteries of the Solar System.* New York:
   Trowbridge Press, 2012.

McCullough, Mark. "Moon Craters." *The New Geologist.* 9.4
   (2014): 8–14. Journal article

Morelli, Margo. *Moon: The Giant Impact Theory.* New York:
   Explorer Publishers, Inc., 2012.

Pacheco, Adrian. *After the Big Bang.* Baltimore: Canton Press,
   2014.

Richards, Abigail. Personal Interview. 4 Nov. 2013. Interview

Taft, Milo J. "How Did the Moon Form? No One Knows for
   Sure." *Youngstown Times.* 18 July 2013: B13. Newspaper article

Tanaka, Takeshi. "Questioning the Giant Impact Theory."
   Science Today. 12.6 (2014): 131–132.
---. *Origins of the Solar System.* Newport, CT: Greens Press, 2012. The symbol --- means the author is the same as for the previous entry.

Vanbrugh, Ella. "In Defense of the Capture Theory." *Theories
   of the Solar System.* Ed. Monique Jones. Los Angeles:
   Spaceline Press, 2013. 280–295. Article or essay from a book

Revise

1 Evaluate Your Work

Have other students read your paper, and ask them for ideas during a peer conference. They can help you improve your writing so it better connects with your audience. Here are a few questions you might ask them:

What to Ask During a Peer Conference

- Is my introduction interesting?
- Does my paper have a clear central idea?
- Does each main idea relate to the central idea?
- Are there any parts that are confusing or don't belong?

> ## Revision in Action

Darrell's Draft

One student's response:

How did the craters on the Moon form? Until fairly recently, scientists didn't know for sure. At first, they thought the Moon's craters came from volcanic explosions. After all, the craters that we see on Earth usually belong to volcanoes. There are many active and inactive volcanoes all over our planet. However, the Moon's craters are flatter than the Earth's and vary in size (Barry 59).

" I thought I'd be reading about the Moon's craters, but this detail is confusing. "

Today, we know craters come from meteorites. The theory that the Moon's craters were impact craters is no longer a theory: it's a fact. When the *Apollo 11* mission came back from the Moon, astronauts brought rocks made of materials that could only have resulted from a meteorite's impact.

" I'm not sure what you want to explain. You should add details to make your central idea more specific. "

" These sentences don't flow. Can you rearrange them? "

2 Mark Your Changes

Think about your classmates' comments as you review your draft. Then make your marks.

Add Text You may need to add

- a question or interesting fact to your introduction
- details to make your central idea specific
- source information you left out.

Move Text Are all your sources in the right place? Does your paper have the best organization? Use ⟲ to move text.

Take Out Text To keep your paper focused and unified, take out the text that doesn't go with your central idea or tell more about a paragraph's main idea.

Reflect

- Does your final draft have a clear central idea?
- Does everything in your report tell about that idea?

Revising Marks

MARK	∧	⟲	⌐	⟿	⁋
WHAT IT MEANS	Insert something.	Move to here.	Replace with this.	Take out.	Make a new paragraph.

Revised Draft

How did the craters on the Moon form? Until fairly recently, scientists didn't know for sure. At first, they thought the Moon's craters came from volcanic explosions. After all, the craters that we see on Earth usually belong to volcanoes. ~~There are many active and inactive volcanoes all over our planet.~~ However, the Moon's craters are flatter than the Earth's and vary in size (Barry 59).

Today, we know craters ~~come from~~ *are formed by the impact of* meteorites. The theory that the Moon's craters were impact craters is no longer a theory: it's a fact. When the *Apollo 11* mission came back from the Moon, astronauts brought rocks made of materials that could only have resulted from a meteorite's impact.

Darrell took out this detail because it didn't relate to the main idea of the paragraph.

Darrell added details to make his central idea more specific.

Darrell moved this sentence to improve the flow of ideas.

Edit and Proofread

After you're satisfied with the content of your research report, read your paper again to fix language errors. This is what you do when you edit and proofread your work:

- **Check the Grammar** Make sure that you have used correct and conventional grammar throughout. In particular, check for correct use of subject and object pronouns. (See page 201W.)

- **Check the Spelling** Spell-check can help, but it isn't always enough. For errors with silent consonants, you'll have to read your work carefully, and perhaps use a dictionary. (See page 202W.)

- **Check the Mechanics** Errors in punctuation and capitalization can make your work hard to understand. In particular, check for correct punctuation and capitalization of sources and titles. (See page 203W.)

Use these marks to edit and proofread your research report.

TechTIP

Your word-processing software probably has a feature that allows you to check your spelling. Click on **Spelling** in your **Tools** window. A screen will then show each misspelled word and how to correct it.

Editing and Proofreading Marks

MARK	WHAT IT MEANS	MARK	WHAT IT MEANS
∧	Insert something.	/	Make lowercase.
∧	Add a comma.	ℯ	Delete, take something out.
∧	Add a semicolon.	¶	Make new paragraph.
⊙	Add a period.	◯	Spell out.
⊙	Add a colon.	∧	Replace with this.
∨ ∨	Add quotation marks.	∼	Change order of letters or words.
∨	Add an apostrophe.	#	Insert space.
≡	Capitalize.	◡	Close up, no space here.

Reflect

- What kinds of errors did you find? What can you do to keep from making them?

GrammarWorkout

Check Subject and Object Pronouns

A **pronoun** is a word that takes the place of a noun. A pronoun often changes its form depending on how it is used in a sentence.

- Use a **subject pronoun** as the subject of a sentence.

   EXAMPLE   Jan is studying astronomy. **She** has a test tomorrow.

- Use an **object pronoun** after an **action verb** or a **preposition**.

   EXAMPLES   We finished the tests, and Mr. Shaw **graded** **them**.

   Jan took the test home **with** **her**.

Subject Pronouns

Singular	Plural
I	we
you	you
he, she, it	they

Object Pronouns

Singular	Plural
me	us
you	you
him, her, it	them

Find the Trouble Spots

American geologist Gilbert observed the Moon with a telescope. Through ~~them~~ *it*, he saw craters of different shapes and sizes. Did meteorites cause it? Gilbert tried to recreate the impacts. ~~You~~ *He* dropped balls and shot bullets into clay and sand. That way they could test his idea.

Find two more pronoun errors to fix.

Edit and Proofread, continued

SpellingWorkout

Check Words with Silent Consonants

Some words have consonants that are not pronounced. Some common silent consonants are *k, w, p,* and *b.*

Silent Consonant	Examples
k	know, kneel, knife, knight
w	write, wrong, wrench
p	psychic, psychology
b	debt, thumb

Sound-alike words can be confusing. Words with silent consonants often sound like words that don't have silent consonants.

With Silent Consonant	Without Silent Consonant
know, knight	no, night
write, wring	right, ring

Find the Trouble Spots

    Our ^knowledge of the universe is improving thanks to scientific research and ^writing. For example, until recently, we didn't no how the craters of the Moon formed. Some geologists thought the craters came from volcanic explosions. Other geologists douted that, and argued that craters came from the impact of meteorites.

Find two more spelling errors to fix.

Mechanics Workout

Check Punctuation and Capitalization of Sources

- For books:

  Capital letters

  Capitals for city and publisher; colon separates names

  Meyers, Kevin. *Mysteries of the Moon.* New York: Harper Collins , 2010.

  Title in *italics*, capital letters for key words

  Comma between publisher and date; ends with period

- For articles:

  Capital letters

  Newspaper title in italics

  Dietrich, Julia. "Crater Q & A." *Rockburg Press.* 14 June 2013: C8.

  Title in quotations, capital letters for key words

  Colon separates issue date and pages

- For Web sites:

  Capital letters

  Title in quotations with capital letters for key words

  Terrence, Marc. "The Moon." *The Space Site.* 23 Oct. 2005.
  4 Jan. 2013. <http://www.spacesite.org/moon.html>.

  URL or online address underscored

  Period between issue and access dates

Find the Trouble Spots

Clemens, Alberto. *Craters of the moon.*
   Seattle: Fletch Press, 2012.

Ono, masako. The surface of the moon. *Moon
   Exploration.* 18 Oct. 2005. 8 May 2013.
   <http://www.moonexploration.net/giantimpact.html>

Find three more capitalization or punctuation errors to fix.

Publish, Share, and Reflect

Now that your research is done and you've written a report that focuses on an interesting topic, you're ready to share the information with your readers.

1 **Publish and Share Your Work**

Because you've taken special care to be sure your report is focused, well-organized, and correctly written, your audience will certainly learn something from it.

Think about publishing your report by

- creating a special binding for it and leaving it in the library for the whole school to read

- posting it on your blog or e-mailing it to friends and family

- sending it to a popular teen magazine

- desk-top publishing your report, enhancing it with photos and graphs to display in your classroom

- using multimedia (see page 205W).

2 **Reflect on Your Work**

After you publish and present your report, take some time to think about it. What went well? What do you think you could do differently for your next research report?

Reflect

- What did I learn about myself while writing?

- How did following the research process help me tell about my topic?

Use Multimedia

Adding multimedia components to your report can help clarify information and keep your audience interested in what you have to say.

Be sure to choose components that will add to, not take the place of, the content of your report. Think about different kinds of multimedia and how they can enhance your report. For example:

Show Images and Graphics

- Show large, eye-catching photographs that relate to your topic.
- Include illustrations that will help explain complex information.
- Use charts or graphs to present a lot of data visually.
- Show maps if they will help your audience visualize a location.
- Play a short clip from a video related to your topic.

Add Music and Sounds

- Present a snippet of speech, or sound bite, by a famous personality: "That's one small step for man, one giant leap for mankind." —*Neil Armstrong*
- Play music from the time period of your report.
- Share parts of recorded interviews with experts on your topic.
- Include the national anthem of the country you are reporting on.

Use Presentation Software or the Internet

- Take advantage of presentation software that lets you make a slide show with images, sound, and text.
- Use the Internet to find and project resources that demonstrate and explain complex concepts.
- Create an original Web site or blog with information and links that your audience can use to learn more about your topic.

Research
RESOURCES

Resource Books

Parts of a Book

When you hear the word *print*, what do you think of? Books! There are many different kinds of books. All books share some features that make it easier for readers to find what they need. Let's look at the parts of a book.

Title Page

The **title page** is usually the first page in a book.

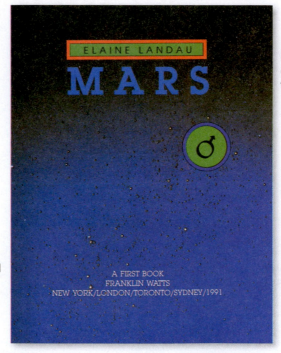

It gives the **title** of the book and the **author**.

It tells the **publisher** and often names the cities where the publisher has offices.

Copyright Page

The **copyright (©) page** gives the year when the book was published.

Check the **copyright** to see how current the information is.

Landau, Elaine
   Mars / by Elaine Landau
     p.cm. — (First book)
   Includes bibliographical references and index.
   Summary: Uses photographs and other recent findings to
     describe the atmosphere and geographic features of Mars.
   ISBN 0-531-20012-4 (lib. bdg)—ISBN 0-531-15773-3 (pbk)
   I. Mars (Planet)—Juvenile Literature. [1. Mars (Planet)]
1. Title.   II. Series.
QB641.L36 1991
523.4'3—dc20   90-13097 CIP AC

Table of Contents

The **table of contents** is in the front of a book. It shows how many chapters, or parts, are in a book. It tells the page numbers where those chapters begin. Look at the chapter names to see which ones might be useful to you.

A table of contents can be much more detailed than the one shown here. For example, it might list sections within chapters, important visuals, or special sections found in the book.

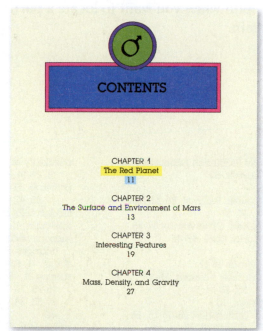

CONTENTS

A **chapter title** tells what the chapter is mostly about.

The **page number** tells where the chapter begins.

Chapter Headings

Once you have found a chapter you are interested in using from the table of contents, you will turn to the chapter. The first page in the chapter will contain a header describing what you will find in the chapter. Often, chapters are numbered.

THE RED PLANET

CHAPTER ONE

The planet Mars appears as a rusty red ball in the nighttime sky. Because of its reddish color, the ancient Romans named the planet after their god of war—Mars. In fact, the fighting god's shield and spear are still used as the planet's symbol.

Mars is one of the nine planets that make up the *solar system*. The solar system consists of the sun and the planets, moons, and other objects that revolve around it. Mars is the fourth planet from the sun. Earth, Mars's neighbor, is the third planet from the sun.

Mars is not a very large planet. Its diameter is about 4,200 miles (6,790 kilometers). That makes Mars a little more than half the size of Earth. The

Parts of a Book, continued

Index

The **index** is usually found at the back of a book. It lists all the important subjects that are discussed in the book in alphabetical order. Use the index to see if the information you seek can be found in the book. After you read a book, the index can also be helpful when you want to locate a particular piece of information again.

Names of people are listed in alphabetical order by their last names.

Sometimes page numbers are in *italics* to show that there is an illustration or photograph on that page.

Related details are often listed for a subject.

Some indexes have words in parentheses that explain more about the subject. For example, these pages tell about the moons of Mars.

Glossary

A **glossary** lists important words used in the book and their meanings. It is found at the back of the book. Use the glossary to help understand specific vocabulary in a book.

Words are listed in alphabetical order.

GLOSSARY

Astronomer– a scientist who studies the stars, planets, and all of outer space

Atmosphere– the various gases that surround a planet or other body in space

Axis– the invisible line through a planet's center around which it spins, or rotates

Crater– an irregular oval-shaped hole created through a collision with another object

Density– the compactness of materials

Equator– an imaginary circle around the center of the Earth, another planet, or the sun

Erosion– the process of being worn away by the action of wind, water, or other factors

55

The **definition** defines, or gives the meaning of, a word.

Types of Resource Books

Atlas

An **atlas** is a book of maps. There are several types of atlases, which are used for different purposes.

A **road atlas** is designed for drivers to use in deciding how to get from one place to another. The maps in a road atlas feature highways, streets, and other driving routes. Places such as cities, towns, and bodies of water are also shown on the road maps. The content of a road atlas might be limited to a small area such as one state, but a road atlas can also cover a huge area like a continent.

A **reference atlas** includes maps and information about every country in the world. Usually, a map of a country is shown on one page, and a second page shows facts and visuals about the country.

Historical atlases are filled with maps that show how people have explored and changed the world through time. These atlases also include interesting facts about history and often have timelines and other related visuals.

▼ road atlas

▼ reference atlas

▼ historical atlas

Since there are several types of atlases, it makes sense that you can find different types of maps inside them, doesn't it? You can use the different maps for different purposes. Let's see what some of them look like.

Physical Maps

A **physical map** shows the geographical features of a place, such as bodies of water and landforms.

Mapmakers often use techniques that make mountains look like they are rising off the page.

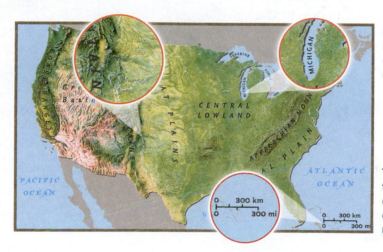

Landforms, like mountains or lakes, are often labeled.

The **scale** shows that this distance on the map is equal to 300 miles on land.

Product Maps

A **product map** uses pictures and symbols to show where products come from or where natural resources are found.

The **compass rose** shows the directions north, south, east, and west.

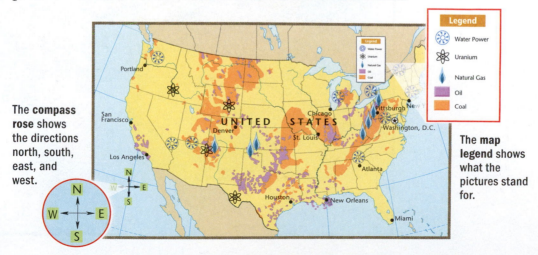

Legend

- Water Power
- Uranium
- Natural Gas
- Oil
- Coal

The **map legend** shows what the pictures stand for.

Types of Resource Books, continued

Political Maps

A **political map** shows the boundaries between countries, states, and other areas. It also shows capitals and other major cities. **Road maps** are usually set up like political maps.

A **grid system** is used on these maps to make it easy to find a particular place. Look up the place name in the index to find the right map and a code to the exact location on the map. For example, L-6 for this map is the square at which the row L and the column 6 intersect. Can you find Orlando somewhere in the square?

Historical Maps

A **historical map** shows when and where certain events happened.

Almanac

An **almanac** is an up-to-date book filled with facts about interesting topics such as inventions, awards, trends, weather, movies, and television. A new almanac is published each year, which is why the information is so current. You can use an almanac to find quick facts about a topic. Because almanacs tend to present information on a vast number of topics, you will find the **index** particularly useful in locating what you need.

INDEX

Solar cars, 60

Solar eclipses, 204

Solar power, 63

Solar system
   exploration of, 203
   facts about, 200–202

Solomon Islands, 162–163
   map, 131; flag, 145

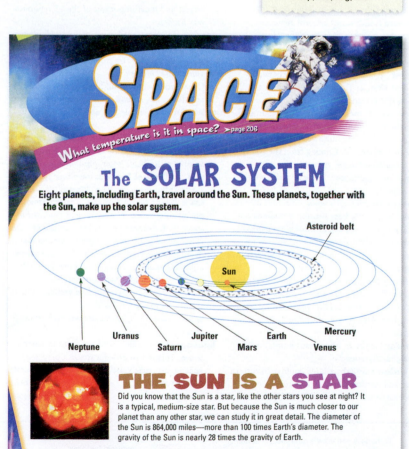

SPACE
What temperature is it in space? ➤page 206

The SOLAR SYSTEM

Eight planets, including Earth, travel around the Sun. These planets, together with the Sun, make up the solar system.

Asteroid belt

Sun

Neptune   Uranus   Saturn   Jupiter   Mars   Earth   Venus   Mercury

THE SUN IS A STAR

Did you know that the Sun is a star, like the other stars you see at night? It is a typical, medium-size star. But because the Sun is much closer to our planet than any other star, we can study it in great detail. The diameter of the Sun is 864,000 miles—more than 100 times Earth's diameter. The gravity of the Sun is nearly 28 times the gravity of Earth.

Types of Resource Books, continued

Dictionary

Think of the **dictionary** as a tool you can use to learn everything you need to know about a word. Dictionaries tell you how to spell, say, and use words. From a dictionary you can learn how to divide a word into syllables, what part of speech a word is, and how to write different forms of a word. You can also learn the history of a word. Look for examples of all of these types of information on these dictionary pages.

 southwards ➤ space shuttle

ward slope of the mountain. *Adjective.*
south·ward (south'wərd) *adverb; adjective.*
southwards Another spelling of the adverb southward: *They drove* ***southwards.*** **south·wards** (south'wərdz) *adverb.*
southwest 1. The direction halfway between south and west. 2. The point of the compass showing this direction. 3. A region or place in this direction. 4. the Southwest. The region in the south and west of the United States. *Noun.*
  ○ 1. Toward or in the southwest: *the southwest corner of the street.* 2. Coming from the southwest: *a southwest wind. Adjective.*
  ○ Toward the southwest: *The ship sailed southwest. Adverb.*
  south·west (south'west') *noun; adjective; adverb.*
souvenir Something kept because it reminds one of a person, place, or event: *I bought a pennant as a souvenir of the baseball game.* **sou·ve·nir** (sü'və nîr' *or* sü'və nîr') *noun, plural* **souvenirs.**
sovereign A king or queen. *Noun.*
  ○ 1. Having the greatest power or highest rank or authority: *The king and queen were the sovereign rulers of the country.* 2. Not controlled by others; independent: *Mexico is a sovereign nation. Adjective.*
  sov·er·eign (sov'ər ən *or* sov'rən) *noun, plural* **sovereigns;** *adjective.*
Soviet Union Formerly, a large country in eastern Europe and northern Asia. It was composed of 15 republics and was also called the U.S.S.R. The

largest and most important of the 15 republics was Russia.
sow¹ 1. To scatter seeds over the ground; plant: *The farmer will sow corn in this field.* 2. To spread or scatter: *The clown sowed happiness among the children.*
  Other words that sound like this are sew and so.
  sow (sō) *verb,* **sowed, sown** *or* **sowed, sowing.**
sow² An adult female pig. **sow** (sou) *noun, plural* **sows.**
soybean A seed rich in oil and protein and used as food. Soybeans grow in pods on bushy plants. **soy·bean** (soi'bēn') *noun, plural* **soybeans.**
space 1. The area in which the whole universe exists. It has no limits. The planet earth is in space. 2. The region beyond the earth's atmosphere; outer space: *The rocket was launched into space.* 3. A distance or area between things: *There is not much space between our house and theirs.* 4. An area reserved or available for some purpose: *a parking space.* 5. A period of time: *Both jets landed in the space of ten minutes. Noun.*
  ○ To put space in between: *The architect spaced the houses far apart. Verb.*
  space (spās) *noun, plural* **spaces;** *verb,* **spaced, spacing.**
spacecraft A vehicle used for flight in outer space. This is also called a spaceship. **space·craft** (spās'kraft') *noun, plural* **spacecraft.**
space shuttle A spacecraft that carries a crew into space and returns to land on earth. The same

space shuttle

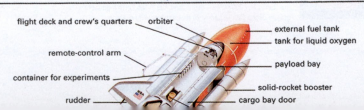

flight deck and crew's quarters — orbiter
— external fuel tank
— tank for liquid oxygen
remote-control arm
— payload bay
container for experiments
— solid-rocket booster
rudder — cargo bay door

space shuttle can be used again. A space shuttle is also called a shuttle.

space station A spaceship that orbits around the earth like a satellite and on which a crew can live for long periods of time.

spacesuit Special clothing worn by an astronaut in space. A spacesuit covers an astronaut's entire body and has equipment to help the astronaut breathe. **space·suit** (spās′süt′) *noun, plural* **spacesuits.**

Astronauts take spacewalks to repair satellites and vehicles.

spacewalk A period of activity during which an astronaut in space is outside a spacecraft. **space·walk** (spās′wôk′) *noun, plural* **spacewalks.**

spacious Having a lot of space or room; roomy; large. —**spa·cious** *adjective* —**spaciousness** *noun.*

spade¹ A tool used for digging. It has a long handle and a flat blade that can be pressed into the ground with the foot. *Noun.*
○ To dig with a spade: *We spaded the garden and then raked it. Verb.*
spade (spād) *noun, plural* **spades;** *verb,* **spaded, spading.**

spade² 1. A playing card marked with one or

thin strings. It is made of a mixture of flour and water. **spa·ghet·ti** (spə get′ē) *noun.*

WORD HISTORY

The word spaghetti comes from an Italian word meaning "strings" or "little cords." Spaghetti looks a bit like strings.

Spain A country in southwest Europe. **Spain** (spān) *noun.*

spamming The sending of the same message to large numbers of e-mail addresses or to many newsgroups at the same time. Spamming is often thought of as impolite behavior on the Internet. **spam·ming** (spa′ming) *noun.*

span 1. The distance or part between two supports: *The span of that bridge is very long.* 2. The full reach or length of anything: *Some people accomplish a great deal in the span of their lives. Noun.*
○ To extend over or across. *Verb.*
span (span) *noun, plural* **spans;** *verb,* **spanned, spanning.**

This bridge spans a wide river.

spaniel Any of various dogs of small to medium size with long, drooping ears, a silky, wavy coat, and short legs. The larger types are used in hunting. **span·iel** (span′yəl) *noun, plural* **spaniels.**

Spanish 1. The people of Spain. The word *Spanish* in this sense is used with a plural verb.
2. The language spoken in Spain. It is also spoken in many countries south of the United States as

Use the **guide words** at the top of each page to help you find the entry word you are looking up. The guide words are the first and last words on the page.

The **entry word** *spacesuit* falls between *space station* and *Spanish* in alphabetical order.

In this dictionary, words in **blue** have corresponding visuals. Special notes about how to use words also appear in blue.

217W

Types of Resource Books, continued

Thesaurus

A **thesaurus** is similar to a dictionary, but instead of giving word meanings, it lists synonyms and antonyms. A thesaurus can be especially useful when you are looking for just the right word to use. For example, you might want to describe how *good* of an experience NASA's Space Camp® is for kids—but without using that tired, overworked adjective. You could look up *good* in a thesaurus and find an entry that looks like this:

Synonyms are words with almost the same meanings.

Antonyms are words with opposite meanings.

fine

good adjective **1** *a good product* FINE, superior, quality; excellent, superb, outstanding, magnificent, exceptional, marvelous, wonderful, first-rate, first-class, sterling; satisfactory, acceptable, not bad, all right; *informal* great, OK, A1, jake, hunky-dory, ace, terrific, fantastic, fabulous, fab, top-notch, blue-chip, blue-ribbon, bang-up, killer, class, awesome, wicked; smashing, brilliant. ANTONYM bad.

2 *a good person* VIRTUOUS, righteous, upright, nding, moral, ethical, high-minded, principled; exemplary,

bad

from Oxford American Writer's Thesaurus. Christine A. Lundberg. By permission of Oxford University Press, Inc.

Which synonym would you decide to use?

A thesaurus can also be helpful when you are trying to decide how to express your thoughts about a big idea or topic. If you can't seem to come up with the right words, look up the subject—for example, *universe*—and see what you find.

universe noun **1** *a collection of stars* COSMOS, creation, nature, heavens, luminaries, constellations, celestial, stellar.

These are only a few of the words listed in one thesaurus for that subject. Just think about how helpful these words might be.

A thesaurus might give more information than simple lists of words.

This thesaurus looks very similar to a dictionary. It includes a definition for each **entry word**. The definition is followed by a **sample sentence** featuring the word. This thesaurus also includes **guide words** at the top of the page.

baby

baby *n.* a very young child or animal: The *baby* is only ten months old.
Synonyms
infant a child too young to walk or talk: You need to carry an *infant*.
newborn a baby that has just been born: The *newborn* and her mother go home from the hospital.

beautiful

beat *n.* a repeated sound, usually with a regular occurrence: Tap your foot to the *beat*.
Synonyms
pounding I could feel the *pounding* of my own heart.
rhythm The *rhythm* of the rain put me to sleep last night.

This thesaurus does not include definitions, only sample sentences.

wakeful adjective **1** *he had been wakeful all night* AWAKE, restless, restive, tossing and turning. ANTONYM asleep.
2 *I was suddenly wakeful* ALERT, watchful, vigilant, on the lookout, on one's guard, attentive, heedful, wary. ANTONYM inattentive.

walk verb **1** *they walked along the road* STROLL, saunter, amble, trudge, plod, dawdle, hike, tramp, tromp, slog, stomp, trek, march, stride, sashay, glide, troop, patrol, wander, ramble, tread, prowl, promenade, roam, traipse; stretch one's legs; *informal* mosey, hoof it; *formal* peram-

Types of Resource Books, continued

Encyclopedia

An **encyclopedia** is a series of books with articles that give facts about many different topics. Each book is called a **volume**. The volumes and articles are arranged in alphabetical order. You can use an encyclopedia for a broad overview of a subject.

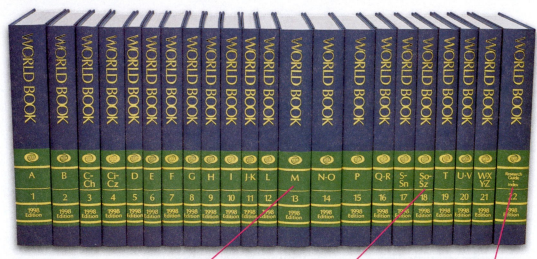

An article about Mars would be in this volume.

This is where you would find information about space travel.

Most encyclopedias have a volume called an **index**. The index lists other related subjects to look up.

Some encyclopedias are on a computer disk. You can read the information from the disk on your computer screen.

Guide words are used on encyclopedia pages to make it easy to flip through and find the specific article you want to read.

Mars 223

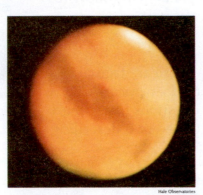

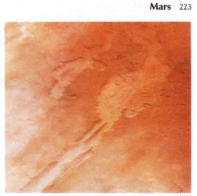

Hale Observatories

NASA

Mars's surface features are visible in a photograph taken from the earth, *left*. The earth's atmosphere makes the picture blurry. A series of canyons called the Valles Marineris (Mariner Valleys) make up the diagonal landform in the photo at the right, taken by the U.S. Viking 1 space probe. This landform is more than 2,500 miles (4,000 kilometers) long.

The **entry word** of an article is its title.

Mars is the only planet whose surface can be seen in detail from the earth. It is reddish in color, and was named Mars after the bloody-red god of war of the ancient Romans. Mars is the only planet other than the earth to produce evidence suggesting that it was once the home of living creatures. However, there is no evidence that life now exists on Mars.

Mars is the fourth closest planet to the sun, and the next planet beyond the earth. Its mean distance from the sun is 141,600,000 miles (227,900,000 kilometers), compared with about 93,000,000 miles (150,000,000 kilometers) for the earth. At its closest approach to the earth, Mars is 34,600,000 miles (55,700,000 kilometers) away. Venus is the only planet in the solar system that comes closer to the earth.

The diameter of Mars is 4,223 miles (6,796 kilometers), a little over half that of the earth. Pluto and Mercury are the only planets smaller than Mars.

Headings tell what each section in an article is about.

Orbit and rotation

Mars travels around the sun in an *elliptical* (oval-shaped) orbit. Its distance from the sun varies from about 154,800,000 miles (249,200,000 kilometers) at its farthest point, to about 128,400,000 miles (206,600,000 kilometers) at its closest point. Mars takes about 687 earth-days to go around the sun.

As Mars orbits the sun, it spins on its *axis,* an imaginary line through its center. Mars's axis is not *perpendicular* (at an angle of 90°) to its path around the sun. The axis tilts at an angle of about 24° from the perpendicular position. For an illustration of the tilt of an axis, see **Planet** (The axes of the planets). Mars rotates once every 24 hours and 37 minutes. The earth rotates once every 23 hours and 56 minutes.

The **author** of each encyclopedia article is chosen because he or she is an expert on the topic.

The contributor of this article is Hyron Spinrad, Professor of Astronomy at the University of California, Berkeley.

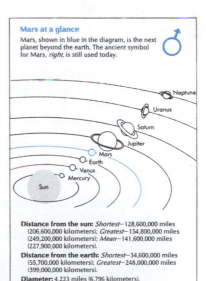

Mars at a glance

Mars, shown in blue in the diagram, is the next planet beyond the earth. The ancient symbol for Mars, *right*, is still used today.

Neptune

Uranus

Saturn

Jupiter

Mars

Earth

Venus

Mercury

Sun

Distance from the sun: *Shortest*—128,600,000 miles (206,600,000 kilometers); *Greatest*—154,800,000 miles (249,200,000 kilometers); *Mean*—141,600,000 miles (227,900,000 kilometers).

Distance from the earth: *Shortest*—34,600,000 miles (55,700,000 kilometers); *Greatest*—248,000,000 miles (399,000,000 kilometers).

Diameter: 4,223 miles (6,796 kilometers).

Length of year: About 1 earth-year and 10½ months.

Rotation period: 24 hours and 37 minutes.

Temperature: −225 to 63 °F (−143 to 17 °C).

Atmosphere: Carbon dioxide, nitrogen, argon, oxygen, carbon monoxide, neon, krypton, xenon, and water vapor.

Number of satellites: 2.

Other Print Resources

Newspapers

A **newspaper** is a daily or weekly series of publications that presents news of interest on the local, state, national, and world levels. People read newspapers to get information. You can use newspapers to find information about current events. You can look at old newspapers to help you write about something that happened in the past.

▲ Yang Liwei, Astronaut of China's First Manned Spaceflight

News Articles

Newspapers contain **news articles**. These are factual accounts of current events. As you read a news article you should find the answers to five key questions (sometimes referred to as the "Five Ws") about the event it describes: *Who? What? When? Where? Why?*

China's Big Plans for Space

The **lead paragraph** gives a summary of the story.

Beijing, China   By 2020, if all goes as planned, China will have put a human on the moon, a space station in orbit around Earth, and a joint China-Russia explorer ship on its way to Mars. For years China has been steadily but quietly building a space program the likes of which we have not seen since the 1960s space race.

In October 2007, China launched a lunar orbiter. China now has a spacecraft orbiting the moon and mapping its surface. China is looking for resources—things like helium-3, a fuel source that might make nuclear power a much safer, cleaner energy source on Earth. By 2017, China hopes to send robots to the moon to collect samples of resources and bring them back to Earth.

China also has big plans for manned space missions. In 2008, China hopes to broadcast a live spacewalk by three taikonauts (the Chinese version of astronauts). China also reportedly has thought about placing people on the moon to work at retrieving the valuable resources it hopes to find there.

Right now, United States officials still believe we are ahead of the Chinese technologically. Yet, as NASA head Michael Griffin has stated, "China will be back on the moon before we are . . . I think when that happens Americans will not like it."

The **headline** grabs readers' attention and gives a quick idea of the story content.

News stories often quote experts, eyewitnesses, and other voices of authority.

Editorials

Most newspapers also usually include **editorials**. These are opinion-based pieces of writing on topics of interest to readers. Editorials often appear in their own section of a newspaper and look different from news stories. This is so that readers will know that editorials present opinions in addition to facts. You can use editorials to give you ideas to write a persuasive essay or to present the opinions of other people.

▲ American Astronaut Scott Carpenter

We Need to Make Astronauts Superstars Again

Americans seem to have become bored with manned space flight. We no longer remain glued to our screens when space shuttles launch, dock at the space station, and land back on Earth. Photos of astronauts floating around in space don't even make the front page of this newspaper!

> The author's **opinion** is clearly stated.

We need to appreciate the incredible accomplishments of our space travelers.

> **Facts** are used to support the opinion.

Back in 1962, *Aurora 7*, the capsule of one of the Mercury rockets, almost didn't make its return to Earth. All kinds of problems occurred during reentry. If there had not been a human on board to correct the problems and make a landing, the capsule and all of its data would have been lost.

Do we truly believe complex space missions are best accomplished without trained humans? More and more I hear about robotics and unmanned probes as the future of U.S. space missions. Why is that happening? Simply put, astronauts are no longer the popular figures they once were, so NASA figures it's easier to do without them.

Only we can give astronauts back the star status they deserve. We can do that by caring about their work. Tune in, read all about it. Send some fan mail. Do whatever you can to tell these heroic men and women—and the people for whom they work—that they really do matter.

> Editorials often end with a specific **call to action**.

Other Print Resources, continued

Magazines

A magazine is a special collection of articles. Some magazines are written about one interest or hobby, such as sports or music. Others are targeted for one group of people—teens or children, for example. Still other magazines, including news and entertainment magazines, are published to appeal to a wide variety of readers.

Magazines are published on a schedule such as monthly or weekly. For example, a monthly magazine publishes a new issue every month. Magazines are sometimes called periodicals. A period is a span of time. You can use magazines for a variety of writing purposes. Past issues of magazines are also helpful in writing about events that happened in the past.

A MASSIVE AIR AND SPACE MUSEUM...

Right by Dulles Airport!

On your next trip to our nation's capital, be sure to set aside some time to visit the Steven F. Udvar-Hazy Center. Located on land that is part of Washington Dulles International Airport, this companion site to the National Air and Space Museum could represent a stellar beginning to your trip or a wonderful grand finale.

The Udvar-Hazy Center originally opened in December 2003, and within six months the Center welcomed its one millionth visitor. Then, in November 2004, the James S. McDonnell Space Hangar opened at the Center. A third structure at the Center, the Donald D. Engen Observation Tower, allows

visitors to view air traffic coming in and out of Dulles.

WHAT CAN YOU SEE?

Both the original Center complex and the McDonnell Space Hangar are remarkable for their size. Given that the goal of the Udvar-Hazy Center was to place actual

The headline and lead paragraph of a magazine article are designed to draw readers' attention.

Headings help to break up the text of magazine articles, which can be several pages long. The headings also tell what the sections are about.

aircraft and space vehicles on display, the hugeness of the spaces involved is no surprise. The original Center is 2½ football fields long and 10 stories high. Visitors walk among many aircraft and view others suspended from the ceiling. Helicopters, the world's fastest jet, and one-of-a-kind experimental planes are just some of the flying machines you can see.

Inside the 53,000-square foot McDonnell Hangar, hundreds of space vehicles are displayed. The centerpiece is the space shuttle *Enterprise*, but rockets, satellites, space capsules, telescopes, and more are housed here as well.

Visitors can also experience IMAX® movies and flight simulators. Daily tours and activities are offered, and diners and shoppers will be pleased to find facilities to suit them as well. An especially interesting feature of the Udvar-Hazy Center is the Wall of Honor. As you enter the Center, you walk along this memorial to our great aviators and space explorers.

WHAT ABOUT THOSE NAMES?

Steven F. Udvar-Hazy is an American billionaire who made his fortune in the aviation industry. Born in Hungary, Steven fled with his family in 1958 to escape the Soviet occupation. Then 12 years old, Steven went on to attend UCLA. He began his own business in 1973. That fabulously successful business leases planes to airlines so that they do not have to buy and sell them on their own.

In 1999, Udvar-Hazy donated $60 million to the National Air and Space

Most magazines use color and plenty of visuals to make the pages more attractive and interesting to readers.

Museum, making him the biggest donor in the history of the Smithsonian. When asked why he gave so much, Udvar-Hazy commented, "I know this new museum will impart to millions of children the same love for aviation that I have, and it will inspire future generations."

Like Udvar-Hazy, James S. McDonnell was an industry leader. As a pioneer in the aerospace industry, McDonnell was a big player in the first American spaceflights. His company built the *Mercury* and *Gemini* rockets which carried the first American astronauts into space.

Donald D. Engen, for whom the observation tower is named, gave to the museum in a different way. Before he was killed in a glider accident in 1999, Admiral Engen worked tirelessly to get the plans for the Center underway. His efforts have been called "legendary" by fellow museum staffers. Without a doubt, Engen would be pleased with how the Center turned out. As for you... you will not want to miss the Center's "out of this world" experience!

"Writing a poem or a
song is like playing with
words."

—Ramona

Model Study

Narrative Poem

Writing poetry is one of the most creative ways you can tell a
story and express yourself. That's because you can use language
in a lot of different ways to get your thoughts, feelings, and
memories on paper.

Sometimes poetry uses precise rhyme patterns or rhythms.
Poems often use **figurative language**, or words that don't mean
exactly what they say. Words in poems create a strong emotional
effect. There are many different kinds of poems.

When you write a narrative poem in **free verse**, you make up
the rules. A poem in free verse does not have to rhyme or have
a set structure. It may also bend or break some of the rules of
grammar or punctuation.

Read the student model on page 227W. It shows the features of a
good free-verse poem.

NARRATIVE POEM

A good narrative poem

☑ focuses on one topic or event

☑ may express feelings about the event

☑ can have a narrator and characters

☑ uses precise words and sensory language to tell about
the event.

Feature Checklist

Out of Tigers

by Isaac Schultz

The title and first stanza introduce the **topic**: endangered tigers.

If the world ran
out of tigers
would I notice?

Would I see
these sleek regal cats, a
grassland of stripes
wilting in the Indian landscape?

The writer uses **vivid, precise words** and **figurative language** for emotional effect.

I could turn
a blind eye

But the tigers
would notice.
Not enough trees
not enough space to live
not enough tigers.

The poem explores the topic without using traditional stanzas, rhyme, or a regular rhythm.

Maybe I
should notice, too.

Student Model

Write a Narrative Poem

WRITING PROMPT From Shakespeare's day through the present, poets have expressed their feelings and told stories about events by writing poetry. What events are important to you?

Think of an event that matters to you. Then write a poem in free verse that

• focuses on one event

• expresses your feelings about the event

• uses precise words and sensory language to tell about the event

• may or may not have a narrator and characters.

Prewrite

1 Choose and Narrow Down Your Topic

Did you choose a topic or an event you feel passionate about? If so, check that it's specific enough. That way it'll be easier to write about, and more interesting for your readers. Here's how Devon narrowed the topic for his poem.

How Devon Narrowed His Topic

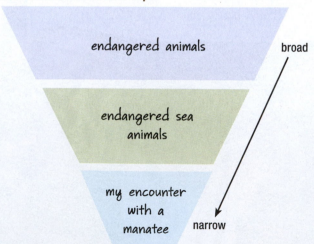

endangered animals — broad

endangered sea animals

my encounter with a manatee — narrow

② Jot Down Ideas and Impressions

What comes to mind when you think of your topic or event?
Jot down everything you think of. You might include drawings
or photos as you brainstorm, too.

glide

paddle tail

gentle and gray

wrinkled face

flowing river

slow movement

rises to breathe

whiskery snout

flippers

Reflect

- Is your topic or event focused?

- Do your details show how you feel about the topic or event?

Draft

Take a look at everything you've jotted down. Now put those words together to form images. Pay attention to how the words sound. Try different words until your draft sounds just right.

- **Play with Words as You Draft** Try different images and different ways of arranging the words to create the best word picture.

> In breathless silence, I wait.
> Then a ripple, a shadow. . .
> A head appears. It's a manatee,
> gliding slowly toward me.

- **Try Different Line Breaks** The way the lines break on the page helps determine how your reader "hears" the poem. Try different ways of breaking the lines.

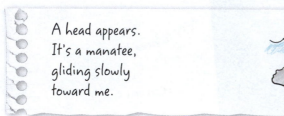

> A head appears.
> It's a manatee,
> gliding slowly
> toward me.

TechTIP

Try inputting your poem in one long line first, and then playing with the line breaks.

- **Play with Rhyme** In free verse, the lines do not have to rhyme, but you can use rhyme within the lines for an appealing sound.

> Gentle, gliding, riding the waves
> the gray manatee
> silently slides, follows the tides

Reflect

- Did you use vivid images that your reader can "see" or imagine?

- Does your language sound appealing?

DRAFTING TIPS

Trait: **Focus and Unity**

If Your Writing Sounds Like a List . . .

When you include a lot of details and images in a poem, it might start to sound like a list of unrelated ideas. Too many disconnected details can make your poem seem unfocused and confusing to your reader.

Zero In on a Part

Start by listing several key details about your subject on separate self-stick notes.

paddling its tail	moving slowly	going underwater to eat	coming back up for air

Then, choose one detail to zero in on. Expand it into several lines or a stanza. Here's how Devon focused on one thing to bring his poem to life:

> Minutes pass
> The water is as smooth as glass
> Suddenly
> The manatee's snout breaks through
> It drinks the air
> Satisfied

Revise

As you get ready to revise your work, keep your audience and purpose in mind. Does your poem tell the story that you want to describe? Will it connect with your audience?

1 **Evaluate Your Work**

Read aloud your poem to a partner and ask him or her to sketch what the poem describes. When you look at the sketch, ask yourself questions:

- **About the Form** Are there enough vivid details in my poem? Does it convey the feelings I want to express?

- **About the Focus and Unity** Do my lines work together to create one powerful image or emotion?

Revision in Action

Devon's Draft

In breathless silence, I wait.
Then I see a ripple in the water and a shadow.
The head of a manatee appears above the water,
And it glides slowly toward me.

With wary eye and whiskery snout,
the creature slides gracefully through the waves
With a gasp, the manatee takes one last breath.
Then satisfied, it dives back down again

Seeing a manatee is a rare sight.
I shiver, also satisfied like the manatee.

Devon's thinks:

"This would be more powerful if I condensed it."

"I have to find a better way of saying this."

"This doesn't even sound like poetry."

2 Mark Your Changes

Consolidate Text Much of the power of telling a story in poetry comes from compressing a lot of meaning into a few words. For that reason, it's a good idea to consolidate your language whenever possible. This means

- replacing wordy phrases with ones that are more compact and economical

- simply deleting unnecessary words—in poetry, fewer words are usually better.

Revising Marks

MARK	∧	↶	↖	↵	ዋ
WHAT IT MEANS	Insert something.	Move to here.	Replace with this.	Take out.	Make a new paragraph.

Revised Draft

In breathless silence, I wait.
Then I see a ripple in the water and a shadow.
    It's a manatee,
A The head of a manatee appears above the water,
And it glides *ing* slowly toward me.

With wary eye and whiskery snout,
the creature slides gracefully through the waves.
With a gasp *ing* the manatee takes one last *another* breath.
Then satisfied, it dives back *sinks* down again.

    The   *I M*   *and wondrous*
Seeing a manatee is a rare sight.
I shiver, *ing I, too, am* also satisfied like the manatee.

Devon deleted words to make the language more compact.

Devon revised two wordy lines.

Devon compressed these lines.

Edit and Proofread

Does your narrative poem paint a vivid picture of your subject? If so, you're now ready to fix language errors. This is what you do when you edit and proofread your work:

- **Check the Grammar** Sometimes poems do not use complete sentences. Look at the way your phrases and sentences are arranged and be sure they are clear. In particular, check how you've used descriptive adjectives. (See page 235W.)

- **Check the Spelling** Spell-check can help, but it's not always enough. Read your poem carefully, especially when adding suffixes like *-ed* and *-ing* to words ending in *y*. (See page 236W.)

- **Check the Mechanics** Although you can bend some rules in poetry, errors in punctuation and capitalization can still make your work hard to understand. If you've chosen to use unconventional mechanics, make sure you can justify your decision. (See page 237W.)

Use these marks to edit and proofread your free-verse poem.

Editing and Proofreading Marks

MARK	WHAT IT MEANS	MARK	WHAT IT MEANS
∧	Insert something.	/	Make lowercase.
∧	Add a comma.	℘	Delete, take something out.
∧	Add a semicolon.	⁋	Make new paragraph.
⊙	Add a period.	◯	Spell out.
⊙	Add a colon.	⌃	Replace with this.
⌄ ⌄	Add quotation marks.	∼	Change order of letters or words.
⌄	Add an apostrophe.	#	Insert space.
≡	Capitalize.	◡	Close up, no space here.

Reflect

- What kinds of errors did you find? What can you do to keep from making them?

Grammar Workout

Check Descriptive Adjectives

Descriptive adjectives are words that describe nouns—people, places, and things. You can use descriptive adjectives to describe

- how something looks, feels, tastes, smells, and sounds

    EXAMPLE The **brown** sparrows have **smooth** feathers and **soft** voices.

- things you can't see or touch.

    EXAMPLE Thinking about this species dying out makes me **depressed**.

Use descriptive adjectives to make your writing more colorful. Choose precise, colorful adjectives to bring people, places, and things to life.

    EXAMPLE The **thick, rough** skin of the manatee protects
    it from the **numbing** cold.

Find the Opportunities

Its <ins>deep</ins> wrinkles
Its <ins>rough, gray</ins> skin
Blend with the waves
Down in the water
Down by the weeds
Down near the bottom
of the bay.

Where else could you add descriptive adjectives in this stanza?

Edit and Proofread, continued

> ### Spelling Workout
>
> # Check Suffixes in Verbs Ending in y
>
> - If the root verb ends in a consonant plus **y**, change the **y** to **i** before adding **-ed**.
>
>   EXAMPLES   supply + -ed ⟶ suppl**ied**
>   carry + -ed ⟶ carr**ied**
>
> - But if the root verb ends in a vowel plus **y**, then you **don't** change the **y** before adding **-ed**.
>
>   EXAMPLES   display + -ed ⟶ displa**yed**
>   enjoy + -ed ⟶ enjo**yed**
>
> - When you add **-ing** to a verb that ends in **y**, keep the **y**.
>
>   EXAMPLES   play + -ing ⟶ pla**ying**
>   cry + -ing ⟶ cr**ying**
>
> ### Find the Trouble Spots
>
> I ~~hurryed~~ **hurried** here
> the manatee's song
> ~~plaiing~~ **playing** in my ear
> But when I sat and studied
> its slow shimmiing
> I fancyed
> A life like its.

Find and fix three more spelling errors.

Mechanics Workout

Check Punctuation in Poems

In free verse, you can bend rules of punctuation and capitalization. But you can't just forget about them! Make sure you can justify any unusual choices. Be creative without confusing your readers.

CONFUSING	**CREATIVE**
Gentle gray	The water stays still
Wrinkled, face,	Suddenly
Paddle tail,	A soft gray head emerges
and flippers.	Drinking air
	Satisfied
	It returns
	To the water.

The confusing example above uses commas in all the wrong places for no reason. The creative example uses line breaks as punctuation. The poem makes sense even without standard punctuation!

Find the Opportunities

The manatee glides dives and slides
Through the water,
She glides
To the bottom
She rises
To the top

She is the majestic
Queen, of the sea
of the waves
of the deep of the darkness.

Correct the punctuation errors, or justify the writer's use of unusual punctuation.

Model Study

Business Letter

A consumer buys or uses products that other people sell. Right now you might buy things like games, snacks, or clothing. You will make major purchases as an adult—things like furniture or a car. As a consumer, you might need to

- ask for information about an item you plan to buy

- make a claim about a product that left you unsatisfied and support your claim with evidence

- request a missing part or a replacement

- thank someone for especially good service.

For each purpose, you might need to write a **business letter**. In a business letter, you use a polite tone and formal language to get your point across.

Read the student model on page 239W. It shows the features of a good business letter.

BUSINESS LETTER

A good business letter

☑ makes a claim and clearly explains the purpose for writing

☑ develops and supports the writer's claim

☑ uses a polite, formal tone

☑ follows the standard business-letter format.

Feature Checklist

8113 Stonebrook Way
Belmont, MA 02478
April 6, 2014

Includes
the sender's
address and
the date.

Includes the
recipient's
address and
a formal
greeting.

Patricia Crawford
Director of Customer Service
Belmont Pet Supply
42 Shaw Street
Belmont, MA 02478

Dear Ms. Crawford:

Makes a
claim about
what the
company
should do.

On March 20, 2014, I purchased a bird feeder from Belmont Pet Supply. I now believe that I should receive a full refund for that bird feeder. I live near the woods and there are many birds in my yard, so I bought your "Bird Gazebo" feeder to hang on my porch.

Starts out
with
information
about the
date and
location of
the purchase.

Marc
explains the
problem in
detail.

Within the first week, I discovered that the plastic was cracked and the bird seed was spilling out everywhere. I tried to repair it with duct tape, but that soon tore in the wind and rain.

According to the box the bird feeder came in, customers are entitled to a full refund for bird feeders that break within one year. I enclose a package with the bird feeder and a copy of my receipt. Please send me a refund of $15.99. Feel free to call me at (555) 376-0943 if you have any questions. Thank you for your time and attention.

Mark gives
evidence
for why he
deserves a
refund and
proposes a
specific
solution.

Marc uses a
polite tone,
and ends
with a
formal
closing
and his
signature.

Sincerely,

Marc Jenson
Marc Jenson

Student Model

Write a Business Letter

WRITING PROMPT As a consumer, it is important to communicate your needs or concerns to businesses. Writing is one way you can make your voice heard. Think of a problem you might want to contact a business about. Then write a business letter that

- explains the problem clearly and makes a claim about what should be done about it
- suggests a possible solution and gives evidence for why this solution is a fair one
- uses a formal, polite tone
- uses proper business-letter format.

Prewrite

Here are some tips for planning your letter.

1 **Plan What You'll Say About the Problem**

Organize your facts. It helps to think about the situation you want to describe and the problems it caused. Use a list of questions and answers to help you remember all the details.

Question	Answer
What did I buy?	A digital camera
When did I buy it?	July 7, 2014
Where did I buy it?	Shutterbug Camera Store, San Diego, California
What was the problem?	It was hard to use. The auto-focus feature did not work.
Why was it a problem?	All of the pictures turned out blurry. The pictures of my trip to the wildlife preserve were ruined.

2 Find Out Whom to Contact

Try to contact a specific person. You can call the company's service department or use the Internet to find out who is responsible for customer service.

TechTIP

The Internet is a great way to find specific contacts for problem-solving. You might even be able to e-mail your "letter."

3 Decide on the Solution You Want

What can the business do to help solve the problem? What will it take to fix the situation? Before you write your letter, make sure you're clear on what you want to ask for.

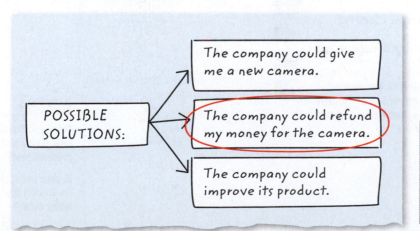

Reflect

- Do you know what you want to say about your problem?

- Have you decided on a solution to your problem?

Draft

Now you're ready to write an effective business letter. Follow these steps:

- **Make Your Letter Look Professional** Format your letter on a computer. Be sure to include your address, the date, and the recipient's name and address. Don't indent the body paragraphs. Use the planner below to set up your letter correctly:

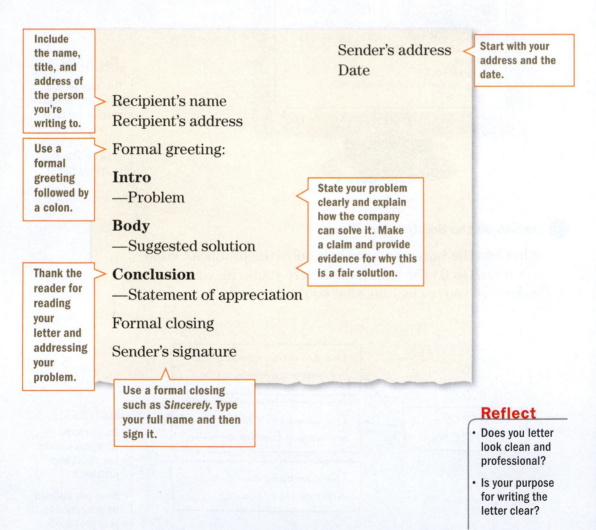

Include the name, title, and address of the person you're writing to.

Use a formal greeting followed by a colon.

Thank the reader for reading your letter and addressing your problem.

Sender's address
Date

Start with your address and the date.

Recipient's name
Recipient's address

Formal greeting:

Intro
—Problem

Body
—Suggested solution

State your problem clearly and explain how the company can solve it. Make a claim and provide evidence for why this is a fair solution.

Conclusion
—Statement of appreciation

Formal closing

Sender's signature

Use a formal closing such as *Sincerely.* Type your full name and then sign it.

Reflect
- Does you letter look clean and professional?
- Is your purpose for writing the letter clear?

DRAFTING TIPS
Trait: **Development of Ideas/Organization**

If You Can't Write Enough...

Do you suffer from "skimpy" writing? If you don't provide enough details or evidence to support a claim, your readers won't understand what you want them to, or they won't believe that your claim is a fair one.

Try Getting into an Argument with Yourself...

When you are challenged to prove your ideas, you can usually think of a lot more to say! To come up with evidence for your claim, imagine what you might say if you were in an argument.

To support a claim with confidence, you have to provide evidence.

It's not our fault!

Prove it!

I deserve a refund for this camera.

It's too late for a refund!

How to Successfully Support a Claim	
1. Explain what led you to make your claim.	4. Leave out any details that do not relate to the problem.
2. Narrate what happened that caused a problem.	5. Reference printed information, such as product manuals or guarantees.
3. Tell when and where the problem took place.	6. Keep a polite, informed, and firm tone.

In a real argument, you tell how you know things to prove your points. In an imaginary argument, you can use your "proof," or evidence, to argue convincingly and support your claim.

Revise

As you revise your work, keep in mind your audience and purpose. Does your writing make your point clear in a respectful way? Does it do what you want it to?

1 Evaluate Your Work

Read your letter to an adult for ideas on how to make it better. When you are done, ask him or her questions:

- **About the Form** Is my tone polite? Are there parts of my writing that should be made more formal?

- **About the Organization** Are the problem and solution clear? Do I get to my point right away? Did I provide clear reasons and evidence for my complaint?

Revision in Action

Ellen's Draft

I am writing to inform you of a problem I have with one of your cameras. It is in the Easy Shot series. The model number is IX63.

I chose this model because the box said it was easy to use and had an auto-focus feature. During a recent trip to a nature preserve, located 50 miles west of Route 110, I found that to be untrue. The instructions inside the box were very confusing and the auto-focus feature did not work. All of my pictures turned out blurry.

According to the instructions, using the auto-focus feature should guarantee clear pictures, but this is just not the case. I am enclosing the faulty camera. I also included my receipt for the camera. I put in my receipt for photo developing, too. Please send me a refund for the camera and the photos.

Ellen's adult advisor says:

"I think your introduction is too wordy and confusing."

"This description of the trip seems unnecessary."

"This is a bit unclear. Maybe you can combine these sentences."

2 **Mark Your Changes**

Consolidate Text Business letters shouldn't be chatty and newsy. You want to give as much information as is necessary, but you want to do it in as little space as possible. Consolidating your text may involve:

- deleting information that's not necessary

- saying things in fewer words

- combining sentences to pack more information in less space.

Use the ⌐ symbol to replace text. Use the ⌐ symbol to delete text.

Reflect
- Are your sentences concise and clear?
- Did you use a formal and polite tone?

Revising Marks

MARK	∧	↶	⌐	⌐	¶
WHAT IT MEANS	Insert something.	Move to here.	Replace with this.	Take out.	Make a new paragraph.

Revised Draft

I am writing to inform you of a problem I have with one of your ~~cameras. It is in the~~ Easy Shot ~~series. The model number is~~ IX63 *camera*.

I chose this model because the box said it was easy to use and had an auto-focus feature. During a recent trip to a nature preserve, ~~located 50 miles west of Route 110~~ I found that to be untrue. The instructions inside the box were very confusing and the auto-focus feature did not work. All of my pictures turned out blurry.

According to the instructions, using the auto-focus feature should guarantee clear pictures, but this is just not the case. I am enclosing the faulty camera. ~~I also included~~ my receipt *and a* ~~for the camera. I put in my~~ receipt for photo developing, too. Please send me a refund for the camera and the photos.

Ellen deleted text and combined sentences to consolidate ideas.

Ellen removed unnecessary details.

Ellen combined sentences to make her conclusion more concise.

Edit and Proofread

After you're satisfied with the content of your business letter, read it again to fix language errors. This is what you do when you edit and proofread your work:

- **Check the Grammar** Correct grammar is especially important when writing a formal business letter. Make sure that you have used correct and conventional grammar throughout. In particular, check for correct use of comparative adjectives. (See page 247W.)

- **Check the Spelling** Spell-check can help, but it isn't always enough. Read your work carefully, especially adjectives with *-er* and *-est* suffixes. Use a dictionary to help you. (See page 248W.)

- **Check the Mechanics** Errors in punctuation and capitalization can make your work hard to understand. In particular, check that you have used a colon after the formal greeting. (See page 249W.)

Use these marks to edit and proofread your business letter.

Editing and Proofreading Marks

MARK	WHAT IT MEANS	MARK	WHAT IT MEANS
∧	Insert something.	⁄	Make lowercase.
∧	Add a comma.	ℒ	Delete, take something out.
⌃	Add a semicolon.	¶	Make new paragraph.
⊙	Add a period.	◯	Spell out.
⊙	Add a colon.	↖	Replace with this.
ⱽ ⱽ	Add quotation marks.	∼	Change order of letters or words.
ⱽ	Add an apostrophe.	#	Insert space.
≡	Capitalize.	◡	Close up, no space here.

Reflect

- What kinds of errors did you find? What can you do to keep from making them?

Grammar Workout

Check Comparative Adjectives

A **comparative adjective** compares two people, places, or things. Follow these rules to form comparative adjectives.

- Add **-er** if the adjective has one syllable. (You may need to change the spelling of some words before adding **-er**. See page 248W.)

  EXAMPLES   I am **older** than you.
  Tigers are **pretty**—even **prettier** than house cats.

- For a long adjective (three or more syllables), use **more** before the adjective.

  EXAMPLE   Tigers are **intelligent,** but are they **more intelligent** than house cats?

- If an adjective has two syllables, use the form that is easier to say.

  EXAMPLES   Siberian Tigers are **fluffier** than Bengal Tigers.
  Siberian Tigers are **more active** than other tigers.

Find the Trouble Spots

The other day I was comparing two cameras in the Tech-Mart store. One camera was ~~more big~~ ^{bigger} and ^{heavier} ~~heavy~~ than the other. But the small, light camera was expensiver than the first. I couldn't decide which one I liked, so I asked the sales clerk for help. She said the camera that was more big takes pictures that are colorfuller.

Find and fix three more errors with comparative adjectives.

Edit and Proofread, continued

> # Spelling Workout

Check Adjectives Ending in -*er* and -*est*

You sometimes need to change the spelling of the base adjective before adding **-er** or **-est**.

- When a one-syllable adjective ends with a vowel and a single consonant, double the consonant before adding **-er** or **-est**.

  EXAMPLES   fat ⟶ fat**t**er ⟶ fat**t**est
                hot ⟶ hot**t**er ⟶ hot**t**est

- When a two-syllable adjective ends in **y,** change the **y** to **i** before adding **-er** or **-est**.

  EXAMPLES   pretty ⟶ prett**i**er ⟶ prett**i**est
                angry ⟶ angr**i**er ⟶ angr**i**est

- When an adjective ends in silent **e,** drop the **e** before adding **-er** or **-est**.

  EXAMPLES   cute ⟶ cuter ⟶ cutest
                white ⟶ whiter ⟶ whitest

Find the Trouble Spots

    The camera was supposed to be the ~~easyest~~ *easiest* model to use, but it had the ~~tinyest~~ *tiniest* directions, so I could barely read them. Each shot came out blurryer than the last. That was the problem that made me madest of all.

Find and fix two additional spelling errors.

MechanicsWorkout

Check Capitalization and Punctuation in Letters

When you write a business letter, pay careful attention to how you capitalize and punctuate the greeting and the closing.

- For the greeting, capitalize *Dear* and the name of the person you are writing to. Use a colon after the person's name.

  EXAMPLE   **D**ear Sir**:**

  Dear Ms. Stevens**:**

- Begin the closing with a capital letter. Add a comma before signing your name.

  EXAMPLE   **R**espectfully**,**

  Elizabeth Mills

Find the Trouble Spots

Ms. nora Porter
5503 Sunset Drive
San Diego, CA 92101

dear Ms. Porter

Please see the attached letter I sent to the manufacturer of a camera I bought at your store. I would like you to be aware of the problems I had with this product. Thank you for your time.

sincerely
Ellen Brooks
Ellen Brooks

Find and fix three more errors in punctuation or capitalization.

Write as a
Friend

Model Study

Friendly Letter

What do you do when you want to communicate with a good friend? Perhaps you get on the phone, send a text message, or compose an e-mail. The format you choose and what you write depends on your purpose for writing. You can write as much or as little as you want and there's no time limit.

When you write a friendly letter, you write to someone you know personally. Because you know the person, you can be chatty and casual, or use an informal tone to share what's going on in your life.

The student model on page 251W shows the features of a good friendly letter.

FRIENDLY LETTER

A good friendly letter

☑ begins with the date in the upper right corner

☑ includes a greeting

☑ uses an informal tone to tell about recent events and about the writer's thoughts and feelings

☑ asks about your friend's life

☑ includes a closing before the signature.

Feature Checklist

Dec. 29, 2014

Dear Tonya,

How have you been? It was great to get your letter last month. I hope your mom's new job is still going well. What are you studying in school right now? In science, we have been studying endangered species. I didn't know so many types of animals were in danger.

One thing we learned was that early this year, six rare birds were added to the endangered-species list. Scientists have been trying to get those birds on the list for nearly fifteen years! I didn't know that listing birds as endangered was so controversial!

I wonder how the birds would feel about that! The birds have names that are as amazing as their descriptions. My favorite is called the black stilt. It is one of the rarest birds in the world, and is black with long, red legs. There are less than 100 left. It's great that scientists have found a way to protect them!

Write again soon and tell me about all the exciting things you've been up to. I can't wait to hear from you!

Your "pen pal,"
Susan

Susan included the **date** in the upper right corner.

In the body of the letter, Susan tells her news.

Susan uses **friendly, informal language** and tells about her feelings.

Susan uses an affectionate **closing** before her signature.

Write a Friendly Letter

WRITING PROMPT You write friendly letters to tell someone close to you about what's been happening in your life.

Think about something interesting or exciting you've done lately. Pick a topic. Then write a friendly letter that includes

- the date in the upper right corner
- a greeting to your friend or relative
- one or more body paragraphs about the event or experience, and your thoughts and feelings about what happened
- questions about your friend's or relative's life or thoughts
- a friendly closing.

Prewrite

Here are some tips for planning and preparing before you write your letter.

1 **Choose One Experience to Write About**

To keep your letter focused, don't try to tell about *everything* that's happened recently. Instead, think about several interesting things you've done, then pick just one to write about. Look how Xavier decided on his topic.

Ideas

—My family's camping trip. ← *My brother wouldn't be interested in this.*

—My trip to the rainforest exhibit at the museum.

—My summer at my Grandma's farm.
  This would take too long to write about.

TechTIP

If your computer has a calendar program, you can use it to keep an e-journal. That way you'll always have material to write to your friends about.

2 Plan How Your Ideas Will Flow

Before you start writing, organize your ideas. Use a graphic organizer like the one below to put your central ideas and details in order.

Xavier's Plan for His Friendly Letter

<u>Central Idea</u>

My trip to the rainforest exhibit at the museum was amazing. I learned a lot about the environment.

<u>Detail 1</u>

Our guide showed us many plants and animals that live only in the rainforest. Some of these can be used to make medicines.

<u>Detail 2</u>

I saw photographs of the canopy of the rainforest, and of animals in their natural habitats.

<u>Detail 3</u>

We learned that rainforests are in danger.

3 Use Your Own Voice

The great thing about writing a friendly letter is that you are free to use your own voice. Choose which style is best for you. Let your feelings come through!

STYLE	EXAMPLE
Cheerful	I can't wait to tell you all about my trip to the museum. The rainforest is so beautiful, and I got to see the most amazing animals.
Informative	During my trip to the museum, I learned just how important the rainforest is to many plant and animal species—and to human beings.
Affectionate	I am so happy to share the details of my trip with you. I know how much you love hearing about the beauty of the rainforest.

Reflect

- Did you decide which style and tone fits your topic?

- Does the order of your details make sense?

Draft

Once you know what you want to say, you can start writing. Your first draft might not be perfect. That's okay—just focus on getting your thoughts down on paper.

- **Use the Right Form** Set up your letter with the date and a greeting.

> November 26, 2014
>
> Dear Domenic,
>
>   At the museum, I learned a lot about the environment, thanks to our guide, who was very friendly and had traveled everywhere. Did you know that tropical rainforests supply 40% of the world's oxygen? They are also home to millions of plants and animals.

Make sure the date appears in the upper right corner of your letter.

- **Use Your Organizer** When you talk about what's been going on in your life, make sure you stay focused on the topic. Use your writing plan to stay on track.

> Our guide took us on a walk through the museum. It was amazing to see photographs of the towering trees. He told us that thousands of species of plants and animals live on the rainforest floor. While walking on the trail, our guide pointed out a bug that looked like it was made of gold! I learned it's called a "ceiba borer beetle."

Xavier used the first detail in his organizer to draft this paragraph.

Reflect

- Read your draft. Does it have all the parts of a friendly letter?

- Are there enough details to make it interesting?

DRAFTING TIPS

Trait: **Development of Ideas/Organization**

If You Have Trouble Developing Your Ideas...

Sometimes, you cannot come up with enough details to express your thoughts and experiences in a friendly letter. You keep trying, but you can't focus on what you want to say.

Try Adding Ba-Da-Bing

When you need to add more details,

- think BA and tell about something you have seen or experienced lately that you think your friend would find interesting

- think DA and tell what you thought about this experience

- think BING and ask what your friend has been up to.

Here's a bare-bones description: I went to an art show.

Now here's how you can enrich it with Ba-Da-Bing.

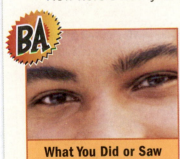

What You Did or Saw	**What You Thought of It**	**What You Want to Know**
I went to a great art show at a sculpture park on the waterfront. Some of the sculptures were floating gently on the water.	I never knew a sculpture could float. I thought this was the coolest part of the exhibit.	How has your painting class been going? Have you been back to the museum in your town for inspiration?

Ba-Da-Bing in Action

Revise

As you get ready to revise your letter, keep in mind the person who will be receiving the letter, and your purpose for writing. Will your letter connect with your "audience"?

1 **Evaluate Your Work**

E-mail your draft to a friend (not the one receiving the letter!). See the Writing Forms section on page 397W for more about e-mail. Ask your friend questions:

- **About the Form** Have I formatted my friendly letter properly?

- **About the Organization** Will it be clear to my friend what I'm talking about and what I'm saying about it?

> ### Revision in Action

Xavier's Draft

Dear Domenic,

At the museum, I learned a lot about the environment thanks to our guide, who was very friendly and had traveled everywhere. Did you know that tropical rainforests supply 40% of the world's oxygen? They are also home to millions of plants and animals. Our guide said the rainforest is in danger because people cut down the trees. We should start a club. The club can focus on ways to save the rainforest.

The museum was great. Let's get together soon to talk about the club. Hope to see you soon!

Your friend,
Xavier

Xavier's friend says:

"This detail about the guide interrupts what you're saying. I'd take it out."

"Can you be more specific about the things the guide told you?"

"This sentence doesn't seem to belong here."

2 Mark Your Changes

Add Text To make your ideas clearer, you may need to add details. Use this mark: ∧

Delete and Consolidate Text You may want to delete excess details to consolidate sentences that seem too wordy or repetitive. Use this mark: ⟿

Rearrange Text You may want to rearrange details into a more effective order. Draw a circle around the information you want to move and then draw an arrow to show where the text should be placed.

Reflect

- Have you added enough details to make your ideas clear?

- Have you set up your friendly letter correctly?

Revising Marks

MARK	∧	↶	⌐	⟿	¶
WHAT IT MEANS	Insert something.	Move to here.	Replace with this.	Take out.	Make a new paragraph.

Revised Draft

Dear Domenic,

At the museum, I learned a lot about the environment, ~~thanks to our guide, who was very friendly and had traveled everywhere.~~ Did you know that tropical rainforests supply 40% of the world's oxygen? They are also home to millions of ˄species of plants and animals. Our guide said the rainforest is in danger because people cut down the trees, ˄which affects every creature's habitat We should start a club. ~~The club can focus~~ ˄that focuses on ways to save the rainforest.

The museum was great. ⟨Let's get together soon to talk about the club.⟩ Hope to see you soon!

Your friend,
Xavier

Xavier deleted unnecessary information.

Xavier added specific details and consolidated ideas to make his writing clear and interesting.

Xavier moved a sentence to improve flow.

Edit and Proofread

After you are satisfied with the content of your friendly letter, read it again to fix any language errors. This is what you do when you edit and proofread your work:

- **Check the Grammar** Even though your tone is informal, your grammar should still be correct to communicate clearly. Make sure that you have used correct and conventional grammar throughout. In particular, check for correct use of adverbs. (See page 259W.)

- **Check the Spelling** Spell-check can help, but it isn't always enough. For adverbs ending in **-ly**, you'll have to read your work carefully, and maybe use a dictionary. (See page 260W.)

- **Check the Mechanics** Errors in punctuation and capitalization can make your work hard to understand. In particular, check that apostrophes are used correctly in contractions. (See page 261W.)

Use these marks to edit and proofread your letter.

Editing and Proofreading Marks

MARK	WHAT IT MEANS	MARK	WHAT IT MEANS
∧	Insert something.	/	Make lowercase.
∧	Add a comma.	℮	Delete, take something out.
∧	Add a semicolon.	¶	Make new paragraph.
⊙	Add a period.	◯	Spell out.
⊙	Add a colon.	⌃	Replace with this.
∨ ∨	Add quotation marks.	∼	Change order of letters or words.
∨	Add an apostrophe.	#	Insert space.
≡	Capitalize.	◡	Close up, no space here.

Reflect

- What kinds of errors did you find? What can you do to keep from making them?

Grammar Workout

Check Adverbs

Adverbs describe verbs, adjectives, or other adverbs. They tell *how*, *when*, or *where*. Adverbs add interest and detail.

- Use an adverb to describe a verb. Many adverbs end in **-ly**.

  EXAMPLE The scientist **attentively** watched the birds in the canopy.

  [verb]

- Use the adverb **more** with another adverb to compare two actions.

  EXAMPLE He studied the leaves **more carefully** than before.

  [verb]

- Use an adverb to make an adjective or another adverb stronger.

  [adjective]

  EXAMPLES I was **quite** fortunate to be able to go on this trip.
  We moved **very** cautiously toward the jaguar.

  [adverb]

Find the Opportunities

When I looked ^*closely* at the tree trunk, I saw something moving. They were ants carrying huge leaves, which seemed like a ^*nearly* impossible feat. But, leafcutter ants are strong and can carry almost ten times their body weight. I was amazed how those little guys worked.

Where else could you add adverbs to enrich this paragraph?

Edit and Proofread, continued

Spelling Workout

Check Adverbs Ending in *-ly*

When you add the suffix **-ly** to an adjective to form an adverb, the spelling of the adjective may change. Follow these rules:

- For adjectives that end in **y**, change the **y** to an **i** before you add **-ly**.

  EXAMPLES   grouchy + -ly   ⟶   grouch**i**ly

  sleepy + -ly   ⟶   sleep**i**ly

- For adjectives that end in **l**, keep the **l** when you add **-ly**.

  EXAMPLE   real + -ly   ⟶   rea**ll**y

- For adjectives that end in **le**, drop the final **le** before you add **-ly.**

  EXAMPLE   possible + -ly   ⟶   possi**bl**y

Find the Trouble Spots

I woke up ~~realy~~ *really* early to be in the first group of the day. ~~Luckyly~~ *Luckily* my plan worked. Our guide gave us a lesson on caving. I accidentaly laughed when I heard that hiking through caves is called "spelunking." Thanks to the lesson, I comfortabley maneuvered though the narrow openings.

Find and fix two more spelling errors.

Mechanics Workout

Check Apostrophes in Contractions

When two words are joined into one, you have a **contraction.**

I + am   ⟶   I'm

are + not   ⟶   aren't

- For contractions formed with a pronoun and the verb **am, are,** or **is,** use an apostrophe to replace the first letter of the verb.

they + are   ⟶   they are   ⟶   they're

it + is   ⟶   it is   ⟶   it's

- Many other contractions are formed with a verb and the word **not.** To form these contractions, use an apostrophe to replace the *o* in **not.**

would + not   ⟶   would not   ⟶   wouldn't

are + not   ⟶   are not   ⟶   aren't

EXCEPTIONS   can + not ⟶ can't [just one *n*]

will + not ⟶ won't [a different word]

Find the Trouble Spots

The dangers of the forest shouldnt be taken lightly.
Since I had'nt visited an area with deadly snakes before,
I did'nt know what to expect. I learned that most snakes
cannt be seen easily because theyr'e camouflaged by
their surroundings. I couldnt see one snake until it
jumped right out at me.

Find and fix four more problems with apostrophes.

Model Study

Story Scene

When you write a **story scene**, you use precise, vivid details to show the time and place of the story action. You want your readers to be able to imagine themselves in the place you're describing.

If you were describing your home, you would give **details** such as how big it is, what the yard and neighborhood are like, and maybe something that makes it unique.

When you write a story scene about a place—real or imagined—you include details to make the subject come to life for your reader.

Read the model on page 263W, which shows the features of a good story scene.

STORY SCENE

A good story scene

✓ hooks the reader with a strong introduction

✓ uses vivid, precise words and sensory details to create a clear image in the reader's mind

✓ shows where and when a story takes place.

Feature Checklist

Yellowstone:
A World Apart

by Allen Marks

Yellowstone is more than a national park. It is a microcosm of almost every landform known. Within its boundaries are mountains with craggy peaks, rugged plateaus, pristine lakes, boundless forests, broad basins, and deep canyons.

But Yellowstone is best known for its geysers and hot springs. You can hardly go anywhere in the park without smelling sulfur from a spring, feeling spray from a geyser, or hearing the gurgle of a babbling brook. There are also reddish-pink mud pots that bloop and spit constantly.

Allen's story scene develops one **central idea**.

Allen uses **vivid, precise words** to provide a clear image of the story scene.

Allen includes **sensory details** to help the reader "see" the setting.

Write a Story Scene

WRITING PROMPT Some places are unforgettable. From the moment you encounter them, you're fascinated. You might feel that way about some place you've been to or a place you've read about or imagined.

Think about a place that could put a person in conflict with nature. (You can describe a real place or invent one.) Then write a story scene that includes

- an introduction that hooks the reader
- sensory details about the appearance of the place
- details that reveal the time period—year or season
- vivid and precise language.

Prewrite

Here are some tips for planning your story scene.

1 Choose a Subject That Interests You

It's best to create a story scene about a place you'll be able to make interesting to your readers. As you plan, think about details you know something about (or can find out about through research).

Jot down several possible ideas and then choose the best one. Noella used a chart like this one:

Ideas	Good and Bad Points
A seaquarium	I liked it, but other people might not be interested.
California Gold Rush	I don't know enough about the time period.
A horse ranch	I once spent the summer at my uncle's horse ranch in Montana.

2 Complete Your Writing Road Map

Think about the purpose of your story scene. It will determine which details you include. If you're creating a scary setting, you'll use different details than if you want to attract readers to visit a place. Use an FATP chart to get clear on your audience and purpose.

FATP Chart

Form: _story scene_

Audience: _classmates_

Topic: _a horse ranch_

Purpose: _to describe a scene at a horse ranch_

3 Brainstorm to Gather Details

Once you have your idea set, brainstorm the details of your story scene. Noella used a web like the one below to gather details to "flesh out" her story scene.

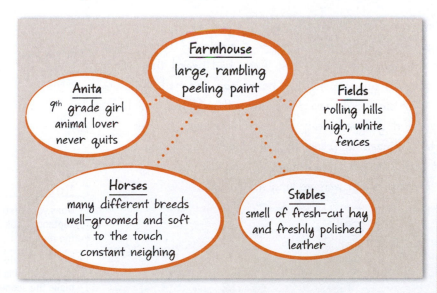

Farmhouse
large, rambling
peeling paint

Anita
9th grade girl
animal lover
never quits

Fields
rolling hills
high, white
fences

Horses
many different breeds
well-groomed and soft
to the touch
constant neighing

Stables
smell of fresh-cut hay
and freshly polished
leather

Reflect

• Have you chosen a place that really interests you?

• Do you need to find more details?

Draft

Once you've brainstormed details and can picture your scene in your mind, it's time to start writing. To begin your draft, use these techniques:

- **Hook Your Readers Right Away** Grab your readers' interest right away. Use a vivid sensory image, a bit of dialogue, or an interesting detail to get your readers' attention.

> The pasture was quiet and still and deserted that crisp fall afternoon. The tranquil silence was pierced only by the young girl's sharp cry of frustration.

Noella begins with a sensory detail that gets readers' attention.

- **Develop Your Description with Details** Adding a lot of details to your writing will make it interesting and help your description "come to life." Think about how to use details to develop your central idea.

From Noella's Draft

> Anita shivered as the wind cut right through her lightweight jacket. Twigs and leaves crunched under the soles of her well-worn boots with every step she took. Anita had heard the whinny of the wild young pony two hours ago and had been following it ever since. Whenever she got within 50 feet of the sleek, tan pony, it galloped away. Pulling up the hood of her jacket, Anita continued to follow the sound of galloping hoofs. "You're not going to get away from me," she told the pony under her breath. "I can wait as long as you can."

Noella uses details to help readers visualize the scene.

Reflect

- Does your first sentence hook the reader?

- Do you include enough details to make the scene come alive?

DRAFTING TIPS

Trait: **Focus and Unity**

If Your Writing Wanders . . .

Sometimes you get your writing going, and it starts drifting in too many directions. You have so many ideas that you don't know which ones to stick with. The result is that your writing wanders and appears to lack focus.

Try Writing a Skeleton Description First

This is not a description of a skeleton! A **skeleton description** is just a super-quick pre-draft that shows just the main points of your description.

Here's an example for Noella's paper:

Skeleton Description

Then, for her actual draft, Noella "exploded" each sentence by adding sensory details to the description.

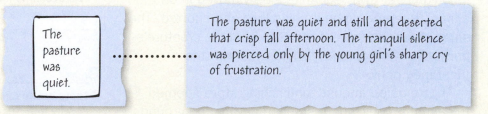

Revise

As you consider how to revise your work, keep in mind your intended audience and your purpose for writing.

1 **Evaluate Your Work**

Read your draft aloud to a partner and ask him or her to make a quick drawing of your story scene. Discuss the drawing, asking questions:

- **About the Form** Does my description paint a complete picture of my story scene? Is it believable?

- **About the Focus and Unity** Have I focused on the details that make this setting stand out? Do all the details go together?

Revision in Action

Noella's Draft

Anita continued to follow the pony as it walked into the foothills surrounding the pasture. The terrain made for tough going, but Anita refused to give up.

At last, the pony stopped to rest in a narrow crevice. Anita felt that she finally had the pony where it couldn't get away. As Anita slowly moved in on the animal, it reared up on its hind legs and snorted. The smell of fear and sweat radiated from the creature's body. Undeterred, Anita locked eyes with the frightened pony.

Anita's quiet, intense, unflinching stare seemed to calm the pony, and it stopped pawing the ground. With eyes still locked, Anita moved in. Girl and pony seemed to be communicating in some mysterious language, known only to them. Anita waited patiently.

Noella's partner says:

" This paragraph could use a few more vivid words to liven it up.**"**

" Will everyone know what a crevice is?**"**

" There are too many details here. Can you condense them?**"**

2 **Mark Your Changes**

Clarify Ideas One main goal of revising your work is to make your ideas as clear as possible for your reader. This may involve

- **adding** sensory details to make your descriptions come alive

- **explaining** or **elaborating** to make sure your reader understands you

- **condensing** or even **deleting** text to keep your reader from becoming distracted or confused.

Reflect

- Does your description include enough sensory detail?

- Are there any unnecessary or repetitive details you could take out?

Revising Marks

MARK	∧	↰	↰	⸜	⁋
WHAT IT MEANS	Insert something.	Move to here.	Replace with this.	Take out.	Make a new paragraph.

Revised Draft

  Anita continued to ~~follow~~ ^{pursue} the pony as it ~~walked~~ ^{cantered} into the ^{rocky} foothills surrounding the pasture. The ^{rugged} terrain made for tough going, but Anita refused to give up.

  At last, the pony stopped to rest in a narrow crevice_{, a large crack in a rock wall}. Anita felt that she had finally had the pony where it couldn't get away. As Anita slowly moved in on the animal, it reared up on its hind legs and snorted. The smell of fear and sweat radiated from the creature's body. Undeterred, Anita locked eyes with the frightened pony.

  Anita's ~~quiet, intense,~~ unflinching stare seemed to calm the pony, and it stopped pawing the ground. With eyes still locked, Anita moved in. Girl and pony seemed to be communicating in some mysterious language, known only to them. Anita waited patiently_{, Knowing that she would triumph in the end.}

Noella changed some words and added details to make her description more vivid.

Noella added a definition of *crevice*.

Noella condensed the details.

Noella added to her ending to make it more satisfying.

Edit and Proofread

Does your story scene paint a vivid picture of the setting you're describing? If so, you're now ready to fix language errors. This is what you do when you edit and proofread your work:

- **Check the Grammar** Make sure that you have used correct and conventional grammar throughout. In particular, check that you've used complete sentences. (See page 271W.)

- **Check the Spelling** Spell-check can help, but it's not enough. For errors with sound-alike words, you'll have to read your work carefully, and perhaps use a dictionary. (See page 272W.)

- **Check the Mechanics** Errors in punctuation and capitalization can make your work hard to understand. In particular, check that you have correctly used commas in lists. (See page 273W.)

Use these marks to edit and proofread your story scene.

TechTIP

Most word-processing programs have a built-in dictionary where you can check the spelling of sound-alike words.

Editing and Proofreading Marks

MARK	WHAT IT MEANS	MARK	WHAT IT MEANS
∧	Insert something.	/	Make lowercase.
∧	Add a comma.	℘	Delete, take something out.
∧	Add a semicolon.	¶	Make new paragraph.
⊙	Add a period.	◯	Spell out.
⊙	Add a colon.	⌒	Replace with this.
⌄ ⌄	Add quotation marks.	∼	Change order of letters or words.
⌄	Add an apostrophe.	#	Insert space.
≡	Capitalize.	◡	Close up, no space here.

Reflect

- What kinds of errors did you find? What can you do to keep from making them?

GrammarWorkout

Check for Complete Sentences

A complete sentence has a subject and a predicate. The **subject** tells *who* or *what* the sentence is about. The **predicate** tells what the subject *does, is,* or *has.*

> **EXAMPLE**   The students | wrote in their diaries every day.
> Subject   Predicate

Sentence fragments are only parts of a complete sentence. They lack a subject or a predicate, or both. When you write, make sure that every sentence has a subject and a predicate.

> **FRAGMENT**   **Her face.** It had a stern and resolute expression.
>
> **COMPLETE
> SENTENCE**   Her face had a stern and resolute expression.

Find the Trouble Spots

Early in the afternoon, Anita went to the barn. To gather the blanket, saddle, and bridle. She went into the first stall. To greet her uncle's old pony. That pony had been her best friend when she was a little girl. Then, she grabbed her gear and headed out. To the pasture. She walked briskly, like she had to perform some important chore.

Find two more
sentence
fragments to
fix.

Edit and Proofread, continued

> ### Spelling Workout
>
> # Check Sound-Alike Words
>
> If you hear the following sentence read aloud, you'll have no trouble understanding it:
>
> > **My teacher took a special coarse at the university because she wants to right stories for children.**
>
> But if you see the sentence written, it's likely you'll be confused. The reason is that there are two sound-alike words.
>
> | Word | Meaning |
> |------|---------|
> | coarse
course | rough, unrefined
a series of lessons |
> | right
write | the opposite of *left*
create, make up |
>
> To find and fix problems with sound-alike words, you have to know which words are the troublemakers. Study the list of common sound-alike words on page 518W.
>
> ### Find the Trouble Spots
>
> > Anita wasn't ~~aloud~~ *allowed* to take the horse on slippery ground, so she tied it to a nearby tree. Slowly, Anita began her *descent* ~~dissent~~ into the creak. She approached the pony warily, until she got to stroke his light-brown main.
>
> Find two more spelling errors to fix.

Mechanics Workout

Check Commas in Lists

When you give a "list" of three or more things in your writing, separate the items with commas. Without commas, the list may be confusing or unclear.

CONFUSING	She was wearing a light-green sweater blue jeans and sneakers.
CLEAR	She was wearing a light-green sweater, blue jeans, and sneakers.

Be sure to use a comma between the next-to-last item in the list and the word *and*. This comma is called a **serial comma**. Without it, your meaning may be unclear.

CONFUSING	Anita was very close to her mom and dad, her best friend Katie and her horse. [Is it Katie's horse, or Anita's?]
CLEAR	Anita was very close to her mom and dad, her best friend Katie, and her horse.

Find the Trouble Spots

Anita borrowed blankets a saddle and a bridle. Then she hurried back to the pony. She strode past the river the farmhouse and the tree with the old tire swing. She hoped the pony hadn't strayed too far.

Find two more places to add commas.

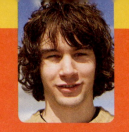

"Talking about a book
I've read helps me
discover things about the
book—and myself."
—Hal

Model Study

Literary Analysis

When you read a good story, you probably want to recommend it to as many people as possible. You can share your thoughts by writing a **literary analysis**.

Think about a book that you really enjoyed. What do you think made the story interesting? What did you like about it? What can you say about the author's style?

When you write a **literary analysis**, you explain why you liked, or didn't like, a story. You write your opinion about different parts of it and support your opinions with evidence from the text.

Read the student model on page 275W. It shows the features of a good literary analysis.

LITERARY ANALYSIS

A good literary analysis

☑ quickly summarizes what you've read

☑ expresses your personal thoughts and opinions about the literature

☑ supports your opinions with reasons and evidence from the text

☑ may mention a life lesson or important truth you learned from reading the text.

Feature Checklist

Conscience and Courage:
Rescuers of Jews During the Holocaust

by Eva Fogelman
Reviewed by Miriam Reed

One of the best books I've read is *Conscience and Courage* by Eva Fogelman. It is a moving account of real heroes and the people they helped.

This book is about people who helped Jews during the Holocaust, the persecution of Jewish people by the Nazi government during the 1930s and 1940s.

The stories in the book focus on the efforts of *gentiles*, or people who weren't of the Jewish faith. Many gentiles helped Jews escape death, often risking their own lives. Some helped one person. Others, like businessmen Oskar Schindler and Raoul Wallenberg, helped hundreds. Without the rescuers' efforts, more of these people would have died.

I was inspired by this book. On page 6, the author analyzes what made people risk their lives to oppose the Nazis. Fogelman explains that in helping others, many people find unexpected strength and courage in themselves.

This book also has a special meaning for me. My Jewish grandparents left for the United States when they were children. As I read Fogelman's accounts, I thought about what would have happened if they had stayed in Germany. So, when I read about people like Schindler, I think that he might have helped them. This thought gives me great comfort.

Student Model

*The writer gives her **personal analysis** of the work.*

The writer expresses her opinion of the book.

The writer sums up why she liked the book and tells how it affected her.

*The writer gives a **brief summary** of the book.*

*The writer uses **evidence** from the book to support her opinion.*

Oskar Schindler saved more than 1,200 Jews from concentration camps by giving them jobs at his factories. ▶

Development of Ideas

 **What's It Like**

If you want to make your voice heard about an important issue, you can write a petition. Then you talk with all the people you know, explain why your cause is important, and ask them to sign the petition and support you. Good writers do the same thing. They gather details and examples to support and develop their ideas.

How Do You Develop Ideas?

When the ideas in a piece of writing are well developed, you feel satisfied. The writer uses reasons and evidence from the book to explain and support ideas and answer questions.

When you write a literary analysis, think about your thoughts, feelings, and opinions. Use details and evidence from the literature to support and explain your opinions.

What Kids Are Made Of

by Kristy Murray
Reviewed by Ken Kirchner

This book is a collection of true stories about kids. I was amazed to learn how much these kids have accomplished. The author tells about a kid named Iqbal from Pakistan. He brought the world's attention to the problem of child labor in his country. Murray also tells about Yehudi, who directed a New York Symphony Orchestra when he was only 11! The stories of these kids inspire me to try to achieve great things on my own.

Ken shares his **feelings** about the book.

Ken uses **evidence** from the book to support his reason for feeling as he does.

Study the rubric below. What is the difference between a paper with a score of 2 and one with a score of 4?

Development of Ideas

	How thoughtful and interesting is the writing?	How well are the ideas or claims explained and supported?
4 Wow!	The writing engages the reader with meaningful ideas or claims and presents them in a way that is interesting and appropriate to the audience, purpose, and type of writing.	The ideas or claims are fully explained and supported. • The ideas or claims are well developed with important details, evidence, and/or description. • The writing feels complete, and the reader is satisfied.
3 Aaah.	Most of the writing engages the reader with meaningful ideas or claims and presents them in a way that is interesting and appropriate to the audience, purpose, and type of writing.	Most of the ideas or claims are explained and supported. • Most of the ideas or claims are developed with important details, evidence, and/or description. • The writing feels mostly complete, but the reader still has some questions.
2 Hmmm.	Some of the writing engages the reader with meaningful ideas or claims and presents them in a way that is interesting and appropriate to the audience, purpose, and type of writing.	Some of the ideas or claims are explained and supported. • Only some of the ideas or claims are developed. Details, evidence, and/or description are limited or not relevant. • The writing leaves the reader with many questions.
1 Huh?	The writing does not engage the reader. It is not appropriate to the audience, purpose, and type of writing.	The ideas or claims are not explained or supported. The ideas or claims lack details, evidence, and/or description, and the writing leaves the reader unsatisfied.

Development of Ideas, continued

Compare Writing Samples

A good literary analysis presents the writer's feelings. It supports the writer's ideas with evidence from the text. Study the two examples of a literary analysis on this page.

Well Developed

In My Hands: Memories of a Holocaust Rescuer

by Irene Gut Opdyke

This book is an autobiography of a truly exceptional woman. When Irene Gut Opdyke was only seventeen, Russians invaded Poland and captured her. After being forced to work for the government, she was able to escape and go to Germany. There, while working as a housekeeper, she used her employer's home to hide Jews from the Nazis. If the Nazis had found them, the Jews would have been sent to concentration camps, and Irene could have been killed. I am inspired by Irene's courage and selflessness. I wonder whether I would have displayed the same courage. I like books like this because they don't just tell a story. They force the readers to ask themselves questions about their own values.

The writer uses a formal style for her analysis and keeps it throughout.

The writer supports her opinion with specific **evidence** showing Irene's courage.

The writer gives a **personal analysis** and gives reasons for her feelings.

Not So Well-Developed

In My Hands: Memories of a Holocaust Rescuer

by Irene Gut Opdyke

This book, *In My Hands: Memories of a Holocaust Rescuer,* tells the story of how the author became a hero. Irene had to leave her country and was forced to work for German officers during WWII. Irene helped Jews hide from Nazis. Had she been caught, she could have been killed. I was inspired by Irene's story. She faced difficult choices.

The writer gives a **personal analysis** but doesn't give enough reasons or evidence to support it. The writing leaves readers with a lot of questions.

Evaluate for Development of Ideas

Now read carefully the literary analysis below. Use the rubric on page 277W to score it.

Rescue: The Story of How Gentiles Saved Jews in the Holocaust

by Milton Meltzer

Reviewed by Kiro Asayo

What do the details tell you about the book?

I have no idea what it is like to have to flee from your home because you might be captured and killed. However, when I read *Rescue: The Story of How Gentiles Saved Jews in the Holocaust* by Milton Meltzer, I understood how important it can be to have a friend and a helping hand. I feel for the Jewish people who had to run from their own homes. I am inspired by the stories of those who helped them.

During the time the Nazis were in power, Adolf Hitler organized the capture and murder of over six million Jews. They were taken from their homes to concentration camps. They were starved, overworked, and frequently murdered.

How well does the writer explain his personal analysis of the book?

The book was inspiring. Even in countries the Nazis controlled, there were some brave people who rebelled. *Rescue* is written like a history book. Usually I prefer to read fictional stories.

Does the writing seem complete? Has the writer answered most of your questions?

To me, the most interesting idea of the book is that the rescuers risked their lives to help people they didn't know at all. If I had been in that position, would I have done the same?

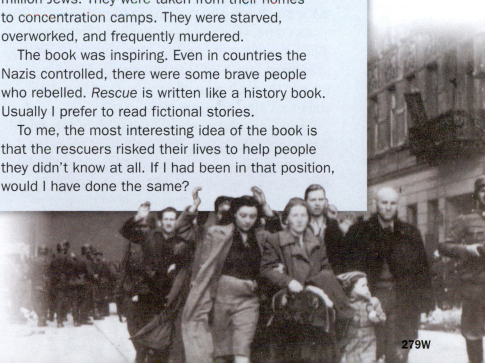

During World War II, the Nazis dominated most of Europe. ▶

Raise the Score

These papers have been scored using the **Development of Ideas Rubric** on page 277W. Study each paper to see why it got the score it did.

Overall Score: 4

Journey to Jo'burg: A South African Story

by Beverly Naidoo
Reviewed by Anthony Jameson

The first sentence gets readers interested in a worthwhile **central idea.**

This is a heartbreaking story of strength and courage. In this short novel, a girl and her younger brother journey on foot to bring their mother home.

The writer gives a **brief summary** of the book.

The main character, Naledi, lives in a village 200 miles from Johannesburg, South Africa's capital. One day, her baby sister Dineo falls sick. Naledi and her younger brother Tiro walk to Johannesburg to alert their mom, who works there as a servant. During their trip, Naledi and Tiro see the terrible reality of *apartheid*, the policy of segregation against black South Africans that lasted from 1948 to 1994.

The writer maintains a formal style throughout.

As I read, I felt very sad, angry, and shocked. Each incidence of *apartheid* the author described was more horrifying than the previous one. Beverly Naidoo's work is easy to read, but it still communicates powerful ideas.

The writer presents his **opinions and reactions** and supports them with **reasons** from the story.

The writer supports his ideas with **specific details and evidence**.

I really enjoyed the hopeful ending of this book. Naledi concludes that she won't be a servant as everybody expects. Instead, she wants to become a doctor and help the people in her village. It is a powerful decision that foresees the end of apartheid. It also shows Naledi's will and courage.

Journey to Jo'burg is a brief but very intense novel. I felt I really understood Naledi and the difficult situation she was going through.

The **conclusion** sums up the writer's analysis and gives his reasons.

Journey to Jo'burg: A South African Story

by Beverly Naidoo

The first sentence gets readers interested in the **central idea.**

This is a heartbreaking story of courage. In this short novel, a girl and her younger brother journey on foot to bring their mother home.

Naledi lives in a village almost 200 miles from Johannesburg, South Africa. One day, her baby sister Dineo falls sick. Naledi and her younger brother Tiro walk to Johannesburg to tell their mom, who works there as a servant. During their trip, Naledi and Tiro observe the terrible reality of *apartheid,* a policy of segregation against black South Africans that lasted from 1948 to 1994.

The writer gives a **brief summary** of the book, but leaves out some information.

The writer maintains a formal style throughout.

As I read I felt many different things. Beverly Naidoo writes in a way that is easy to read but still communicates powerful ideas.

I really liked the ending of the book. Naledi decides that she wants to become a doctor and help the people in her village. It is an inspiring decision that shows her strength.

I really liked this book. I enjoyed every page.

The writer includes some specific **evidence** to support his opinion, but he leaves the reader with a few questions.

The **conclusion** wraps up the writer's **opinions** but feels incomplete.

RAISING *THE SCORE*

The reader is left with questions because the writing is not complete. Where should the writer add more evidence to support his opinions?

Raise the Score, continued

The beginning is dull. The writer needs to state the **central idea** in a more interesting way.

Journey to Jo'burg: A South African Story

by Beverly Naidoo

This is a good story. In this book, a girl and her brother go on a journey to bring their mom home.

Naledi lives in a village far away from Johannesburg, South Africa. Naledi and her younger brother decide to walk to Johannesburg. *Apartheid* was a policy of segregation in South Africa. Johannesburg is one of many places that followed the system of apartheid. It was interesting to learn about life under apartheid.

The writer needs to rephrase these details and add others to create a **brief summary** of the book.

I was really moved by the simplicity of this story. I mean, like really, who should have to put up with the stuff like Naledi and Tiro had to?

Parts of the book were really sad, like when Naledi and her mom take Dineo to the hospital. This happens towards the end of the book. I felt bad for the people who had to go through a similar situation in their lives.

The writer gives his **opinions,** but it's not clear why he feels this way. The **reasons and evidence** are vague and uninteresting.

The writer drops the formal tone of a literary analysis and resorts to slang.

The book has a hopeful ending. Naledi decides she will become a doctor when she grows up.

I liked the book a lot. It made me want to know more about South Africa.

The **conclusion** feels incomplete.

RAISING THE SCORE

The writer needs to develop his ideas with specific examples and evidence. How could he support his opinions and improve the introduction and conclusion?

Journey to Jo'burg: A South African Story

by Beverly Naidoo

The beginning is dull and has no **central idea**.

In this book, a girl and her brother go on a journey to Johannesburg in South Africa.

Naledi lives in a village far away from Johannesburg, South Africa. Naledi and her younger brother decide to walk to Johannesburg. During their trip, Naledi and Tiro must deal with *apartheid*.

The **summary** is too general and vague.

The writer gives his **opinions** but doesn't support them with reasons and evidence from the story.

I liked this story. Naledi had to go through a lot of tough situations. I admire her because she was so brave.

Parts of the book are very sad. I felt bad for her family.

The book has a hopeful ending.

I really liked this book. I admire Naledi a lot.

The **conclusion** does not feel complete.

RAISING *THE SCORE*

The writer needs to give specific details about the book and support his opinions with reasons and evidence. What kinds of details could he add?

Good Beginnings and Good Endings

What's It Like ?

A good beginning and a good ending are like bookends that hold up your writing. A good beginning makes readers want to read more. A good ending wraps up what you've said and helps your readers remember.

Starting Out Right

Here are some ideas for grabbing your reader's interest right away:

- Start with a question.

> What would you do if you and your family were forced to leave your home? What if you were then separated from members of your family? This is exactly what Elie Wiesel writes about in his book <u>Night</u>.

- Start with a statistic.

> Between 1933 and 1945, Adolf Hitler organized the capture and murder of six million Jews. Elie Wiesel was one of the survivors. In his book <u>Night</u>, he tells the story of his horrifying experiences.

- Start with a quotation.

> "Never shall I forget that night, the first night in camp, which has turned my life into one long night, seven times cursed and seven times sealed," says Elie Wiesel in his book <u>Night</u>. He makes this long night painfully vivid for readers.

- Start with a personal connection.

> When I read Elie Wiesel's book <u>Night</u>, I felt a connection to his story. My grandmother grew up in Poland during World War II. She knew some of her neighbors were being deported. She told me about how she felt the day her best friend didn't come to school.

The sample below shows a bad beginning. How could you improve it, using one of the techniques you've just learned about?

> Well, I read a book by a really good author, and it was awesome. I got so much out of it. I liked it. I think you will, too. The main character is our age. But his problems are a lot more serious than ours.

Elie Wiesel was deported to the concentration camp at Auschwitz when he was a teenager. As an adult, he has written extensively about his experiences. ▶

Good Beginnings and Good Endings, continued

Finishing Strong

A good ending scores major points with readers. You've worked hard to share your ideas. Now the ending should help them remember what you've said. Here are some ways to do that:

- End by going back to your main point.

> Wiesel's <u>Night</u> shows that after people survive something tragic, they need time to even begin to heal. Sad memories continue to haunt them even after the tragedy is over.

- End by summarizing your ideas and supporting them with reasons and evidence.

> <u>Night</u> has showed me the personal effects of the Holocaust. Wiesel helped me understand what it was like to experience such a horrible thing firsthand. He showed what it is to be a true survivor.

The United States Holocaust Memorial Museum is in Washington, D.C. ▼

- End with a question. You can answer a question you asked at the start or ask a new one.

> How was Elie Wiesel able to survive? I don't know how anyone could under such horrifying conditions. Wiesel's strength was amazing.

- End with a personal example, providing reasons and evidence as needed.

> <u>Night</u> has personal meaning for me for another reason. Last year I visited the Holocaust Museum. I was able to meet a survivor and hear her story. I was amazed that she not only lived through such experiences but has also chosen to share them with people like me. I had that same feeling after reading this book.

- End with a quote. It can be from a famous person, from the book, or from someone you admire.

> In the final passage of his book, Elie Wiesel states, "From the depths of the mirror, a corpse gazed back at me. The look in his eyes, as they stared into mine, has never left." He showed that the memory of the concentration camp would never leave him. What I've learned from his book will never leave me.

The sample below shows a weak ending. How could you improve it using one of the techniques you've just learned about?

> This was a really good story. I liked it. It made me think about how hard it is to survive in tough situations. You should read it, too.

Explain and Support Your Ideas

What's It Like ?

When you spread a tasty tomato sauce on a pizza and add a lot of toppings, you have a dish that everyone wants to eat. Applause for the chef! You can get applause for your writing, too, if you develop your ideas as deeply as a deep dish pizza and pile it high with details.

Backing Up What You Say

When you write a literary analysis, your purpose is to tell how the book made you feel and what you took away from it. If you don't include enough evidence to support your ideas, you won't get your points across.

So what can you do to meet your purpose? Once you have a beginning that captures your readers' interest, keep your audience reading by adding enough specific details and evidence to explain and support your ideas.

Tech TIP

Save your ideas, drafts, and other resources in a single file folder on your computer. This will make it easier for you to find everything when you need it.

◀ Visitors to the Anne Frank ▶ House in Amsterdam can see the annex Anne and her family lived in from 1942 to 1944.

Try some of these techniques to explain and support your ideas:

- Include facts, evidence, and specific details.

> Miep Gies helped hide Anne Frank's family for nearly two years. During that time, Anne lived in a room only 16 feet long by 6 feet wide. There she wrote one of the most famous diaries in the world.

These **specific details** come straight from the story.

- Add examples from the literature.

> In her book, Miep Gies recalls Anne as a smart and strong-minded young lady. Despite her difficult circumstances, Anne still liked to dream big. She put up pictures of movie stars on her walls and wrote in her diary about her hopes and goals.

Explain and Support Your Ideas, continued

- Add direct quotations from the literature as evidence.

> Ms. Gies was not the only hero who risked her life to help others. More than twenty thousand Dutch people helped hide Jewish families. Ms. Gies states, "My story is a story of very ordinary people during extraordinary, terrible times."

The writer uses a **quotation** from the book as evidence.

- Add your own thoughts as reasons to support your ideas.

> I was so impressed with how humble Ms. Gies was about her story. She didn't help the Frank family in order to get attention or praise. She helped them because she saw a family in need. That type of selfless behavior is very admirable. Next time I see a person in need, I will take a cue from Ms. Gies and do what I can to help.

These **personal reasons** help support the writer's ideas.

◄ Miep Gies at the 1995 dedication ceremony at Anne Frank Elementary School in Dallas, Texas

Evaluate for Support

Read carefully the literary analyses below. Decide how you could make them better.

The writer uses a **quotation**. Where else would you like to see the author's own words?

> Anne Frank Remembered provides a personal look at the life of Anne Frank and the efforts of Miep Gies. The reader learns about the experiences of the Jews and their rescuers as Ms. Gies tells her personal story. Ms. Gies says, "There is nothing special about me." But really there are lots of things that are special about her.

The writer uses **general words** to describe Ms. Gies. What specific details or evidence could you replace them with?

> Ms. Gies felt she could have done more to help people. She says, "It was not enough." But Ms. Gies helped the Franks and other Jewish families in many ways. With assistance from others, Ms. Gies gave people what they needed to survive. She did a lot.

What could you add or change to develop ideas in this paragraph?

◄ In 1941, before going into hiding, the Frank family attends the wedding of Miep and Jan Gies.

Write a Literary Analysis

WRITING PROMPT   What's your favorite book or story—and why is it your favorite? Maybe there's a particular character in it that you relate to really well. Or maybe you learned an important life lesson from it. Think of a book that's important to you. Then write a literary analysis that includes

- a beginning that captures the reader's interest
- a brief summary of the book
- your personal analysis of, or opinions about, the book
- an explanation of why it's important to you
- reasons and evidence to support your ideas
- a satisfying conclusion.

Prewrite

1 **Choose a Book That Means a Lot to You**

Write about literature that is important to you. If you feel strongly about your subject, your writing will be more interesting. Jot down a few possibilities.

My Favorite Books

Dead Engine Kids: World War II Diary of John J. Briol, B-17 Ball Turret Gunner by John J. Briol

The Freedom Writers Diary: How a Teacher and 150 Teens Used Writing to Change Themselves and the World Around Them by the Freedom Writers and Erin Gruwell

Baghdad Diaries: A Woman's Chronicle of War and Exile by Nuha Al-Radi

② Record Your Thoughts About the Book

Reread or review the book. Record your overall opinion, your favorite parts, and important ideas.

> **Book**
> The Freedom Writers Diary by the Freedom Writers and Erin Gruwell
>
> **Thoughts and reactions**
> I can relate to Ms. Gruwell and her students. Where I live, there are people from many different backgrounds. We sometimes have trouble getting along.
>
> **What's good about it?**
> The book really showed how writing changed people's lives. Ms. Gruwell's writers all went on to college. No one ever thought they could do that.
>
> **Would I recommend this to others? Why or why not?**
> Yes, because people can relate to a true story of people learning to get along, despite their differences.

Daneeka's Notes for Her Paper

③ Gather Support for Your Opinions

Look at the text carefully. Use an opinion chart to help you organize and support your opinions with evidence.

> **Opinion**
> People from different backgrounds can learn to focus on what they have in common.
>
> **Support**
> — Gruwell found an offensive caricature of an African American.
> — She decided to speak about prejudice during the Holocaust.
> — She had her students read diaries written by other victims of prejudice and respond in their own diaries.
> — Eventually they held a "read-a-thon for tolerance."

Reflect

- Do your notes explain why this book matters to you?

- Can you support your opinions with specific details and evidence?

Draft

Once you know what you want to say, start writing your draft. Use your notes and charts to make your first draft go smoothly. Keep the story or book you're writing about nearby. That way you can refer to it while you write.

- **Start With a Good Beginning** Think of how to get your reader's attention in the first sentence. You might use a question, a fact, or a quotation.

> Have you ever had a teacher who makes learning real and alive for you? That's what Ms. Gruwell did for her students at Wilson High School. Then she told their story in <u>The Freedom Writers Diary</u> so that you and I could learn from her, too.

Daneeka used a thought-provoking question to hook the reader.

- **Develop Ideas with Support** As you write, use your graphic organizer to help you develop your ideas with details and evidence from the story. If you feel "stuck," stop and look through the book again for inspiration.

From Daneeka's Draft

People from different backgrounds can learn to focus on what they have in common. I believe that more than ever after reading the story of Ms. Gruwell and her students.

It all started when Ms. Gruwell found students passing around a caricature of a student in her class. It really upset her. Right then she decided to teach them about prejudice. She wanted them to understand its effects.

Ms. Gruwell explained how similar caricatures of Jewish people were widely distributed during the Holocaust. The class discussion showed Ms. Gruwell's students how prejudice can have real, disastrous effects. They became interested in learning more about prejudice—and tolerance.

Daneeka used her opinion chart to organize and support ideas in her paper.

Reflect

- Read your draft. Do you explain what the book means to you?

- Do you support your ideas with specific details and evidence?

DRAFTING TIPS

Trait: **Development of Ideas**

If Your Writing Is Vague. . .

If you don't support your ideas with clear, specific details and supporting evidence, your readers won't understand what you're trying to say.

Try Drawing a Target Diagram First

You want readers to understand why the book matters to you. To develop your ideas, answer these questions on a **target diagram**.

1. What is the book or story mostly about?

2. What details stand out for you?

3. What are the important events or high points?

4. What life lesson did you learn?

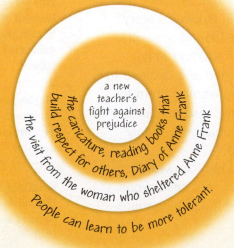

Daneeka's Target Diagram

Revise

As you consider how to revise your work, keep in mind your intended audience and your purpose for writing.

1 **Evaluate Your Work**

Share your draft with friends or classmates. Survey their opinions. Ask them questions:

- **About the Form** Is your paper engaging? Is it clear what the book is about and why you liked it (or didn't like it)?

- **About the Development of Ideas** Did you support your ideas with enough evidence and details from the book? Do your readers still have any questions?

Revision in Action

Draft

People from different backgrounds can learn to focus on what they have in common. I believe that more than ever after reading Ms. Gruwell's story.

It all started when Ms. Gruwell found students passing around a caricature of a student in her class. It really upset her. Right then she decided to teach them about prejudice. She wanted them to understand its effects. Ms. Gruwell explained how similar caricatures of Jewish people were widely distributed during the Holocaust.

The class discussion showed Ms. Gruwell's students how prejudice can have real, disastrous effects. They became interested in learning more about prejudice—and tolerance.

Daneeka's classmates say:

" Why was Ms. Gruwell so upset? Kids make fun of each other all the time."

" Maybe you could explain more about how prejudice is harmful."

" What did the kids in the class do? I want to hear more about that."

2 **Mark Your Changes**

Clarify Ideas Most of the time, clarifying your ideas will mean adding more text. You may need to add

- an **explanation** of an idea or a concept

- **background information** that will help your reader understand what you're saying

- **supporting** reasons and evidence from the book, to help you prove a point.

Reflect

- Have you included enough evidence for your opinions?

- Does your paper keep readers' interest from beginning to end?

Revising Marks

MARK	∧	↶	⌐	⤙	¶
WHAT IT MEANS	Insert something.	Move to here.	Replace with this.	Take out.	Make a new paragraph.

Revised Draft

People from different backgrounds can learn to focus on what they have in common. I believe that more than ever after reading Ms. Gruwell's story.

It all started when Ms. Gruwell found students passing around ~~a~~ ∧*an offensive* caricature of ~~a~~ ∧*an African American* student in her class. It really upset her. Right then she decided to teach them about prejudice. She wanted them to understand ~~its effects~~ *the effect that ethnic slurs can have.* Ms. Gruwell explained how similar caricatures of Jewish people were widely distributed during the Holocaust. *when the Nazis killed six million European Jews, as well as members* ∧*of other minority groups.* *Nazi propaganda influenced the attitudes of ordinary Germans.*

The class discussion showed Ms. Gruwell's students how prejudice can have real, disastrous effects. They became interested in learning more about prejudice—and tolerance. *in their journals.* *They read other works that dealt with these subjects and responded Eventually they held a "read-a-thon for tolerance.*

Daneeka gave reasons for why the caricature wasn't a harmless joke.

She added details about the role of propaganda during the Holocaust.

She added evidence from the book about what the students learned.

Edit and Proofread

Once you know that your literary analysis gets the point across, read it again to fix language errors. This is what you do when you edit and proofread your work.

- **Check the Grammar** Make sure that you have used correct and conventional grammar throughout. In particular, check that you've used conjunctions correctly in compound and complex sentences. (See page 299W.)

- **Check the Spelling** Spell-check can help, but it isn't always enough. To find errors in words with tricky sounds, it is best to use a dictionary. (See page 300W.)

- **Check the Mechanics** Errors in punctuation and capitalization can make your work hard to understand. In particular, check that you've used commas and semicolons correctly in compound and complex sentences. (See page 301W.)

Use these marks to edit and proofread your literary analysis.

Editing and Proofreading Marks

MARK	WHAT IT MEANS	MARK	WHAT IT MEANS
∧	Insert something.	／	Make lowercase.
∧	Add a comma.	ℓ	Delete, take something out.
∧	Add a semicolon.	¶	Make new paragraph.
⊙	Add a period.	◯	Spell out.
⊙	Add a colon.	⤶	Replace with this.
⌄ ⌄	Add quotation marks.	～	Change order of letters or words.
⌄	Add an apostrophe.	#	Insert space.
≡	Capitalize.	◡	Close up, no space here.

Reflect

- What kinds of errors did you find? What can you do to keep from making them?

GrammarWorkout

Check Compound and Complex Sentences

An **independent clause** has a subject and a verb and can stand alone as a sentence. To form a **compound sentence,** use *and, but,* or *or* to join two independent clauses. Use a comma before the conjunction.

EXAMPLES   I really enjoy writing in my journal**, and** I would love to publish it one day.

I want to share my writing**, but** I would keep some parts to myself.

A **dependent clause** also has a subject and a verb, but it can't stand alone. To form a **complex sentence,** you can use certain conjunctions to connect a dependent clause to an independent clause. *Although*, *because*, and *since* are a few of the conjunctions you can use.

EXAMPLE   Lady Murasaki became well known because her diary was published.

Find the Opportunities

Last week my class to the library ⨯ ˌ *and* I borrowed a book my teacher recommended. It was *The Freedom Writers Diary.* It is very interesting ⨯ *because* It is written by students. Ms. Gruwell wanted her students to express their feelings. She wanted them to do it on paper. I liked many parts of the book. The part about Miep Gies was my favorite.

What other complex or compound sentences can you form?

Edit and Proofread, continued

> ## SpellingWorkout
>
> # Check Words You Have to Know or Look Up
>
> Some words you can figure out how to spell; others you just have to know.
>
> For example, if you were hearing the word *dragon* for the first time, chances are you could figure out how to spell the first syllable, *drag-*. But how could you figure out that second syllable? How could you know that the correct spelling is *dragon* and not *dragan* or *dragun* or *dragin*?
>
> You might know the spelling is *dragon* because you've seen the word many times before and have memorized the spelling. If you had not seen it before, you'd have to look up the correct spelling in a dictionary.
>
> That's because the sound that the *o* makes in *dragon* (sounds kind of like *uh*) can be spelled with any vowel in English.
>
>   **EXAMPLES**   around   pixel   limit   possum
>
> This sound happens very often in the unstressed syllable of a two-syllable word, and it can give you spelling nightmares. So, do whatever it takes to learn those tricky spellings. For example, to learn *dragon*, you might imagine the *o* as the eye of a dragon.
>
> ### Find the Trouble Spots
>
>   *The Everyday Diary* is a ~~chorel~~ choral book. It was written by a teacher and her students. It tells ~~ybout~~ about how the teacher motivated her students to write down whatever happened in their lives. Some students just wrote in pencel in their notebooks. Others turned it into a majer projet and kept files on their computers.
>
> Find and fix four more spelling errors.

Mechanics Workout

Check Punctuation in Longer Sentences

- Unless the clauses of a **compound sentence** are very short, you need a comma before the conjunction *and*, *or*, or *but*.

  EXAMPLE   He wrote many books**,** and some won prizes.

- It's possible to form a **compound sentence** without *and*, *or*, or *but*, but you must use a semicolon (**;**). If you use a comma, you'll have a run-on sentence, which is incorrect.

  EXAMPLE   He wrote many books**;** some won prizes.

  INCORRECT   He wrote many books**,** some won prizes.

- With a **complex sentence**, if the dependent clause (the one with the conjunction) comes first, you need to separate the clauses with a comma. A comma is not needed if the dependent clause comes last.

  EXAMPLES   While traveling through Asia**,** Ms. Wills wrote a book.

                  Ms. Wills wrote a book while traveling through Asia.

Find the Trouble Spots

Ms. Gruwell asked her students to read *The Diary of Anne Frank*. The students loved the story ⌃ and Anne's thoughtful writing inspired them. The students realized that Anne was strong in the face of tragic circumstances, they connected to her struggle. The teacher pointed out how Anne dealt with bigotry and the students realized they had to deal with this issue too.

Find and fix two more punctuation errors.

Publish, Share, and Reflect

Your final draft expresses your thoughts and feelings about a book that matters to you. Why not share your thoughts with other readers, too?

① Publish and Share Your Work

You might want to make your analysis public, just as professional book reviewers do. Here are a few ways to share it with a wide audience:

- Post it on a blog or the author's Web site.

- Submit your work to your school newspaper or literary magazine.

- Look for Web sites that publish essays and reviews by teens, and send your work in.

- Read your work aloud to your class.

Since the subject of your work is personal, you might prefer to keep it fairly private. If so, you might

- give a copy to a close friend or family member

- read it aloud in a book group.

② Reflect on Your Work

Keep thinking about your work after it's finished. Did you get your message across?

- Does your writing say something about *you* as well as the book?

- Did you learn more about why this book is an important piece of literature?

Think about other books you'd like to write about, too.

TechTIP

"Dress up" your final paper. Use special fonts for your headings and captions.

Reflect

- Did I learn more about why this book means a lot to me?

- Did I express my feelings well in my analysis?

How to Conduct a Book-Club Meeting

If you want to share your work with your friends, you might hold a book-club meeting in which you invite people to discuss their opinions about a book. You may even want to turn this group into a book-club group that reads the same books and meets regularly to discuss them.

To hold a book-club meeting:

1. Invite group members to your house or to another convenient location. (Public libraries often have a conference room you can reserve.)

2. Remind group members to bring copies of the book or story. They can put sticky notes on pages they want to refer to for evidence. They can also bring notes or reports they wrote about it.

3. If you like, find and use a printed discussion guide for the book. Ask your teacher or librarian to help you find one. You can also make up questions of your own or have each group member suggest a question in advance.

" *The Freedom Writers Diary* is a book about conflict that changed me. It made me understand how people can learn to resolve differences. "

4. Ask someone to be the group leader, or do the job yourself. The leader's job is to make sure everyone gets a chance to talk.

5. Be a good listener. Listen to the opinions of others with a open mind. Be prepared to change your opinion if new evidence warrants it.

6. Keep the discussion orderly. Focus on one topic at a time. Don't break up into separate conversations.

7. If you have started a book group, decide on the next book you want to read and discuss. Pick a meeting date, and agree to read the book before that date.

"Writing can help you find
out why things happen. It's
a good exercise for your
brain!"
—Camille

Model Study

Cause-and-Effect Paragraph

When you write paragraphs, you state your main idea in a topic
sentence. The other sentences in the paragraph support the
main idea with details and examples.

A **cause-and-effect paragraph** states the main idea and then
uses the details to explain why something happened. A **cause** is
a reason something happened. An **effect** is the result of a cause.

CAUSE-AND-EFFECT PARAGRAPH

A good cause-and-effect paragraph

☑ presents one or more causes

☑ presents one or more effects that result from the causes.

Feature Checklist

Depending on your topic, you can choose different ways to
organize a cause-and-effect paragraph:

- Explain how one cause led to one effect or to many effects.

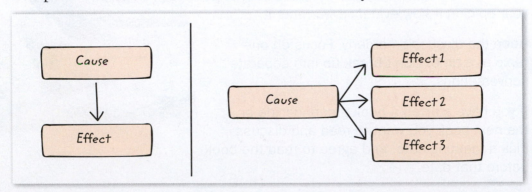

- Explain how one effect resulted from several causes.

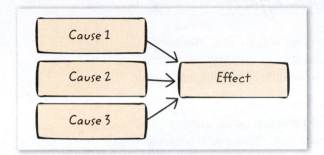

- Explain a cause-and-effect chain. The chain is formed because one event causes the next event to happen, then that event causes another event, and so on.

To show cause and effect, writers often use signal words such as *because, since, due to,* and *so.*

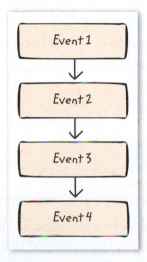

Model Student Grounded!
by Martin Rogers

Nadia let someone copy her math test (cause), so she was grounded (effect).

My older sister, Nadia, is a math genius. Since Nadia is so good in math, she tutors some of her classmates and even helps the teacher explain difficult lessons. My parents are really proud of her. Yet last week, Nadia was caught showing her math test to a classmate. Because of this, Nadia has to miss recess for a month and is grounded for two months. She is furious!

Martin uses **signal words** to show causes and effects.

Student Model

Write About Causes and Effects

WRITING PROMPT Sometimes people act unfairly. They may want special treatment that they don't deserve, or they may tell other people to do their work for them. Sometimes, it might seem like life itself is unfair.

Think about an experience in your past that was unfair, whether because of people's actions or just bad luck. Choose your audience and form. Then write a cause-and-effect paragraph that

- explains what happened and why
- tells what the effects of the event were and how they were unfair
- shows the chain of effects that began from a single important event.

Prewrite

Here are some tips for planning your paragraph.

1 Choose a Topic, Audience, and Form

Quickly brainstorm a few topics. Think of memories that stand out for you. The cause of the unfairness, as well as its effects, should be clear. Choose your audience and form. With whom will you communicate? How?

Topic	Audience	Form
Our soccer team lost the championship on a bad call.	The soccer league board of directors	Letter of complaint
Terry's computer broke down, and I had to work all weekend to finish our report.	My friend	E-mail
The fee for being in the school band was raised.	Community	School newspaper article

2 Organize Ideas

Use a **cause-and-effect chain** like Miriam's to organize your thoughts. Write the first event in the top box. In the second box, write the effect of the first event. Then, think about how that effect became a cause. What else happened because of it?

Miriam's Plan for Her Paragraph

> **Event 1**
> Two days before our report was due, Terry's computer broke.

> **Event 2**
> Terry asked me to research the images for our report.

> **Event 3**
> I worked the entire weekend to research images and finish the report.

> **Event 4**
> Terry felt bad and came to help me on Sunday evening.

> **Event 5**
> We finished our report, but we could have done a better job.

Cause-and-Effect Chain

Reflect

- Is the experience you have chosen important enough to write about?

- Does your plan show how each event led to the next?

Draft

Now that you have some great ideas to work with, it's time to draft! You will use your graphic organizers and your prewriting to make your first draft go smoothly.

No two writers write in exactly the same way, so decide what works best for you. Drafting is about getting ideas down, not getting it perfect on the first try. You can change and rearrange things later. Using a computer makes it easier.

- **Start with a Good Topic Sentence** Write a topic sentence that suggests that you will be talking about an event that was unfair.

> When I heard Terry's worried voice on the phone, I knew my weekend was about to change for the worse.

- **Add Causes and Effects** Include causes and effects from your cause-and-effect chain. Show how the experience affected you as a person. Use signal words to alert the reader about how causes are linked to effects. Miriam used her cause-and-effect chain to write her draft.

From Miriam's Draft

> Terry announced that his computer was broken. He'd waited until the last minute to research the images for our report—so now he couldn't possibly do it. I sighed, and agreed to do the research myself.

Reflect

- Read your draft. Does it clearly show how the event was unfair?

- Does it show how each event led to the next?

DRAFTING TIPS
Trait: **Development of Ideas**

If Your Writing Is Not Connected . . .

Sometimes you get so focused on writing your paragraph that you forget to show how events are connected. The result is that your writing feels jerky, like riding on a bumpy road.

Take Time for Transitions

Transitions can help you avoid those bumps and jerks. They let the reader know what to expect next. Time-order words are one kind of transition, but other kinds can also answer your readers' questions:

When did this happen?	Why did this happen?	Is this important?
After a while	As a result	As a matter of fact
Immediately	Because	In fact
Soon	Since	Most important

Miriam might use transitions in her story like this:

From Miriam's Draft

> As soon as I heard Terry's worried voice on the phone, I knew I was in for trouble. Terry announced that he would not be able to complete the image-search part of our report because his computer had broken down. Even worse, I hadn't finished the writing portion, so now I had to do double duty.

As you write your paragraph, think about how to use transitions to make your events flow smoothly.

Revise

As you consider how to revise your work, keep in mind your intended audience and your purpose for writing. Does your writing do what you want it to do? Will it connect with your audience?

1 **Evaluate Your Work**

Read your draft aloud to yourself. Listen as if you were someone else, to see what can be improved. As you read your work, ask yourself questions:

- **About the Form** Were the causes and effects clear? Did I use helpful signal words?

- **About the Development of Ideas** Do I need to explain ideas or give background information to make my paragraph clearer?

> ## Revision in Action

Miriam's Draft

Terry announced that his computer was broken. He'd waited until the last minute to research the images for our report—so now he couldn't possibly do it! I sighed, and agreed to do the research myself. My family bought a computer last year. On Sunday afternoon, Terry came to help, so I could finally slow down a bit! Since I also had to finish writing my part of the report, I had to work both Saturday and Sunday. Terry and I worked together until late, and we finished the report. It's too bad we had to rush. The whole report felt like we just threw it together and I knew it wasn't as good as we wanted it to be. I wished we had time to do a better job.

Miriam thinks:

" **I should explain more about why we were so worried.** "

" **This detail is not necessary.** "

" **This ending doesn't flow well. It is wordy and confusing.** "

2 Mark Your Changes

Add Text To make the links between causes and effects clearer, you may need to add text. Use a caret: ∧.

Delete and Consolidate Text You may also want to take out details that aren't important to the chain of causes and effects, or remove words that restate the same idea. Use a delete mark: ⸜⸝.

Rearrange Text Sometimes, things are unclear because they are presented in the wrong order. To move text, circle it and draw an arrow to show where you want it to go.

Revising Marks	**MARK**	∧	↩	⌐	⸝	¶
	WHAT IT MEANS	Insert something.	Move to here.	Replace with this.	Take out.	Make a new paragraph.

Revised Draft

Terry announced that his computer was broken. He'd waited until the last minute to research the images for our report—so now he couldn't possibly do it. I sighed, and agreed to do the research myself. ~~The report was due in two days, so I knew I had to step up and solve the problem.~~ ~~My family bought a computer last year.~~ On Sunday afternoon, Terry came to help, so I could finally slow down a bit! ⟨Since I also had to finish writing my part of the report, I had to work both Saturday and Sunday.⟩ Terry and I worked together until late, and we finished the report. ~~It's too bad~~ *But since* we had to rush. ~~The whole report felt like we just threw it together and~~ I knew it wasn't as good as we wanted it to be. ~~I wished we had time to do a better job.~~

Miriam added and deleted details to make her ideas clearer.

Miriam moved a sentence to make the cause-and-effect chain clearer.

Miriam consolidated three sentences to avoid wordiness.

Edit and Proofread

When you're happy with the content of your cause-and-effect paragraph, read your paper again to fix language errors. This is what you do when you edit and proofread your work.

- **Check the Grammar** Make sure that you have used correct and conventional grammar throughout. In particular, check for the correct use of participles as adjectives. (See page 313W.)

- **Check the Spelling** Spell-check can help, but it isn't always enough. Read your work carefully. Look especially for misspelled sound-alike words. (See page 314W.)

- **Check the Mechanics** Errors in punctuation and capitalization can make your work hard to understand. In particular, check that you've correctly used apostrophes in contractions. (See page 315W.)

Use these marks to edit and proofread your cause-and-effect paragraph.

TechTIP

Use the **Find** feature on your computer to look for apostrophes. That way, you can quickly check that they are placed correctly.

Editing and Proofreading Marks

MARK	WHAT IT MEANS	MARK	WHAT IT MEANS
∧	Insert something.	/	Make lowercase.
∧	Add a comma.	℘	Delete, take something out.
⌃	Add a semicolon.	¶	Make new paragraph.
⊙	Add a period.	◯	Spell out.
⊙	Add a colon.	⌒	Replace with this.
⌄ ⌄	Add quotation marks.	∼	Change order of letters or words.
⌄	Add an apostrophe.	#	Insert space.
≡	Capitalize.	◡	Close up, no space here.

Reflect

- What kinds of errors did you find? What can you do to keep from making them?

Grammar Workout

Participles as Adjectives

- Verbs have four principal parts. Two of the parts are called **participles**.

Present	Present Participle	Past	Past Participle
confuse	confusing	confused	confused
write	writing	wrote	written

- You can also use the **present participle** or **past participle** of a verb as an **adjective** to describe a noun or pronoun.

  EXAMPLES   Confused, I asked the teacher to repeat the assignment.

  I had to ask the teacher to repeat the confusing assignment.

- If the **participle** starts a sentence, be sure to use a **comma** after it to show a break and keep the meaning clear.

  EXAMPLE   Nodding, Ms. Franklin explained the assignment again.

Find the Trouble Spots

   On Monday, the teacher asked us to read our ~~wrote~~ *written* reports aloud. Mary exhausted had spent all weekend working on it. Standing Mary seemed ready and confident enough to give her report. But her shake hands showed how nervous she was. With a soothing voice, the teacher was able to calm her down. Determining, Mary started reading her report.

Find three more places to fix participles used as adjectives.

Edit and Proofread, continued

Spelling Workout

Check Sound-Alike Words

If you hear the following sentence read aloud, you'll have no trouble understanding it:

> Their is a cat on you're roof that needs too be rescued.

But if you see it written, it's likely that you'll be confused. That is because certain words in English sound alike but are spelled differently. Study these frequently misused and misspelled words.

Word	Meaning
your **you're**	possessive adjective for the pronoun **you** contraction meaning "you are"
their **they're** **there**	possessive adjective for the pronoun **they** contraction meaning "they are" refers to a place
to **two** **too**	a preposition an amount, or number, of something adverb meaning "also"

Find the Trouble Spots

> **There**
> ~~They're~~ wasn't enough time, but we had to try anyway.
>
> I told Terry, "I'll start researching now. Can you read me
> **your**
> ~~you're~~ notes so far?"
>
> Terry's notes were very helpful, but their was still a lot
> for me two do. I looked at the calendar and sighed. They're
> was a soccer game on Sunday that I really wanted to play.

Find three more spelling errors to fix.

Mechanics Workout

Check Apostrophes in Contractions

You can put two words together to make a **contraction**. An **apostrophe** shows where one or more letters have been left out.

Verb Phrase	Contraction
I + am	I'm
they + are	they're
he + is	he's
she + is	she's
do + not	don't
does + not	doesn't
did + not	didn't
are + not	aren't
is + not	isn't
was + not	wasn't
were + not	weren't

> she + is = she's
> should + not = shouldn't

- To form a contraction with a verb and the word **not**, use an apostrophe to replace the **o** in **not**.

  could + not = couldn~~o~~t = couldn't

- To form a contraction with a pronoun and the verb **is, am,** or **are,** use an apostrophe to replace the first letter of the verb.

  you + are = you~~a~~re = you're
  it + is = it~~i~~s = it's

Use **you're** and **it's** to stand for **you are** and **it is**. The apostrophes keep readers from confusing these words with **your** and **its**.

Find the Trouble Spots

"I am going to work on the images, " I told Terry." ~~Your~~ ^{You're} going to write the introduction."

"Are you sure ~~its~~ ^{it's} not too late to look for all those images?" asked Terry. "Your already doing so much work!"

"Its not your fault if the computer broke," I answered.

Find and fix two more problems with apostrophes.

Model Study

Cause-and-Effect Essay

When you write a **cause-and-effect essay**, you explain what happened and why. You can focus more on the causes or on the effects, but organize your essay in a clear way.

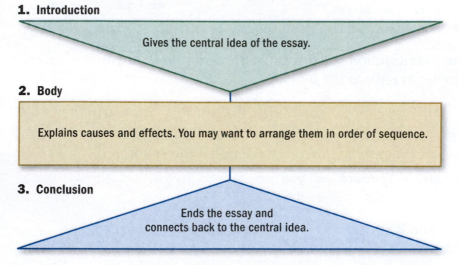

1. Introduction

Gives the central idea of the essay.

2. Body

Explains causes and effects. You may want to arrange them in order of sequence.

3. Conclusion

Ends the essay and connects back to the central idea.

Read the student model on page 317W. It shows one good way to structure a cause-and-effect essay.

CAUSE-AND-EFFECT ESSAY

A good cause-and-effect essay

☑ presents one or more causes that lead to one or more effects

☑ includes an introduction, a body, and a conclusion.

Feature Checklist

Lincoln's Election in 1860

by Víctor López

The **introduction** states the **central idea** of the essay.

Abraham Lincoln's moderate positions and his support from the Republican party, along with strong political divisions in the United States, all helped to bring about Lincoln's election in 1860.

The writer presents many **causes** that led to a single **effect**.

Americans were deeply divided on slavery. Lincoln opposed extending slavery into new territories. However, he did not advocate equal rights for African Americans. Nor did he press for complete abolition. Because his position was moderate, he appealed to many Northern voters.

The **body** of the essay presents causes and effects.

Signal words help the reader identify causes and effects.

The support of the new Republican party also helped. Many Republican leaders disagreed with one another, but joined together to support Lincoln. As a result, Republicans voted solidly for him.

Finally, Lincoln was helped by the strong political divisions among Americans. Three other candidates ran against him. Only 40 percent of voters chose Lincoln. The rest of the vote was split among the other candidates. Therefore, although Lincoln did not win a majority of votes, he won the election.

The **conclusion** wraps up the essay and ties back to the central idea.

Although he became a great president, Lincoln's path to the White House was not easy. His moderate positions, strong support from his party, and a divided political atmosphere led to his success.

Student Model

From 1861 to 1865, Abraham Lincoln served as the 16th President of the United States. ▶

Voice and Style

If you want to play basketball on a hot summer day, you wear light, comfortable clothing. If you want to take a walk in the snow, you wear warm, bulky clothing to keep you warm. Writing is similar. What you write—and how you write it—changes depending on the situation. Before you write, ask yourself why you are writing, and who will read it.

Make Your Writing Sound Like You

What does it mean to say that a writer has a strong voice or effective style? Simple: it means the writer uses language so well that you know exactly what the writer means, and you don't feel bored or confused.

You adjust your voice for different audiences and purposes, but you always want to sound like yourself. Below, the writer wants her audience to support her idea. Which voice is more effective for her purpose?

Friendly and Informal

I think we need to support this amendment to the Education Reform Act. Maybe we could brainstorm ideas for a letter to our representatives in Congress. I think it's kind of a neat idea.

Formal, but Not Stiff

I think the amendment to the Education Reform Act will greatly improve our school. That is why I suggest we meet to write a letter to our representatives in Congress. This will help make our voice heard.

Study the rubric on page 319W. What is the difference between a paper with a score of 2 and one with a score of 4?

Voice and Style

	Does the writing have a clear voice and is it the best style for the type of writing?	Is the language interesting and are the words and sentences appropriate for the purpose, audience, and type of writing?
4 Wow!	The writing <u>fully</u> engages the reader with its individual voice. The writing style is best for the type of writing.	The words and sentences are interesting and appropriate to the purpose and audience. • The words are precise and engaging. • The sentences are varied and flow together smoothly.
3 Ahh.	<u>Most</u> of the writing engages the reader with an individual voice. The writing style is mostly best for the type of writing.	<u>Most</u> of the words and sentences are interesting and appropriate to the purpose and audience. • Most words are precise and engaging. • Most sentences are varied and flow together.
2 Hmm.	<u>Some</u> of the writing engages the reader, but it has no individual voice and the style is not best for the writing type.	<u>Some</u> of the words and sentences are interesting and appropriate to the purpose and audience. • Some words are precise and engaging. • Some sentences are varied, but the flow could be smoother.
1 Huh?	The writing does <u>not</u> engage the reader.	<u>Few or none</u> of the words and sentences are appropriate to the purpose and audience. • The words are often vague and dull. • The sentences lack variety and do not flow together.

Voice and Style, continued

Compare Writing Samples

An effective voice uses vivid words and a variety of sentence types to engage the reader. It also lets the writer's personality come through. Study the two samples of cause-and-effect writing on this page.

Engaging

Precise words make the writing engaging.

The Highway-Safety Bill

Last year, two members of Congress sponsored a bill to make U.S. highways safer. The bill was approved by both House and Senate. Only yesterday, the President signed it, too. The bill has finally become a law.

Because of this law, states will receive financing for billions of dollars to rebuild worn-out stretches of highway. Where will this money go? Funds can be spent to rebuild unsteady bridges. States can widen and repave roads. Narrower suburban roads can be transformed into superhighways.

The writer mixes short and long sentences and different sentence types.

Not Engaging

Too many **repeated words** make the writing sound dull.

The Highway-Safety Bill

Last year, some people in Congress supported a highway bill. The bill was approved in the House and the Senate, and the President approved it, too. This means the bill has now become a law.

Because of this law, states will get a lot of money to build roads. They can rebuild bridges so that they don't fall down. They can fix roads so that they are wide and smooth. They can use the money to make smaller roads into good highways.

The sentences sound very similar. Using too many statements makes the writing boring.

Evaluate for Voice and Style

Now read carefully the cause-and-effect essay below. Use the rubric on page 319W to score it.

An Important Decision for America

The 1954 case known as *Brown versus Board of Education* was important. The court ruled that separate schools for blacks and whites were unequal and unconstitutional. Some Southern whites were mad. But people who supported equal rights were encouraged to fight for more social changes.

Since many Southern schools were segregated, the decision got some Southerners really mad. Some said they would rather close their schools than let African Americans go to white schools. Many Virginia schools closed in protest. Some political figures—such as George Wallace, who later became the governor of Alabama—continued to oppose the decision well into the 1960s. Can you believe it?

People who believed in equal rights for all Americans thought the decision was great. Because the Court supported equality in education, civil rights supporters hoped that the Court would support other forms of equal rights, too. The civil rights movement gained more support as a result of the Brown case.

The Brown decision was important. Although it made some people angry, it allowed students of all races to attend the same schools, and it gave hope to supporters of equal rights.

Are the sentences varied? Do they flow well together?

Is the writer's word choice engaging and interesting? Which words would you replace?

Does the writer use a consistent tone? Are there any places where the language is too formal or too casual?

Although the first session of the Court convened in 1790, the Supreme Court Building wasn't constructed until the 1930s. ▶

Raise the Score

These papers have been scored using the **Voice and Style Rubric** on page 319W. Study each paper to see why it got the score it did.

Until 1913, ▲ senators were not elected by the general public.

Overall Score: 4

The 17th Amendment

Anthony Aldridge

Today, United States senators are elected by the public. However, this was not always the case. Before 1913, senators were chosen by legislators.

This process caused problems. Sometimes state legislators could not agree on one senator. They would send two senators to Washington, D.C.—but which one would serve in office? While a decision was being made, important legislation was delayed or discarded. Moreover, corruption brewed. State legislators took bribes in exchange for a Senate seat.

Members of Congress knew the process had to be changed. It had to be if the Senate was to truly provide for fair and equal representation for each state.

The 17th Amendment, passed in 1913, brought that change. Now the public elects two senators from each state. Once elected to a six-year term, each senator has a vote in law-making decisions.

The amendment improved the voting system by making it more just. After 1913, candidates had to reach out to the public through campaigning. They needed to appeal to the needs of thousands of citizens instead of just a few hundred legislators.

The **informative voice** fits the subject and purpose.

The writer mixes short and long sentences and includes different sentence types.

Specific words keep the reader engaged.

The 17th Amendment

Today, United States senators are elected by the public. However, this was not always the case. Before 1913, senators were chosen by legislators.

This process caused problems. Sometimes state legislators could not agree on one senator. They would send two senators to Washington, D.C. Then it would take time to decide which one would ==serve==. That ==delayed== important legislation. Moreover, ==corruption== kept getting worse and State legislators took money in trade for Senate seats.

Members of Congress knew the process had to be changed. It had to be if the Senate was to truly provide for fair and ==equal representation== for each state.

The 17th Amendment, passed in 1913, brought that change. Now the public elects two senators from each state. Once elected to a six-year ==term==, each senator has a vote in law-making decisions.

The amendment improved the voting system by making it more just. After 1913, candidates had to reach out to the public through ==campaigning==. They needed to get the attention of thousands of citizens instead of just a few hundred legislators.

The **informative voice** fits the writer's subject and purpose.

Some of the sentences vary in length, but many begin the same way.

The writer uses some **specific, precise words**, but could use more.

RAISING *THE SCORE*

The writer needs to vary the sentences more and replace some words to make the writing livelier. What changes can the writer make?

Raise the Score, continued

The writer uses an **informal tone,** which is not appropriate for the audience.

The 17th Amendment

These days, United States senators are picked by the public. It wasn't always like that. Until 1913, senators were picked by state legislators.

At first, the process for getting senators into office was to have state legislators pick them. Sometimes this process caused problems. Sometimes state legislators picked more than one senator because they could not agree. Both senators would go to Washington, D.C. But, only one was picked to work in the Senate. Sometimes, while a decision was being made, work stopped. Sometimes worse things happened. Money was offered to people to give them a seat in the Senate. There have always been crooked people!

Members of Congress knew the process had to be changed to improve the Senate.

The 17th Amendment, passed in 1913, brought that change. Now the public elects two senators from each state. Each has one vote.

The change made the system better. Candidates had to get support from lots of people across a big state.

The writer uses too many sentences that **begin the same way**. That makes the writing boring.

The writer uses too many **vague words**.

RAISING THE SCORE

The writer needs to use language that's more precise and less repetitive. Which words should the writer replace? How can the writer vary the sentences?

The 17th Amendment

Today, U.S. senators are picked by the voters. They were not always picked by the voters. They used to be picked by state legislators.

Sometimes there were problems. Sometimes state legislators could not agree on a senator. They would pick more than one. Both senators would go to Washington, D.C. Only one could do the job. They had to pick who. While they picked, the work stopped. Over time, more problems happened. People would try all sorts of things to get a Senate seat. Can you believe that? The Senate really needed to fix things up!

The 17th Amendment fixed everything. The public had to pick two senators. Senators got one vote.

The amendment made things better. Candidates needed lots of people to like them, not just the people in Washington.

The tone is **inconsistent**. It lacks an individual voice and style.

The writer **repeats the same dull words** over and over.

The language is **vague** and not engaging. The sentences do not flow together well.

RAISING *THE SCORE*

The writer does not engage the reader. How can the writer make sentences more interesting and engaging?

Choose the Right Voice

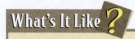

What's It Like?

Would you send a "Get Well" card for a birthday? Or a "Happy Holidays" card to a cousin who is about to get married? No—you choose a card that fits the occasion. You do the same thing when you choose your voice as a writer. Your voice changes depending on the topic, audience, and purpose.

Adapt Your Voice to Your Form and Topic

To decide which voice you will use, think about the form of your writing. Compare the voice used in each of the forms below.

Friendly Letter

> Dear Kristin,
>   Are you going on the trip to the courthouse on Thursday? I'm really looking forward to it! I want to find out how I can become a lawyer when I grow up.

Flyer

LEARN ABOUT THE LAW

Have you ever thought about becoming a lawyer?

The Student Government Association is sponsoring a trip to the county courthouse during Thursday's half-day. We'll be meeting with Judge Louisa Amato and District Attorney Ron Miller.

You can adapt your voice for your topic, too. The voice you use for a serious topic, such as the importance of civil rights legislation, would be different from the voice you use for an account of a field trip to Washington, D.C.

Adapt Your Voice for Different Audiences

When you're writing to a friend, it's okay to use an informal voice. For other audiences, like your teacher or the editor of the local newspaper, a formal voice is better. Study the examples below.

Formal

> Because of a 1966 Supreme Court decision, suspects have the right to remain silent. This decision was based on the Fifth Amendment of the Constitution.

Informal

> Do you watch cop shows on TV? Then you know the Miranda Warning: "You have the right to remain silent."

The writer addresses the reader directly.

Adapt Your Voice to Your Purpose

When you write to inform, you use a different voice than you use when you are trying to persuade. How does the writer below change the voice to fit the purpose?

To Inform

> Before anyone suspected of a crime is questioned, police are required by law to give the Miranda Warning. This warning reminds citizens that they have the right to remain silent and to have an attorney present during questioning.

To Persuade

> You never know when you might be in the wrong place at the wrong time. Protect yourself! You must learn the Miranda Warning by heart so you know your rights.

The writer uses a command and the word "must."

Choose the Right Voice, continued

The writer was asked to write an article to motivate her fellow students to attend a special event. Compare the article with the writer's FATP chart. Does the writing fit the form, audience, topic, and purpose?

During the Vietnam War, young people struggled to gain a political voice. ▼

FATP Chart

Form: _newspaper article_

Audience: _students and teachers_

Topic: _the 26th amendment_

Purpose: _to persuade_

A Celebration of Young People's Right to Vote

by Alyssa Gill Stuart

Why should we care about the 26th Amendment to the Constitution? The 26th Amendment gives 18-year-olds the right to vote. For most of us, that's only a few years away.

The 26th Amendment was ratified during the Vietnam War. At that time, the draft sent 18-year-olds to Vietnam, but the voting age was still 21. As the conflict got worse, people realized that if soldiers could give their lives for their country, they should have a voice in their government. The amendment was ratified in 1971.

Several American cities celebrate the anniversary of this landmark decision.

Walt Whitman Middle School will also celebrate this year. On the last day of school, State Senator John Trowbridge will visit to tell the story of the 26th Amendment. He will also show news footage from the Vietnam years.

If you don't care much about voting, this event might change your mind. Come learn more about the amendment that gave teens the right to vote.

Is the writer's tone appropriate for an audience of students?

How effectively does the writer persuade readers? What words might make the article more convincing?

This essay for class should explore how the 26th Amendment came into being and what effects it had. Did the writer meet the goal? What changes would you recommend?

"Old Enough to Fight, Old Enough to Vote."

by Leshawn Charles

The 26th Amendment to the U.S. Constitution grants 18-year-olds the right to vote. Its ratification came during one of the most difficult moments in American history.

Between 1959 and 1975, the United States was involved in a war in Vietnam. Many soldiers who took part in the Vietnam War were very young, since the draft recruited soldiers from the age of 18. At the time the conflict started, the minimum voting age was 21.

More than 58,000 American troops lost their lives in the Vietnam War. This prompted the American people to question the voting age. If 18-year-olds were old enough to go to war, why were they still too young to vote? Many soldiers protested, using slogans such as, "Old enough to fight, old enough to vote."

Thanks to this debate, the 26th Amendment was ratified on July 1st, 1971. All 18-year-olds were granted the right to vote in state and national elections. As a result, young people finally had a voice in their government. Their role in the destiny of the United States had been acknowledged.

Is the writer's tone appropriate?

Did the writer use specific, precise words?

Are the details informative?

Are the sentences varied enough to make the writing interesting and engaging?

Use Figurative Language

What's It Like ?

Have you ever told a friend that your backpack "weighs as much as a pile of bricks"? If you have, you've used figurative language—not exactly true, but expresses just how you feel!

"This is really heavy!"

Make Language Come Alive

Writers use figurative language—idioms, similes, and metaphors—to say things in vivid and imaginative ways. Figurative language makes your writing engaging and interesting.

Figurative Language: Idioms

In an **idiom**, the phrase as a whole means something different from what the words mean by themselves. The writer below used an **idiom** to make his explanation more interesting.

> Supporters worked **24-7** to get the 26th Amendment ratified. Finally, 18-year-olds were granted the right to vote in state and national elections in July of 1971.

Idiom	What You Really Mean
We campaigned 24-7.	We campaigned constantly.
Voting is nothing to sneeze at.	Voting should be taken seriously.
She put her heart into the election.	She put all her effort into the election.

Warning: Using too many idioms can make your writing sound not only informal, but unoriginal.

See how the **idioms** emphasize this writer's points:

Electoral College

Are you really in the know when it comes to presidential elections? When you cast your vote, you're really helping to select the Electoral College that will elect the president. They are special electors who are chosen by the popular vote. Each state has as many electoral votes as it has members of Congress. During an election, the jury is out until the Electoral College makes its decisions. Once in a blue moon, a candidate loses the popular vote, but wins the electoral vote.

Where can the writer add idioms to spice up this paragraph about the Bill of Rights?

TechTIP

Keep lists of idioms in a file on the computer to refer to when you need to spice up your writing!

The Bill of Rights

The first ten amendments to the U.S. Constitution were passed in 1791. They protect all Americans. The problem comes when you have to apply them. For example, do school newspapers enjoy freedom of the press? Is burning the flag considered free speech? If we didn't have the Bill of Rights, citizens would be helpless.

◄ The right to vote is guaranteed by the U.S. Constitution.

Use Figurative Language, continued

Figurative Language: Similes

A **simile** compares two unlike things using the words *like* or *as*. Which paragraph gives a more vivid impression of someone voting?

Without Similes

> After signing in with a volunteer, I surveyed the room. Soon I spotted an open booth. It was sitting in the far corner of the room. I approached the booth and slipped inside. I closed the curtain and took out my ballots.

With Similes

> After signing in with a volunteer, I surveyed the room like a cat on the prowl. Soon I spotted an open booth. It was sitting like an outcast in the far corner of the room. I approached the booth and slipped inside as smooth as butter. I closed the curtain and took out my ballots.

Read the **similes** in the passage below. Then look for places where the writer could add more similes.

> Students poured into the assembly hall like bees returning to a hive. As sudden as a clap of thunder, a gavel sounded. Everyone sat down and became quiet. Then the first candidate for Senior Class President approached the podium. Fred Miller promised to push for longer study halls. Some in the audience clapped like their hands were sunburned. Then Sally Franklin talked about stronger dress codes. A few students applauded. Finally, Marcus Smith raced up to the podium. He promised to eliminate any food in the cafeteria that tasted bad. The applause was as loud as a rock concert.

Figurative Language: Metaphors

Like a simile, a **metaphor** compares two things, but it does not use the words *like* or *as* to make the comparison. Instead, it says that one thing is the other thing. How does the paragraph with metaphors help you better "see" a political convention?

Without Metaphors

A political convention has a lot of sights and sounds. Thousands of people applaud their favorite candidates. They wave flags, hold up signs, and cheer each time they hear their candidate speak. The convention hall is packed with groups of people who want to show support for their party.

With Metaphors

A political convention is an orchestra of sights and sounds. Thousands of people are advertisements for their favorite candidates. They wave flags, hold up signs, and cheer each time they hear their candidate speak. An ocean of color, the convention hall is packed with groups of people who want to show support for their party.

Read the **metaphors** in the passage below. Then look for places where the writer could add more metaphors.

John Wilson, a candidate for mayor of Baylorville is the people's sweetheart. He has a charisma that appeals to old and young alike. Skateboard parks are monsters to some, but Wilson is willing to consider building one. He's also said that he'll provide shuttle buses to concerts and other community events—free of charge. The downtown area, a real junkyard, is of great concern to the community. John Wilson wants to work with business owners to clean it up. John Wilson is great, and it's unlikely anyone can defeat him.

Write a Cause-and-Effect Essay

WRITING PROMPT Causes and effects shape your life and your world. Think about issues in your community that have changed as a result of a vote, a petition, or a campaign. What effects of active citizenship can you see?

Think of an important change in your community. Explore what caused the change. Or consider that change a cause and think of the effects it brought about. Write a five-paragraph cause-and-effect essay that

- explains in the introduction what change occurred
- explains in the body the causes and effects
- wraps up the ideas in the conclusion.

Prewrite

Here are some tips for planning your essay.

1 **Choose a Topic**

Choose an issue whose causes and effects are clear. You can brainstorm ideas by asking yourself questions.

Ideas	Cause-and-effect questions	Possible causes or effects
school started offering healthier food	What effect did this have?	Students became interested in nutrition
Indiana had a kids' election	What happened because of this?	Kids got more involved in politics
Zach Bonner helps victims of Hurricane Charley	Why did this happen?	Zach Bonner learned about children's homes being destroyed in the hurricane

2 Write Your Central Idea

The central idea is the most important thing you have to say in your essay. You can state it in the first paragraph. That will help you focus on your topic.

> Zach Bonner was shocked to hear about the conditions homeless children lived in, so he started raising awareness among other kids.

Tamika states her central idea.

3 Organize Your Thoughts

Use a Cause-and-Effect Chart like Tamika's to put your thoughts in order.

Tamika's Cause-and-Effect Chart

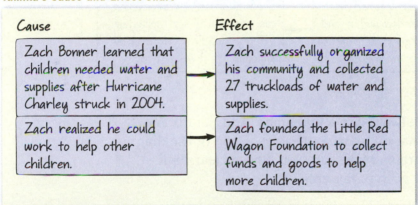

Cause	Effect
Zach Bonner learned that children needed water and supplies after Hurricane Charley struck in 2004.	Zach successfully organized his community and collected 27 truckloads of water and supplies.
Zach realized he could work to help other children.	Zach founded the Little Red Wagon Foundation to collect funds and goods to help more children.

◄ A Category 4 storm, Hurricane Charley caused extensive damage when it made landfall in Florida in 2004.

Reflect

- Do the details support your central idea?

- Does your plan clearly show causes and effects?

Draft

Now that you have a topic to work on, it's time to draft! Remember, your draft doesn't have to be perfect. You will have time later on to make all the changes you need.

Use your Cause-and-Effect Chart and your prewriting to make your first draft go smoothly.

- **Focus on One Event at a Time** If you try to cover everything at once, you might lose your focus. Choose one cause and effect to work with at a time.

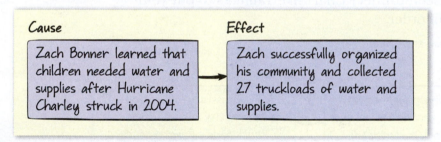

Cause

> Zach Bonner learned that children needed water and supplies after Hurricane Charley struck in 2004.

Effect

> Zach successfully organized his community and collected 27 truckloads of water and supplies.

- **Expand Each Event into a Paragraph** Add details and other information to expand each section of the diagram into a paragraph. Make sure you have a clear topic sentence for each paragraph.

- **Use Signal Words** Use signal words such as *because*, *since*, and *as a result* to show the reader how causes are linked to effects.

From Tamika's Draft

> Zach Bonner learned about children who had been affected by Hurricane Charley in 2004. The children did not have drinking water and other basic commodities. Because he cared about these children, he organized his community to donate water. Together, they sent 27 truckloads of supplies to hurricane victims.

Reflect

- Does each paragraph show at least one clear cause and effect?

- Did you use cause-and-effect signal words?

DRAFTING TIPS
Trait: **Voice and Style**

If Your Writing Sounds Flat . . .

You don't want your essay to sound flat and boring. To spice things up, use specific, precise words to capture—and keep—your reader's interest.

Try Using the Intensity Scale First

"Weighing" your words on an Intensity Scale will help you choose precise, colorful language. Here's how it works:

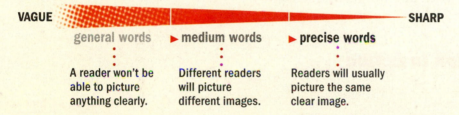

VAGUE .... **SHARP**

general words ▶ **medium words** ▶ **precise words**

A reader won't be able to picture anything clearly.	Different readers will picture different images.	Readers will usually picture the same clear image.

When you use words that fall toward the right end of the scale, your writing will be clear, sharp, and interesting!

VAGUE .... **SHARP**

girl ▶ **rider** ▶ **resolute rider**

Try it. Use an Intensity Scale to find the most colorful, vivid words to tell about your causes and effects. Here's how Tamika used an Intensity Scale to make her cause-and-effect essay more exciting:

Tamika's Intensity Scale

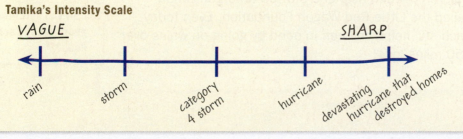

VAGUE   *SHARP*

rain   storm   category 4 storm   hurricane   devastating hurricane that destroyed homes

Revise

As you consider how to revise your work, keep in mind your intended audience and your purpose for writing.

1 **Evaluate Your Work**

Read your draft aloud to a partner. As you read, your partner will fill out a cause-and-effect graphic organizer. Ask your partner to consider these questions:

- **About the Form** Are causes and effects clearly linked to each other? Do they need to be explained better?

- **About the Voice and Style** Are the voice and style right for the audience and purpose? Does the essay need more vivid and interesting words?

Revision in Action

Draft

> Recently I learned about a young boy who believed he could make a difference. His name is Zach Bonner.
> Zach learned about children whose houses had been hit by a hurricane. Zach cared, and he convinced his community to gather drinking water for the children. Together they gave 27 truckloads of water and other supplies. The children did not have drinking water.
> Zach didn't stop there. He saw other areas where children needed help and started an organization called the Little Red Wagon Foundation. Even today Zach still helps children in need by going on walks over 250 miles long!

Tamika's partner says:

" This is too general. Can you be more specific?"

" You could combine sentences here. Also, the last sentence seems out of place."

" Can you tell more about what Zach does?"

2 Mark Your Changes

Clarify Text Make your draft clearer and more engaging by

- replacing dull, vague words with precise, specific words

- supplying more details and explanations

- adding signal words to clarify causes and effects.

Consolidate Text When you consolidate text, you make it shorter by

- taking out unnecessary details or repeated ideas

- saying the same thing with fewer words

- combining sentences.

Revising Marks

MARK	∧	↶	↖	＿ᰂ	⁋
WHAT IT MEANS	Insert something.	Move to here.	Replace with this.	Take out.	Make a new paragraph.

Revised Draft

Recently I learned about ~~a young boy~~ **a six-year-old boy** who believed he could make a difference. His name is Zach Bonner. **in the lives of other children.**

Zach learned about children whose houses had been ~~hit~~ **struck** by a hurricane. **Because** Zach cared, ~~and~~ he convinced his community to ~~gather~~ **donate** ~~drinking water for the children.~~ ~~Together they gave~~ 27 truckloads of water and other supplies. The children did not have drinking water.

Zach didn't stop there. He saw other areas where children needed help ~~and~~ **so he** started ~~an~~ **a nonprofit** organization called the Little Red Wagon Foundation. Even today Zach still helps children in need by going on **marathon** walks over 250 miles long! **Thanks to these initiatives, Zach raises money and awareness.**

The writer used more precise words to make her ideas clearer.

The writer added signal words, combined sentences, and moved a sentence.

The writer added specific words and details.

Edit and Proofread

After you're satisfied with the content of your cause-and-effect essay, read your paper again to fix language errors. This is what you do when you edit and proofread your work:

- **Check the Grammar** Make sure that you have used correct and conventional grammar throughout. In particular, check for correct use of participial phrases. (See page 341W.)

- **Check the Spelling** Spell-check can help, but it isn't always enough. Read your work carefully, especially words with Greek and Latin roots. You can use a dictionary to check. (See page 342W.)

- **Check the Mechanics** Errors in punctuation and capitalization can make your work hard to understand. In particular, check for commas before and after participial phrases and appositives. (See page 343W.)

Use these marks to edit and proofread your cause-and-effect essay.

TechTIP
As you proofread, use the highlighter feature of your word processing program to mark words and phrases to check.

Editing and Proofreading Marks

MARK	WHAT IT MEANS	MARK	WHAT IT MEANS
∧	Insert something.	/	Make lowercase.
∧	Add a comma.	℘	Delete, take something out.
∧	Add a semicolon.	¶	Make new paragraph.
⊙	Add a period.	◯	Spell out.
⊙	Add a colon.	↖	Replace with this.
⌄⌄	Add quotation marks.	∼	Change order of letters or words.
⌄	Add an apostrophe.	#	Insert space.
≡	Capitalize.	◡	Close up, no space here.

Reflect
- What kinds of errors did you find? What can you do to keep from making them?

Grammar Workout

Participial Phrases

- A **participle** can stand alone before a noun or pronoun or begin a group of words called a participial phrase .

  EXAMPLES   **Concerned about lost homes**, Zach did something.

- Use participial phrases to combine sentences or add details.

  EXAMPLE   Zach talked to his mom. He was **wanting some advice.**

  Wanting some advice, Zach talked to his mom.

  Zach, **wanting some advice**, talked to his mom.

- Participial phrases are set off by commas unless the participial phrase ends a sentence and the information is not necessary for understanding the meaning.

  EXAMPLES   Mom spoke to Zach, **knowing how concerned he was.**

  Zach felt better with his mom **offering suggestions.**

- Place a participial phrase near the word it describes to avoid a "dangling" or "misplaced" modifier.

  Misplaced: I learned about the hurricane listening carefully.

  Correct: Listening carefully, I learned about the hurricane.

Find the Trouble Spots

Know*~ing* his mom was special, Zach was sure she would help him. Realizing Zach was serious, she helped start the Little Red Wagon Foundation. Zach also started a Web site determined to share ideas. Navigating there, you can learn how to help. Inspired by Zach children everywhere are thinking more about how they can help others.

Find two more errors in the use of participial phrases.

Edit and Proofread, continued

> ## Spelling Workout

Check Words with Greek and Latin Roots

Many words in English come from Greek or Latin roots. Here are some examples:

Latin Root	Meaning	Common words
ann	year	anniversary, annually
civi	citizen	civil, civilization
cogn	know	cognitive, cognition
temp	time	tempo, temporary, contemporary

Greek Root	Meaning	Common words
demo	people	epidemic, demographic
path	feeling, suffering	sympathy
philo	strong caring or love for	philharmonic, philosophy
poli	city	politics, political, politician

Knowing Greek and Latin roots can often help you spell a word correctly—or help you know when it's spelled incorrectly.

EXAMPLE   The word ~~phillosophy~~ *philosophy* means "love of knowledge."

Find the Trouble Spots

Because of his ~~empithy~~ *empathy* for other children, Zach Bonner became a ~~filanthropist.~~ *philanthropist* He spends hundreds of hours anually on projects addressing the problems faced by contemporary communities. Zach has been reckognized by President Bush for his efforts. In a demmocracy, having a sense of sivic responsibility can make a difference.

Find four more misspelled words. Which Greek or Latin root can help you spell each correctly?

MechanicsWorkout

Check Commas

- A **participial phrase** describes a noun or pronoun. If it begins a sentence, use a comma to separate it from the main clause. If it is in the middle, set it off with commas

  EXAMPLE   **Impressed by Zach's accomplishments**, President Bush met with him during a visit to Florida.

  President Bush, **impressed by Zach's accomplishments**, met with him during a visit to Florida

  If a participial phrase ends a sentence, use a comma before it if the added details are nonrestrictive, or unnecessary.

  EXAMPLE   Zach watched the arrival of Air Force One, **landing smoothly on the runway.**

  Do not use a comma if the added details are restrictive.

  EXAMPLE   Zach enjoyed the handshake given by the president.

- An **appositive** is a noun or phrase that tells more about a noun. Appositives are also set off by commas.

  EXAMPLE   She wrote a letter to the editor of her local paper, **The Herald Gazette.**

Find the Trouble Spots

Concerned about the homeless Zach has become an activist. His non-profit organization the Little Red Wagon Foundation raises money for homeless children. Aided by Zach's efforts hundreds of homeless children have received help. You can visit his Web site www.lrwf.com.

Find two more places to add commas.

Publish, Share, and Reflect

You've worked hard to write and revise a cause-and-effect essay that is well organized, shows clear cause-and-effect relationships, and uses an effective voice. Now it's time to share it!

1 Publish and Share Your Work

When you publish your writing, you put it in a final form and share it. How you publish it depends on your purpose and audience.

You might choose to share your essay with just a few friends by reading it aloud to them privately. Or, if you want to reach a wider audience, you might

- present it orally in your social studies class
- post it on a blog or Web site
- send it to your school or town newspaper
- publish it in your school or class newsletter.

No matter how you publish your essay, you can use the word-processing software on your computer to add finishing touches.

2 Reflect on Your Work

Even after you've published your work, you might make additional changes later on. Reflect about what went well for this assignment and what areas you want to keep working on as a writer.

Reflect

- Is my writing clear and focused?
- Did writing about causes and effects help me understand my topic better? What did I learn from writing this essay?

How to Stay Focused

When presenting your essay, it is important to create and maintain a clear focus so that your audience can follow and understand your ideas.

To give a successful presentation:

1. **Plan** Read your essay on your own. Make notes about the key details you want to focus on. Mark the places where you should read with added emphasis. Add related descriptions and examples that can further support your key points.

2. **Practice** To make sure your presentation is focused, practice in front of a partner beforehand. Check that you effectively placed emphasis on your key ideas by asking your partner to explain what you presented. You may also want to videotape yourself and watch your performance to evaluate how you can improve your focus.

3. **Deliver** Briefly introduce your essay and describe what you plan to focus on. Then present your essay to your audience. Remember to:

   - Read at a steady rate that your audience can easily listen to and understand.

   - Pronounce each word clearly and correctly.

   - Speak at an appropriate volume that is not too soft or too loud. You should alter your volume when adding emphasis, but always make sure your audience can hear you.

   - Make eye contact with your listeners throughout your presentation.

" What effects has the *Brown versus Board of Education* case had on the way we go to school today?"

"When I feel strongly
about something, I try
to get others to believe
as I do."

—Kwami

Model Study

Public Service Announcement

What causes do you care about? Healthier food? More school
sports? Cleaner air? You can become an advocate for your cause.
An advocate is someone who publicly supports a cause or policy.
You can be an advocate in your everyday life. You could, for
example, wear a "Bike for Life" T-shirt to show support for cleaner
air. You can also write as an advocate. One way to do this is to write
a public service announcement.

A public service announcement is a short message or position
statement that is delivered to an audience. Most public service
announcements are broadcast on radio, television, or other media.
Like other speeches, a good public service announcement engages
the audience and tries to persuade people to agree with a position.

Read the student model on page 347W. It shows the features of a
good public service announcement.

PUBLIC SERVICE ANNOUNCEMENT

A good public service announcement

☑ captures the listener's interest with a clearly stated position

☑ tells how the position differs from alternate or opposing positions

☑ supports the position with logical reasons and relevant evidence

☑ uses transition words and phrases to show how the ideas are
related

☑ starts out with a formal tone and maintains it throughout

☑ provides a conclusion that follows from the stated position.

Feature Checklist

Vending for Health

by Carl Carpenter

If you get snacks from our school's vending machines, you're not doing your body any favors. Our school's vending machines need to offer healthy choices. According to a government study, vending machines offering sugary-sweet drinks, chips, and cookies negatively impact students' bodies. With rising obesity rates, it's important to have healthy foods and drinks available throughout the day.

Many schools depend on the income they earn from vending machines to help support other activities. They fear losing that money if the vending machines are stocked with healthy foods because students won't buy them. However, once students get used to the healthy alternatives, they will buy them—with no loss of income for the school.

The cafeteria is now serving healthy meals, so the vending machines should follow suit by replacing high-calorie snacks that have no nutritional value with fresh fruits and whole-grain snacks. We students need to sign a petition to get healthy foods into our vending machines as soon as possible.

Student Model

The writer presents his **opinion**.

The writer cites **evidence** from a reliable source.

The writer acknowledges an **opposing view** and counters it.

The writer uses **transition words** to connect ideas.

The writer ends with a strong **conclusion**.

Write Effective Sentences

Combine Sentences

Good writing has a rhythm to it. The sentences are varied and interesting to read. If your writing sounds choppy, try to combine some sentences.

Short, Choppy Sentences

Organic foods are better for you than conventional foods. They are grown using natural fertilizers. Farmers use fewer pesticides in the growing process. This makes produce less toxic.

One Way to Combine the Sentences

Organic foods are better for you than conventional foods. *because* They are grown using natural fertilizers. Farmers use fewer pesticides in the growing process. *which* This makes produce less toxic.

This writer combined sentences 1 and 2 and sentences 3 and 4.

Another Way to Combine the Sentences

Organic foods are better for you than conventional foods. They are grown using natural fertilizers. *and* ~~Farmers use~~ fewer pesticides ~~in the growing process. This~~ *which* makes produce less toxic.

This writer combined sentences 2–4.

Organic farms use natural materials such as compost to fertilize the soil. ▶

Vary Your Sentences

Your writing will be livelier if you make some sentences short and others long. That way you can create a nice rhythm and flow. Use different kinds of sentences, too.

Boring

Organic Foods

People should eat more organic foods. Organic foods are grown with only natural fertilizers. They have no harmful pesticides in them. Pesticides can harm your body and the air and soil. You can tell if you are buying an organic product by reading the label. A government agency called the Organic Standards Board looks over products to see if they are made of organic ingredients. Products made of all organic ingredients are certified "100% organic." Products made of 95% organic ingredients are certified "organic." Companies are allowed to put the certification on their packaging.

All the sentences are statements and are about the same length.

Interesting

Why Go Organic?

Do you want to look and feel better? Consider changing your diet to include more organic foods. Because organic products are grown with only natural fertilizers, they have no harmful pesticides in them. How can you tell you're getting an organic product? Read the label! The Organic Standards Board, a government agency, evaluates the ingredients in a product to see how much is really organic. In order for a product to be labeled "100% organic," it must contain only organic ingredients. Products made of 95% organic ingredients can be labeled "organic." So, read and eat right.

The writer mixes short and long sentences and uses a question, an exclamation, and a command.

Write Effective Sentences, continued

Streamline Your Sentences

To keep your readers interested, avoid using too many words. Readers shouldn't get lost between the beginning and the end of a sentence.

> **Overloaded Sentence, Streamlined**
>
> People in lower Manhattan should visit the farmers' market in Union Square. It sells delicious and wholesome fruits and vegetables, ~~many of which are grown organically without artificial pesticides or chemicals, and these foods~~ *which* are very good for you, ~~unlike most of the foods sold in big supermarkets~~.

Don't write three or four words where just one will do.

> **Wordy Sentences, Streamlined**
>
> People in our town should support opening a farmers' market near the old piers. Farmers' markets have been around since the 1920s ~~due to the fact that~~ *because* people enjoy getting a variety of fresh foods. Back ~~in that day and age~~ *then*, farmers' markets were mainly in big cities like Los Angeles.

Instead of . . .	Use . . .
a large number of	many
at the present time	now
due to the fact that	because
in this day and age	now

The Farmers' Market in Los Angeles, California, started in the 1930s. ▶

Another way to streamline sentences is to combine them with **appositives**. An appositive renames a noun or pronoun.

Choppy Sentences

Our farmers' market should be named Gilmore Farmers' Market to honor the man who founded the idea. E. B. Gilmore was responsible for the original farmers' market in Los Angeles, California. He was a businessman. He got an idea for a store. It was a place where farmers and artisans could sell goods directly to the public. It was a new kind of store. It was a farmers' market.

Streamlined with Appositives

Our farmers' market should be named Gilmore Farmers' Market to honor the man who founded the idea. E. B. Gilmore, a businessman, was responsible for the original farmers' market in Los Angeles, California. He got an idea for a store, a place where farmers and artisans could sell goods directly to the public. Soon the city gave birth to the farmers' market, a new kind of store.

Keep Your Sentences Parallel

When you compare or list more than one item, use similar, or parallel, grammatical forms.

Not Parallel

Farmers realized it made more sense to offer their goods directly than selling them to stores.

Parallel

Farmers realized it made more sense to offer their goods directly than to sell them to stores.

Not Parallel

The Farmers' Market has hosted music gigs, parades, and children can pet farm animals there.

Parallel

The Farmers' Market has hosted music gigs, parades, and petting zoos.

How would you edit this sentence to make it parallel?

Not Parallel

People not only came to the market to shop, but it also became entertainment.

Write a
Public Service Announcement

WRITING PROMPT What issue or cause in your school or community do you think needs to be solved? What can you do to support the cause or resolve the issue? How can you get others involved in supporting the cause, too?

Think about a cause that you've recently supported or are currently supporting. Write a public service announcement that

- captures your listeners' attention by describing the cause up front
- supports the cause with logical reasons and relevant evidence
- provides transitions to show how the ideas are related
- concludes with a call to action, telling listeners what they can do.

Prewrite

Here are some tips for planning your public service announcement.

1 Choose a Topic

Brainstorm a list of issues you'd like resolved or causes you'd like supported. Think of ones that you really care about.

Write down a few possibilities and then choose the best one. Mara made a list like this one.

Ideas	Good and Bad Points
increase my allowance so that I can buy healthier food	too personal; not interesting to anyone but me
build a community composting site	too broad and technical— requires too much research
shop at the local farmers' market	I know a lot about this—love the fresh fruits and veggies; know they're healthy

② Get to the Point

A public service announcement needs to quickly engage the audience. Mara's purpose for writing is to convince her audience that they should shop at local farmers' markets. She started with a thought-provoking question and then moved right on to her position.

> Do you want to feed your family the best and support your community at the same time? If so, you should shop at farmers' markets in your area.

③ Organize Your Ideas

A public service announcement expresses ideas about issues. Sometimes people will disagree with you, so plan how to respond to possible objections.

Mara's Plan for Her Public Service Announcement

Position Statement: People should search out and shop at local farmers' markets to benefit their families and communities.

Good Reason	Objection	Counterclaim
Fresh produce is healthier. →	Produce at farmers' markets is costly. →	Reduce what's spent on soft drinks and junk food to cover added cost.

Strongest Reason	Objection	Counterclaim
Shopping at farmers' markets benefits your family and local businesses. →	It takes too much time away from the family to make the extra stop. →	Take the whole family. Younger kids can go on a treasure hunt; older ones can compare prices.

Reflect

- Do you state your position clearly and right up front?

- Do you respond to possible objections to your position?

Draft

Now that you've organized your ideas, it's time to start writing.

- **State Your Position** Remember to hook your reader's attention and then get right to your point.

- **Prove Your Point** Add your reasons and evidence.

> Farmers' markets are good for you and for your community. They are good for you because the produce you buy there is fresher and more free of chemicals than what you can buy at the supermarket. Businesses near the farmers' markets also benefit. They have reported profit increases of 10–15 percent on market days.

Mara gives reasons and evidence to support her ideas.

- **Address Opposing Views** Respond to possible objections.

> Many people object to the high cost of fresh, organically grown produce. But those people can probably reduce what they spend on sugary drinks and unhealthy snacks to make up for the cost of buying fresh fruits and vegetables.

Mara responds to possible objections.

- **Ask for Agreement or Action** In your conclusion, state what you want your audience to do. Be clear and specific.

> Shopping for produce at a farmers' market is a win-win situation. Your family benefits from eating healthier foods, and you help support local farmers and business owners. So, get out and shop those farmers' markets!

Reflect

- Is your position clearly stated?

- Did you use a formal style to address the public?

DRAFTING TIPS
Trait: **Voice and Style**

If Your Writing Sounds Boring...

Boring writing lacks punch. If you don't get your listeners' attention with vivid words, you won't be able to make your point in a public service announcement.

Boring

> Fungi and insects can <u>hurt</u> tomato plants. Tomato growers <u>must use</u> strong pesticides to <u>stop</u> the crops from being <u>damaged</u>.

Try Picking Verbs with a Punch

When you change bland, overused verbs to vivid and specific ones, you can really spice up your writing.

Interesting

> Fungi and insects can <u>attack</u> tomato plants. Tomato growers <u>rely on</u> strong pesticides to <u>prevent</u> the crops from being <u>destroyed</u>.

The following chart shows a few of the verbs you can pick to make your writing more lively and interesting. A thesaurus is also a great resource for finding precise, vivid verbs.

Instead of...	Try...
eat	munch, gulp, devour, consume
help	aid, assist, relieve, improve
protect	defend, guard, shield, safeguard, shelter
complain	protest, grumble, criticize, whine
support	back up, provide, corroborate, confirm
impact	influence, affect, bear on

Revise

As you revise your public service announcement, remember your audience and purpose. Will your writing do what you want it to do? Will it connect with your audience?

1 **Evaluate Your Work**

Let a partner read your public service announcement and give you feedback. Ask your partner questions about your writing:

- **About the Form** Is my writing well organized? Is my position, or opinion, clear? Did I provide strong support for my position, or opinion?

- **About the Voice and Style** Does my announcement hook your interest? Are the word choices precise? Are there places where I could write with more punch?

Revision in Action

From Mara's Draft

What's a good reason to shop at farmers' markets? They are a good place to get whole foods. Whole foods are ones that are processed as little as possible. They are free from artificial additives. An apple picked right off the tree is a whole food. As Americans try to get healthier, they try to include more whole foods in their diets. Fruits and vegetables grown without pesticides or chemical fertilizers are whole foods. You don't have to be a vegetarian to eat whole foods. Whole-wheat bread, brown rice, and bran muffins are also whole foods. They are made from unprocessed whole grains. Whole foods are better for you. They taste better, too.

Mara's partner says:

" You used the word *good* in the first two sentences. "

" You could combine sentences here. "

" Your conclusion should relate back to your position. "

2 Mark Your Changes

Add or Replace Text You may need to add or replace text to make your public service announcement more persuasive. Use these marks ∧, ⌐ to add:

- facts, examples, and other evidence to support your position

- clear reasons to support your position

- a more interesting opening sentence

- a stronger conclusion.

Reflect

- Is your position clear?

- Do you need to add, replace, or rearrange text to improve your voice and style?

Revising Marks

MARK	∧	↶	⌐	⌐	¶
WHAT IT MEANS	Insert something.	Move to here.	Replace with this.	Take out.	Make a new paragraph.

Revised Draft

What's a good reason to shop at farmers' markets? They are a ~~good place to get~~ *great source for* whole foods. Whole foods are ones that are processed as little as possible. They are *and that* free from artificial additives. An apple picked right off the tree is a whole food. As Americans ~~try~~ *strive* to get healthier, they try to include more whole foods in their diets. Fruits and vegetables grown without pesticides or chemical fertilizers are whole foods. You don't have to be a vegetarian to eat whole foods. Whole-wheat bread, brown rice, and bran muffins are also whole foods. *because* They are made from unprocessed whole grains. Whole foods are *not only* better for you. They taste better, too. *And they are available at farmers' markets.*

Edit and Proofread

When you've made your public service announcement as strong as possible, the last step is to fix your language errors. This is called editing and proofreading your work.

- **Check the Grammar** Make sure that you have used correct and conventional grammar throughout. In particular, check for correct use of the present perfect tense. (See page 359W.)

- **Check the Spelling** Spell-check on a computer can be helpful, but it won't catch all your spelling mistakes. It is important to read your work carefully so you can check the spelling of words ending with -y. (See page 360W.)

- **Check the Mechanics** Mistakes in punctuation and capitalization can make your work hard to understand. In particular, pay attention to how you have used punctuation to indicate breaks or pauses. (See page 361W.)

Use these marks to edit and proofread your persuasive essay.

Editing and Proofreading Marks

MARK	WHAT IT MEANS	MARK	WHAT IT MEANS
∧	Insert something.	/	Make lowercase.
∧	Add a comma.	℘	Delete, take something out.
∧	Add a semicolon.	¶	Make new paragraph.
⊙	Add a period.	◯	Spell out.
⊙	Add a colon.	⌃	Replace with this.
⌄ ⌄	Add quotation marks.	∼	Change order of letters or words.
⌄	Add an apostrophe.	#	Insert space.
≡	Capitalize.	◡	Close up, no space here.

GrammarWorkout

Check Present Perfect Tense

Use the **present perfect tense** to tell about an action that started in the past but is still going on. Or use the present perfect tense to describe an action that happened in the past but you are not sure when.

- The present perfect tense is formed with the helping verb **has** or **have** plus the **past participle** of a verb.

  EXAMPLE   We **have started** a vegetable garden.

- For regular verbs, the past participle ends with **-ed**. However, **irregular verbs** use special forms for their past participles. See the Grammar Handbook for a list of irregular verbs.

  EXAMPLE   Mrs. Wise **has prepared** her yard for planting.

  She **has grown** tomatoes and cucumbers for years.

- Be sure that you use the correct form of the helping verb when you use the present perfect tense. Use **has** with singular nouns or the pronouns **he**, **she**, or **it**. With all other nouns and pronouns, use **have**.

  EXAMPLE   She ~~have~~ ^{has} given many of the vegetables to the hungry.

Find the Trouble Spots

Mrs. Wise has enjoy^{ed} growing vegetables since she was a teenager. Once the cucumbers and tomatoes has ripened, she brings them to class. Many students have took the vegetables home before. Even the Food Bank on Oak Street has waited for Mrs. Wise to come by. It have received fresh vegetables from her every year.

Find and fix three other present perfect tense errors.

Edit and Proofread, continued

> ### Spelling Workout
>
> # Spelling Words Ending with -y
>
> Follow these spelling rules to add endings to words that end with *-y*.
>
> - If a word ends in a consonant + *y*, change the *y* to *i* before you add *-es*, *-ed*, *-er*, or *-est*.
>
>   **EXAMPLES** carry carries try tried heallthy healthier
>
> - For words that end with a vowel + *y*, just add *-s* or *-ed*.
>
>   **EXAMPLES** stay stayed key keys boy boys
>
> - If you add *-ing* to a verb that ends in *-y*, do not change the *y* to **i**.
>
>   **EXAMPLES** empty emptying cry crying satisfy satisfying
>
> ### Find the Trouble Spots
>
> Many towns and cit~~y~~ies have food banks. Like other charitis, food banks are nonprofit organizations. That means that they don't make money, or a profit, from what they do. Food banks collect food for familyies who can't buy enough food to avoid hunger. Volunteers check and take in food donations. They also pick up dryed and canned food from people's homes. Food bank volunteers are tring to make a difference in people's lives.
>
> Find four more spelling errors to fix.

Mechanics Workout

Check Commas, Ellipses, and Dashes

- Use commas to separate items in a series or extra information. Commas indicate when to slow down or pause, which helps your reader clearly understand your ideas.

  CONFUSING Food volunteers and shelters help the poor.
  CLEAR Food**,** volunteers**,** and shelters help the poor.

  CONFUSING Working at the soup kitchen I give people hot meals.
  CLEAR Working at the soup kitchen**,** I give people hot meals.

- Use ellipsis marks (…) to show that some words are left out in a quotation. Or use them to show an unfinished thought or pause.

  EXAMPLES The article says, "In Millsville, the shelters aren't big enough **. . .** we need a larger facility."

  Maybe the building on Maple Street **. . .**

- Use dashes to set off extra information or a sudden break in thought. Use one dash if the break is at the end of a sentence; use two if the break is in the middle.

  EXAMPLES I believe each person—including me—must help.
  Will the city do something?—I wonder.

Find the Trouble Spots

> The building on Maple Street perfect for a shelter is in the middle of town. It's only a block from the grocery store clinic and bus station. Many of us at least I hope think it would be a good location. Coming up for a vote at the next meeting that proposal should pass.

Find and fix six errors with commas, ellipses, and dashes.

Model Study

Persuasive Essay

Are there issues that you care deeply about? Well, writing as a citizen is one way to share your opinions. You try to persuade readers to agree with you. With a good persuasive essay, you may even convince your readers to take action.

PERSUASIVE ESSAY

A good persuasive essay

☑ states the writer's position on the issue

☑ appeals to logic using evidence

☑ appeals to emotions using persuasive language

☑ addresses the opposing argument

☑ ends with a call to action.

Read the persuasive essay on the following pages. The writer opens with some background information about the issue, and then states her position. She goes on to present reasons for her position and persuade others to take action.

Getting Out There

by Melinda Santos

What do the grades on a report card say? They likely show how well a student has learned his or her subjects, and that's important. However, just as important is what students have done to help others. More and more schools around the nation are finding ways to help students volunteer. Many teenagers would gladly offer their time to the community, if given the chance. I think our school should give students that chance by working with the Rockville Soup Kitchen to create a student volunteer program.

A soup kitchen is an ideal place for students to volunteer. Hundreds of people in our community cannot afford a warm meal every day. With the help of adult supervisors, we could help feed people from all over the city. Although working in a food kitchen is a big job, I think our student body is up for the challenge. Our responsibilities might range from preparing food to serving it. Teachers can include skills in our curriculum that students can use at the soup kitchen. Isn't helping the hungry and the homeless as important as learning math and science?

Student Model

The writer provides background on the issue and states her **position**.

The writer gives **reasons** to support her position.

The writer includes **appeals to readers' emotions**.

► Volunteers serve food at a soup kitchen. ►

Persuasive Essay, continued

Working in the soup kitchen will not only provide help to the homeless, but it will also help students feel better about themselves. This is one reason young people should be involved in community service. Studies show that volunteering can be good for people's mental health. It can give us a sense of purpose.

Furthermore, volunteering can improve our physical health, too. For example, a recent study by researchers at Boston College showed people with chronic, or long-lasting, pain have felt better after volunteer work. Shouldn't we make helping others a habit now?

The soup kitchen can also help students connect with the community. Many of us have never met a homeless person. Some have, but were unsure of how to help them. Students need guidance and information on how they can help others. Students interested in volunteering should ask the school to form a volunteer program for the Rockville Soup Kitchen.

The writer gives additional reasons supported by **facts**.

The writer appeals to logic with a **statistic**.

The writer offers a way for **readers to take action**.

Young people help out in a soup kitchen. ▶

Some people may think that middle school students are too young to do volunteer work, or not interested enough. But with a little guidance and encouragement, students are willing and able to help needy people in their communities. For example, every month, a group of students from Jamestown Middle School spends a Saturday stocking shelves in their city's soup kitchen. Last November, many students from our own school participated in the Thanksgiving Food Drive. Other schools include volunteering in their class work. The students of Dunley Middle School researched local volunteer organizations as part of their social studies curriculum. Through their research, students learned about many ways they could help their communities.

Our school already does a lot for students, but it can also help us do a lot for the community. Many people in our city need and deserve help, and we deserve a chance to take action. All it would take is a few hours a month. I urge the school board to work with the Rockville Soup Kitchen to establish a student volunteer program. Kids want to make a difference.

Additional reasons and examples support the writer's argument.

The writer ends by restating her **position** and including a **call to action**.

Appeal to Logic

In a public debate, it is your job to convince your audience that your position is right. You do this by giving reasons for your opinions. You do the same thing when you write persuasively. You appeal to your reader's logic with solid reasons supported by facts and evidence.

Build Strong Arguments

Include the following to appeal to your reader's sense of logic.

Solid Reasons

Back up your point of view with two or three solid reasons. You can start with your strongest reason, or begin with the weakest and build up.

Most Convincing Reason
↓
Less Convincing Reason
↓
Least Convincing Reason

Facts and Statistics

Adding facts and statistics makes your argument more convincing.

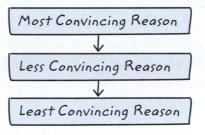

Young volunteers play an important role in keeping the Mitchell Mobile Meals program running. Between September 2006 and September 2007, 20% of the volunteers were under 18.

To make your reasons more convincing, you can add supporting examples.

> Many organizations for the elderly encourage students to volunteer. Mitchell Mobile Meals on Forster Street, for example, is staffed completely by young people. Lamar Stevens, who is in charge of the kitchen, says that they can always use more teens to help cook and package meals. Others can make phone calls to check up on the people who receive the meals.

Backup from an Expert

You can also include an expert's opinion to support your own.

> We must be sure that the elderly get enough to eat. America's Second Harvest recently reported a study focused on hunger among the elderly. It stated that elderly individuals who do not eat regular meals are twice as likely to experience health problems.

Read the example below. How could the writer include appeals to logic to make the argument more convincing?

Meals on the Go

Many elderly Americans depend on meal-delivery services. Since it may be difficult for them to walk or drive to local food banks, meals are brought to them. Volunteers prepare and package meals. Then they are delivered to the homes of elderly people in need. Many elderly people would go hungry if it were not for these programs.

Where could the writer add facts, statistics, or expert opinions?

Appeal to Emotion

Has a melody ever made you smile, cry, tap your feet, or get up and dance? Not only does music "move" you emotionally, it can literally get you moving. In writing, appeals to emotion are like music. Strong appeals can affect readers' feelings and move people to take action.

Use Persuasive Language

Use words that show you believe in your opinion. Don't overdo it, though. Using words that are too harsh is a turn-off. Show that you care about the issue, but make sure you sound reasonable. Check out the examples below. What makes the middle one the most effective?

Not Enough Emotion

> Volunteering for a local mobile meal program could give you a chance to help your community.

Effective Appeal to Emotion

> Mobile meal programs help ensure that older people won't go hungry. Please do your part to help.

Too Emotional

> Older people need mobile meal programs or they will starve. How can you stand back and let that happen?

Use Personal Examples

You can appeal to emotions by including personal stories. These stories can come from people affected by an issue. Remember that these examples don't replace facts and statistics. But they're a great way to make readers care more about what you are saying.

Personal Example

> Receiving a meal can brighten a senior's day. "It's nice to have volunteers stop by," says Dotty Meyer, 77, a participant in Glenbrook's mobile meal program.

Personal Example

> Some seniors would have no other source of food. Arthur Baxter lives ten miles from the nearest grocery store and is no longer allowed to drive a car. He cannot afford to have his meals delivered to him from a commercial service.

Read the model below. How could it be improved?

Meals on the Move

The Sunnyside Mobile Meal program has been helping seniors in our community since 1973. It currently serves 60 seniors and has a large waiting list. Many of the people on the waiting list are in serious need. To reach these seniors, Sunnyside needs more volunteers.

You don't have to drive a car to be a volunteer. Help is also needed in the kitchen to cook and package meals. By volunteering, you can help serve the physical and emotional needs of the community.

How could the writer change the language to appeal to readers' emotions? Where could he add a personal example?

Support Your Arguments

No matter how beautiful a house is, it won't stand up without a solid foundation. A good argument is like a house. It needs to be supported by solid evidence, or it won't stand up. As you construct your argument, think about how you can support it with reasons and evidence.

Gather Evidence

Evidence supports your opinions. Use evidence from various sources to convince your audience of your argument. You might include evidence based on your own experience, facts and statistics, or even expert opinions.

Use a graphic organizer like the one below to organize your evidence. It will also reveal whether you need more ideas.

Argument	Evidence
Food drives can help feed lots of people.	Recent data shows there are over 35 million Americans who have difficulty paying for groceries.
Donating is not difficult to do.	There are several ways to help your local food banks. You can donate money, food, or time.
Food drives are important and necessary.	Rising food costs have made it harder for food banks to feed the hungry.

As you write your essay, use your list of reasons and evidence. Make sure you include appeals to readers' logic and to their emotions. Use these techniques:

- Support your reasons with facts.

> According to America's Second Harvest, there were 195 member food banks in 2007. They distributed more than two billion pounds of food to needy people.

- Develop your reasons with details.

> In 2006, more than 25 million people participated in a charitable food program. Children made up 36% of that total.

- Use persuasive language to get readers on your side.

> Shouldn't we all do what we can to help others in our country? We have the power to make a real difference.

Read the example below. How could the writer improve it?

Fighting Hunger

Doing all you can to feed the hungry is a valuable service. There are many different ways to feed those in need. Food banks across the nation need funds, volunteers, and donations.

Some Americans already contribute food every year, but many more could still join them. Maybe they do not realize what a difference they can make, but something as simple as donating a can of food can make life better for someone in need.

How could the writer make this argument more convincing? What support could he add?

Use Charts, Tables, and Pictures

What's It Like

Would you go on a vacation without bringing a camera along? Of course not! You take photographs so you can remember your trip and so other people can see what it was like. You can also use visuals in persuasive writing. Charts, tables, and photographs can make persuasive writing clearer and more memorable.

Add Visuals to Your Writing

You can develop your ideas by adding visuals such as charts, tables, and pictures. Graphics get readers' attention. They can also help make complicated ideas clear.

- Use a graph or table to present data or statistics.

- Present information in a pie chart like the one below.

Location of Hungry Americans

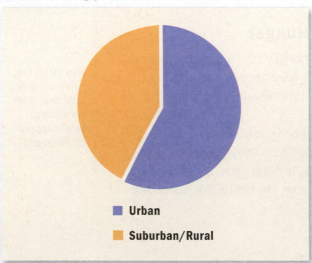

■ Urban
■ Suburban/Rural

- Another way to strengthen your arguments is to include pictures or photographs. Pictures can show your readers exactly what you mean.

Donating to the Food Bank

Most people donate canned goods and other food items around the holidays. The biggest spike in food donations begins around Thanksgiving and lasts through the winter holidays. Unfortunately, hungry people need food all year round. This is why I urge you to donate to the Metropolitan Food Bank today.

The image below on the left shows the types of food we're currently accepting at the Metropolitan Food Bank. The image on the right shows our hardworking volunteers doing their best for the community. We have been receiving incredible help in the past years. Do you want to pitch in?

The Metropolitan Food Bank accepts a variety of foods for distribution by our volunteers.

*Tech*TIP

Use a scanner to turn photographs or other images into electronic files you can insert in your paper.

Write a Persuasive Essay

WRITING PROMPT What we eat has changed from a personal choice to a public issue. What should schools and restaurants do to encourage healthier eating? How would you persuade others to agree with your opinion?

Think of a food-related issue you feel strongly about. Then write a persuasive piece. Choose a form to fit your purpose. You might write a persuasive letter, article, speech, or other form. Your persuasive piece should include

- background information about the issue
- a clear statement of your position on the issue
- reasons and evidence to support your position
- a call to action asking readers to do something about the issue.

Prewrite

❶ Choose an Issue and a Position

It's important to choose an issue you really care about. Next, decide what your position on the issue is—and what you want people to do about it. Raúl listed several ideas, then chose the best one for his essay:

> ### Issues I care about
> Soup kitchens—Our community should open a volunteer soup kitchen.
> Healthier cafeteria food—Our school should provide healthier options in the cafeteria.
> Vegetarian options—Local restaurants should serve more meatless dishes so vegetarians will not have to go to specialty restaurants.

Raúl decided to write his essay as an article for his school newspaper.

2 Gather Evidence to Support Your Position

Learn more about your topic. Do research to make sure that you know the issue very well. Then, write down evidence based on personal experience, facts and statistics, and expert opinions. Use a chart to organize your evidence.

Argument	Evidence
Our cafeteria's menu choices are unhealthy.	Students eat fries, sloppy joes, chips, and fried chicken 5 days a week! Too much fried food and sugar has a negative impact on students' health.
Healthier cafeteria food would help students maintain a healthy weight and teach them good eating habits.	Students will choose healthy food if it is convenient and available. Fresh fruit always sells out quickly on the days it's available.

TechTIP

List reasons, facts, and examples as phrases or sentences. Then use **cut** and **paste** from the **Edit** menu to move details around as you need to.

3 Organize Your Main Supporting Points

Now that you've done the research, what are the strongest reasons you'll use to support your position?

POSITION:
Our school should provide healthier food choices in the cafeteria.

REASON 1:
Unhealthy school lunches contribute to childhood obesity and related health problems.

REASON 2:
Students who are concerned about their weight would not need to skip lunch to avoid unhealthy food.

REASON 3:
Healthy cafeteria food would promote a healthier lifestyle for students in and out of school.

Reflect

- Do you have a clear position on your issue?

- Is there enough evidence to support your opinion?

Draft

You've thought about the issue, done some research, and organized your reasons and evidence. Now it's time to start writing. Use your planning to create a strong argument.

- **Write an Introduction** Start off by giving your readers a little background about the issue. Then, state your position clearly in **one sentence**.

From Raúl's Draft

> Take a look around your school cafeteria at lunch time. Notice what students are eating. You'll probably see a lot of junk food. The school cafeteria often resembles a fast-food restaurant. A lot of the food is fried, greasy, and sugary. We must replace those foods with healthier options.

Raúl introduces readers to the issue and then clearly states his **position**.

- **Build Your Case** Present your arguments and your supporting evidence to the reader. Use your list of reasons and evidence to write the essay. Appeal to your reader's logic and emotions.

- **End with a Strong Conclusion** In your last paragraph, restate your position and main supporting reasons. Then, end with a **call to action**! You've gotten readers to care about the issue—now tell them what they can do about it.

From Raúl's Draft

> We need to help our students stay healthy. The best way to do that is to offer healthier food in the school cafeteria. It's been proven that well-nourished students are more alert and learn better. Now it's time to take that knowledge and use it! Write letters to school administrators, asking for healthier lunch options. Boycott school lunches and bring your own until we see changes in the menu. We need and deserve better and healthier food choices.

Reflect

- Does the introduction give background information?

- Did you build your case with reasons and evidence?

- Did you end with a call to action?

DRAFTING TIPS
Trait: **Voice and Style**

If Your Writing Isn't Convincing Enough . . .

In a verbal conversation, communication is back and forth. You say your opinion, hear what others think, and have a chance to respond. But when you're writing, you can't hear your readers' thoughts. That's why it's important to consider how they'll respond to your arguments. Then you can be prepared with answers.

Try Taking the Other Side

You've taken a side on the issue. Chances are, not everyone will agree with you! Try looking at it from another point of view. How would someone who disagrees with you challenge your arguments? How could you respond?

Argument	Challenge	Response
Students need healthier food in their school cafeterias.	Healthy food is too expensive. Some schools can't afford to provide healthier choices.	If schools provide healthy food, cafeteria sales will increase because more parents will be willing to let their children eat school lunches.

Once you have predicted what some possible challenges might be, you can prepare your response. Use a calm, reasonable tone. By including a response in your essay, you show your reader how well-thought-out your argument really is.

Revise

As you revise your work, think about your audience and purpose. Is your writing persuasive enough to convince your readers to take action?

1 **Evaluate Your Work**

Switch drafts with a partner and debate the points in both of your essays. Consider these questions:

- **About the Form** Are the arguments clear, convincing, and well supported? Is there a call to action?

- **About the Voice and Style** Does the writer's voice come through? Are the sentences varied and interesting?

> ## *Revision in Action*

From Raúl's Draft

Raúl's partner says:

> Take a look around your school cafeteria at lunch time. Notice what students are eating. You'll probably see a lot of junk food. The school cafeteria often resembles a fast-food restaurant. A lot of the food is fried, greasy, and sugary. We must replace those foods with healthier options.
>
> Obesity in children and teens has become a serious problem over the past 15 years. It is a problem because children are eating unhealthy food in large portions. School cafeterias serve too many unhealthy foods. They serve fried foods and sugary desserts. We need to improve children's health and bring down obesity rates. But schools keep feeding their students junk. We need to change that.

" **This paragraph has too many statements.** "

" **Can you be more specific about what students are eating?** "

" **These sentences are wordy and repetitive. Maybe you could combine them.** "

2 Mark Your Changes

Clarify To make you text clearer, you may need to

- add facts, examples, and details to support or explain your position

- replace vague words or dull phrases with more precise or colorful language.

Consolidate Streamlining your text can make your arguments clearer and more convincing. You may need to

- delete repetitive or wordy phrases and dull words

- combine sentences to make your writing more sophisticated.

Reflect

- Do your arguments make sense? Do you need to add more support?

- Does the writing in your essay sound like you?

Revising Marks

MARK	∧	↶	⌐	↝	¶
WHAT IT MEANS	Insert something.	Move to here.	Replace with this.	Take out.	Make a new paragraph.

Revised Draft

Take a look around your school cafeteria at lunch
time. ~~Notice what students are eating.~~ *What do you see the students eating?* You'll probably
see a lot of ~~junk food~~ *fries, sloppy joes, fried chicken, and soda*. The school cafeteria often
resembles a fast-food restaurant. ~~A lot of~~ the food
is fried, greasy, and sugary. We must replace those
foods with healthier options.

Obesity in children and teens has become a serious
problem over the past 15 years~~.~~? ~~It is a problem~~
because ~~children are eating unhealthy food in large~~ *we eat too much junk food.*
~~portions~~. School cafeterias ~~serve too many unhealthy~~ *encourage bad eating habits by serving*
~~foods. They serve~~ fried foods and sugary desserts.
~~We need~~ to improve children's health and bring down *How are we going*
obesity rates. ~~But~~ *if* schools keep feeding their students
junk~~.~~? We need to change that.

Raúl varied his sentences by changing a statement to a question. He also replaced a general phrase with specific words to make his meaning clearer.

Raúl deleted repetitive language and consolidated ideas by combining sentences.

Edit and Proofread

When you've made your argument as strong as possible, the last step is to fix your language errors. This is called editing and proofreading your work.

- **Check the Grammar** Make sure that you have used correct and conventional grammar throughout. In particular, check for any shifts in the verb voice and mood. (See page 381W.)

- **Check the Spelling** Spell-check on a computer can be helpful, but it won't catch all your spelling mistakes. It is important to read your work carefully and use a dictionary to check words with *q, ie,* and *ei.* (See page 382W.)

- **Check the Mechanics** Mistakes in punctuation and capitalization can make your work hard to understand. In particular, pay attention to how you have used capitalization with proper adjectives. (See page 383W.)

Use these marks to edit and proofread your persuasive essay.

Editing and Proofreading Marks

MARK	WHAT IT MEANS	MARK	WHAT IT MEANS
∧	Insert something.	╱	Make lowercase.
∧	Add a comma.	℘	Delete, take something out.
∧	Add a semicolon.	¶	Make new paragraph.
⊙	Add a period.	◯	Spell out.
⊙	Add a colon.	⟵	Replace with this.
⌄ ⌄	Add quotation marks.	∼	Change order of letters or words.
⌄	Add an apostrophe.	#	Insert space.
≡	Capitalize.	◡	Close up, no space here.

Reflect

- What kinds of errors did you find? What can you do to keep from making them?

Grammar Workout

Check for Consistent Verb Voice and Mood

Avoid shifting the voice and mood of your verbs. Keep them consistent. Otherwise, your readers—and you—might get confused.

- Choose the active voice or passive voice, not both. For more about the voice of verbs, see the Grammar Handbook.

EXAMPLE   We watched a documentary about fast food. Afterward, ~~the film was rated by~~ the class. *rated the film*

~~The french fries are eaten by~~ Jim, but he doesn't like them. *eats the French fries*

- Choose which verb mood you want to use, such as the indicative. imperative, or subjunctive, and stick to it! Look in the Grammar Handbook on pages 480W–481W for more about verb moods.

EXAMPLE   After Mary surveys the class about favorite fast food places, give us the results. If you read carefully, ~~don't~~ miss the facts. If I were you, I exercise more. *she gives* *you won't* *would*

Find the Trouble Spots

> If children don't eat right and exercise now, they become *could* overweight as adults. The weights of 6-foot-tall American men was said by researchers to have increased 30% since the 1990s. That means that the average weight had increased steadily for 150 years. Expect it. Scientists think that the average American's weight will go up even more by 2030.

Fix the two sentences that show a shift in the verb voice or mood.

Edit and Proofread, continued

Spelling Workout

Check Words with *q*, *ie*, and *ei*

Some words follow spelling rules you can almost always count on.

- The letter **q** nearly always has the letter **u** right after it. Some proper nouns are exceptions.

EXAMPLES	quit, quarter, quest
EXCEPTIONS	Iraq, Qatar

- The letter **i** usually comes before the letter **e**. However, this changes when the letters come after the letter **c**, or when they sound like long **a**.

EXAMPLES	friend, relief, achieve
EXCEPTIONS	ceiling, conceited, sleigh, weight

Find the Trouble Spots

The nutritional qᵘality of food greatly impacts a person's health. Due to large portions and an unhealthy diet, Americans wiegh more than ever. Obesity rates in children are qickly rising. Many people beleive that schools should serve healthier food to students.

Find two more spelling errors to fix.

MechanicsWorkout

Check Capitalization of Proper Adjectives and Academic Courses

- **Proper Adjectives** Proper adjectives are adjectives that come from proper nouns. For example, adjectives based on the name of a country or continent are proper adjectives.

  EXAMPLES **Japanese** food
  African dance

  Always capitalize proper adjectives.

  EXAMPLES I love **Latin American** music.
  We had to write a **Shakespearean** sonnet.

- **Academic Courses** When writing about the title of a specific class, capitalize the name of the class. Do not capitalize the names of general fields of study.

  EXAMPLES My sister is taking **Introduction to Psychology** in college.

  I have to take three semesters of **math** before I can graduate.

Find the Trouble Spots

We started learning about the obesity crisis in american society in my ~~s~~Social ~~s~~Studies class. The next day, Mrs. Paz, who teaches history, asked us to research food production in the U.S. Then, my Science teacher had us write a report comparing the calories in a typical american and mexican dinner.

Find three more capitalization errors to fix.

Publish, Share, and Reflect

By now your persuasive essay is organized and convincing, and it lets your voice come through. The next step is to share it with readers.

1 Publish and Share Your Work

Your essay won't persuade anyone if you don't share it! When you publish your writing, think about the best way to present your ideas to your audience.

You might want to make your essay public, especially if it addresses an issue that affects your community. To share your essay with a wide audience, consider these ways of publishing:

- Post it on a blog or Web site.
- Publish it in your school newspaper.
- Read it aloud at a school assembly.
- Send it as a letter to the editor of your local newspaper.
- Send it as a letter to your mayor or your representative in Congress.

Alternatively, you may share it with a smaller audience, such as your family, your friends, or your class. However you choose to share it, think about ways to make it clear and informative. For instance, you might

- use tables to present detailed information
- use bulleted lists to summarize major points.

2 Reflect on Your Work

Keep thinking about what you wrote! You took the time to research and write about an issue that matters to you. Stay informed about the topic, and revisit your essay if you want to make changes.

Reflect

- What did I learn about the issue from writing about it?

- Has my position on this issue changed at all?

How to Present a Persuasive Essay

When presenting your essay, it is important to decide on the facts and examples that best support your opinion.

To give a successful presentation:

1. **Plan** Read your essay to yourself. Make notes about the key facts and examples that you want your audience to understand. Mark those places so that you know where to read with extra emphasis. Try to add some more interesting facts and examples that your audience has probably not heard before.

2. **Practice** To make sure your facts and examples are presented logically, practice in front of a partner beforehand. Check that you effectively placed emphasis on your key ideas by asking your partner to explain what you presented. You may also want to make a video recording of yourself and watch your performance to evaluate how well you can get your points across.

3. **Deliver** Briefly introduce your topic and clearly state your opinion. Then present your essay to your audience. Remember to:

- Read at a steady rate that your audience can easily listen to and understand.

- Pronounce each word clearly and correctly.

- Speak at an appropriate volume that is not too soft or too loud. You should alter your volume when adding emphasis, but always make sure your audience can hear you.

- Make eye contact with your listeners throughout your presentation.

" No one should go hungry. We need to help feed the homeless and the hungry."

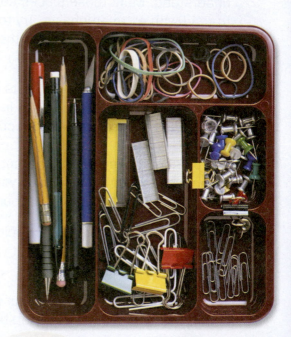

Writing FORMS

Advertisements

Autobiography

Biography

Book Review

Character Sketch

Description

Directions

E-mail

Essays

Interview

Job Application

Letters

Literary Response

Newspaper

Personal Narrative

Play

Poetry

Procedure

Story

Web site

Workplace and
Consumer Resources

Advertisements

Print Ad

Advertisements are a powerful form of persuasion. They can be used to "sell" almost anything—food, clothes, vacation spots, even political candidates. Print ads appeal to readers by combining text with eye-catching visual images.

"Whistle" was a soft drink popular in the 1920s. ▼

Attracts readers' attention with images

Uses descriptive words to appeal to consumers

The Best on the Beach!

At the end of a perfect swim—"Whistle". It's great! And refreshing! And dee-licious! Something to be glad about? You said it! It's bottled sunshine.
Just drift to some nearby place where you can pucker up your lips and

WHISTLE

TV Ad Script

Advertisements on television get viewers' attention and present a brief, persuasive message, often with catchy phrases and vivid images. Some ads try to sell a product. Others, like the public service announcement (PSA) below, try to persuade viewers to take action on a community concern.

Crushed aluminum cans ready for recycling ▶

"Recycling" PSA

Scene: A living room with doorway to the kitchen visible in background. JAMAL is taking a nap on the couch in the living room.

KEVIN begins wrestling a heavy garbage bag from the trash can in the kitchen. JAMAL wakes up.

JAMAL (*annoyed*): Why does taking out the trash have to make so much noise?

KEVIN: It's all these soda cans.

JAMAL: What are those doing in the garbage?

KEVIN: Making noise, I guess.

KEVIN puts the heavy bag down. It drops loudly.

JAMAL: No, I mean, why are they in the trash when they aren't garbage? Those cans could be melted down and reused. Recycling metal cans saves energy and resources.

Cut to a recycling bin full of cans.

VOICE-OVER: If it clinks, it's not garbage. Recycle.

Cut to CCFEA logo and URL.

VOICE-OVER: For more information about recycling in your neighborhood, visit our Web site. Paid for by Concerned Citizens for Environmental Activism.

Stage directions tell what happens on-screen.

Dialogue defines what the actors will say.

A clear persuasive message often uses brief, memorable language.

Autobiography

An autobiography is the story of someone's own life. When you write an autobiography, you tell about the experiences that made you who you are today.

At age 7, Firoozeh Dumas moved to the U.S. from Iran. ▶

Often includes background about family history and childhood experiences

Moving to America was both exciting and frightening, but we found great comfort in knowing that my father spoke English. Having spent years regaling us with stories about his graduate years in America, he had left us with the distinct impression that America was his second home. My mother and I planned to stick close to him, letting him guide us through the exotic American landscape that he knew so well. We counted on him not only to translate the language but also to translate the culture, to be a link to this most foreign of lands. . .

Uses first-person pronouns.

Once we reached America, we wondered whether perhaps my father had confused his life in America with someone else's. Judging from the bewildered looks of store cashiers, gas station attendants, and waiters, my father spoke a version of English not yet shared with the rest of America. His attempts to find a "vater closet" in a department store would usually lead us to the drinking fountain or the home furnishings section. Asking my father to ask the waitress the definition of "sloppy Joe" or "Tater Tots" was no problem. His translations, however, were highly suspect. Waitresses would spend several minutes responding to my father's questions, and these responses, in turn, would be translated as "She doesn't know." Thanks to my father's translations, we stayed away from hot dogs, catfish, and hush puppies, and no amount of caviar in the sea would have convinced us to try mud pie.

Tells about specific memorable events.

Biography

A biography tells the story of someone else's life. Long biographies can appear in books. Shorter ones may appear in magazines, encyclopedias, or Web sites.

▲ This engraving shows pioneers traveling West in the 1800s.

Laura Ingalls Wilder
born Feb. 7, 1867,
Lake Pepin, Wis., U.S.;
died Feb. 10, 1957,
Mansfield, Mo.

Laura Ingalls Wilder

Laura Ingalls grew up in a family that moved frequently from one part of the American frontier to another. Her father took the family by covered wagon to Minnesota, Iowa, Missouri, Kansas, Indian Territory, and Dakota Territory. At age 15 she began teaching in rural schools. In 1885 she married Almanzo J. Wilder, with whom she lived from 1894 on a farm near Mansfield, Missouri. Some years later she began writing for various periodicals.

Prompted by her daughter, Wilder began writing down her childhood experiences. In 1932 she published *Little House in the Big Woods*, which was set in Wisconsin. After writing *Farmer Boy* (1933), a book about her husband's childhood, she published *Little House on the Prairie* (1935), a reminiscence of her family's stay in Indian Territory. The "Little House" books were well received by the reading public and critics alike.

Wilder continued the story of her life in *On the Banks of Plum Creek* (1937), *By the Shores of Silver Lake* (1939), *The Long Winter* (1940), *Little Town on the Prairie* (1941), and *These Happy Golden Years* (1943). Her books remain in print.

450

Often describes the subject's life and work, using chronological order

Time words and dates cue the order of events.

Book Review

Sometimes you read a book that you just have to tell others about. You can tell about it by writing a book review.

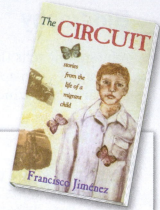

The *Circuit*

by Francisco Jiménez

Reviewed by Vicente P.

The first paragraph tells what the book is mostly about, or its main idea.

The Circuit is about a boy, Panchito, from a family of poor migrant farmworkers. He loves school. But Panchito works in the fields, and his family moves from town to town, so he can't go to school very often. When he does go to school, sometimes he has to start in the middle of the school year. It's hard for him because he is a stranger in the class and he doesn't speak or understand English well.

The next section tells how you feel about the book and why.

I like this book. My dad is in the army, so my family moves a lot. I know how Panchito feels being the new kid in class. I feel sorry for him because just when he starts to like a place and he makes friends there, he has to leave. I know how that feels, too.

The final paragraph tells the most important idea you learned from the book.

This book makes me thankful that I don't have to work hard like Panchito. And, even though my family moves a lot, I'm thankful that I always have a home and enough to eat. I also realize that I'm lucky because I speak English and I get to go to school.

Character Sketch

A character sketch may appear in fiction or nonfiction writing. It's like a quick word portrait of another person. A character sketch may portray a real person or a fictional character.

THIS BOY'S LIFE | Tobias Wolff   15

Dwight was a short man with curly brown hair and sad, restless brown eyes. He smelled of gasoline. His legs were small for his thick-chested body, but what they lacked in length they made up for in spring; he had an abrupt, surprising way of springing to his feet. He dressed like no one I'd ever met before—two-tone shoes, hand-painted tie, monogrammed blazer with a monogrammed handkerchief in the breast pocket. Dwight kept coming back, which made him chief among the suitors. My mother said he was a good dancer—he could really make those shoes of his get up and go. Also he was very nice, very considerate.

I didn't worry about him. He was too short. He was a mechanic. His clothes were wrong. I didn't know why they were wrong, but they were. We hadn't come all the way out here to end up with him. He didn't even live in Seattle; he lived in a place called Chinook, a tiny village three hours north of Seattle, up in the Cascade Mountains. Besides, he'd already been married. He had three kids of his own living with him, all teenagers. I knew my mother would never let herself get tangled up in a mess like that.

Includes **descriptive details** about appearance, actions, and personality

The writer tells his opinion of the character.

Description

A description uses specific details to help readers picture whatever is being described. Use words that appeal to the reader's senses.

Includes vivid sensory details

It was one of those super-duper cold Saturdays. One of those days that when you breathed out your breath kind of hung frozen in the air like a hunk of smoke and you could walk along and look exactly like a train blowing out big, fat, white puffs of smoke.

It was so cold that if you were stupid enough to go outside your eyes would automatically blink a thousand times all by themselves, probably so the juice inside of them wouldn't freeze up. It was so cold that if you spit, the slob would be an ice cube before it hit the ground. It was about a zillion degrees below zero.

It was even cold inside our house. We put sweaters and hats and scarves and three pairs of socks on and still were cold. The thermostat was turned all the way up and the furnace was banging and sounding like it was about to blow up but it still felt like Jack Frost had moved in with us.

Word pictures create a memorable image of this very cold day.

Directions

Directions tell how to play a game, how to get somewhere, or how to make something. When you write directions, the most important thing to do is to put the steps in order.

Game Directions

The **beginning** tells how many people can play.

The **middle** tells how to play the game.

The **end** tells how to win the game.

Rock, Paper, Scissors

Number of players: 2

How to Play: First make a fist with one hand. Next, shake your fist three times as you say *rock, paper, scissors.* Then do one of these:
  –Keep a fist for *rock*
  –Put two fingers out for *scissors*
  –Put your palm down for *paper*
Finally, look at your hands to see who wins.

Who Wins: Rock beats scissors, scissors beats paper, and paper beats rock. Play again if both players have the same hand position.

Order words show the steps.

Directions to a Place

Direction words tell people which way to go.

To get to the theater, turn left out of the parking lot. Go four blocks past the school, to Citrus Street. Turn right. The theater is on the left. It's a yellow building with a big, white sign.

Describing words help someone find the correct place.

Directions for Making Something

The title tells the name of the food.

The ingredients and amounts of each thing you need are listed.

The steps are in order.

What's Cooking

Shrimp and Vegetable Stir Fry

Ingredients

3/4 pound shrimp

2 tablespoons canola oil

3/4 cup sliced mushrooms

1/2 cup sliced onion

1/2 cup sliced green pepper

1/4 cup chopped cabbage

1/4 cup teriyaki sauce

1 cup quick-cook brown rice

2 cups water

1. Boil water in a pot. Add the rice and cook for 20 minutes.
2. Heat oil in a large skillet.
3. Place vegetables in the skillet. Cook 5 minutes or until tender, stirring frequently.
4. Remove vegetables from the skillet.
5. Place shrimp in the skillet and cook 3 minutes.
6. Add vegetables back in with the shrimp.
7. Add teriyaki sauce and heat until the sauce is warm.
8. Spoon the stir fry over the rice. Serves 10.

E-mail

People write e-mail messages for many different reasons—to chat with friends and family, communicate with coworkers, sometimes even to apply for a job. Therefore, e-mails can be as informal as a note left on the fridge or as formal as a business letter—make sure you get the tone right!

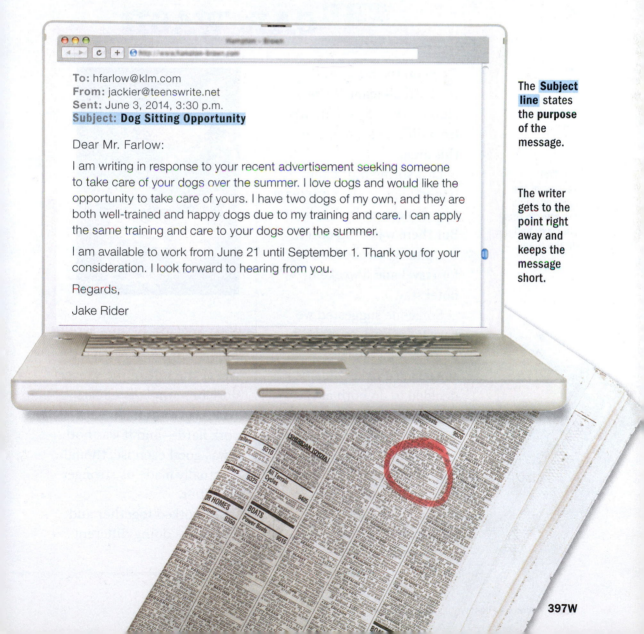

To: hfarlow@klm.com
From: jackier@teenswrite.net
Sent: June 3, 2014, 3:30 p.m.
Subject: Dog Sitting Opportunity

Dear Mr. Farlow:

I am writing in response to your recent advertisement seeking someone to take care of your dogs over the summer. I love dogs and would like the opportunity to take care of yours. I have two dogs of my own, and they are both well-trained and happy dogs due to my training and care. I can apply the same training and care to your dogs over the summer.

I am available to work from June 21 until September 1. Thank you for your consideration. I look forward to hearing from you.

Regards,

Jake Rider

The **Subject line** states the **purpose** of the message.

The writer gets to the point right away and keeps the message short.

Essays

Cause-and-Effect

A cause-and-effect essay tells why something happened. When you write a cause-and-effect essay, you may focus mainly on causes or mainly on effects, or you may discuss both.

THE CAR WASH

The introduction in column 1 introduces the topic.

The first section of the body explains the effects the car wash had on the team.

I'm on the Stingrays Softball team. We're a club team made up of girls from different schools in this area.

Last spring our team hoped to go to the club team tournament up in Pleasanton. But there was a big entry fee, plus we needed money for travel and a weekend hotel stay.

Someone suggested we have a car wash to make money. Someone else suggested a bake sale. We decided to do both at the same time, on two weekends.

Family members, coaches, and volunteers helped organize the event and prepare food for it. But we girls did all of the car washing!

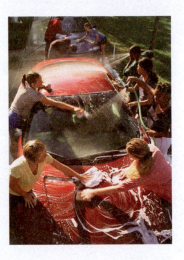

WHAT WE GOT, BESIDES MONEY

We had the car wash/bake sale at the side of the grocery store in town. Lots of cars came, so we really had to work hard—and it was hot! It was good exercise, though. It actually made us stronger and fitter.

We worked together and took turns doing different

tasks. This made us feel more like a team, which helped us play better later.

We sacrificed our free time for the car wash, but even before that we hardly ever went out to shop, eat, or see movies. We needed to save up for our trip. This experience made us realize what time and money are really worth.

We all love softball. After all we had to go through, we really appreciated that we got the chance to play it.

THE COMMUNITY IMPACT

People were generous. Some even paid extra, more than the price of the car wash or the food.

Because of the car wash, more people found out about our team and started coming to our games to support us. The stands were usually packed with fans!

It made us realize how much people care. We wanted to do well for all the fans who supported us, so we tried even harder to win.

I almost forgot. The "event" was a huge success. We made more than enough money for the trip, so we were able to buy some new equipment we badly needed.

We didn't win the tournament, but we came in second, which was amazing for a team just starting out. We had a great season. Now we can't wait for this season to begin. And it all started with a car wash!

The second section explains other effects of the car wash, including the effect on the community.

The conclusion leaves the reader with something to think about.

Essays, continued

Comparison-Contrast

A comparison-contrast essay describes how two things are alike and different. You may choose to describe one item completely before you move on the next. Or, you might organize your essay according to the specific points you're comparing.

RECREATION

TWO CHOICES, NO EXCUSES

The introduction names the **two things** being compared.

We all know we need to exercise. What can we do when school's out? Of course, if the weather's nice, you can always walk your dog, or play tennis or basketball on the outdoor courts at school. In our town, we can go to the **Community Center** or **Teen Center**, too. What's the difference, you ask?

The body has section heads and point-by-point organization.

INSIDE AND OUT

The Community Center has a large multi-purpose room, which serves as a gym, a dance hall, theater, and banquet room. You can play basketball or table tennis, or take karate, dance, and other classes there. There's another room with a pool table. Outside, there's a playground for younger kids, but older kids can exercise on the equipment, too.

Each section covers the main similarities and differences.

The Teen Center has a music room, and a pool table and table-tennis table in separate rooms.

Outdoors, there's one basketball hoop, a sand volleyball court, and the main feature: a huge skate park.

ATMOSPHERE

All ages are welcome at the community Center, so you never know who you might run into there. Special classes and activities are offered for kids ages 5–12 and senior citizens ages 55 and up.

The Community Center gym

Depending on the activity in the main room, it may be "quiet time" for kids or seniors, there may be music playing for a dance or singing class, or there may be a basketball game or table tennis tournament going on. <mark>In contrast</mark>, all the posters, bulletin-board information, games, and activities at the Teen Center are for kids ages 13–18. Music isn't permitted out in the skate park, but teens can share their music in the music room.

WHERE YOU SHOULD GO

The Community Center offers lots of activities, but not all at the same time. If you want to play a game on a wood court, check the schedule for basketball hours, or join the Youth Basketball League.

<mark>However</mark>, if you're a teen, and you just want to shoot baskets and hang out with kids your age, go to the Teen Center. It is always open after school and on weekends. If you want to skate, it's the *only* place to go.

These <mark>transition words</mark> show a contrast.

The conclusion sums up the major differences to help the reader make a decision.

The skate park is open to all ages.

Persuasive Essay

Writing as a citizen often involves writing to persuade. In a persuasive essay, you try to convince others to agree with your position on an important issue—and to take action.

What position does Mike take in his essay? What arguments does he use to try to convince his readers?

The opening provides background on the issue. States the writer's **position**.

The body gives **reasons** for the writer's position and provides supporting evidence.

End the Curfew Now
Mike Bozarth

The city officials in San Antonio believe that imposing a curfew on teenagers makes our city a better place. I disagree. Lifting the curfew would help local businesses by encouraging people to visit downtown stores at night. Furthermore, it would help make our city safer and reduce crime. It would also reward the city's hard-working students by allowing them to hang out with their friends at more comfortable times of day. Ending the curfew would improve life in San Antonio.

Ending the curfew would benefit our city's economy. Right now, our town is nearly empty at night because there aren't any teenagers around. But if the curfew were lifted, more people would spend time shopping downtown at night. That would help local businesses to grow and encourage stores to stay open longer. Longer store hours, in turn, would lead to better wages and more jobs available for retail workers.

Furthermore, although many people think the curfew reduces crime, it actually doesn't. In fact, since the curfew began last year, vandalism and theft have been on the

A view of San Antonio, Texas, at sunset ▶

rise. Officer Cheryl Williams of the San Antonio Police Department says that most of these crimes occur in quiet areas when no one's around. So, if more people were outside during the evenings, our town would be safer. People would think twice about committing a crime, since more potential witnesses, including teenagers, would be around to report it.

Finally, dropping the curfew would benefit the city's students. Right now, by the time they finish their homework and want to see their friends, it's too late to do anything. Some people say, "Why can't teenagers hang out downtown after school?" The problem with that suggestion is that it's really hot here in Texas. In the daytime, when it's 100 degrees outside and super sunny, people just want to stay in. At night, it's cooler, and the sun isn't hurting your skin. Students should be allowed to enjoy a nighttime social life.

The curfew law penalizes good kids and does nothing to benefit local businesses or to make our city safer. People should write to the mayor and urge her to lift the curfew on teens. It's the right thing to do.

Persuasive essays often include a response to an anticipated objection.

The conclusion includes a **summary** of the writer's ideas and a **call to action**.

Interview

An interview presents a conversation in question-and-answer format. When you write an interview, prepare your questions beforehand and record carefully the answers of the person you are interviewing.

Molding Troubled Kids into Future Chefs
An Interview with Neil Kleinberg
by Kathy Blake

Neil Kleinberg is the culinary-arts training manager at a tiny, 12-seat, takeout cafe operated by Covenant House, a shelter for runaway teenagers in New York City. Kleinberg says his job at Ezekiel's Cafe involves being father, mother, brother, counselor, teacher, and adviser, as well as a tough boss to the 17- to 21-year-old trainees who work with him.

Starts with background information about the person interviewed

How do you work as executive chef and culinary-arts trainer?

A place this small doesn't need an executive chef. My real job is teaching. Ezekiel's Cafe exists to give kids who live at Covenant House hands-on training in food service so they can get good jobs. Of course, when you say Covenant House, you know that these are kids with troubled pasts who need a lot of training in life skills, not just job skills. We screen the kids to try to get the ones who really have the desire to work in the industry, because to work this hard takes a lot of commitment.

When did you know you wanted to cook?

I always wanted to be a chef, and this was before it was trendy. When I was a kid growing up in Brooklyn, I'd go to Lundy's, which was the largest restaurant in the world at one time, and I'd think, "I want to be the chef here someday." That's why I tell the kids to be careful what they wish for! I got my wish, and it was really hard work. We did 1,500 dinners on Saturday nights. I essentially gave up my life for two years.

Was that immediately before you went to Ezekiel's?

Yes. I'd worked really hard my whole career; and when I left Lundy's, I needed some soul-searching time. So I took about a month and a half off and traveled to Australia, Thailand, and Europe. When I got back, I wanted to teach, but I still wanted to cook. I knew I'd always been good at directing people.

Lists the interviewer's questions and the interviewee's responses

Job Application

Many companies ask job candidates to fill out applications before they can be considered for a position. When you fill out a job application, make sure that the information is clear, accurate, and easy to read.

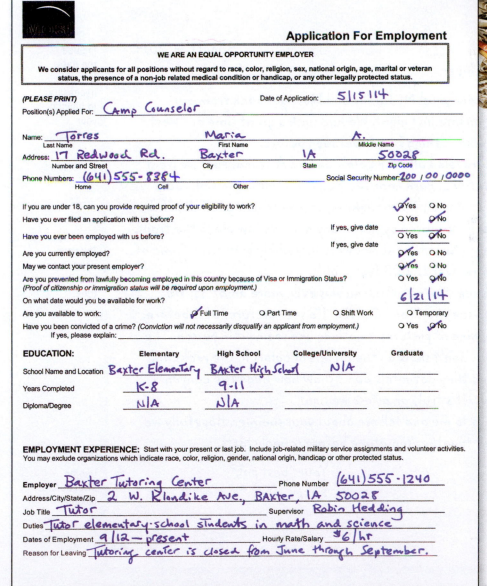

Application For Employment

WE ARE AN EQUAL OPPORTUNITY EMPLOYER

We consider applicants for all positions without regard to race, color, religion, sex, national origin, age, marital or veteran status, the presence of a non-job related medical condition or handicap, or any other legally protected status.

(PLEASE PRINT)

Position(s) Applied For: _Camp Counselor_   Date of Application: _5|15|14_

Name: _Torres_ (Last Name)   _Maria_ (First Name)   _A._ (Middle Name)

Address: _17 Redwood Rd._ (Number and Street) _Baxter_ (City) _IA_ (State) _50028_ (Zip Code)

Phone Numbers: _(641)555-8384_ (Home)   (Cell)   (Other)   Social Security Number: _200 / 00 / 0000_

If you are under 18, can you provide required proof of your eligibility to work? ☑Yes ○No

Have you ever filed an application with us before? ○Yes ☑No   If yes, give date _____

Have you ever been employed with us before? ○Yes ☑No   If yes, give date _____

Are you currently employed? ☑Yes ○No

May we contact your present employer? ☑Yes ○No

Are you prevented from lawfully becoming employed in this country because of Visa or Immigration Status? ○Yes ☑No
(Proof of citizenship or immigration status will be required upon employment.)

On what date would you be available for work? _6|21|14_

Are you available to work: ☑Full Time   ○Part Time   ○Shift Work   ○Temporary

Have you been convicted of a crime? *(Conviction will not necessarily disqualify an applicant from employment.)* ○Yes ☑No
    If yes, please explain: _____

EDUCATION:

	Elementary	High School	College/University	Graduate
School Name and Location	Baxter Elementary	Baxter High School	N/A	
Years Completed	K-8	9-11		
Diploma/Degree	N/A	N/A		

EMPLOYMENT EXPERIENCE: Start with your present or last job. Include job-related military service assignments and volunteer activities. You may exclude organizations which indicate race, color, religion, gender, national origin, handicap or other protected status.

Employer _Baxter Tutoring Center_   Phone Number _(641)555-1240_

Address/City/State/Zip _2 W. Klondike Ave., Baxter, IA 50028_

Job Title _Tutor_   Supervisor _Robin Hedding_

Duties _Tutor elementary-school students in math and science_

Dates of Employment _9/12 — present_   Hourly Rate/Salary _$6/hr_

Reason for Leaving _Tutoring center is closed from June through September._

Provides personal information

Writes "N/A" in any section that does not apply

Tells about past work experience

Letters

Friendly

In a friendly letter, you write to someone you know, using an informal tone. A friendly letter often tells about recent events in the writer's life.

August 31, 2014

Dear Amber,

How are you? My family and I just got back from our vacation late last night. We had such a great time out west. It was like nothing I had ever seen before.

We traveled all over Colorado and Arizona. First we went to a National Park near the Rocky Mountains in Colorado. We hiked all day until I thought my legs were going to fall off. I was really surprised by how many deer we saw along the trails. The mountains themselves were incredibly beautiful. Some of them are over 12,000 feet high!

Believe it or not, Arizona was even more amazing. We went to see the Grand Canyon. I'd seen pictures of it before, but looking at pictures is nothing like seeing it in person. The pictures don't show all the different colors in the rocks and soil, and they definitely don't show how huge the canyon really is. It's truly an awesome sight.

Write to me and tell me about your summer. Hopefully we can get together sometime before school starts.

Your "best pal,"
Kelsey

Include the date. It is not necessary to include your address.

Tell your news in an informal tone.

Use an affectionate closing.

Inquiry/Request

When you write a letter of inquiry or request, you ask for specific favors, materials, or information. Use business-letter format.

242 Crescent Ln.
Oceanside, CA 91147
July 14, 2014

Mr. Nelson Tatupu
Recreation Dept.
Fallbrook City Hall
27 Leatherneck St.
Fallbrook, CA 92648

Dear Mr. Tatupu:

I am writing to request information about your city's Youth Football team, the Rebels. I will be moving to Fallbrook soon, and I have heard that your community has an excellent Youth Football program. I would like to learn more about it.

Please send me more information about the program, including age and weight requirements for players. Please also send me an application to join the team.

Thank you very much for your time. I look forward to hearing from you.

Sincerely,

Robert Truitt

Robert Truitt

Includes your address as well as the date

States the reason for writing

Requests specific information or materials

Closes formally with full signature

Praise

A letter of praise expresses appreciation for the actions of a person. When you write to offer praise, be specific about why you are pleased.

37 Scotson Road
Parkville, OR 97086
October 6, 2014

Mr. Fred Simms
Parkville Youth Athletic League
1100 Carey Lane
Parkville, OR 97086

Dear Coach Simms:

   Thank you so much for your patience, caring, and hard work this summer. Your efforts have made my teammates and me into better players and made this year's baseball season one to remember.

   When the season started, most of us didn't know each other, and we didn't work together very well. In only a few weeks, you brought us together and taught us how to play as a team. Under your coaching, my skills greatly improved. Even when I made a bad play in the field, you didn't get upset. Instead, you taught me how I could learn from my mistakes and do better next time.

   Thanks again for making this baseball season so memorable. I can't wait to play on your team again next year!

Sincerely,
Tony Lopez
Tony Lopez

Tells why
the person
mattered to
the writer

Provides
specific
details

Problem-Solving

Consumers write problem-solving letters to inform a company or organization about a problem. State your complaint and explain how the problem can be solved.

714 Almond Road
Fresno, CA 93707
August 1, 2014

Mr. Gary Zimmer, Chairman
Green Grass Teen Craft Fair Committee
43 Howard Avenue
Fresno, CA 93707

Dear Mr. Zimmer:

On June 23, 2014, I paid to reserve a table to sell my handmade jewelry at the upcoming Green Grass Teen Craft Fair. However, I recently read on your Web site that the date of the fair has been moved forward a week. Unfortunately, I will be out of town during the festival's new date, and I will not be able to attend.

I am enclosing a copy of my approved reservation application and my receipt. I would like you to send me a refund for the price of my reservation.

Thank you for your time and attention. Please feel free to call me at 559-555-6784 with any questions.

Sincerely,

Beth Vaden
Beth Vaden

Politely states the complaint

Tells how the writer wants the problem resolved

Often includes contact information

Literary Response

A response to literature is similar to a literary analysis, but it focuses more on the writer's personal, individual reactions to the work. You still need to support your response with concrete details from the text.

When I Was Puerto Rican
by Esmeralda Santiago

Reviewed by Jennifer K.

States opinion and summarizes the book

This is a delightfully woven story of immense passion and unconquerable spirit. In this extraordinary autobiography, Santiago, an immigrant to New York from rural Puerto Rico, tells the story of her trials and triumphs, defeats and heartaches, in vivid detail.

Santiago grew up in what her *mami* calls "savage" conditions, dutifully obeying her parents as they constantly moved. Her greatest relocation occurred when a "metal bird" flew her, her mother, and two of her siblings to the rough city of New York. . . .

Using words as her medium, Santiago paints a beautiful picture of her life. I smelled the spices and herbs emanating from the special Puerto Rican dishes her *mami* prepared. Mesmerized, I watched as her *abuela* delicately stitched her needlework. . . . Santiago writes with such clarity and fierceness that it is impossible for any person not to see, feel, and understand what she went through in her remarkable journey.

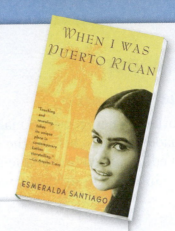

Santiago's unique style is easy to follow. When I read the book, I was immediately hooked and could not stop until I read the last word. The stories are interesting and full of insight. Santiago addresses fears and trials of all people. I especially related to her conflicts with her cultural identity. Anyone who has lived in between two cultures can relate to her story. Santiago wrote, "When I returned to Puerto Rico after living in New York for seven years, I was told I was no longer Puerto Rican. . . . In writing the book I wanted to get back to that feeling of Puertoricanness I had before I came here. Its title reflects who I was then, and asks, who am I today?"

Santiago's book provides a sense of hope. The narrator is transformed from a confused and frightened child into a spirited woman full of courage and hope. Her success in life—acceptance into New York City's High School of Performing Arts and graduating from Harvard with highest honors—proves she is capable of achieving her dreams.

Santiago's strong will and courage are evident throughout her story. *When I Was Puerto Rican* describes the remarkable journey that her life has been.

Describes the writer's emotional response to the book

Newspaper

Editorial

An editorial is a newspaper or magazine article that is written to persuade people to believe the same way you do. When you write an editorial, tell how you feel about something. That's your opinion. Give facts to support your opinion.

Opinions about the subject are in the first paragraph.

Next, facts expand on the opinion.

February 6, 2014

Save the Gentle Manatees

Our manatees need protection from speeding boats. If we don't keep boat speeds slow, more and more of these gentle beasts will die.

A few members of the City Council want to pass a law that will increase boat speeds in some waterways where manatees live. When boats go too fast, the manatees can't get out of the way of the dangerous boat propellers in time.

We need to tell the City Council that saving the manatees is important to us. Increasing boat speeds is not. You can take action no matter where you live. Call, write, fax, or e-mail City Council members. Ask them to support protection for manatees and their home, and to *keep existing slow speed zones in our waters*! Any type of letter or call helps!

The end tells what people can do to help, and states your opinion again.

News Article

A news article tells about a recent event. It covers the "5 Ws": who, what, where, when, and why. A news article uses an "inverted pyramid" structure: it states the main points in the beginning, and then provides less important details in later paragraphs.

EVACUATION ROUTE

Tropical Storm Florence Forms in Atlantic

Weather system intensifies but poses no immediate threat to land

States the main point

MIAMI, FL—Tropical Storm Florence formed today in the open Atlantic, becoming the sixth named storm of the 2014 hurricane season.

Tells what happened and when

Florence had top sustained winds near 40 mph, 1 mph over the 39 mph threshold for a tropical storm, and it was expected to slowly intensify over the next few days, according to the National Hurricane Center.

Tells where and who might be affected

Its tropical storm force winds extended 115 miles from its center, but posed no immediate threat to land.

At 11 a.m., the storm was centered 935 miles east of the Lesser Antilles and was moving west at about 12 mph, forecasters said.

Florence follows Tropical Storm Ernesto, which was briefly the season's first hurricane before hitting Florida and North Carolina last week as a tropical storm.

At least nine deaths have been attributed to Ernesto, and the aftereffects were still being felt early today. About 75,000 people remained without power in New York's Westchester County.

Last year's Atlantic storm season set a record with 28 named storms and 15 hurricanes.

Often connects the story to a broader subject

May include photos and captions

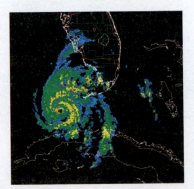

Radar image of hurricane approaching west coast of Florida

Classified Ads

Classified ads are short notices that are classified, or put into groups. For example, the "New Today" section groups those items that are appearing for the first time. Look at these ads.

Help Wanted

For Sale

Wanted to Buy

New Today

DOGGY DAY CARE: Wanted dog lover w/time to care for energetic dog 2-3 days per week. 555-1759, lv. msg.

UNICYCLE: Brand new! We can't ride it! $80 OBO. Call 555-2521.

WANTED: Used longboard, 8 ft. or longer. Call Marc 555-8653.

People pay for classified ads by the line, so they use abbreviations.

Abbreviation	Meaning
w/	with
lv. msg.	leave message
obo.	or best offer
ft.	feet

Personal Narrative

When you write a personal narrative, you tell a story about something that happened to you. Because the story is about you, you'll use the words *I*, *me*, and *my* a lot.

Urff

The **beginning** tells what the event was.

One afternoon, two summers ago, I was walking on the beach. I was looking out at the bay, daydreaming.

Suddenly, something pushed me on my chest, and I fell back a step. A big, hairy dog had just put wet paw prints on my shirt! "Urff!" he barked playfully. Dogs are always romping on the beach. I figured his owner was nearby. I petted the dog. Then I started to walk again.

The writer tells her **feelings** about the event.

The **middle** gives details about the event.

After a few steps, I noticed the dog was walking beside me. "Go on, now," I said. I tried to gently shoo him away with my hand. I looked around for his owner, but no one seemed to be calling for him.

This happened a couple more times, but he kept following me. He followed me as I left the beach and walked home. He followed me into my house and room, where he slept that night by my bed.

The writer gives **details** that describe what happens.

The **end** tells what finally happened.

The next day, my mom made me take him to the shelter. I checked on him after a month. No one had claimed him. So I took him home. (Mom said, "OK," after much begging by me.) And Urff has been my best friend ever since.

Play

A play is a story that is acted on stage. Real people, or actors, pretend to be characters in the story.

The actors perform the play *Annie* **on stage**.

The **audience** watches the play in a **theater**.

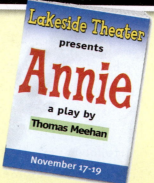

The author of a play is called a **playwright**. The playwright writes the script.

The actor's part in a play is called a **role**.
The girl is performing the role of Annie.

This **scene**, or part of the play,
takes place in the city. The
scenery shows what this place
looks like. The scenery can
change between scenes.

The actors wear different **costumes** to look
like their characters. **Props**, or objects on
stage, help the action seem more real.

Play, continued

You can turn any story into a play. Follow these steps.

1. Start with a story. Make one up or choose one from a book.

THE LEGEND
OF THE
CHINESE ZODIAC

In ancient times, the Jade Emperor wanted to name each year in the twelve-year cycle after an animal. He couldn't decide which animals to honor, however. He invited all the animals on earth to participate in a race. The first twelve to finish the race would each have a year named for them. The rat won the race; the ox was second. The tiger, rabbit, dragon, snake, horse, sheep, monkey, rooster, dog, and boar were the next ten animals to cross the finish line. The Jade Emperor named a year for the animals in the order they finished.

2. Turn the story into a script. The script names the characters and the setting. It describes what the characters say and do.

THE LEGEND OF THE CHINESE ZODIAC   19

ACT TWO

The Race

CHARACTERS: *the Jade Emperor, rat, ox, tiger, rabbit, dragon, snake, horse, sheep, monkey, rooster, dog, boar*

SETTING: Long ago, in front of the Jade Emperor's palace. There is a starting line on the ground. The Jade Emperor is telling all the animals the rules of the race.

JADE EMPEROR *(loudly, to get everyone's attention):* Listen! Listen! We are going to start the race soon. First, I want to explain the course and the rules.

BOAR *(raising his hand):* Will we be allowed to stop for water along the way?

JADE EMPEROR: *Please let me tell you the rules of the whole race before you ask questions. (pointing at the line on the ground) This is the starting line. You must have all of your toes behind this line.*

SNAKE *(raising his tail):* What if you don't have toes?

JADE EMPEROR *(Surprised):* Good point.

Name each character and write the **dialogue**, or the words the characters say.

Use **stage directions** to tell how the characters should say lines or move around.

3. Perform the play. Choose people to play the characters. Have them use the script to practice. Then put on the play.

Poetry

Rhymed Verse

Rhymed verse follows a set rhyme scheme and often uses a regular rhythm as well.

Stopping By Woods on a Snowy Evening

by Robert Frost

Whose woods these are I think I know.	*a*
His house is in the village, though;	*a*
He will not see me stopping here	*b*
To watch his woods fill up with snow.	*a*
My little horse must think it queer	*b*
To stop without a farmhouse near	*b*
Between the woods and frozen lake	*c*
The darkest evening of the year.	*b*
He gives his harness bells a shake	*c*
To ask if there is some mistake.	*c*
The only other sound's the sweep	*d*
Of easy wind and downy flake.	*c*
The woods are lovely, dark, and deep,	*d*
But I have promises to keep,	*d*
And miles to go before I sleep,	*d*
And miles to go before I sleep.	*d*

This poem has an interesting rhyme pattern, shown by the letters.

Free Verse

Free verse has no fixed rhythm and uses irregular rhyme or no rhyme at all. However, free verse often includes other poetic devices, such as repetition, imagery, or figurative language.

MOTHER

by Maya Angelou

During the years when you knew nothing
And I knew everything, I loved you still.
Condescendingly of course,
From my high perch
Of teenage wisdom.
I grew older and
Was stunned to find
How much knowledge you had gleaned
And so quickly.

Poetry, continued

Haiku

A haiku is a brief poem that focuses on a single image or emotion. The haiku form originated in Japan and often describes images found in nature. The form traditionally uses three lines with five, seven, and five syllables, respectively.

by the noonflower
a rice-pounder cools himself:
a sight so moving
                    —*Bashō*

the cathedral bell
is shaking a few snowflakes
from the morning air
                    —*Nicholas Virgilio*

heat before the storm:
a fly disturbs the quiet
of the empty store
                    —*Nicholas Virgilio*

A bitter morning:
sparrows sitting together
without any necks.
                    —*James Hackett*

Concrete Poem

A concrete poem is written so the words make a picture of what they are describing.

(a poem to be read from the bottom up)

this great oak

into the coming night

its capillary ends

its garbled limbs

against the hazy light

now stretches

to stand winter and the wind

from wells far
underground

with strength

girthed itself

upon a trunk

upon a branch

upon a sprig

upon a leaf

spring by spring

a century ago

from under land

this tree unrolled

Simple as a flower

–Dawn L. Watkins

Procedure

A procedure is a list of steps that must be followed to complete a task. When you write a procedure, clearly describe, in order, what needs to be done.

Headings help organize the instructions.

Gives clear, specific, step-by-step instructions

PROCEDURE FOR HOUSE SITTER

When Entering

Open door and close it quickly. Rufus will try to escape if the door is left open!

In the Morning

1. Give Rufus fresh water and dry kibble.
2. Play with Rufus and let him outside for $\frac{1}{2}$ hour.
3. Water plants on kitchen windowsill.
4. Feed fish with flakes next to tank.
5. Bring in the morning's newspaper and leave on kitchen table.

In the Afternoon

1. Bring in the day's mail and leave on kitchen table.
2. Feed Rufus $\frac{1}{2}$ can of dog food.
3. Play with Rufus and walk him for at least 20 minutes.
4. Check the tomato plants and place any ripe tomatoes on the kitchen table.

When Leaving

1. Close windows.
2. Turn off lights and fans.
3. Don't forget to lock the door and deadbolt.

Emergency Phone Numbers

Mr. & Mrs. Rhoades (cell): (212) 555-7834
Dr. Sternberg (vet): (212) 555-4700
Annandale Police Dept.: (212) 555-2299

Story

Writers use their imaginations and make up different types of stories to entertain their readers. They decide where a story will happen, who will be in it, and what will happen.

Parts of a Story

Every story happens in a place at some time. That place and time are called the **setting**.

The people or animals in a story are called the **characters**. In most stories, the characters speak. Their words are called **dialogue**.

Saturday morning in our apartment

Come by this afternoon to see if you have won.

Anything is possible, but don't count on winning the bike, Alex.

woman from the bike store

Alex and his mom

The things that happen in a story are the events. The order, or **sequence of events**, is called the **plot**.

1. Mom filled out a form for the bike drawing.

2. We went to the bike store.

MOUNTAIN BIKE WINNER Alex Sanchez

3. I saw a huge sign that said I won!

Realistic Fiction

Some stories have characters that seem like people you know. They happen in a place that seems real. These stories are called realistic fiction because they tell about something that could happen in real life.

Another Saturday Morning

The **characters** are like people you know.

The events in the **plot** could really happen.

Mom and I were eating breakfast Saturday morning when a woman knocked on the door to our apartment.

"Hello," she said. "I'm from Bikes and Stuff. We're having a drawing for a mountain bike. Would you be interested in signing up?" Mom agreed and filled out a form for me.

"Come by this afternoon to see if you have won," the woman said.

"Anything is possible, but don't count on winning the bike, Alex," Mom said when the woman left.

So I forgot all about the bike and started reading my new book. Before I knew it, Mom came in the room and said it was time to go to the bike store.

When I walked in, the first thing I saw was a huge sign that said: *Mountain bike winner: Alex Sanchez!* I couldn't believe it!

They put my name and photograph in the newspaper in an ad for Bikes and Stuff. That was the day I learned anything is possible on a Saturday morning.

The **setting** is in a time and a place you know.

The **dialogue** sounds real.

Historical Fiction

Historical fiction is a story that takes place in the past during a certain time in history. Some of the characters may be real people, and some of the events really happened. Even so, the story is fiction because the writer made it up.

The characters act and talk like the people in that time did.

January 13, 1778

Today when we returned the laundry to the army headquarters, I was astounded to see only General Washington in the parlor, no other officers. I know not where Billy Lee was. The General was sharpening his quill with his penknife. He looked up at us and smiled.

"Thank you, Abigail. Thank you, Elisabeth," he said.

I curtsied, unable to speak. How did he know our names?

He looked at us with kind eyes—they're gray-blue—then he returned to his pen and paper. Mrs. Hewes says Mr. Washington writes at least fifteen letters a day, mostly to Congress. He is pleading for food, clothing, and other supplies for the soldiers, she told us.

It can have **real people** and **made-up characters** who lived during that time.

Fantasy

A fantasy is a story that tells about events that couldn't possibly happen in real life. Here is part of a fantasy about some children playing a very unusual board game.

JUMANJI | Chris Van Allsburg   15

At home, the children spread the game out on a card table. It looked very much like the games they already had.

"Here," said Judy, handing her brother the dice, "you go first."

Peter casually dropped the dice from his hand.

"Seven," said Judy.

Peter moved his piece to the seventh square.

"'Lion attacks, move back two spaces,'" read Judy.

"Gosh, how exciting," said Peter, in a very unexcited voice. As he reached for his piece he looked up at his sister. She had a look of absolute horror on her face.

"Peter," she whispered, "turn around very, very slowly."

The boy turned in his chair. He couldn't believe his eyes. Lying on the piano was a lion, staring at Peter and licking his lips. The lion roared so loud it knocked Peter right off his chair. The big cat jumped to the floor. Peter was up on his feet, running through the house with the lion a whisker's length behind. He ran upstairs and dove under a bed. The lion tried to squeeze under, but got his head stuck. Peter scrambled out, ran from the bedroom, and slammed the door behind him. He stood in the hall with Judy, gasping for breath.

"I don't think," said Peter in between gasps of air, "that I want . . . to play . . . this game . . . anymore."

"But we have to," said Judy as she helped Peter back downstairs. "I'm sure that's what the instructions mean. The lion won't go away until one of us wins the game."

The characters can be like real people.

Some of the events could never happen in real life.

Web Site

A Web site can be personal or professional and can be about any subject. Web sites often include images, sound files, video, and links to related pages or sites.

As a Web-site "writer" you have to think "in time."
What happens when you click a link?
How do you get back "home" after listening to a song?

Workplace and Consumer Resources

Instruction Manual

Most products come with directions, often in the form of an **instruction manual**, or booklet. The instruction manual usually describes the product's parts and features and tells how to use the product.

Some products, especially more complicated ones, come with two sets of instructions. A short **quick-start guide** may give you the most essential information, so you can start using the product and its basic features right away. The quick-start guide may be as short as a single page (sometimes a big page!).

The complete instruction manual is sometimes called a **user manual**. A good instruction manual covers everything you might want to know about the product, both right away and later on.

USER MANUAL

LIGHTNING STAR
GAME SYSTEM

USER MANUAL

CONTENTS

1: LightningStar 3 Parts and Features
3: Setting Up Your LightningStar 3
4: Loading and Playing Games
7: Using the Controller: Basics
9: Using the Controller: Advanced Play
11: Multiplayer Games
13: Online Play
15: Wireless Play (requires accessories sold separately)
16: Troubleshooting
18: Important Warnings and Safeguards
Back Cover: Customer Support

LIGHTNING STAR

GAME SYSTEM

QUICK-START GUIDE

Set-Up

IIn order to start the LightningStar game system, first insert the accompanying cd-rom into your computer. The program will automatically install the necessary software onto your computer. Follow the steps in the Installation Wizard. Your system may need some additional support software to effectively run your LightningStar game system. If this is the case, the system will automatically link you to the site to download the appropriate software for free, as long as you have an active internet connection.

Once you have completed the steps, you will be ready to calibrate, or set up, your LightningStar joystick. Directions on how to calibrate your joystick will follow installation.

Basic Play

LightningStar is a game in which you will explore various solar systems to hunt for life on other planets. Once life is located, you will help the civilizations move forward by helping them develop new tools and methods. For example, in the solar system for Star X587, the planet Zevob has a population that has not yet discovered farming. Your task is to teach the Zevobians about farming, as well as to help the population develop tools to stop the invading Nostrarians who are from a nearby planet.

Play continues until populations from all of the planets under your supervision have developed useful tools and are no longer at war with others.

Tips

The following tips will help you have the most successful journey through your stars and planets:

- Use the tutorial to walk you through your first planet encounter.
- You can always ask the planet guide to walk you through a difficult task.
- You must solve the problems of the planet you are on before you can travel to another

planet or solar system.
- Multiple planets in a solar system may have life. Be sure to check all of the planets before moving to the next solar system.

Troubleshooting Checklist

LightningStar game system is a quick-installation game system. If you are unable to start or control your game system, check the following:

- Make sure that the joystick is plugged into an active USB port and is turned on.
- Check that the system successfully installed missing software components during the installation process. To ensure this has been done properly, re-install the CD-ROM and go through the installation process once more. If the system sends you an error message for any necessary software, check if your computer has the correct operating system needed to play LightningStar.
- Be sure to calibrate your joystick and set the various controls so that you know what each button does. Improperly calibrated joysticks can have control problems during a game.
- For more troubleshooting help, please visit our Web site or call us at 1-800-555-3939.

Workplace and Consumer Resources, continued

Warranty

When you buy a product, you hope it will keep working the way it's supposed to. But what if it doesn't? Most products come with a written **warranty** that states what the manufacturer will do if something goes wrong. It's a good idea to check out the warranty before you buy the product, so you'll know what kind of protection you're getting.

A warranty will usually spell out the following:

• What is (and is not) covered

• How long the warranty period lasts

• What the consumer needs to do to take advantage of the warranty.

WARRANTY

LIMITED WARRANTY FOR THE LIGHTNINGSTAR GAME SYSTEM

LightningStar warrants to the original purchaser that the LightningStar 3 game system shall be free of defects in material and workmanship for a period of one (1) year from the original date of purchase (the "Warranty Period"). LightningStar will, at its sole discretion, repair or replace a defective system returned during the warranty period in accordance with the instructions below. No other warranty is expressed or implied.

Tells what the warranty covers and how long the warranty period lasts

This warranty shall not apply if the game system has been damaged, misused, or altered after purchase. This warranty does not cover accessories purchased separately.

Tells what is *not* covered

To arrange for service under this warranty, visit the Customer Service section of our Web site or call the toll-free number listed in the User Manual. You will need to have the product serial number available when you contact us. You will also need a copy of your original purchase receipt when you send the system in for repair. You are responsible for shipping charges to our repair facility. LightningStar is not responsible for units lost or damaged in transit to or from our repair facility.

Tells what to do if you need to use the warranty

Employment Advertisements

When it's time to get your first job, an important source of information for you will be the **Classified** section of your local newspaper. Employers place advertisements for workers they need to hire in this section. By reading an **employment advertisement** carefully, you can find out details about the job, including hours, tasks, qualifications, and how to apply. Look for each of these pieces of information in the ad below.

Retail Sales

Out of This World gift shop seeks P/T person (eves and weekends) to assist customers as they browse and buy. Our one-of-a kind shop offers a wide range of space-oriented items, and we seek someone who is enthusiastic about our products. Good math skills, friendly personality, and dependability required. Min. wage with attractive sales bonus. Apply in person at City Mall, Saturdays (9:00 a.m.–noon).

Most advertisers use standard abbreviations. *P/T* stands for *part-time*.

Employment Contract

Once you are hired for a job, you might be asked to sign an **employment contract**. This is a legal document, so you will want to read it very carefully before you sign it. The purpose of an employment contract is to ensure that you and your employer agree on the terms of your employment. It usually states when your employment begins, what the expectations are for you on the job, what your starting pay will be, and what special benefits (such as paid vacation) you will receive. A sample is provided below.

EMPLOYMENT AGREEMENT

This Employment Agreement (hereinafter "Agreement") is entered into on December 5, 2014, by and between The Daily Herald (The "Employer") and Starry Jackson (The "Employee").

Employer and Employee each agree with the other as follows:

1. **EMPLOYMENT**   Employer has agreed to employ Employee for the position of Newspaper Delivery Person, and Employee has agreed to accept such employment. Employee's duties shall include collating and delivering papers and collecting payment from customers.

2. **TERM**   The term of this Agreement shall begin December 6, 2014, and shall continue until terminated in accordance with the terms set forth below.

3. **COMPENSATION**   For services provided, Employer shall employ Employee at a rate of $8.25/hour. The Employee shall be paid weekly. The remuneration is subject to all required withholdings, paid in accordance with Employer's regular payroll policies and procedures.

4. **PROBATION**   The probationary period is 3 months.

5. **VACATION**   Vacation time can be taken at the employee's discretion, with notice to The Daily Herald.

6. **HOURS OF WORK**   The Employee agrees that the working hours are flexible with a minimum of 15 hours per week.

7. **CONDUCT**   Employee agrees that during the time of employment with Employer, the Employee shall adhere to all rules, regulations, and policies established by the Employer for the conduct of its employees. Employee agrees to devote his/her full time, attention, and energies to the business of the Employer.

8. **TERMINATION**   The employment of the Employee by the Employer may be terminated by either the Employer or the Employee upon the giving of 14 days prior written notice to the other party. The employment of the Employee by the Employer may be immediately terminated upon the occurrence of any of the following events:

   a. In the event the Employee shall willfully and continuously fail or refuse to comply with the standards, rules, regulations, and policies established by the Employer.

   b. In the event the Employee shall be guilty of fraud, dishonesty, or any other misconduct in the performance of the Employee's duties on behalf of the Employer.

   c. In the event the Employee shall fail to perform any provision of this Agreement to be performed by the Employee.

9. **GOVERNANCE**   This Agreement shall be governed by the Laws of the State of Florida. The parties hereby indicate by their signatures below that they have read and agree with the terms and conditions of this Agreement in its entirety.

Employer: Employee:

_____   _____
Signature   Signature

_____   _____
Name/Title   Printed Name

_____   _____
Date   Date

ONE OF THE HARDEST PARTS of writing is organizing your ideas. You can use graphic organizers and idea organizers to plan and organize what you are going to write. Idea organizers can help you plan how to present your ideas. They help the reader (and the writer—you!) follow your thinking process. You can use graphic organizers to narrow your writing topic or to remember the sequence of your ideas before writing.

Find out more about the different kinds of graphic organizers and idea organizers.

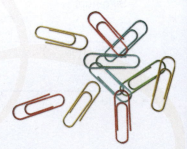

Writing ORGANIZERS

Writing Organizers

Logical Order

Logical order makes the most sense when you want to group ideas that have something in common, or you want to organize them by importance.

Topic and Main Idea Diagram

A diagram like this can help you plan the focus for each paragraph in an essay.

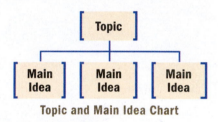

Topic and Main Idea Chart

Main Idea and Detail Diagrams

For each paragraph in the essay, try one of these diagrams to plan the details you'll include.

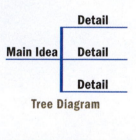

Tree Diagram

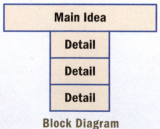

Block Diagram

Category Chart

Try sorting information into groups or categories.

Carlos and Me

Category

Helped me	Caused me problems
helped me pass math class	was rude to my parents
convinced me to try out for the football team	never shows up on time
lent me money to buy concert tickets	went to the concert with someone else

Category Chart

Example

Hypothesis-and-Results Chart

You could use a chart like this to explain the results of a survey.

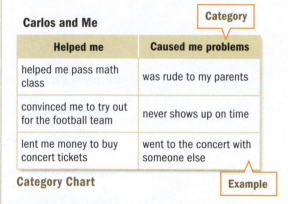

Question:	Hypothesis:
What percentage of teens at Washington High School sometimes lie to their best friends?	Most teenagers at Washington High lie to their best friends occasionally.
	Data:
	50 teens surveyed
	30 have lied about minor things (60%)
	5 have lied about something important (10%)
	15 always tell their best friends the truth (30%)
Conclusions:	**Observations:**
70% of teens sometimes lie to their best friends.	Most teens will not lie to their best friends about something important.

Hypothesis-and-Results Chart

Outline

You can also use an outline to help you organize your ideas logically. List the main ideas and supporting details, using roman numerals, capital letters, numbers, and lowercase letters.

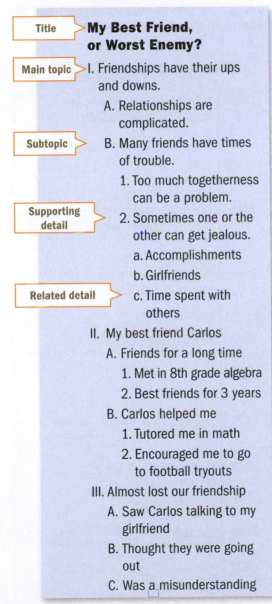

Title

My Best Friend, or Worst Enemy?

Main topic

I. Friendships have their ups and downs.

   A. Relationships are complicated.

Subtopic

   B. Many friends have times of trouble.

     1. Too much togetherness can be a problem.

Supporting detail

     2. Sometimes one or the other can get jealous.

      a. Accomplishments

      b. Girlfriends

Related detail

      c. Time spent with others

II. My best friend Carlos

   A. Friends for a long time

     1. Met in 8th grade algebra

     2. Best friends for 3 years

   B. Carlos helped me

     1. Tutored me in math

     2. Encouraged me to go to football tryouts

III. Almost lost our friendship

   A. Saw Carlos talking to my girlfriend

   B. Thought they were going out

   C. Was a misunderstanding

Outline

Order-of-Importance Diagrams

Sometimes you'll want to organize your ideas by how important they are.

1. You can organize from most important to least important.

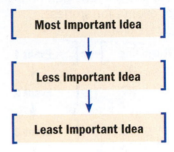

2. Or, you can organize from least important to most important.

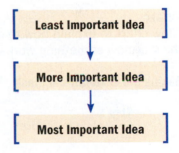

Chronological Order

To tell about events in the order in which they happen or to explain the steps in a process, use chronological order.

Sequence Chain

A diagram like this one can help you plan plot events for stories.

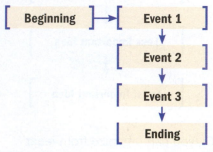

[**Beginning**] → [**Event 1**]

↓

[**Event 2**]

↓

[**Event 3**]

↓

[**Ending**]

Sequence Chain

Flow Chart

Use a flow chart to explain how to do something or how something works.

Making a 3-D Theatrical Mask

Step 1
A cast of the actor's face is made.

↓

Step 2
The cast is then used to shape the features of the mask.

↓

Step 3
This new character's "face" is then used to make a mold for the final mask.

↓

Step 4
Latex rubber is poured into the mold to create the mask.

↓

Step 5
The mask is then painted and attached to the actor with a special glue.

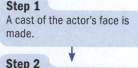

Flow Chart

Time Line

Use a time line to help you keep track of when important events happened.

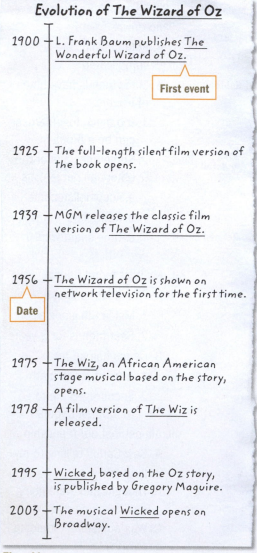

Evolution of *The Wizard of Oz*

1900 — L. Frank Baum publishes *The Wonderful Wizard of Oz.*

> **First event**

1925 — The full-length silent film version of the book opens.

1939 — MGM releases the classic film version of *The Wizard of Oz.*

1956 — The Wizard of Oz is shown on network television for the first time.

> **Date**

1975 — *The Wiz*, an African American stage musical based on the story, opens.

1978 — A film version of *The Wiz* is released.

1995 — *Wicked*, based on the Oz story, is published by Gregory Maguire.

2003 — The musical *Wicked* opens on Broadway.

Time Line

Spatial Order

For a description, try using spatial order to tell what you see—from left to right, from near to far, or from top to bottom, for example.

Picture Diagram

Try labeling a picture—or drawing one—to show how you'll organize details for a description.

Picture Diagram

beat-up hat

plaster nose

rope belt

hay stuffing

busted shoes

Circle Diagram

Whether you want to describe an area from the inside to the outside or vice versa, try using a circle diagram to show your plan.

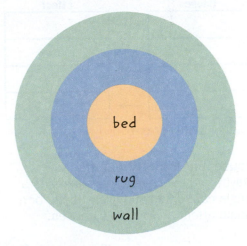

bed

rug

wall

Circle Diagram

Showing Causes and Effects

When you write about causes and effects, you explain what happens and why.

Cause-and-Effect Chart

Sometimes a cause leads to a single effect. You might want to show each cause and its effect in a chart.

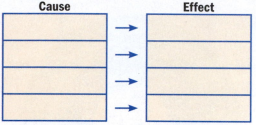

Cause-and-Effect Chart

Cause-and-Effect Diagrams

Maybe what you want to explain has a single cause and multiple effects, or a single effect and multiple causes.

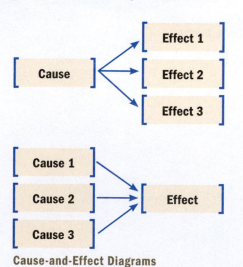

Cause-and-Effect Diagrams

Cause-and-Effect Chain

Sometimes causes and effects form a chain of linked events. One event causes the next event to happen.

Event 1:
I lose my cell phone.

Event 2:
I cannot call my friend, so I can't give her directions to the party.

Event 3:
Without directions, my friend gets lost. She is late for the party.

Event 4:
My friend misses the music and dancing.

Cause-and-Effect Chain

Showing Comparisons

Plan what you'll say about how people, places, or things are alike or different. It'll be easy to see the comparisons if you show your ideas side by side.

T Chart

Use a T Chart to help you compare and contrast specific characteristics of a topic.

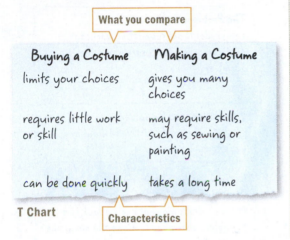

T Chart

Venn Diagram

A Venn diagram uses overlapping circles to compare and contrast.

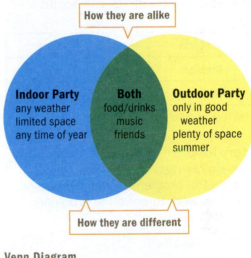

Venn Diagram

Showing Goals and Outcomes

Whether you want to share your own personal accomplishments or create a story about a fictional character, try organizing your ideas by goal and outcome.

Goal	Actions	Obstacles	Outcome
I wanted to get the lead role in the school play.	I found out the date and time of the audition.	I had a cold on the day of the audition.	My friend got the lead role. I got a minor part.
	I prepared a monologue.	I kept coughing during my monologue.	
	I attended the audition and performed the monologue.	My best friend tried out for the lead, too.	

Goal-and-Outcome Chart

What stands in the way?

Showing Problems and Solutions

Both fiction and nonfiction often present problems and solutions.
In your writing, organize the ideas by first telling why something is a
problem and then how the problem is or can be solved.

Problem-and-Solution Chart

A chart like this one works best for
nonfiction in which there are several
problems, each with its own solution.

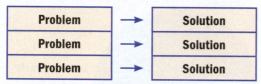

Problem-and-Solution Chart

Story Map

Use a story map to show your
characters' problems, or conflicts, and
how they work to solve the problems.

> **Title:** Finding a Place
> **Author:** Jasmine Porter
>
> **Characters:** Cathy, Cathy's German host
> family, Anke, other students
> **Setting:** Munich, Germany
>
> **Problem:** Cathy feels lonely.
> ↓
> **Event 1:** Cathy signs up for a study-abroad
> program and goes to Germany.
> **Event 2:** She has trouble fitting in because she
> doesn't speak German.
> **Event 3:** She meets and befriends a German
> student named Anke.
> ↓
> **Solution:** Anke helps Cathy improve her
> German and meet more people.

Story Map

Essay Map

For an essay, complete a map to help
you organize and explain your ideas.

> **The Problem**
> Few students are submitting works for
> publication in the literary magazine The
> Scribbler

↓

> **Why It Needs to Be Solved**
> The Scribbler can't survive without any
> work to publish.

↓

> **The Solution**
> Many students may not know about The
> Scribbler, so we need to make the magazine
> more visible.

↓

> **How the Solution Works**
> The staff will
> • add a page about The Scribbler to the
>   Fowler High School Web site.
> • put a notice in the school newspaper.
> • ask English teachers to let students submit
>   work to The Scribbler for extra credit.

↓

> **Conclusion**
> If more students know about the literary
> magazine, there'll be an increase in the
> number of submissions.

Problem-and-Solution Essay Map

Showing Your Position

When you write to argue, you want to convince people to agree with you. So, to be sure you've included all the important and persuasive details, use a chart or a diagram to plan what you'll say.

Opinion Chart

You can use an opinion chart to organize the reasons and supporting evidence for your opinion.

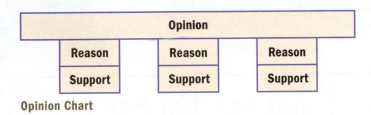

Opinion Chart

Position-and-Support Diagram

Sometimes people will disagree with you. When this happens, you need to plan how to respond to their objections with rebuttals, or counterclaims.

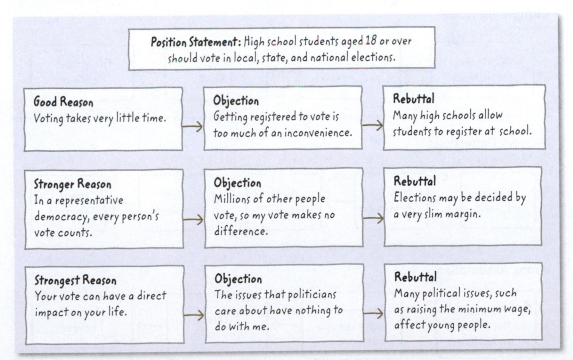

Position-and-Support Diagram

Idea Organizers

Choose an Organizer

Idea organizers can help you plan how to present your ideas. They help the reader (and the writer—you!) follow your thinking process.

The Story of My Thinking

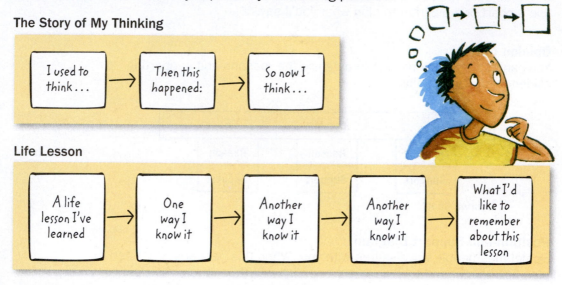

Life Lesson

Comparing Notes

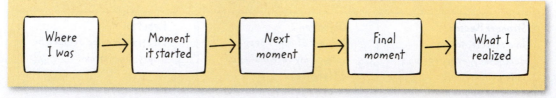

Memory Reflections

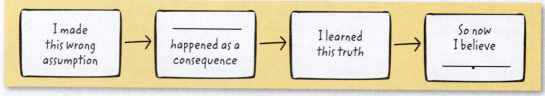

Wrong Assumption

Sensory Associations

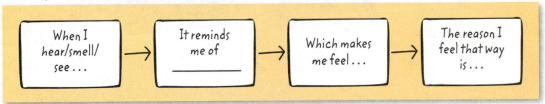

When I hear/smell/see... → It reminds me of ___ → Which makes me feel... → The reason I feel that way is...

Something Big

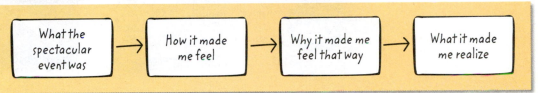

What the spectacular event was → How it made me feel → Why it made me feel that way → What it made me realize

Finding Out for Sure

I've never been sure if... → But I've always suspected that... → Because once I experienced... → Which made me think that... → And finally I realized that...

Making a Change

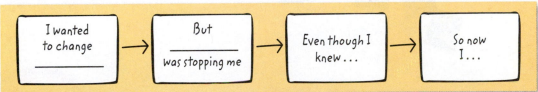

I wanted to change ___ → But ___ was stopping me → Even though I knew... → So now I...

Learning from Mistakes

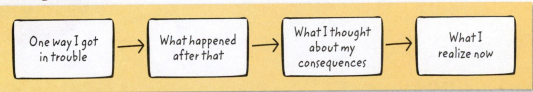

One way I got in trouble → What happened after that → What I thought about my consequences → What I realize now

Grammar, Usage, AND Spelling

Sentences

A sentence is a group of words that tells a complete thought.

Subjects and Predicates

A **subject** tells who or what the sentence is about. A **predicate** tells something about the subject. A sentence must have both of these parts to be a **complete sentence**. If one part of a sentence is missing, a **fragment** is the result.

Complete and Simple Subjects and Predicates	Examples
The **complete subject** includes all the words in the subject.	**Many people** visit our national parks. **My favorite parks** are in the West.
The **simple subject** is the most important noun or pronoun in the complete subject.	Many **people** visit our national parks. My favorite **parks** are in the West.
The **complete predicate** includes all the words in the predicate.	Visitors **explore caves in Yellowstone Park**. Some people **climb the unusual rock formations**.
The **simple predicate** is the **verb**. It is the most important word in the predicate.	Visitors **explore** caves in Yellowstone Park. Some people **climb** the unusual rock formations.

Compound Subject and Compound Predicate	Examples
A **compound subject** is two or more simple subjects joined by **and** or **or**.	**Yosemite and Yellowstone** are both in the West. Either **spring or fall** is a good time to visit.
A **compound predicate** has two or more verbs joined by **and** or **or**.	At Yosemite, some people **fish and swim**. My family **hikes** to the river **or stays** in a cabin.

Complete Sentences and Fragments

Sentences and Fragments	Examples
Begin a complete sentence with a capital letter, and end it with a period or other end mark.	These parks / have many tourist attractions. *subject*　　　*predicate*
A **fragment** is a sentence part that is incorrectly used as a complete sentence. For example, the fragment may be missing a subject. Add a subject to correct the problem.	**Incorrect:** Beautiful waterfalls. **Correct:** Many parks have beautiful waterfalls.
Writers sometimes use fragments on purpose to emphasize an idea or for special effect.	I did not camp in bear country. **No way. Too dangerous**.

Subject-Verb Agreement

The subject and verb of a sentence or clause must agree in number.

Subject-Verb Agreement	Examples
Use a **singular subject** with a **singular verb**.	Another popular **park is** the Grand Canyon.
Use a **plural subject** with a **plural verb**.	We **were amazed** by the colors of its cliffs.
If the simple subjects in a **compound subject** are connected by **and**, use a plural verb. If they are connected by **or**, look at the last simple subject. If it is singular, use a **singular verb**. If it is plural, use a **plural verb**.	<u>Rafts</u> and a <u>boat</u> **are** available for a trip down the canyon. These **rafts** or this <u>boat</u> **is** the best way to go. This **boat or** these <u>rafts</u> **are** the best way to go .
The **subject** and **verb** must agree, even when other words come between them.	The **bikers** in the park **are looking** for animals.

Sentence Structures

Clauses	Examples
A **clause** is a group of words that has both a **subject** and a **predicate**.	California's population / grew during the 1840s. *subject* *predicate*
An **independent clause** can stand alone as a complete sentence.	California's population / increased. *subject* *predicate*
A **dependent clause** cannot stand alone as a complete sentence because it begins with a subordinating conjunction. A dependent clause can be combined with an independent clause to form a complete sentence.	**because** gold / was found there during that time California's population grew because gold was found. *independent clause* *dependent clause*
An **adjective clause** gives more details about the noun or pronoun that it describes.	The news **that gold had been found** spread fast.
An **adverb clause** gives more details about the verb, adjective, or adverb that it describes.	**When someone found gold**, people celebrated.

Sentence Structures, continued

Simple Sentences	Examples
A **simple sentence** is one independent clause with a subject and a predicate. It has no dependent clauses.	Supplies / were scarce. The miners / needed goods and services.

Compound Sentences	Examples
When you join two independent clauses, you make a **compound sentence**. • Use a comma and a **coordinating conjunction** to join independent clauses. • Use a semicolon to join independent clauses that are short and closely related.	People opened stores, **but** supplies were scarce. People went hungry; there was no food.
Joining independent clauses without a conjunction or proper punctuation creates a **run-on sentence**.	**Incorrect:** The miners were hungry supplies were scarce. **Correct:** The miners were hungry, and supplies were scarce.

Complex Sentences	Examples
To make a **complex sentence**, join an independent clause with one or more dependent clauses. If the dependent clause comes first, put a **comma** after it.	Many writers visited camps **where miners worked**. *independent* *dependent* **While the writers were there**, they wrote stories about the miners.

Compound-Complex Sentences	Examples
You can make a **compound-complex sentence** by joining two or more independent clauses and one or more dependent clauses.	Many miners never found gold, **but** they stayed in California **because they found other jobs there**. *dependent*

Sentence Structures, continued

Phrases	Examples
A **phrase** is a group of related words that does not have both a subject and a verb. Phrases add details to sentences.	The team won the game **in overtime**. **With only seconds left**, the quarterback scored.
A **prepositional phrase** starts with a preposition and ends with a noun or a pronoun. (See page 461W [Level A], 487W [Level B], or 483W [Level C] for a list of prepositions.) It includes all the words in between. The noun or pronoun is the **object of the preposition**.	I live **near the Chávez Community Center**. *preposition* *object of preposition* Tom wants to walk there **with you and me**. *preposition* *objects of preposition*
Prepositional phrases can function either as **adjectives** or as **adverbs**. • They function as adjectives when they modify a noun or pronoun. • They function as **adverbs** when they modify a verb, an adjective, or another adverb.	The **guy in the yellow shirt and khaki pants** is my friend Joel. He is **excited about the new Chávez Center**. He wants to **come with us**.
A **participial phrase** begins with a participle. A **participle** is a word made from a verb but used as an adjective (**sizzling** burgers, **burned** hot dogs) Most participles end in **-ing** or **-ed**. A participle phrase includes the participle and its modifiers. Place the phrase next to the noun it describes.	**Correct:** **Standing by the grill**, he soon had the hamburgers cooked to perfection. **Incorrect:** He soon had the hamburgers cooked to perfection standing by the grill.

Parenthetical Phrases and Appositives	Examples
A **parenthetical phrase** adds nonessential information to a sentence. You can leave out a nonessential phrase without changing the meaning of the sentence. Use commas to set off a nonessential phrase.	Most miners did not, **in fact**, find gold. Gold, **every miner's dream**, lay deeply buried.
An **appositive phrase** renames the noun next to it. An appositive phrase usually comes after the noun or pronoun it refers to.	James Marshall, **a mill worker**, started the Gold Rush when he found gold nuggets in 1848.

Sentence Functions

Sentence Types	Examples
A **statement** ends with a period.	The football game was on Friday. The coach made an important announcement.
A **question** ends with a question mark.	Who heard the announcement? What did the coach say?
An **exclamation** shows surprise or strong emotion. It ends with an exclamation mark.	That's fantastic news! I can't believe it!
In an **imperative** sentence, or command, the subject **you** is implied. It is not stated. • An imperative sentence usually begins with a verb and ends with a period. • If an imperative sentence shows strong emotion, it ends with an exclamation mark.	Give the team my congratulations. **Be** on time. Beat the opponent!

Negative Sentences	Examples

A **negative sentence** uses a **negative word** to say "no."
 	
 Negative Words
 	
 no   nobody   never
 not   nothing   no one
 none   nowhere
 	
 Use only one negative word in a sentence. Two negatives in one sentence is called a **double negative**. Two negatives cancel each other out. **I did not see no one** means **I saw someone**.
	The game in Hawaii was **not** boring!
	 Nobody in our town missed it on TV.
	 Our team **never** played better.
	 Nothing is better than watching your team win!
	 None of us could stop cheering.
	
	 Incorrect:
	 The cheering **did not** never stop.
	
	 Correct:
	 The cheering **never** stopped
	 The cheering **did not** stop.
	
	                       anything
	 The other team could not do ~~nothing~~ right.
	
	               any
	 Their team never scored ~~no~~ points.

Conditional Sentences	Examples
Conditional sentences tell how one action depends on another action. These sentences often use conditional or modal verbs. **Conditional Verbs** can could might will would	**If** our team returns today, **then** we will have a party. **Unless** it rains, we can have the party outside. If you have time, **could** you invite the mayor? The mayor **might** come to the party **if** he is available.

Combining Sentences

Good writers use many different types of sentences. You can combine short, related sentences in different ways.

Combined Sentences	Examples
You can use **appositives**.	Samuel Brannan was a newspaper publisher. He told everyone about the discovery of gold. Samuel Brannan, **a newspaper publisher**, told everyone about the discovery of gold.
You can use **participial phrases**.	The search for gold was dangerous. The miners stood in rushing streams. The search for gold was dangerous for miners **standing in rushing streams**.
You can use **prepositional phrases**.	The trip to California was difficult. People traveled in covered wagons. The trip to California **by covered wagon** was difficult.
You can join clauses. Use **coordination** to join clauses of equal weight, or importance.	Gold was often found next to streams, **and** it was also found deep beneath the earth.
Use **subordination** to join clauses of unequal weight, or importance. Put the main idea in the main clause and the less important detail in the dependent clause.	The miners were called '49ers. *main idea* Many miners arrived in 1849. *less important detail* The miners were called '49ers because they arrived in 1849.

Parts of Speech

All the words in the English language can be put into one of eight groups. These groups are the eight **parts of speech**. You can tell a word's part of speech by looking at how it functions, or the way it is used, in a sentence. Knowing about the functions of words can help you become a better writer.

The Eight Parts of Speech	Examples
A **noun** names a person, place, thing, or idea.	**Erik Weihenmayer** climbed the highest **mountain** in the **world**. The **journey** up **Mount Everest** took **courage**.
A **pronoun** takes the place of a noun.	**He** made the journey even though **it** was dangerous.
An **adjective** describes a noun or a pronoun.	Erik is a **confident** climber. He is **strong**, too.
A **verb** can tell what the subject of a sentence does or has. A **verb** can also link a noun or an adjective in the predicate to the subject.	Erik also **skis** and **rides** a bike. He **has** many hobbies. Erik **is** an athlete. He **is** also blind.
An **adverb** describes a verb, an adjective, or another adverb.	Illness **slowly** took his eyesight, but it **never** affected his spirit. His accomplishments have made him **very** famous. He has been interviewed **quite** often.
A **preposition** shows how two things or ideas are related. It introduces a prepositional phrase.	Erik speaks **to** people **around** the world. **In** his speeches, he talks **about** his life.
A **conjunction** connects words or groups of words.	Courage **and** skill have carried him far. He has one disability, **but** he has many abilities.
An **interjection** expresses strong feeling.	**Wow**! What an amazing person he is! **Hurray**! He reached the mountaintop.

Nouns

A **noun** names a person, animal, place, thing, or idea.
There are different kinds of nouns.

Common and Proper Nouns	Examples
A **common noun** names a general person, place, thing, or idea.	A **teenager** sat by the **ocean** and read a **magazine**.
Capitalize a common noun only when it begins a sentence.	**Magazines** are the perfect thing to read at the beach.
A **proper noun** names a specific person, place, thing, or idea. Always capitalize a proper noun.	**Jessica** sat by the **Pacific Ocean** and read *Teen Talk* magazine.

Regular Plural Nouns	Examples
Plural nouns name more than one person, place, thing, or idea. Add **–s** to most nouns to make them plural.	My favorite **guitar** was made in Spain, but I also like my two American **guitars**.

Other nouns follow different rules to form the plural.

Forming Noun Plurals

When a Noun Ends in:	Form the Plural by:	Examples
ch, **sh**, **s**, **x**, or **z**	adding -**es**	box—box**es** brush—brush**es**
a consonant + **y**	changing the **y** to **i** and adding -**es**	story—stor**ies**
a vowel + **y**	just adding -**s**	boy—boy**s**
a single **f** or **fe**	changing the **f** or **fe** to **v** and adding -**es** **Exceptions**	leaf—lea**ves** knife—kni**ves** belief—belief**s** chief—chief**s** scarf—scarf**s**/scar**ves**
a vowel + **o**	adding -**s**	radio—radio**s** kangaroo—kangaroo**s**
a consonant + **o**	adding -**s** or -**es**. Some words take -**s**, some words take -**es**, some take both -**s** and -**es**.	photo—photo**s** radio—radio**s** potato—potato**es** tomato—tomato**es** tornado—tornado**s**/ tornado**es** zero—zero**s**/zero**es**

Irregular Plural Nouns	Examples
Some nouns are **irregular**. These nouns do not follow the rules to form the plural.	At first only one **person** came, but within an hour there were many **people**.

Forming Plurals of Irregular Nouns

For some irregular nouns, change the spelling to form the plural.	one child many **children**	one man several **men**	one mouse a few **mice**
	one foot many **feet**	one ox ten **oxen**	one tooth three **teeth**
	one goose some **geese**	one person two **people**	one woman most **women**
For other irregular nouns, keep the same form for the singular and the plural.	one deer two **deer**	one fish many **fish**	one sheep twelve **sheep**

Possessive Nouns	Examples
Possessive nouns show ownership or relationship of persons, places, or things.	**Ted's** daughter made the guitar. The **guitar's** tone is beautiful.
Follow these rules to make a noun possessive: • Add **'s** to a singular noun or a plural noun that does not end in **s**. • Add an apostrophe after the final **s** in a plural noun that ends in **s**.	When she plays the piano, it attracts **the children's** attention. Three **musicians'** instruments were left on the bus.

Noun Phrases	Examples
A **noun phrase** is made up of a noun and its modifiers. Modifiers are words that describe, such as adjectives.	**The flying frog** does not actually fly. It glides on **special skin flaps**. Thailand is a **frog-friendly habitat**.

Articles

An **article** is a word that helps identify a noun.

Articles	Examples
A, **an**, and **the** are **articles**.	It is **an** amazing event when **a** flying frog glides in **the** forest.
A and **an** are **indefinite articles**. Use **a** or **an** before a noun that names a nonspecific thing.	**A flying frog** stretched its webbed feet. **An owl** watched from a nearby tree.
• Use **a** before a word that starts with a consonant sound.	a **f**oot a **p**ool a **n**est a **r**ainbow a **u**nion (*u* is pronounced like *y*, a consonant)
• Use **an** before a word that starts with a vowel sound.	an **e**gg an **a**nimal an **i**dea an **o**cean an **h**our (The *h* is silent.)
The is a **definite article**. Use **the** before a noun that names a specific thing.	Leiopelmids are **the** oldest kind of frog in **the** world. They are survivors of **the** Jurassic period.

Pronouns

A **pronoun** takes the place of a noun or refers to a noun.

Subject Pronouns	Examples
Use a **subject pronoun** as the subject of a sentence. | **Singular**	**Plural**
I	we
you	you
he, she, it	they		**Antonio** is looking forward to the dance. **He** is trying to decide what to wear. The **dance** starts at 7:00. **It** ends at 10:00.
The pronoun **it** can be used as a **subject** to refer to a noun. ***But:*** The pronoun **it** can be the subject without refering to a specific noun.	The **dance** starts at 7:00. **It** ends at 10:00. **It** is important to arrive on time. **It** is fun to see your friends in formal clothes.

Object Pronouns

Use an **object pronoun** after an action verb or after a preposition.

Singular	Plural
me	us
you	you
him, her, it	them

Examples

Tickets are on sale, so buy **them** now.

Antonio invited Caryn. He has flowers for **her**.

Possessive Pronouns

A **possessive pronoun** shows who or what owns something or belongs with something.

A **singular possessive pronoun** shows that one person owns or has something.

A **plural possessive pronoun** shows that more than one person owns or has something.

Singular	Plural
mine	ours
yours	yours
his, hers, its	theirs

Examples

The photographs belong to **John and Marissa**. The photographs are **theirs**.

John has a new camera. The camera is **his**.

I made a video of the event. The video is **mine**.

Have you seen my laptop, Mom?
Yes, that laptop is **yours**.

John, **Marissa**, and **I** posted the photos online. The online photos are **ours**.

Have you seen our photos yet, Zack?
Yes, **yours** are the best!

Demonstrative Pronouns

A **demonstrative pronoun** points out a specific person, place, thing, or idea. Use the correct pronoun to talk about things that are near you or far from you.

	Singular	Plural
Near	this	these
Far	that	those

Examples

This is a good phone. It takes great photos. Look at **these**!

These on my phone are photos of my friends. **This** is my friend, Michael.

Those on the wall are photographs of my grandparents. **That** is a photo of my grandmother when she was young.

Pronouns, continued

Indefinite Pronouns	Examples
Use an **indefinite pronoun** when you are not talking about a specific person, place, or thing.	**Someone** has to lose the game. **Nobody** knows who the winner will be.

Some Indefinite Pronouns

	Examples
These **indefinite pronouns** are always singular and need a **singular verb**. anybody either neither one anyone everybody nobody somebody anything everyone no one someone each everything nothing nothing	**Something is** happening on the playing field. We hope that **everything goes** well for our team.
These **indefinite pronouns** are always plural and need a **plural verb**. both few many several	**Many** of us **are** hopeful.
These **indefinite pronouns** can be singular or plural. all any most none some Look at the phrase that follows the indefinite pronoun. If the noun or pronoun in the phrase is plural, use a **plural verb**. If it is singular, use a **singular verb**.	**Most** of the players **are** tired. **Most** of the game **is** over.

Relative Pronouns	Examples
A **relative pronoun** introduces **a relative clause**. It connects, or relates, the clause to a word in the sentence.	**Relative Pronouns** who what which whom whoever whatever whose whomever whichever
Use **who**, **whom**, or **whose** for people. The pronouns **whoever** and **whomever**, also refer to people.	The student **who** was injured is Joe. We play **whomever** we are scheduled to play.
Use **which**, **whichever**, **what**, and **whatever** for things.	Joe's wrist, **which** is sprained, will heal.
Use **that** for people or things.	The trainer **that** examined Joe's wrist is sure. The injury **that** Joe received is minor.

Reflexive and Intensive Pronouns	Examples

Reflexive and **intensive pronouns** refer to nouns or other pronouns in a sentence. These pronouns end with –**self** or –**selves**.

I will go to the store by **myself**.

Singular	Plural
myself	ourselves
yourself	yourselves
himself, herself, itself	themselves

Use a **reflexive pronoun** when the object **refers back to the subject**.

To surprise her technology teacher, **Kim** taught **herself** how to create a website on the computer.

Use an **intensive pronoun to emphasize a noun or a pronoun** in a sentence.

The technology **teacher himself** learned some interesting techniques from Kim.

Agreement and Reference	Examples

When nouns and pronouns **agree**, they both refer to the same person, place, or thing. The **noun** is the **antecedent**, and the **pronoun** refers to it.

Rafael and Felicia visited a local college. **They** toured the campus.

antecedent   pronoun

A pronoun must agree (match) in **number** with the noun it refers to.
- **Singular pronouns** refer to one.
- **Plural pronouns** refer to more than one.

Rafael plays violin. **He** enjoyed the music school.

The teenagers were impressed. **They** liked this college.

Pronouns must agree in **gender** with the nouns they refer to. Use **she**, **her**, and **hers** to refer to females. Use **he**, **him**, and **his** to refer to males.

Felicia told **her** uncle about the college visit.

Her uncle told **her** that **he** received **his** graduate degree from that school.

When you write, check that your pronouns refer to the correct noun. To correct sentences with unclear or vague pronouns, you can edit the sentence and remove the pronoun, or replace the pronoun with a noun.

Unclear:	Bill told Rafael **he** would like the teachers. *Is **he** Uncle Bill or Rafael?*
Clear:	Bill said that Rafael would like the teachers.
Unclear:	At the college, **they** give violin lessons. *Who gives the lessons?*
Clear:	At the college, musicians give violin lessons.

Adjectives

An **adjective** describes, or modifies, a noun or a pronoun. It can tell what kind, which one, how many, or how much.

Adjectives	Examples
Adjectives provide more detailed information about a noun. Usually, an adjective comes before the noun it describes.	Deserts have a **dry** climate.
But an adjective can also come after the noun.	The climate is also **hot**.
Number words are often used as adjectives.	While I was out in the desert I saw **one** roadrunner, **two** Gila monsters, and **six** cacti.
Sometimes the number word tells the **order** that things are in.	The **first** day, I just saw some lizards. The **second** day, I got to see a coyote!

Proper Adjectives	Examples
A proper adjective is formed from a proper noun. It always begins with a capital letter.	Major deserts are found in Africa, Asia, and the Americas. The largest **African** desert is the Sahara.

Possessive Adjectives	Examples
A **possessive adjective** replaces an owner's name. It matches the gender and number of owners.	I have notes about an interesting desert animal. **My** notes are mostly about the Gila monster. A **Gila monster** has a painful bite. **Its** bite is poisonous. **Mia's** report is about a bird called a Roadrunner. **Her** report includes photographs of the bird.

Singular	Plural
my	our
your	your
his, her, its	their

big huge gigantic

Adjectives That Compare	Examples
Comparative adjectives help show the similarities or differences between two nouns.	Deserts are **more fun** to study **than** forests.
To form the comparative of one-syllable adjectives, add -**er**, and use **than**. Use **more ... than** if the adjective has three or more syllables.	The Sechura Desert in South America is small**er than** the Kalahari Desert in Africa. Is that desert **more interesting than** this one?
Superlative adjectives help show how three or more nouns are alike or different.	Of the Sechura, Kalahari, and Sahara, which is **the largest**?
To form the superlative of one-syllable adjectives, add -**est** and use **the**. Use **most** if the adjective has three or more syllables.	Which of the three deserts is the **smallest**? I think the Sahara is **the most beautiful**.
Irregular adjectives form the comparative and superlative differently. good better best bad worse worst much/many more most little less/fewer least	I had **the best** time ever visiting the desert. But the desert heat is **worse than** city heat. There was **less** traffic **than** before. There were **fewer** buses on the road.
Some two-syllable adjectives form the comparative with either -**er** or **more** and the superlative with either -**est** or **most**. Do not use both more and -er with the same adjective.	Desert animals are usually **more lively** at night than during the day. Desert animals are usually **livelier** at night than during the day. **Incorrect:** Desert animals are usually **more livelier** at night than during the day.

Adjective Phrases and Clauses	Examples
An **adjective phrase** is a group of words that work together to modify a noun or a pronoun. A phrase has no verb.	Plants **in the desert** have developed adaptations.
An **adjective clause** also works to modify a noun or a pronoun. Unlike an adjective phrase, an adjective clause has a subject and a verb.	The saguaro, **whose flowers bloom at night**, soaks up surface water after it rains. Desert plants **that have long roots** tap into water deep in the earth.

Verbs

Every complete sentence has two parts: a subject and a predicate. The subject tells who or what the sentence is about. The predicate tells something about the subject. For example:

The dancers / **performed** on stage.

subject   predicate

The **verb** is the key word in the predicate because it tells what the subject does or has. Verbs can also link together words in the subject and the predicate.

Action Verbs	Examples
An **action verb** tells what the subject of a sentence does. Most verbs are action verbs.	Dancers **practice** for many hours. They **stretch** their muscles and **lift** weights.
Some **action verbs** tell about an action that you cannot see.	The dancers **recognize** the rewards that come from their hard work.

Linking Verbs	Examples
A **linking verb** connects, or links, the subject of a sentence to a word in the predicate. Forms of the verb *be* are most commonly used, but other verbs are used as well. **Forms of the Verb *Be*** 	am	are	were
is	was	| **Other Linking Verbs** | appear	seem	become
feel	smell	taste
look				
The word in the predicate can describe the subject.	Their feet **are** calloused.
Or the word in the predicate can rename the subject.	These dancers **are** athletes.

Helping Verbs	Examples
Some verbs are made up of more than one word. They need help to show exactly what is happening.	Ballet **is considered** a dramatic art form. *helping verb* *main verb*
The action word is called the **main verb**. It shows what the subject does, has, or is.	This dance form **has been evolving** over the years. *helping verbs* *main verb*
Any verbs that come before the **main** verb are the **helping verbs**.	Ballet **must have been** very different in the 1500s. *helping verbs* *main verb*

Helping Verbs

Forms of the Verb *Be*	Forms of the Verb *Do*	Forms of the Verb *Have*
am was is were are	do did does	have had has

Other Helping Verbs	
To express ability: **can, could**	I **can** dance.
To express possibility: **may, might**, **could**	I **might** dance tonight.
To express necessity or desire: **must**, **would**	I **must** dance more often.
To express certainty: **will, shall**	I **will** dance more often.
To express obligation: **should, ought to**	I **should** practice more often. I **ought to** practice more often.

Helping verbs agree with the subject.	Baryshnikov **has performed** around the world. Many people **have praised** this famous dancer.
When used, the adverb *not* always comes between the **helping verb** and the main verb.	If you **have** not **heard** of him, you can watch the film *Dancers* to see him perform.
In questions, the subject comes between the **helping verb** and the **main verb**.	**Have** you **heard** of Mikhail Baryshnikov?

Verb Tense: Past, Present, Future

The **tense** of a verb shows when an action happens.

Present Tense Verbs	Examples
The **present tense** of a verb tells about an action that is happening now.	Greg **checks** his watch to see if it is time to leave. He **starts** work at 5:00 today.

Habitual Present Tense Verbs	Examples
The **habitual present tense** of a verb tells about an action that happens regularly or all the time.	Greg **works** at a pizza shop. He **makes** pizzas and **washes** dishes.

Past Tense Verbs (Regular and Irregular)	Examples
The **past tense** of a verb tells about an action that happened earlier, or in the past.	Yesterday, Greg **worked** until the shop closed. He **made** 50 pizzas.
• The past tense form of **regular verbs** ends with -**ed**.	He **learned** how to make a stuffed-crust pizza. Then Greg **chopped** onions and peppers.
• **Irregular verbs** have **special forms** to show the past tense. See pages 454W-455W [Level A], 480W-481W [Level B], 476W-477W [Level C]. Here are some examples of irregular verbs:	Greg **cut** the pizza. It **was** delicious. We **ate** all of it!

Present Tense	Past Tense
cut	cut
am, is, are	was, were
eat	ate

Future Tense Verbs	Examples
The **future tense** of a verb tells about an action that will happen later, or in the future. To show future tense, use:	Greg **will ride** the bus home after work tonight.
• the helping verb **will** plus a main verb	Greg's mother **will drive** him to work tomorrow. On Friday, he **will get** his first paycheck.
• **am**, **is**, or **are** + **going to** + a main verb	He **is going to take** a pizza home to his family. They **are going to eat** the pizza for dinner.

Verb Tense: Perfect Tenses

All verbs in the **perfect tenses**—**present perfect**, **past perfect**, and **future perfect**—have a helping verb and a form of the main verb that is called the **past participle**.

Present Perfect Tense Verbs	Examples
The **present perfect tense** of a verb uses the helping verb **has** or **have** plus the past participle.	
Use the present perfect tense to tell about something that happened at an unknown time in the past.	I **have looked** things up on the Internet.
You can also use the present perfect tense to tell about something that happened in the past and may still be going on.	The public **has used** the Internet since the 1980s.
For **regular verbs**, the past participle ends in -**ed**. **Present Tense** like **Past Participle** liked	I like the Internet. I **have** always **liked** the Internet.
Irregular verbs have **special forms** for the past participle. **Present Tense** know **Past Participle** known	I know a lot about the Internet. I **have known** about it for a long time.

Past Perfect Tense Verbs	Examples
The **past perfect tense** of a verb tells about an action that was completed before some other action in the past. It uses the helping verb **had**.	My grandmother **had graduated** from high school before computers were even invented!

Future Perfect Tense Verbs	Examples
The **future perfect tense** of a verb tells about an action that will be completed at a specific time in the future. It uses the helping verbs **will have**.	By the end of next year, 100,000 people **will have visited** our website.

Verb Forms

The **form** a verb takes changes depending on when the action happened—in the present, the past, or the future. It also depends on whether the action is in progress.

Progressive Verbs	Examples
The **progressive** verb forms tell about an action that occurs over a period of time.	
The **present progressive** form of a verb tells about an action as it is happening. • It uses the helping verb **am**, **is**, or **are**. The main verb ends in -**ing**.	They **are expecting** a big crowd for the fireworks show this evening. **Are** you **expecting** the rain to end before the show starts?
The **past progressive** form of a verb tells about an action that was happening over a period of time in the past. • It uses the helping verb **was** or **were** and a main verb. The main verb ends in -**ing**.	They **were thinking** of canceling the fireworks. A tornado **was heading** in this direction.
The **future progressive** form of a verb tells about an action that will be happening over a period of time in the future. • It uses the helping verbs **will be** plus a main verb. The main verb ends in -**ing**.	The weather forecasters **will be watching** for tornados. I hope that they **will** not **be canceling** the show.

Transitive and Intransitive Verbs	Examples
Action verbs can be transitive or intransitive. A **transitive verb** needs an **object** to complete its meaning and to receive the action of the verb.	**Not complete**: **Complete**: Many cities **use** Many cities **use** fireworks.
The object can be a **direct object**. A direct object answers the question *Whom?* or *What?*	**Whom**: The noise **surprises** the audience. **What**: The people in the audience **cover** their ears.
An **intransitive verb** does not need an object to complete its meaning.	**Complete**: The people in our neighborhood **clap**. They **shout**. They **laugh**.
An **intransitive verb** may end the sentence, or it may be followed by other words that tell how, where, or when. These words are not objects since they do not receive the action of the verb.	The fireworks **glow** brightly. Then, slowly, they **disappear** in the sky. The show **ends** by midnight.

Active and Passive Voice of Verbs	Examples
Sentences have nouns or pronouns and verbs. You use verbs to tell about actions. You use nouns or pronouns to tell about the subject. The subject does the action. The voice of a verb depends on the subject in a sentence.	*doer* *receiver* Many cities **hold** fireworks displays on the Fourth of July. *receiver* *doer* Fireworks displays **are held by** many cities on the Fourth of July.
A verb is in the **active voice** if the subject does, or performs, the action. The subject is the doer.	
A verb is in the **passive voice** if the subject does not perform the action. The subject is the receiver. A verb in the passive voice always includes a form of the verb be (am, is, are, was, were) and the past participle of the main verb.	*receiver* Fireworks displays **are held** every Fourth of July.
How does a reader know who does the action? Sometimes the subject is included in a phrase. Sometimes the subject is not mentioned in the sentence.	
The first words in a sentence usually get more attention from the reader. Using active or passive voice impacts the focus, or emphasis, of writing.	
Use the **active voice** when you want more emphasis on the subject.	*doer* The mayor **picked** a safe location.
Use **passive voice** when you want less emphasis on the subject. This happens when: • the object, or receiver of the action, is more important than the subject • the subject is not known, not important, or obvious • the writer prefers not to mention who did the action (the subject). For example, the writer might not want to blame a specific person or group.	*receiver* A safe location **was picked** by the mayor. The fireworks **were made** in the U.S. An error **was made** in the location choice last year.
When you write for a specific audience or purpose, you choose a tone. Your tone can be formal or informal.	Formal Tone: The mayor **approved** the location for this year's fireworks display.
Use **active voice** when you write in either a formal tone or an informal tone.	Informal Tone: The mayor **picked** a really awesome location for this year's fireworks.
When you use passive voice, your writing sounds more objective and impersonal. Use passive voice when you write in a more formal tone.	The location for this year's fireworks display **was approved** by the mayor.

Verb Forms, continued

A **two-word verb** is a verb followed by a preposition. The meaning of the two-word verb is different from the meaning of the verb by itself.

Some Two-Word Verbs

Verb	Meaning	Example
break	to split into pieces	I didn't **break** the window with the ball.
break down	to stop working	Did the car **break down** again?
break up	to end	The party will **break up** before midnight.
	to come apart	The ice on the lake will **break up** in the spring.
check	to make sure you are right	We can **check** our answers at the back of the book.
check in	to stay in touch with someone	I **check in** with my mom at work.
check up	to see if everything is okay	The nurse **checks up** on the patient every hour.
check off	to mark off a list	Look at your list and **check off** the girls' names.
check out	to look at something carefully	Hey, Marisa, **check out** my new bike!
fill	to place as much as can be held	**Fill** the pail with water.
fill in	to color or shade in a space	Please **fill in** the circle.
fill out	to complete	Marcos **fills out** a form to order a book.
get	to receive	I often **get** letters from my pen pal.
get ahead	to go beyond what is expected	She worked hard to **get ahead** in math class.
get along	to be on good terms with	Do you **get along** with your sister?
get out	to leave	Let's **get out** of the kitchen.
get over	to feel better	I hope you'll **get over** the flu soon.
get through	to finish	I can **get through** this book tonight.
give	to hand something to someone	We **give** presents to the children.
give out	to stop working	If she runs ten miles, her energy will **give out**.
give up	to quit	I'm going to **give up** eating candy.

Verb	Meaning	Example
go	to move from place to place	Did you **go** to the mall on Saturday?
go on	to continue	Why do the boys **go on** playing after the bell rings?
go out	to go someplace special	Let's **go out** to lunch on Saturday.
look	to see or watch	Don't **look** directly at the sun.
look forward	to be excited about something	My brothers **look forward** to summer vacation.
look over	to review	She **looks over** her test before finishing.
look up	to hunt for and find	We **look up** information on the Internet.
pick	to choose	I'd **pick** Lin for class president.
pick on	to bother or tease	My older brothers always **pick on** me.
pick up	to increase	Business **picks up** in the summer.
	to gather or collect	**Pick up** your clothes!
run	to move quickly	Juan will **run** in a marathon.
run into	to unexpectedly see someone	Did you **run into** Chris at the store?
run out	to suddenly have nothing left	The cafeteria always **runs out** of nachos.
stand	to be on your feet	I have to **stand** in line to buy tickets.
stand for	to represent	A heart **stands for** love.
stand out	to be easier to see	You'll **stand out** with that orange cap.
turn	to change direction	We **turn** right at the next corner.
turn up	to appear	Clean your closet and your belt will **turn up**.
	to raise the volume	Please **turn up** the radio.
turn in	to go to bed	On school nights I **turn in** at 9:30.
	to present or submit	You didn't **turn in** the homework yesterday.
turn off	to make something stop	Please **turn off** the radio.

Verb Forms, continued

Irregular verbs do not follow the same rules for changing form as the "regular" verbs do. These verb forms have to be memorized. Here are some irregular verbs.

Irregular Verb	Past Tense	Past Participle
be: am, is, are	was, were	been
beat	beat	beaten
become	became	become
begin	began	begun
bend	bent	bent
bind	bound	bound
bite	bit	bitten
blow	blew	blown
break	broke	broken
bring	brought	brought
build	built	built
burst	burst	burst
buy	bought	bought
catch	caught	caught
choose	chose	chosen
come	came	come
cost	cost	cost
creep	crept	crept
cut	cut	cut
dig	dug	dug
do	did	done
draw	drew	drawn
drink	drank	drunk
drive	drove	driven

Irregular Verb	Past Tense	Past Participle
eat	ate	eaten
fall	fell	fallen
feed	fed	fed
feel	felt	felt
fight	fought	fought
find	found	found
fly	flew	flown
forget	forgot	forgotten
forgive	forgave	forgiven
freeze	froze	frozen
get	got	gotten
give	gave	given
go	went	gone
grow	grew	grown
have	had	had
hear	heard	heard
hide	hid	hidden
hit	hit	hit
hold	held	held
hurt	hurt	hurt
keep	kept	kept
know	knew	known
lead	led	led
leave	left	left

Forms of Irregular Verbs

Irregular Verb	Past Tense	Past Participle
let	let	let
light	lit	lit
lose	lost	lost
make	made	made
mean	meant	meant
meet	met	met
pay	paid	paid
prove	proved	proved, proven
put	put	put
read	read	read
ride	rode	ridden
ring	rang	rung
rise	rose	risen
run	ran	run
say	said	said
see	saw	seen
seek	sought	sought
sell	sold	sold
send	sent	sent
set	set	set
shake	shook	shaken
show	showed	shown
shrink	shrank	shrunk
sing	sang	sung

Irregular Verb	Past Tense	Past Participle
sink	sank	sunk
sit	sat	sat
sleep	slept	slept
slide	slid	slid
speak	spoke	spoken
spend	spent	spent
stand	stood	stood
steal	stole	stolen
stick	stuck	stuck
sting	stung	stung
strike	struck	struck
swear	swore	sworn
swim	swam	swum
swing	swung	swung
take	took	taken
teach	taught	taught
tear	tore	torn
tell	told	told
think	thought	thought
throw	threw	thrown
wake	woke, waked	woken, waked
wear	wore	worn
win	won	won
write	wrote	written

Verbals

A **verbal** is a word made from a verb, but used as a different part of speech.

Gerunds	Examples
A **gerund** is a verb form that ends in **-ing**, and is used as a noun. A gerund can be: • the subject of a sentence. Only use gerunds as the subject when the verb is singular. • a direct object of a verb • an object of a preposition • a predicate nominative, or word in the predicate that renames the subject.	**Cooking** is Jorge's favorite hobby. He enjoys **cooking**. Jorge is very talented at **cooking**. His talent is **cooking**. subject predicate
A **gerund phrase** is made up of the gerund, its modifiers, and other words that complete its meaning. Use gerunds to vary your sentences. Notice how this writer made improvements by including gerunds.	Jorge makes **creating delicious meals** look easy. As you learn how to cook, ~~it is a good idea for you~~ *following* ~~to take the time to follow~~ a recipe step-by- *is important* step. But once you have successfully created the dish a few times, try *experimenting* ~~to do different things with it~~. Add or change ingredients to make the dish your own.

Infinitives	Examples
An **infinitive** is a verb form that begins with the word **to**.	
• An infinitive can be used as a noun. It can be the **direct object of a verb**.	Jorge likes **to cook**. *noun: direct object*
Sometimes an infinitive can be the **subject** of the sentence. When it is the subject, the verb is singular.	**To cook** is Jorge's passion. *noun: subject*
• An infinitive can also be an **adjective** or an **adverb**.	His beef tamales are a sight **to see**. adjective
	Jorge cooks **to relax**. adverb
Remember, a phase is a group of related words. An **infinitive phrase** is made up of the infinitive, its modifiers, and other words that complete its meaning.	Jorge likes **to create his own special dishes**. infinitive infinitive phrase

Participles	Examples
A **participle** is a verb form that is used as an adjective.	
• For regular verbs, a participle ends in -**ing** or -**ed**.	His **sizzling** fajitas taste delicious. He makes them with **sliced** steak.
• For irregular verbs, a participle takes the past participle form.	Jorge also makes tasty **frozen** desserts.
A **participial phrase** begins with a participle and includes all the words that complete its meaning.	**Starving for a good lunch**, we ask Jorge to cook. participle participial phrase
Always place a participial phrase next to the noun it describes so the meaning is clear.	**Correct:** He prepared ground beef **mixed with spices**. *Incorrect:* **Mixed with spices**, he prepared ground beef. **Correct: Standing by the grill**, he cooked hamburgers. *Incorrect:* He cooked hamburgers, **standing by the grill**.

Verb Moods

Sometimes writers state facts. Other times, they give commands or express wishes. To show what they intend by the action in sentences, writers use different **verb moods**.

Indicative Mood	Examples
The **indicative mood** is the most common verb mood. Indicate means "to show" or "point out." The indicative mood points out something that exists or is true in real life. Use the indicative mood to • describe events • state a fact or make a statement • express beliefs, thoughts, and ideas that are possible in real life.	Our class studied the solar system. Jupiter is the largest planet. Thinking about space travel is interesting.

Imperative Mood	Examples
Imperative means "necessary or required," so sentences that use the **imperative mood** • make requests • give commands • give advice. Remember, complete sentences include a subject and a predicate. Sometimes the subject is not directly stated, it is implied. Most of the time, sentences using the imperative mood have an implied subject: *You*.	Let me see what you've done so far. Sit down. Take a break for a while. (You) Work with your partner.

Interrogative Mood	Examples
To interrogate means "to question." Use the **interrogative mood** to • make requests for action • ask for information.	Will you show me those photographs now? How many rings does the planet Saturn have?

Conditional Mood	Examples
The **conditional mood** expresses what could or might happen as a result of another event.	**If Ian goes online**, he will find a lot of facts about Saturn.
Sentences in the conditional mood use the words *if, might, could,* or *would* to express possibilities.	**If he sees what Saturn looks like, he **could** make a model of it.
Sentences using the conditional mood can reflect:	
• facts	A meteoroid will evaporate **if** it collides with Earth's atmosphere.
• activities that are repeated	**If** Ian takes notes, he'll remember what he learned.
• future events or plans	**If** Ian does well on his report, he could get a good grade.

Subjunctive Mood	Examples
The **subjunctive mood** expresses ideas that are not facts, such as wishes or possibilities.	
Sentences using the subjunctive mood tell about things that someone	
• wants to happen	The teacher asks that teams **be** ready by 2 p.m.
• predicts will happen	**If** we aren't ready, the teacher will not have time to finish the presentation.
• imagines happening	**If we were** ready early, she **might** give us more reading time
The subjunctive often	
• uses the words: *if, might, could, would, should*	**I would** do it **if** I had the time. But I don't have the time.
• follows the verbs: *ask, demand, doubt, request, suggest,* or *wish*	Mary **suggests** that we stay late each day this week.
• begins with the phrases: *if I /you/we/they/ were; it is important that; it is necessary that*	**It is important that** he decide as soon as possible.
	If I were to bring a meteor to class, **I would** definitely get an A!
Always use **were**, not **was**, when you use the **if** clause with a form of the verb **be**.	were If I ~~was~~ an alien, I would live on Saturn.

Contractions

A **contraction** is a shortened form of a verb plus the word *not*, or of a verb-and-pronoun combination.

Contractions	Examples	
Use an **apostrophe** to show which letters have been left out of the contraction.	is not = isn't can not = can't	I would = I'd They are = They're
In contractions made up of a verb and the word **not**, the word **not** is usually shortened to **n't**.	I **can't** stop eating these cookies!	

Adverbs

An **adverb** describes a verb, an adjective, or another adverb.

Adverbs	Examples
Adverbs answer one of the following questions: • How? • Where? • When? • How often?	**Carefully** aim the ball. Kick the ball **here**. Try again **later** to make a goal. Cathy **usually** scores.
An adverb can come before or after a **verb**.	Our team **always wins**. The whole team **plays well**.
An adverb can modify the meaning of an **adjective** or another **adverb**.	Gina is **really good** at soccer. She plays **very well**.

Adverbs That Compare	Examples
Some **adverbs** compare actions. Add -**er** to compare the actions of two people. Add -**est** to compare the actions of three or more people.	Gina runs **fast**. Gina runs **faster** than Maria. Gina runs **the fastest** of all the players.
If the adverb ends in -**ly**, use **more** or **less** to compare two actions.	Gina aims **more carefully** than Jen. Jen aims **less carefully** than Gina.
Use **the most** or **the least** to compare three or more actions.	Gina aims **the most carefully** of all the players. Jen aims **the least carefully** of all the players.

Prepositions

A **preposition** comes at the beginning of a prepositional phrase. **Prepositional phrases** add details to sentences.

Uses of Prepositions				Examples
Some prepositions show **location**.				The Chávez Community Center is **by my house**.
behind	between	inside	outside	The pool is **behind the building**.
below	by	near	over	
beside	in	on	under	
Some prepositions show **time**.				The Teen Club's party will start **after lunch**.
after	before	during	until	
Some prepositions show **direction**.				Go **through the building** and **around the fountain** to get **to the pool**.
across	down	out of	toward	The snack bar is **down the hall**.
around	into	through	up	
Some prepositions have **multiple uses**.				We might see Joshua **at the party**.
about	among	for	to	Meet me **at my house**.
against	as	from	with	Come **at noon**.
along	at	of	without	

beside under with

down in behind until

among across about on to

before through toward from above over

of between without after

around into at against for

Conjunctions

A **conjunction** connects words or groups of words.

Conjunctions	Examples
A **coordinating conjunction** connects words, phrases, or clauses. To show similarity: **and** To show difference: **but**, **yet** To show choice: **or** To show cause/effect: **so**, **for** To put negative ideas together: **nor**	Irena **and** Irving are twins. I know Irena, **but** I do not know Irving. They will celebrate Friday **or** Saturday night. I have a cold, **so** I cannot go to the party. My mother will not let me go, **nor** will my father.
Correlative conjunctions are used in pairs. The pair connects phrases or words.	**Some Correlative Conjunctions** both … and not only … but also either … or whether … or
A **subordinating conjunction** introduces a **dependent clause** in a complex sentence. It connects the **dependent clause** to the main clause.	**Some Subordinating Conjunctions** after before till although if until
A **conjunctive adverb** joins two independent clauses. Use a semicolon before the conjunction and a comma after it.	**Some Conjunctive Adverbs** besides however then consequently moreover therefore

Interjections

An **interjection** expresses strong feeling or emotion.

Interjections	Examples
An **interjection** shows emotion. If an interjection stands alone, follow it with an exclamation point.	**Help!** **Oops!** **Oh boy!**
An interjection used in a sentence can be followed by a comma or an exclamation mark. Use a comma after a weak interjection. Use an exclamation mark after a strong interjection.	**Oh**, it's a baby panda! **Hooray**! The baby panda has survived!

Grammar Troubleshooting Guide

In this section, you will find helpful solutions to common problems with sentences and parts of speech.

Sentences: Problems and Solutions

Sentence Fragments

Problem:
An infinitive phrase is punctuated as a complete sentence.

Solution:
Add a complete sentence to the phrase.

Incorrect:
To show students alternative ways to learn.

Correct:
To show students alternative ways to learn, Mr. Harris organized the trip.

Problem:
A clause starting with a relative pronoun is punctuated as a complete sentence.

Solution:
Add a subject and predicate to the sentence.

Incorrect:
Who might be interested in going on the trip.

Correct:
Anyone who might be interested in going on the trip should see Mr. Harris.

Problem:
A prepositional phrase is punctuated as a complete sentence.

Solution:
Add a sentence to the prepostional phrase.

Incorrect:
When traveling overseas.

Correct:
When traveling overseas, always try to speak to people in their native language.

Run On Sentences

Problem:
Two or more independent clauses are run together with no punctuation.

Solution:
Change one of the clauses into a dependent clause. Rewrite the sentence as two sentences.

Incorrect:
I first played guitar at twelve I thought I was great I knew very little then.

Correct:
When I first played guitar at twelve, I thought I was great. However, I knew very little then.

Problem:
Two independent clauses are joined with a conjunction, but without a comma.

Solution:
Use a comma before the conjunction.

Incorrect:
I continued to take lessons and I realized that I had much to learn to become a good guitarist.

Correct:
I continued to take lessons, and I realized that I had much to learn to become a good guitarist.

Parts of Speech: Problems and Solutions

Nouns

Problem: The sentence has the wrong plural form of an irregular noun.	**Incorrect:** Many **deers** live there.
Solution: Rewrite the sentence using the correct plural form. Check a dictionary.	**Correct:** Many **deer** live there.
Problem: The noun should be possessive, but it is not.	**Incorrect:** The beginning should capture the **readers** interest.
Solution: Add an apostrophe to make the noun possessive.	**Correct:** The beginning should capture the **readers'** interest.

Pronouns

Problem: The pronoun does not agree in number or gender with the noun it refers to.	**Incorrect:** Mary called Robert, but **they** did not answer **him**.
Solution: Match a pronoun's number and gender to the number and gender of the noun it is replacing.	**Correct:** Mary called Robert, but **he** did not answer **her**.
Problem: A pronun does not agree in number with the indefinte pronoun it refers to.	**Incorrect:** Everyone brought **their book** to class.
Solution: Make the pronoun and the word it refers to agree in number, so that both are singular or plural.	**Correct:** Everyone brought **his or her book** to class. OR All the students brought **their books** to class.
Problem: It's hard to tell which noun in a compound subject is referred to or replaced.	**Incorrect:** Ana and Mia own a car, but only **she** drives it.
Solution: Replace the unclear pronoun with a noun.	**Correct:** Ana and Mia own a car, but only **Ana** drives it.

Pronouns, continued

Problem: An object pronoun is used in a compound subject. Remember that subjects do actions and objects receive actions.	**Incorrect:** My brother and **me** rebuild car engines. object pronoun
Solution: Replace the object pronoun with a subject pronoun.	**Correct:** My brother and **I** rebuild car engines. subject pronoun
Problem: A subject pronoun is used in a compound object.	**Incorrect:** Leticia asked my brother and **I** to fix her car. subject pronoun
Solution: Replace the subject pronoun with an object pronoun.	**Correct:** Leticia asked my brother and **me** to fix her car. object pronoun
Problem: A subject pronoun is used as the object of a preposition.	**Incorrect:** Give your timesheet to Colin or **I**. subject pronoun
Solution: Replace the subject pronoun with an object pronoun.	**Correct:** Give your timesheet to Colin or **me**. object pronoun

Adjectives

Problem: The sentence contains a double comparison, using both an -er ending and the word *more*.	**Incorrect:** Joseph is **more older** than he looks.
Solution: Delete the incorrect comparative form.	**Correct:** Joseph is **older** than he looks. OR Joseph is more old than he looks.
Problem: The wrong form of an irregular adjective appears in a sentence that makes a comparison.	**Incorrect:** Cal feels **worser** since he ran out of medicine.
Solution: Replace the wrong form with the correct one. Check a dictionary.	**Correct:** Cal feels **worse** since he ran out of medicine.
Problem: The adjective *good* is used to modify a verb.	**Incorrect:** Julia did **good** on her test.
Solution: Rewrite the sentence using the adverb *well*, or add a noun for the adjective to describe.	**Correct:** Julia did well on her test. OR Julia did a good **job** on her test. noun

Verbs

Problem:	Incorrect:
In a sentence with two verbs, the tense of the second verb doesn't match the first.	Yesterday, Alberto **called** me and **says** he has tickets for the game.
Solution:	**Correct:**
Keep the verb tense the same unless there is a change in time, such as from past to present.	Yesterday, Alberto **called** me and **said** he has tickets for the game.
Problem:	**Incorrect:**
The past tense form of an irregular verb is formed incorrectly.	We **bringed** our portable TV to the game.
Solution:	**Correct:**
Replace the wrong form with the correct one. Check a dictionary.	We **brought** our portable TV to the game.
Problem:	**Incorrect:**
The participle form is used when the past-tense form is required.	After the game, we **run** over to Marcia's house.
Solution:	**Correct:**
Replace the wrong form with the correct one. Check a dictionary.	After the game, we **ran** over to Marcia's house.

Adverbs

Problem:	Incorrect:
An adverb is used to modify a noun or pronoun after the linking verb *feel*.	I feel **badly** about the mistake. adverb
Solution:	**Correct:**
Rewrite the sentence using an adjective.	I feel **bad** about the mistake. adjective
Problem:	**Incorrect:**
An adverb is used but does not modify anything in the sentence.	**Hopefully**, I didn't make too many mistakes on the test.
Solution:	**Correct:**
Rewrite the sentence using the adverb as a verb.	**I hope** I didn't make too many mistakes on the test.
Problem:	**Incorrect:**
Two negative words are used to express one idea.	We **don't** have **no** aspirin.
Solution:	**Correct:**
Change one negative word to a positive word.	We **don't** have **any** aspirin.

Capitalization

Knowing when to use capital letters is an important part of clear writing.

First Word in a Sentence	Examples
Capitalize the first word in a sentence.	**W**e are studying the Lewis and Clark expedition.

In Direct Quotations	Examples
Capitalize the first word in a **direct quotation**.	Clark said, "**There is great joy in camp**."
	"**We are in view of the ocean**," he said.
	"**It's the Pacific Ocean**," he added.

In Letters	Examples
Capitalize the first word used in the **greeting** or in the **closing** of a letter.	**D**ear Kim,
	Your friend,

In Titles of Works	Examples
All important words in a **title** begin with a capital letter. Articles (*a*, *an*, *the*) and short prepositions such as *at*, *for*, *of*, and *on* are not capitalized unless they are the first or last word in the title.	**book:** *The Longest Journey* **poem:** "Leaves of Grass" **magazine:** *Flora and Fauna of Arizona* **newspaper:** *The Denver Post* **song:** "The Star-Spangled Banner" **game:** Exploration! **TV series:** "The Gilmore Girls" **movie:** *The Lion King* **play:** Fiddler on the Roof **work of art:** Mona Lisa

Pronoun *I*	Examples
Capitalize the pronoun *I* no matter where it is located in a sentence.	**I** was amazed when **I** learned that Lewis and Clark's expedition was over 8,000 miles.

Capitalization, continued

Proper Nouns and Adjectives	Examples
Common nouns name a general person, place, thing, or idea. Proper nouns name a particular person, place, thing, or idea. All the important words in a **proper noun** start with a capital letter.	**Common Noun:** team **Proper Noun:** **C**orps of **D**estiny
Proper nouns include the following: • names of people and their titles Do not capitalize a title if it is used without a name. • family titles like *Mom* and *Dad* when they are used as names. • names of organizations • names of languages and religions • months, days, special days, and holidays • names of academic courses • historical events and documents	**S**tephanie **E**ddins **C**aptain **M**eriwether **L**ewis The **captain's** co-leader on the expedition was William Clark. "William Clark is one of our ancestors," **Mom** said. I asked my **mom** whose side of the family he was on, hers or my **dad's**. United Nations History Club Wildlife Society Spanish Christianity Islam April Sunday Thanksgiving Algebra I World History Physics Boston Tea Party Bill of Rights
Names of geographic places are proper nouns. Capitalize street, city, and state names in mailing addresses.	**Cities and States:** Dallas, Texas **Regions:** New England **Streets and Roads:** Main Avenue **Bodies of Water:** Pacific Ocean **Countries:** Ecuador **Landforms:** Sahara Desert **Continents:** North America **Public Spaces:** Muir Camp **Buildings, Ships, and Monuments:** *Titanic* **Planets and Heavenly Bodies:** Neptune
A **proper adjective** is formed from a **proper noun**. Capitalize proper adjectives.	Napoleon Bonaparte was from **Europe**. He was a **European** leader in the 1800s.

Abbreviations of Proper Nouns

Abbreviations of geographic places are also capitalized.

Words Used in Addresses

Avenue	Ave.	Drive	Dr.	North	N.	Street	St.
Apartment	Apt.	East	E.	Place	Pl.	Suite	Ste.
Boulevard	Blvd.	Highway	Hwy.	Road	Rd.	West	W.
Court	Ct.	Lane	Ln.	South	S.		

State Names

Alabama	AL	Indiana	IN	Nebraska	NE	South Carolina	SC
Alaska	AK	Iowa	IA	Nevada	NV	South Dakota	SD
Arizona	AZ	Kansas	KS	New Hampshire	NH	Tennessee	TN
Arkansas	AR	Kentucky	KY	New Jersey	NJ	Texas	TX
California	CA	Louisiana	LA	New Mexico	NM	Utah	UT
Colorado	CO	Maine	ME	New York	NY	Vermont	VT
Connecticut	CT	Maryland	MD	North Carolina	NC	Virginia	VA
Delaware	DE	Massachusetts	MA	North Dakota	ND	Washington	WA
Florida	FL	Michigan	MI	Ohio	OH	West Virginia	WV
Georgia	GA	Minnesota	MN	Oklahoma	OK	Wisconsin	WI
Hawaii	HI	Mississippi	MS	Oregon	OR	Wyoming	WY
Idaho	ID	Missouri	MO	Pennsylvania	PA		
Illinois	IL	Montana	MT	Rhode Island	RI		

Abbreviations of Personal Titles

Capitalize abbreviations for a personal title. Follow the same rules for capitalizing a personal title.

Mr.	Mister	**Mrs.**	Missus	**Dr.**	Doctor
Jr.	Junior	**Capt.**	Captain	**Sen.**	Senator

Punctuation

Punctuation marks are used to emphasize or clarify meanings.

End Marks	Examples
Use a **period** at the end of a statement or a polite command. Or use a period after an indirect question. An indirect question tells about a question you asked.	Georgia read the paper to her mom**.** Tell me if there are any interesting articles**.** She asked if there were any articles about the new restaurant on Stone Street near their house**.**
Use a **question mark** at the end of a question. Or use a question mark after a question that comes at the end of a statement.	What kind of food do they serve**?** The food is good, isn't it**?**
Use an **exclamation mark** after an interjection. Or use an exclamation mark at the end of a sentence to show you feel strongly about something.	Wow**!** The chicken parmesan is delicious**!**

Semicolon	Examples
Use a **semicolon**:	
• to separate two simple sentences used together without a conjunction	A group of Jim's classmates plan to attend the reading**;** he hopes to join them.
• before a conjunctive adverb that joins two simple sentences. Use a comma after the adverb.	Jim wanted to finish reading Josie Ramón's book this evening**;** however, he forgot it at school.
• to separate a group of words in a series if the words in the series already have commas	After school, Jim has to study French, health, and math**;** walk, feed, and brush the dog**;** and eat dinner.

Colon	Examples
Use a **colon**:	
• after the greeting in a business letter	Dear Sir or Madam**:**
• to separate hours and minutes	The restaurant is open until 11**:**30 p.m.
• to start a list	If you decide to hold your banquet here, we can**:** 1. Provide a private room 2. Offer a special menu 3. Supply free coffee and lemonade.

Comma	Examples
Use a comma:	
• before the **coordinating conjunction** in a compound sentence	Soccer is a relatively new sport in the United States, **but** it has been popular in England for a long time.
• to set off words that interrupt a sentence, such as an **appositive phrase** that is not needed to identify the word it describes	Mr. Okada, **the soccer coach,** had the team practice skills like passing, **for example,** for the first hour.
• to separate three or more items in a **series**	Shooting, passing, and dribbling are important skills.
• between coordinate adjectives, or adjectives of equal rank, that tell about the same noun	The midfielder's quick, unpredictable passes made him the team's star player.
• after an **introductory phrase or clause**	**In the last game,** he made several goals.
• before someone's exact words and after them if the sentence continues	Mr. Okada said, "Meet the ball after it bounces," as we practiced our half-volleys.
• before and after a **clause** if the clause is not necessary for understanding the sentence	At the end of practice, **before anyone left,** Mr. Okada handed out revised game schedules.
• before a question at the end of a statement	You talked to Mr. Okada, **didn't you?**
• to set off the name of a person someone is talking to	Mr. Okada said, "That's not how you do it, **Jimmy.**"
Use a comma in these places in a letter:	
• between the city and the state	Milpas, AK
• between the date and the year	July 3, 2008
• after the greeting of a personal letter	Dear Mr. Okada,
• after the closing of a letter	Sincerely,

Punctuation, continued

Apostrophe	Examples
Use an **apostrophe** to punctuate a **possessive noun**.	
If there is one owner, add **'s** to the owner's name, even if the owner's name ends in **s**.	Mrs. Ramos**'s** sons live in New Mexico.
If there is more than one owner, add **'** if the plural noun ends in **s**. Add **'s** if it does not end in **s**.	Her sons**'** birthdays are both in January. My children**'s** birthdays are in March.
Use an **apostrophe** to replace the letters left out of a contraction.	could n~~o~~t = couldn**'t** he ~~woul~~d = he**'d**

Hyphen	Examples
Use a **hyphen** to:	
• connect words in a number and in a fraction	**One-third** of the people surveyed used at least **thirty-two** gallons of water every day.
• join some words to make a compound word	A **15-year-old** boy and his **great-grandmother** have started an awareness campaign.
• connect a letter to a word	They designed a **T-shirt** for their campaign.
• divide words at the end of a line. Always divide the word between two syllables.	Please join us today in our awareness **campaign**. It's for the good of the planet.

Dash	Examples
Use a **dash** to show a break in an idea or the tone in a sentence.	Water—a valuable resource—is often taken for granted.
Or use a dash to emphasize a word, a series of words, a phrase, or a clause.	It is easy to conserve water—wash full loads of laundry, use water-saving devices, fix leaky faucets.

Ellipsis	Examples
Use an **ellipsis** to show that you have left out words.	A recent survey documented ... water usage.
Or use an ellipsis to show an idea that trails off.	I don't know ... so much waste ...

Quotation Marks	Examples
Use **quotation marks** to show:	
• a speaker's exact words	"Listen to this!" Jim said.
• the exact words quoted from a book or other printed material	The announcement in the paper was: "The writer Josie Ramón will be at Milpas Library on Friday."
• the title of a song, poem, short story, magazine article, or newspaper article	Her famous poem "Speaking" appeared in the magazine article "How to Talk to Your Teen."
• the title of a chapter from a book	She'll be reading "Getting Along," a chapter from her new book.
• words used in a special way	We will be "all ears" at the reading.

Italics and Underlining	Examples
When you are typing or using a computer, use **italics** for the names of:	
• magazines and newspapers	I like to read *Time* magazine and the *Daily News*.
• books	They help me understand our history book, *The U.S. Story*.
• plays	Did you see the play *Abraham Lincoln in Illinois*?
• movies	It was made into the movie *Young Abe*.
• musicals	The musical *Oklahoma!* is about Southwest pioneers.
• music albums	*Greatest Hits from Musicals* is my favorite album.
• TV series	Do you like the singers on the TV show *American Idol*?
If you are using handwriting, underline.	

Parentheses	Examples
Use **parentheses** around extra information in a sentence.	The new story (in the evening paper) is very interesting.

Using Words Correctly

This section will help you to choose between words that are often confused or misused.

a lot • allot

A lot means "many" and is always written as two words, never as one word. *Allot* means "to assign" or "to give out."

I have **a lot** of friends who like to eat.

We **allot** one hour for lunch.

a while • awhile

The two-word form *a while* is often preceded by the prepositions *after*, *for*, or *in*. The one-word form *awhile* is used without a preposition.

Let's stop here for **a while**.

Let's stop here **awhile**.

accept • except

Accept is a verb that means "to receive." *Except* can be a verb meaning "to leave out" or a preposition meaning "excluding."

I **accept** everything you say, **except** your point about music.

advice • advise

Advice is a noun that means "ideas about how to solve a problem." *Advise* is a verb and means "to give advice."

I will give you **advice** about your problem today, but do not ask me to **advise** you again tomorrow.

affect • effect

Affect is a verb. It means "to cause a change in" or "to influence." *Effect* as a verb means "to bring about." As a noun, *effect* means "result."

Sunshine will **affect** my plants positively.

The governor is working to **effect** change.

The rain had no **effect** on our spirits.

ain't

Ain't is not used in formal English. Use the correct form of the verb *be* with the word *not*: *is not*, *isn't*; *are not*, or *aren't*.

We **are not going** to sing in front of you.

I **am not going** to practice today.

all ready • already

Use the two-word form, *all ready*, to mean "completely finished." Use the one-word form, *already*, to mean "previously."

We waited an hour for dinner to be **all ready**.

It is a good thing I have **already** eaten today.

alright • all right

The expression *all right* means "OK" and should be written as two words. The one-word form, *alright*, is not used in formal writing.

I hope it is **all right** that I am early.

all together • altogether

The two-word form, *all together*, means "in a group." The one-word form, *altogether*, means "completely."

> It is **altogether** wrong that we will not be **all together** this holiday.

among • between

Use *among* when comparing more than two people or things. Use *between* when comparing a person or thing with one other person, thing, or group.

> How can we share one piece of pizza **among** the four of us?

> We will split the money **between** Sal and Jess.

amount of • number of

Amount of is used with nouns that cannot be counted. *Number of* is used with nouns that can be counted.

> The **amount of** pollution in the air is increasing.

> A record **number of** people attended the game.

assure • ensure • insure

Assure means "to make certain." *Ensure* means "to guarantee." *Insure* means "to cover financially."

> I **assure** you that he is OK.

> I will personally **ensure** his safety.

> If the car is **insured**, the insurance company will pay to fix the damage.

being as • being that

Neither of these is used in formal English. Use *because* or *since* instead.

> I went home early **because** I was sick.

beside • besides

Beside means "next to." *Besides* means "plus" or "in addition to."

> Located **beside** the cafeteria is a vending machine.

> **Besides** being the fastest runner, she is also the nicest team member.

bring • take

Use *bring* to speak of transporting something to where you are now. Use *take* to speak of transporting something to a place where you're not now.

> **Bring** the snacks here to my house, and then we'll **take** them to the party at Ann's.

bust • busted

Neither of these is used in formal English. Use *broke* or *broken* instead.

> I **broke** the vase by accident.

> The **broken** vase cannot be fixed.

can't • hardly • scarcely

Do not use *can't* with *hardly* or *scarcely*. That would be a double negative. Use only *can't*, or use *can* plus a negative word.

I **can't** get my work done in time.

I **can scarcely** get my work done in time.

capital • capitol

A *capital* is a place where a government is located. A *capitol* is the actual building the government meets in.

The **capital** of the U.S. is Washington, D.C.

The senate met at the **capitol** to vote.

cite • site • sight

To *cite* means "to quote a source." A *site* is "a place." *Sight* can mean "the ability to see" or it can mean "something that can be seen."

Be sure to **cite** all your sources.

My brother works on a construction **site**.

Dan went to the eye doctor to have his **sight** checked.

The sunset last night was a beautiful **sight**.

complement • compliment

Complement means "something that completes" or "to complete." *Compliment* means "something nice someone says about another person" or "to praise."

The colors you picked really **complement** each other.

I would like to **compliment** you on your new shoes.

could have • should have • would have • might have

Be sure to use "have" not "of" with words like *could*, *should*, *would*, and *might*.

I **would have** gone, but I didn't feel well last night.

council • counsel

A *council* is a group organized to study and plan something. To *counsel* is to give advice to someone.

The city **council** met to discuss traffic issues.

Mom, please **counsel** me on how to handle this situation.

different from • different than

Different from is preferred in formal English and is used with nouns and noun clauses and phrases. *Different than*, when used, is used with adverbial clauses.

My interest in music is **different from** my friends.

Movies today are **different than** they used to be in the 1950s.

farther • further

Farther refers to a physical distance. *Further* refers to time or amount.

> If you go down the road a little **farther**, you will see the sign.

> We will discuss this **further** at lunch.

fewer • less

Fewer refers to things that can be counted individually. *Less* refers to things that cannot be counted individually.

> The farm had **fewer** animals than the zoo, so it was **less** fun to visit.

good • well

The adjective *good* means "pleasing," "kind," or "healthy." The adverb *well* means "ably."

> She is a **good** person.

> I am glad to see that you are **well** again after that illness.

> You have performed **well**.

immigrate to • emigrate from

Immigrate to means "to move to a country." *Emigrate from* means "to leave a country."

> I **immigrated to** America in 2001 from Panama.

> I **emigrated from** El Salvador because of the war.

it's • its

It's is a contraction of *it is*. *Its* is a possessive word meaning "belonging to it."

> **It's** going to be a hot day.

> The dog drank all of **its** water already.

kind of • sort of

These words mean "a type of." In formal English, do not use them to mean "partly." Use *somewhat* or *rather* instead.

> The peanut is actually a **kind of** bean.

> I feel **rather** silly in this outfit.

lay • lie

Lay means "to put in a place." It is used to describe what people do with objects. *Lie* means "to recline." People can *lie* down, but they *lay* down objects. Do not confuse this use of *lie* with the verb that means "to tell an untruth."

> I will **lay** the book on this desk for you.

> I'm tired and am going to **lie** on the couch.

> If you **lie** in court, you will be punished.

learn • teach

To *learn* is "to receive information." To *teach* is "to give information."

> If we want to **learn**, we have to listen.

> She will **teach** us how to drive.

leave • let

Leave means "to go away." *Let* means "to allow."

> **Leave** the keys on the kitchen table.

> I will **let** you borrow my pen.

like • as

Like can be used either as a preposition or as a verb meaning "to care about something." *As* is a conjunction and should be used to introduce a subordinate clause.

> She sometimes acts **like** a princess. But I still **like** her.

> She acts **as** if she owns the school.

loose • lose

Loose can be used as an adverb or adjective meaning "free" or "not securely attached." The verb *lose* means "to misplace" or "to be defeated."

> I let the dog **loose** and he is missing.

> Did you **lose** your homework?

> Did they **lose** the game by many points?

passed • past

Passed is a verb that means "to have moved ahead of." *Past* is a noun that means "the time before the present."

> I **passed** my English test.

> Poor grades are in the **past** now.

precede • proceed

Precede means "to come before." *Proceed* means "to go forward."

> Prewriting **precedes** drafting in the writing process.

> Turn left; then **proceed** down the next street.

principal • principle

A *principal* is "a person of authority." Principal can also mean "main." A *principle* is "a general truth or belief."

> The **principal** of our school makes an announcement every morning.

> The **principal** ingredient in baking is flour.

> The essay was based on the **principles** of effective persuasion.

raise • rise

The verb *raise* always takes an object. The verb *rise* does not take an object.

> **Raise** the curtain for the play.

> The curtain **rises**.

> I **rise** from bed every morning at six.

real • really

Real means "actual." It is an adjective used to describe nouns. *Really* means "actually" or "truly." It is an adverb used to describe verbs, adjectives, or other adverbs.

> The diamond was **real**.

> The diamond was **really** beautiful.

set • sit

The verb *set* usually means "to put something down." The verb *sit* means "to go into a seated position."

> I **set** the box on the ground.

> Please **sit** while we talk.

than • then

Than is used to compare things. *Then* means "next" and is used to tell when something took place.

> She likes fiction more **than** nonfiction.

> First, we will go to the bookstore; **then** we will go home.

they're • their • there

They're is the contraction of *they are*. *Their* is the possessive form of the pronoun *they*. *There* is used to indicate location.

> **They're** all on vacation this week.

> I want to use **their** office.

> The library is right over **there**.

> **There** are several books I want to read.

this • these • that • those

This indicates something specific that is near you. *These* is the plural form of *this*. *That* indicates something specific that is farther from you. *Those* is the plural form of *that*.

> **This** book in my hand belongs to me. **These** pens are also mine.

> **That** book over there is his. **Those** notes are his, too.

where

It is not necessary to use *at* or *to* with *where*.

> **Where** are you going?

> **Where** is Ernesto?

who • whom

Who is a subject. *Whom* is an object. If you can replace *who* or *whom* with *he*, *she*, *they*, or *it*, use *who*. If you can replace the word with *him*, *her*, or *them*, use *whom*.

> **Who** is going to finish first?

> My grandmother is a woman to **whom** I owe many thanks.

who's • whose

Who's is a contraction of *who is*. *Whose* is the possessive form of *who*.

> **Who's** coming to our dinner party?

> **Whose** car is parked in the garage?

you're • your

You're is a contraction of *you are*. *Your* is a possessive pronoun meaning "belonging to you."

> **You're** going to be late if you don't hurry.

> Is **your** backpack too heavy?

Spelling Handbook

Spelling. It's one of those subjects that seem to make a lot of people anxious. You now—like going to the dentist or taking a pop quiz. It's time to take control of spelling and turn worries into word work!

The truth is that spelling can be fun, especially when you see yourself getting better and better at it. It's also true that once you learn the spelling basics, you will know how to spell six out of seven words. That's right! Most words follow spelling patterns. Most words obey spelling rules. Tricky words are definitely in the minority.

Don't just read this guide. Apply it! Think like a speller. Here are some ideas:

- Start your own lists of related words.

- Make other lists of unusual words.

- Become a pattern finder. As you figure out a pattern, write the rule down in your own words.

- Create your own dictionary for words that are tricky for you.

- Make up your own ways to remember a tough word.

Write it all down, and watch your personal spelling guide grow right along with your spelling skills!

Don't forget every speller's best friend—the dictionary! ▶

Learning New Words

Follow six steps when you are learning how to spell a new word.

STEP 1: Look at the word carefully.

STEP 2: Say the word aloud. Look at the word as you say it, and listen to yourself saying it.

STEP 3: Picture the whole word in your mind.

STEP 4: Spell the word aloud, letter by letter.

STEP 5: Write the word. Use your memory.

STEP 6: Check the word. You can use a dictionary, a computer spell checker, or a word list.

If you find errors in **STEP 6**, circle them. Write the word correctly. Then repeat the steps again for the word.

Use all Your Senses

Good spellers remember how words look and how they sound. When you are learning how to spell a new word, you should also get the rest of your senses involved. Try these ideas to use all of your senses together:

Ideas for Learning New Words

See it. Really study the word. Look at every letter.

Hear it. As you study the word, say it aloud. Say each sound and notice how it matches the letters.

Work it. As you say each sound, tap your finger or foot. As you look at each letter, write it in the air.

Feel it. Write the word slowly. Shape the letters carefully. Imagine writing the word in sand to really feel it!

Making Words Your Own

Every person has trouble spelling some words. The secret is to help yourself remember these troublesome words. You can make up your own memory tools that fit your way of thinking. Here are some examples.

Rhymes

Here's a famous rhyme to use when deciding whether to use *ie* (brief) or *ei* (receive).

> "*i* before *e*
> except after *c*
> or when sounded *a*
> as in *neighbor* and *weigh* . . .
> and *weird* is just weird!"

Acronyms

Think of a word that begins with each letter. The words in the correct order should be easy for you to remember.

> **EXAMPLES** **because**
>
> **b**ig **e**lephants **c**an **a**lways **u**nderstand **s**mall **e**lephants
>
> **rhythm**
>
> **r**hythm **h**elps **y**our **t**wo **h**ips **m**ove
>
> **ocean**
>
> **o**nly **c**ats' **e**yes **a**re **n**arrow

Explanations

Think of a clever way to remember *why* letters appear or not in a word.

> **EXAMPLES** **argument**
>
> "I lost an *e* in an argument."
>
> **dessert**
>
> "It has two *s*'s for sweet stuff!"
>
> **necessary**
>
> "It is *necessary* for a shirt to have one collar (one *c*) and two sleeves (two *s*'s)."

Stories

Make up a story that will help you remember how to spell a word.

EXAMPLES   **cemetery**
I got scared walking through the cemetery and yelled, "e-e-e!" as I ran away. (The word *cemetery* has three *e*'s.)

separate
A lady was married to a man named Sep. One day she saw a rat. She yelled, "Sep! A rat! E!"

The best memory tools are the ones you make up. Here are examples from students' personal spelling guides.

from Grace's Memory Tricks

When I get a bargain, I feel like I gain money.

from Alphonso's Explanations

The desert is too dry to grow more than one s.

from Anna's Amazing Acronyms

said: Sailor Al is daring.

from Julian's Spelling Stories

My aunt always says that I have "cute scarlet cheeks." (Scarlet is another word for red.) When I am embarrassed, my two scarlet cheeks turn really red. The word embarrassed takes two r's and two s's, to match my two red or scarlet cheeks.

Reflect

• Which memory tool looks most fun?

• Which memory tool would probably work best for me because of how I am able to remember things?

Finding and Fixing Errors

Spelling and the Writing Process

You focus on spelling during the editing and proofreading stage of writing. But what should you do while drafting? When you are drafting, let your ideas flow. Keep writing even if you are unsure of how to spell a word. When you want to write a word and are unsure of the spelling, follow these steps:

1. Recall spelling rules you know. Think about related words and how they are spelled.

2. Write the word down.

3. Circle the word so you remember to check the spelling.

Check Your Spelling

Read your paper carefully, word by word. Study each spelling. Think about the rules you know. Remember, six out of every seven words follow common spelling rules.

How do you know if a word is spelled wrong? Trust what you know. If you are not sure, circle it. Many of the words you circle and check may be spelled correctly! There are common errors that many writers make. Look out for these problems:

- Missing letters
- Missing syllables
- Flipped letters
- Words that sound alike
- Sounds that can be spelled many different ways

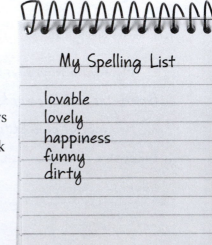

My Spelling List

lovable
lovely
happiness
funny
dirty

Whether you work alone or with a partner, keep track of the words that you misspell. Create a personal spelling list. Review the words on a regular schedule and you will see your spelling improve.

Bryon used these spelling tips to find the errors in his personal narrative.

Byron's First Draft

I really enjoyed our family reunion this summer. More than 20 of us got together at Clear Lake for the Fourth of July. There were some surprises. My Uncle Al hadn't seen me for two years, and he was amazed by my hieght. There were three new babys born since last year's reunion, including twin girls! Other things at the reunion were expected, includeing great food, lots of laughs, fun games, and warm feelings.

Byron thinks:

" This word follows the *i* before *e* rule, but it just doesn't look right."

" I need to think about how to make a word that ends in y plural."

You should always check your own spelling. It's also helpful to have a friend or classmate check your work. Remember we all have different words that challenge us. Ask your friend to circle words to check. Talk about the words. Work together to use a dictionary to find the correct spellings.

Byron's Edited Draft

I really enjoyed our famly reunion this summer. More than 20 of us got together at Clear Lake for the Fourth of July. There were some surprises. My Uncle Al hadn't seen me for two years, and he was amazed by my height. There were three new babies born since last year's reunion, including twin girls! Other things at the reunion were expected, includeing great food, lots of laughs, fun games, and warm feelings.

" I remember to really say the middle syllable to myself so I don't leave it out: *fam·i·ly.*"

" Remember to drop the e before adding an ending that starts with a vowel."

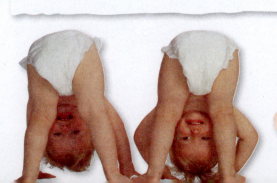

Making Sound-Spelling Connections

English words are made up of combinations of more than 40 different sounds. You can expect each sound to be spelled by certain letters. (Yes, there are exceptions!) Let's start with vowel sounds.

LONG VOWELS	
Spellings	**Example Words**
i ie igh i_e _y	**i**tem p**ie** n**igh**t f**i**n**e** cr**y**
o oa ow o_e	**o**pen s**oa**p gr**ow** v**o**t**e**
u ew ue ui u_e oo	**u**nit f**ew** bl**ue** fr**ui**t p**u**r**e** t**oo**th

OTHER VOWELS	
Spellings	**Example Words**
au aw	**au**thor sh**aw**l
al all	**al**so b**all**
ow ou	c**ow** sc**ou**t
oy oi	t**oy** b**oi**l
oo u	f**oo**t b**u**sh
ar	y**ar**d
er ir ur	ov**er** b**ir**d c**ur**l
or	h**or**n
a e i o u	**a**bout **e**ffect rabb**i**t sec**o**nd circ**u**s

Now let's look at consonant sounds.

CONSONANT SOUNDS	
Spellings	**Example Words**
ch _tch	chin patch
d	did
f ph	first graph
g	gum
h	hen
j g _dge	jump giant fudge
k c ck	king camp luck
x	six
qu	quack
l	left
m mb	make lamb

CONSONANT SOUNDS	
Spellings	**Example Words**
n kn	name know
p	pond
r wr	red wrist
s c	safe pencil
sh	shell
t	time
th	thank
th	this
v	van
w	wash
wh	when
y	yell
z s	zebra news

Breaking Words Down

One great way to learn how to spell a word is to break it into parts. You can break words into **syllables**. Learn how to spell each syllable. Then put them together.

Syllable Rules (Look in the middle of the word. Look for the patterns named below. Say the word aloud.)	Examples
The VCV Rule: **A consonant between two vowels** If the first vowel is long, the break usually comes before the consonant. If the first vowel is short, the break usually comes after the consonant.	**before:** be·fore **vacant:** va·cant **music:** mu·sic **cabin:** cab·in **wagon:** wag·on **linen:** lin·en
The VCCV Rule: **Two consonants between vowels** The break comes between the consonants, unless the consonants work together to make one sound (as in *sh* and *th*).	**blanket:** blan·ket **perhaps:** per·haps **picture:** pic·ture **fashion:** fash·ion **weather:** weath·er
The VCCCV Rule: **Three consonants between vowels** The break comes between the two consonants that work together to make a sound and the third consonant.	**pumpkin:** pump·kin **exchange:** ex·change **instead:** in·stead **although:** al·though
Compound Words: Always divide a compound word between the two smaller words forming it.	**afternoon:** after·noon **driveway:** drive·way **skateboard:** skate·board

Look for these patterns in longer words, too. For example:

possible: pos·si·ble

controversy: con·tro·ver·sy

responsibility: re·spon·si·bil·i·ty

Making Words Plural

Once you learn how to spell a word, you also need to learn how to get it right in its different forms. For example, when you make nouns plural, you might need to make some spelling changes.

Plural Rules	Examples
Make most nouns plural by adding –s to the end.	author ⟶ authors crowd ⟶ crowds principal ⟶ principals niece ⟶ nieces
If the word ends in s, sh, ch, x, or z, add –es.	business ⟶ businesses brush ⟶ brushes speech ⟶ speeches fox ⟶ foxes waltz ⟶ waltzes
If the word ends in a consonant followed by y, change the y to i and add –es.	category ⟶ categories puppy ⟶ puppies library ⟶ libraries fly ⟶ flies
If the word ends in a vowel followed by y, just add –s.	birthday ⟶ birthdays toy ⟶ toys turkey ⟶ turkeys key ⟶ keys
If the word ends in a consonant followed by o, add –es.	hero ⟶ heroes potato ⟶ potatoes
If the word ends in a vowel followed by o, just add –s.	video ⟶ videos radio ⟶ radios
Words that end in f or fe are tricky. Sometimes you change the f to v and add –es. Sometimes you just add –s.	knife ⟶ knives half ⟶ halves roof ⟶ roofs belief ⟶ beliefs

Making Words Plural, continued

Some words have irregular plural forms. They do not follow the normal rules for creating plurals.

Singular	Plural	Singular	Plural
auto	autos	man	men
axis	axes	medium	media
basis	bases	mouse	mice
child	children	oasis	oases
crisis	crises	ox	oxen
criterion	criteria	parenthesis	parentheses
datum	data	piano	pianos
Eskimo	Eskimos	radius	radii
focus	foci	solo	solos
foot	feet	stimulus	stimuli
goose	geese	tooth	teeth
index	indices	woman	women

Some words are used for both the singular and the plural forms: deer, fish, moose, series, sheep, traffic, trout, wheat.

Knowing Your Roots

Many English words came from other languages. In many modern English words, you can see Greek and Latin roots. In some cases, you can find the same root in several words. So, if you learn how to spell these common roots, you will be on your way to knowing how to spell many words!

Root	Origin	Meaning	Examples
act	Latin	do	action, enactment
alter	Latin	other	alternate, alternative
anim	Latin	life	animated, inanimate
ann	Latin	year	annual, anniversary
aqua	Latin	water	aquarium, aquatic
ast	Greek	star	astronaut, astronomy
aud	Latin	hear	auditorium, audible
bio	Greek	life	biography, biology
cred	Latin	believe	credit, incredible
cycl	Greek	circle	bicycle, recycle
dic	Latin	speak	dictate, verdict
form	Latin	shape	uniform, transform
geo	Greek	earth	geologist, geography
gram	Greek	written	grammar, telegram
loc	Latin	place	location, local
meter	Greek	measure	thermometer, diameter
nat	Latin	born	native, national
phon	Greek	sound	phonics, telephone
poli	Greek	city	politics, cosmopolitan
port	Latin	carry	portable, import

Root	Origin	Meaning	Examples
rect	Latin	straight	rectangle, erect
rupt	Latin	break	erupt, interrupt
san	Latin	health	sane, sanitary
sci	Greek	know	science, conscious
sign	Latin	mark	signal, signature
spec	Latin	see	spectacles, inspect
struct	Latin	build	instruct, destruction
terr	Latin	land	terrace, territory
tract	Latin	pull	tractor, subtract
trib	Latin	give	contribution, attribute
vac	Latin	empty	vacant, evacuate
var	Latin	different	variety, variable

Adding Inflected Endings

Other word forms are made when certain endings, called **inflected endings**, are added. These endings include –*ed*, -*ing*, –*er*, and –*est*. Sometimes the spelling of a word changes when these endings are added.

Inflected Endings Rules	Examples		
If the word ends with one vowel and two consonants, just add the ending.	weigh	→	weighed, weighing
	grand	→	grander, grandest
If the word ends with two vowels and one consonant, just add the ending.	repair	→	repaired, repairing
	great	→	greater, greatest
If the word ends in silent e, drop the e before adding the ending.	acquire	→	acquired, acquiring
	safe	→	safer, safest

Inflected Endings Rules, continued	Examples, continued
If the word ends in one vowel and one consonant (except *x*), double the consonant before adding the ending	trim → trimmed, trimming wet → wetter, wettest
If the word ends in *y*, change the *y* to *i* before adding –*ed*, –*er*, or –*est*. However, keep the *y* if you are adding –*ing*.	study → studied easy → easier, easiest study → studying
If the word ends in *c*, add a *k* before the ending.	panic → panicked, panicking

Adding Suffixes and Prefixes

Other **suffixes** (the letters after the root word) can also change the spelling of a word.

Suffix Rules	Examples
If the word ends in silent *e*, drop the *e* before adding a suffix that starts with a vowel. However, if the suffix starts with a consonant, just add it to the word.	lie + -ar → liar white + -en → whiten life + -less → lifeless confine + ment → confinement
If the word ends in a consonant and *y*, change the *y* to *i* before adding the suffix.	pretty + -ly → prettily silly + -ness → silliness
If the word ends in a vowel and *y*, just add the suffix.	enjoy + -ment → enjoyment play + -ful → playful
If the word ends in *le*, drop the final *le* before adding the suffix –*ly*.	able + -ly → ably comfortable + -ly → comfortably
If the word ends in *l*, just add –*ly* to the end.	usual + -ly → usually annual + -ly → annually

When it comes to **prefixes** (the letters before the root word), you are lucky. You do not have to memorize any spelling rules to add prefixes! The spelling of a word does not change when you add a prefix.

Prefix Examples
disagree, impossible, reheat, unable

Knowing the Long and Short of It

Compound Words

- A **compound word** is made up of two smaller words. The compound word has a new meaning.

- Most of the time, you just put the two short words together without changing their spellings. These are called **closed compounds**.

- Sometimes compound words are **open compounds**. They are spelled with a space between the two words.

- **Hyphenated compounds** use a hyphen to join the two words.

- When a compound word is used as an adjective or adverb, it is usually hyphenated, except when part of the compound is an adverb ending in –*ly*.

Examples
sailboat
high school
well-known

Examples
baseball
homework
raincoat

Examples
potato chips
vacation home
health food

Examples
ice-cold
brand-new
long-term

Examples
The track meet was an all-day event.

Exception
The badly injured woman was taken away in an ambulance.

Contractions

When two words are joined into one with a loss of one or more letters, the word is called a **contraction**. The missing letter is replaced by an apostrophe.

- Many contractions are formed with a pronoun and the verb forms *am, are, is, have,* or *will.*

  EXAMPLE

  I + am ⟶ I'm

  we + are ⟶ we're

  he + is ⟶ he's

  they + have ⟶ they've

  she + will ⟶ she'll

- Many other contractions are formed with a verb and the word *not*. To make this kind of contraction, an apostrophe replaces the *o* in *not*.

  EXAMPLES

  could + not ⟶ couldn't

  does + not ⟶ doesn't

  EXCEPTIONS

  can + not ⟶ can't (just one n)

  will + not ⟶ won't (a different word)

Making Spelling Generalizations

You can memorize certain rules about spelling patterns within words. These rules are nearly always true, so they are known as **generalizations**.

Generalizations	Examples	Exceptions
ie or *ei* for the long e sound: Write *i* before e except right after c.	chief, relief, shield, receive	weird, seize, either, leisure, neither
words ending with a syllable pronounced "shent": This ending is spelled *cient*.	efficient sufficient ancient	
the letter *q*: Always follow the letter *q* with *u*.	quantity, quiet, request, inquiry, antique	Iraq, Iraqi, Qatar
the schwa sound followed by /l/ at the end of a word: These two sounds combined at the end of the word will be spelled –*le*, -*el*, or –*al*.	staple, jewel, dental	
c: the /k/ or /s/ sound When *c* is followed by e, i, or y, it makes the sound /s/. When *c* is followed by a, o, or u, it makes the sound /k/.	celery, city, fancy camera, copy, cushion	
words ending with a short vowel followed by /k/: The /k/ sound is spelled ck.	pack, check, sick, lock, buck	
words ending with a short vowel followed by /j/: The /j/ sound is spelled *dge*.	badge, ledge, ridge, dodge, fudge	
words ending with /v/: Final /v/ is spelled *ve*.	brave, dive, cove	names like Tel Aviv and Isaac Asimov
words with endings pronounced /shon/: This final syllable is spelled *cion*, *sion*, or *tion*. If the base word has a *t*, the spelling is –*tion*. If the base word has a *d* or an *s*, the spelling is –*sion*.	suspicion, tension creation delete, deletion decide, decision confuse, confusion	attend, attention

Learning to Spell Tricky Words

Some words are tricky because they just don't follow the rules or sound-spelling connections. Other words are confusing because they sound alike but are spelled differently and have different meanings. These words are called **homophones**. Still other words are easily confused because they sound similar.

Lists of homophones and easily confused words are started here. On the next page, see more lists of common words that don't follow the rules. Add your own words to these lists as you come across them. Remember to make the words your own by coming up with good ways to connect their meanings to their spellings.

Homophones and Meanings	Examples
all together (in a group) altogether (completely)	It is **altogether** wrong that we will not be **all together** this holiday.
capital (a place where a government is located) capitol (the actual building the government meets in)	We saw the senate vote in their chambers at the **capitol** during our tour of the **capital**.
cite (to quote a source) site (a place) sight (the ability to see or something that can be seen)	Be sure to **cite** your sources. My brother works on a construction **site**. The sunset last night was a beautiful **sight**.
council (a group organized to study and plan something) counsel (to give advice to someone)	The city **council** asked a lawyer to come and **counsel** them about civil rights.
it's (a contraction of *it is*) its (a possessive word meaning "belonging to it")	**It's** true that the dog drank all of **its** water already.
passed (to have moved ahead of) past (the time before the present)	In the **past** my brother drove too fast and often **passed** cars when he shouldn't.
principal (a person of authority or main) principle (a general truth or belief)	Our school **principal** makes announcements every morning. The **principal** ingredient in baking is flour. The essay was based on the **principles** of effective persuasion.
they're (contraction of *they are*) their (possessive form of the pronoun *they*) there (used to indicate location)	**They're** all on vacation this week. I want to use **their** office. The library is right over **there**.

Homophones and Meanings	Examples
who's (contraction of *who is*) whose (possessive from of *who*)	**Who's** coming to our dinner party? **Whose** car is parked in the garage?
you're (contraction of *you are*) your (possessive pronoun meaning "belong to you")	**You're** going to be late if you don't hurry. Is **your** backpack too heavy? **from Grace's Memory Tricks** My principal is my PAL. A ruLE can be called a principLE.

Easily Confused Words and Meanings	Examples
accept (to receive) except (to leave out or excluding)	I **accept** everything you say **except** your point about music.
advice (ideas about how to solve a problem) advise (to give advice)	I will give you **advice** about your problem today, but do not ask me to **advise** you again tomorrow.
affect (to cause a change in or to influence) effect (to bring about or the result)	Sunshine will **affect** my plants in a positive way. The rain will have a good **effect** on my plants, too.
assure (to make certain) ensure (to guarantee) insure (to cover financially)	I **assure** you that he is OK. I will personally **ensure** his safety. If the car is **insured**, the insurance company will pay to fix the damage.
beside (next to) besides (in addition to)	A parking lot is right **beside** the store. **Besides** being the fastest runner, she is also the nicest team member.
farther (refers to a physical distance) further (refers to time or amount)	If you go down the road a little **farther**, you will see the sign. We will discuss this **further** at lunch.
loose (free or not securely attached) lose (to misplace or to be defeated)	The dog got **loose** and now he is missing. First I **lose** my homework, and then we **lose** the game!
precede (to come before) proceed (to go forward)	Prewriting **precedes** drafting in the writing process. Please **proceed** carefully on the icy sidewalk.
than (used to compare things) then (next)	She likes to read fiction more **than** nonfiction. First, we will go to the bookstore; **then** we will go home.

Learning to Spell Tricky Words continued

Some of the most common words in the English language do not follow spelling rules. Check out these examples from the 25 most frequently used words:

are	*have*	*of*	*on*	*to*	*they*	*you*	*was*

You see these words so often that you tend to learn them by sight. You memorize what they look like. For this reason, these common words are sometimes called *sight* words.

A list is started here of other tricky words that just don't follow the usual rules and patterns. These words come from the 1,000 most common words in the English language and from lists of words that students your age often misspell. You will probably have more words that are tricky for you to spell for one reason or another. Add those words to this list.

A	C	F	K	O
above	century	father	knowledge	ocean
accurate	certain	favorite		often
ache	chocolate	February	**L**	once
again	city	foreign	language	one
aisle	clothes	four	laughed	only
although	color	friend	listen	opposite
among	come	from		other
ancient	conquer		**M**	
answer	conscience	**G**	many	**P**
anxious	control	give	marriage	people
any	cough	gone	material	persuade
	country	great	meant	picture
B		group	measure	piece
balloon	**D**	guard	minute	put
bargain	design	guess	money	
beautiful	determine		mother	**Q**
become	discipline	**H**	mountain	quarterly
been	does	heard	move	quarter
both	done	height		
bought			**N**	**R**
brilliant	**E**	**I**	necessary	receipt
brought	earth	iron	none	restaurant
building	early	island	notice	rhythm
bury	engine			route
busy	enough	**J**		
buy	evening	jealousy		
	experience			

S	T	V	XYZ
said	though	vacuum	yacht
says	thought	valley	young
several	through	various	youth
shoes	toward	very	
should	trouble	villian	
sign			
soldier	**U**	**W**	
some	usually	want	
southern		watch	
special		water	
sugar		Wednesday	
sure		were	
surface		what	
		where	
		whose	
		woman	
		work	
		would	

My Word List

mansion

gorgeous

daughter

fruit

chalk

Index of Skills and Strategies

At-A-Glance Index

Acknowledgments

Bill Smith Studios: Design and artwork of "Space" from *The World Almanac for Kids 2003.* Copyright © Bill Smith Studios. Used by permission.

Encyclopædia Britannica: Reprinted with permission from Encyclopædia Britannica, © 2008 by Encyclopædia Britannica, Inc.

John Eng: Quote from Dr. John Eng was originally published in "Taking on a monster" by Terri Somers from the *San Diego Union-Tribune*, April 29, 2005. By permission.

Grove/Atlantic, Inc.: *This Boy's Life* © 1989 by Tobias Wolff. Used by permission of Grove/Atlantic, Inc.

James W. Hackett: "A bitter morning" by James W. Hackett from hacketthaiku.com. Reprinted by permission.

Henry Holt and Company: "Stopping by Woods on a Snowy Evening" by Robert Frost from *The Poetry of Robert Frost*, edited by Edward Connery Lathem. Copyright 1923, 1969 by Henry Holt and Company. Copyright 1951 by Robert Frost. Reprinted by permission of Henry Holt and Company, LLC.

Highlights for Children: "Oak" by Dawn Watkins. Copyright © 1997 by Highlights for Children, Inc., Columbus, Ohio. Reprinted by permission.

Houghton Mifflin Harcourt Publishing Company: Excerpt from *Jumanji* by Chris Van Allsburg. Copyright © 1981 by Chris Van Allsburg. Reprinted by permission of Houghton Mifflin Harcourt Publishing Company. All rights reserved.

Marshall Cavendish Corporation: Reprinted from *Juvenile Diabetes* by Johannah Haney with permission of Marshall Cavendish.

McGraw-Hill: "southward" through "Spanish" from the *Macmillan Dictionary for Children.* Copyright © 1997 by Simon & Schuster and was originally published in the McGraw-Hill School Dictionary.

National Geographic Society: Cover of the *Family Reference Atlas of the World, Second Edition.* Copyright © 2007 National Geographic Society. All rights reserved.

Cover of *National Geographic Historical Atlas of the United States.* Copyright © 2004 National Geographic Society. All rights reserved.

Cover of the *National Geographic Road Atlas, Adventure Edition.* Published by National Geographic Maps in association with MapQuest, Inc. Copyright © 2007 by MapQuest, Inc. and Adventure section copyright © 2007 National Geographic Society. Cover photo by Steve Casimiro. All rights reserved.

Oxford University Press: "good" from *Oxford American Writer's Thesaurus.* Copyright © 2004 by Oxford University Press. Used by permission of Oxford University Press, Inc.

Random House, Inc.: Excerpt from *Mother* by Maya Angelou, copyright © 2006 by Maya Angelou. Used by permission of Random House, Inc.

Excerpt from *The Watson's Go to Birmingham* – 1963 by Christopher Paul Curtis. Copyright © 1995 by Christopher Paul Curtis.

"Funny in Farsi" excerpt was originally titled "Hot Dogs and Wild Geese," from *Funny in Farsi* by Firoozeh Dumas, copyright © 2003 by Firoozeh Dumas. Used by permission of Villard Books, a division of Random House, Inc.

Scholastic Library Publishing, Inc.: "Mars" by Elaine Landau. All rights reserved. Reprinted by permission of Franklin Watts an imprint of Scholastic Library Publishing, Inc. Background image on title page is from NASA.

Scholastic, Inc.: Adapted from *Dear America: The Winter of Red Snow: The Revolutionary War Diary of Abigail Jane Stewart* by Kristiana Gregory. Copyright © 1996 by Kristiana Gregory. Reprinted by permission of Scholastic Inc.

SUNY Press: Reprinted by permission from *Basho's Haiku: Selected Poems of Matsuo Basho* by Matsuo Basho, translated by David Landis Barnhill, the State University of New York Press © 2004, State University of New York. All rights reserved.

Teen Ink Magazine: "Book Review of When I Was Puerto Rican by Esmeralda Santiago" by Jennifer K. Reprinted with permission of Teen Ink Magazine and teenink.com

Anthony Virgilio: "heat before the storm" and "the cathedral bell" by Nicholas Virgilio from *Selected Haiku* (Second Edition) by Nicholas Virgilio co-published by Burnt Lake Press and Black Moss Press, copyright © 1988 Nicholas A. Virgilio. Reprinted by permission by Anthony Virgilio.

World Almanac Education Group: "Space" from the *World Almanac for Kids 2003.* Copyright © 2002 World Almanac Education Group. All rights reserved. Used by permission.

The YGS Group: "Molding Troubled Kids into Future Chefs" by Kathy Blake. Used with permission of Nation's Restaurant News © 2008 All Rights Reserved. "Tropical Storm Florence Forms in Atlantic" by The Associated Press, September 5, 2006. Used with permission of The Associated Press © 2008 All Rights Reserved.

Photography

Cover ©JH Pete Carmichael/Riser/Getty Images. **Back cover** ©Loeiza JACQ/Gamma-Rapho via Getty Images. **2–3W** ©David R. Frazier Photolibrary Inc./Alamy. **2W** ©MM Productions/Corbis. **4W** ©Tony Anderson/stone/Getty Images. **7W** ©Thinkstock/Corbis. **8W** ©David Young-Wolff/PhotoEdit. **11W** ©Jean-Pierre Lescourret/Corbis. **13W** ©Richard Klune/Corbis. **13W** ©Atlantide Phototravel/Corbis. **15W** ©Frank Gaglione/Digital Vision/Getty Images. **16W** ©Martin O'Neill. **18W** ©MedioImages/Corbis. **19W** ©BananaStock/Jupiter Images. **20W** ©Larry Hirshowitz/Corbis. **21W** ©National Geographic. **21W** ©National Geographic. **21W** ©Michael Lewis/National Geographic Collection National Geographic. **22W** ©Tom & Dee Ann McCarthy/Bridge/Corbis. **23W** ©Paul Harizan/Getty Images. **23W** ©Shannon Fagan/Flirt/Corbis. **23W** ©Ariel

Illustration

Fine Art

Common Core State Standards

CHAPTER 1: The Building Blocks of Writing

Project 1: Paragraph Structure: Ways to Organize

pages	Lesson	Code	Standards Text
2W–13W	Sentences and Paragraphs: Model Study and Writing Strategy: Organize Your Paragraphs		Write informative/explanatory texts to examine a topic and convey ideas, concepts, and information through the selection, organization, and analysis of relevant content.
		W.8.2.a	Introduce a topic clearly, previewing what is to follow; organize ideas, concepts, and information into broader categories; include formatting (e.g., headings), graphics (e.g., charts, tables), and multimedia when useful to aiding comprehension.
14W–15W	Paragraph: Plan and Write	W.8.2	Write informative/explanatory texts to examine a topic and convey ideas, concepts, and information through the selection, organization, and analysis of relevant content.
		W.8.2.a	Introduce a topic clearly, previewing what is to follow; organize ideas, concepts, and information into broader categories; include formatting (e.g., headings), graphics (e.g., charts, tables), and multimedia when useful to aiding comprehension.
		W.8.2.b	Develop the topic with relevant, well-chosen facts, definitions, concrete details, quotations, or other information and examples.
		W.8.4	Produce clear and coherent writing in which the development, organization, and style are appropriate to task, purpose, and audience.
		W.8.5	With some guidance and support from peers and adults, develop and strengthen writing as needed by planning, revising, editing, rewriting, or trying a new approach, focusing on how well purpose and audience have been addressed.
		W.8.10	Write routinely over extended time frames (time for research, reflection, and revision) and shorter time frames (a single sitting or a day or two) for a range of discipline-specific tasks, purposes, and audiences.

Common Core State Standards, continued

Common Core State Standards, continued

Pages	Lesson	Code	Standards Text
32W–39W	Personal Narrative: Draft	W.8.3	Write narratives to develop real or imagined experiences or events using effective technique, relevant descriptive details, and well-structured event sequences.
		W.8.3.a	Engage and orient the reader by establishing a context and point of view and introducing a narrator and/or characters; organize an event sequence that unfolds naturally and logically.
		W.8.3.b	Use narrative techniques, such as dialogue, pacing, description, and reflection, to develop experiences, events, and/or characters.
		W.8.3.d	Use precise words and phrases, relevant descriptive details, and sensory language to capture the action and convey experiences and events.
		W.8.3.e	Provide a conclusion that follows from and reflects on the narrated experiences or events.
		W.8.4	Produce clear and coherent writing in which the development, organization, and style are appropriate to task, purpose, and audience.
		W.8.5	With some guidance and support from peers and adults, develop and strengthen writing as needed by planning, revising, editing, rewriting, or trying a new approach, focusing on how well purpose and audience have been addressed.
		W.8.10	Write routinely over extended time frames (time for research, reflection, and revision) and shorter time frames (a single sitting or a day or two) for a range of discipline-specific tasks, purposes, and audiences.
40W–41W	Writing Strategy: Write Effective Sentences		Write narratives to develop real or imagined experiences or events using effective technique, relevant descriptive details, and well-structured event sequences.
		W.8.3.c	Use a variety of transition words, phrases, and clauses to convey sequence, signal shifts from one time frame or setting to another, and show the relationships among experiences and events.
		W.8.5	With some guidance and support from peers and adults, develop and strengthen writing as needed by planning, revising, editing, rewriting, or trying a new approach, focusing on how well purpose and audience have been addressed.

Common Core State Standards, continued

Project 2: Use the Writing Process, continued

Pages	Lesson	Code	Standards Text
42W–47W	**Personal Narrative: Revise**		Write narratives to develop real or imagined experiences or events using effective technique, relevant descriptive details, and well-structured event sequences.
		W.8.3.a	Engage and orient the reader by establishing a context and point of view and introducing a narrator and/or characters; organize an event sequence that unfolds naturally and logically.
		W.8.3.c	Use a variety of transition words, phrases, and clauses to convey sequence, signal shifts from one time frame or setting to another, and show the relationships among experiences and events.
		W.8.3.d	Use precise words and phrases, relevant descriptive details, and sensory language to capture the action and convey experiences and events.
		W.8.4	Produce clear and coherent writing in which the development, organization, and style are appropriate to task, purpose, and audience.
		W.8.5	With some guidance and support from peers and adults, develop and strengthen writing as needed by planning, revising, editing, rewriting, or trying a new approach, focusing on how well purpose and audience have been addressed.
48W–56W	**Personal Narrative: Edit and Proofread**	W.8.5	With some guidance and support from peers and adults, develop and strengthen writing as needed by planning, revising, editing, rewriting, or trying a new approach, focusing on how well purpose and audience have been addressed.
		W.8.6	Use technology, including the Internet, to produce and publish writing and present the relationships between information and ideas efficiently as well as to interact and collaborate with others.
		W.8.10	Write routinely over extended time frames (time for research, reflection, and revision) and shorter time frames (a single sitting or a day or two) for a range of discipline-specific tasks, purposes, and audiences.
		L.8.1	Demonstrate command of the conventions of standard English grammar and usage when writing or speaking.
		L.8.2	Demonstrate command of the conventions of standard English capitalization, punctuation, and spelling when writing.
		L.8.2.c	Spell correctly.

Common Core State Standards, continued

Chapter 2 The Writing Process, continued			
Project 2: Use the Writing Process, continued			
Pages	**Lesson**	**Code**	**Standards Text**
		L.8.3	Use knowledge of language and its conventions when writing, speaking, reading, or listening.
57W	**Grammar Workout: Check for Correct Sentences**	L.8.1	Demonstrate command of the conventions of standard English grammar and usage when writing or speaking.
		L.8.3	Use knowledge of language and its conventions when writing, speaking, reading, or listening.
58W	**Spelling Workout: Check Plural Nouns**	L.8.2	Demonstrate command of the conventions of standard English capitalization, punctuation, and spelling when writing.
		L.8.2.c	Spell correctly.
59W	**Mechanics Workout: Check Sentence Punctuation**	L.8.2	Demonstrate command of the conventions of standard English capitalization, punctuation, and spelling when writing.
60W–63W	**Personal Narrative: Publish, Share, and Reflect**	W.8.5	With some guidance and support from peers and adults, develop and strengthen writing as needed by planning, revising, editing, rewriting, or trying a new approach, focusing on how well purpose and audience have been addressed.
		W.8.6	Use technology, including the Internet, to produce and publish writing and present the relationships between information and ideas efficiently as well as to interact and collaborate with others.
64W–65W	**Presentation Manual: Use Multimedia**	SL.8.1	Engage effectively in a range of collaborative discussions (one-on-one, in groups, and teacher-led) with diverse partners on grade 8 topics, texts, and issues, building on others' ideas and expressing their own clearly.
		SL.8.1.a	Come to discussions prepared, having read or researched material under study; explicitly draw on that preparation by referring to evidence on the topic, text, or issue to probe and reflect on ideas under discussion.
		SL.8.1.c	Pose questions that connect the ideas of several speakers and respond to others' questions and comments with relevant evidence, observations, and ideas.
		SL.8.2	Analyze the purpose of information presented in diverse media and formats (e.g., visually, quantitatively, orally) and evaluate the motives (e.g., social, commercial, political) behind its presentation.

Common Core State Standards, continued

Common Core State Standards, continued

Common Core State Standards, continued

Project 4: Write as a Storyteller

pages	Lesson	Code	Standards Text
80W–89W	**Modern Fairy Tale: Model Study and Writing Trait: Organization**	W.8.4	Produce clear and coherent writing in which the development, organization, and style are appropriate to task, purpose, and audience.
		W.8.5	With some guidance and support from peers and adults, develop and strengthen writing as needed by planning, revising, editing, rewriting, or trying a new approach, focusing on how well purpose and audience have been addressed.
		W.8.10	Write routinely over extended time frames (time for research, reflection, and revision) and shorter time frames (a single sitting or a day or two) for a range of discipline-specific tasks, purposes, and audiences.
90W–91W	**Writing Strategy: How to Make Your Ideas Flow**		Write narratives to develop real or imagined experiences or events using effective technique, relevant descriptive details, and well-structured event sequences.
		W.8.3.c	Use a variety of transition words, phrases, and clauses to convey sequence, signal shifts from one time frame or setting to another, and show the relationships among experiences and events.
		W.8.5	With some guidance and support from peers and adults, develop and strengthen writing as needed by planning, revising, editing, rewriting, or trying a new approach, focusing on how well purpose and audience have been addressed.
92W–93W	**Writing Strategy: How to Connect Your Paragraphs**		Write narratives to develop real or imagined experiences or events using effective technique, relevant descriptive details, and well-structured event sequences.
		W.8.3.c	Use a variety of transition words, phrases, and clauses to convey sequence, signal shifts from one time frame or setting to another, and show the relationships among experiences and events.
		W.8.5	With some guidance and support from peers and adults, develop and strengthen writing as needed by planning, revising, editing, rewriting, or trying a new approach, focusing on how well purpose and audience have been addressed.
94W–97W	**Modern Fairy Tale: Prewrite**		Write narratives to develop real or imagined experiences or events using effective technique, relevant descriptive details, and well-structured event sequences.
		W.8.3.d	Use precise words and phrases, relevant descriptive details, and sensory language to capture the action and convey experiences and events.

Common Core State Standards, continued

Project 4: Write as a Storyteller

Pages	Lesson	Code	Standards Text
		W.8.5	With some guidance and support from peers and adults, develop and strengthen writing as needed by planning, revising, editing, rewriting, or trying a new approach, focusing on how well purpose and audience have been addressed.
98W–99W	Modern Fairy Tale: Draft	W.8.3	Write narratives to develop real or imagined experiences or events using effective technique, relevant descriptive details, and well-structured event sequences.
		W.8.3.a	Engage and orient the reader by establishing a context and point of view and introducing a narrator and/or characters; organize an event sequence that unfolds naturally and logically.
		W.8.3.b	Use narrative techniques, such as dialogue, pacing, description, and reflection, to develop experiences, events, and/or characters.
		W.8.3.c	Use a variety of transition words, phrases, and clauses to convey sequence, signal shifts from one time frame or setting to another, and show the relationships among experiences and events.
		W.8.3.d	Use precise words and phrases, relevant descriptive details, and sensory language to capture the action and convey experiences and events.
		W.8.3.e	Provide a conclusion that follows from and reflects on the narrated experiences or events.
		W.8.5	With some guidance and support from peers and adults, develop and strengthen writing as needed by planning, revising, editing, rewriting, or trying a new approach, focusing on how well purpose and audience have been addressed.
		W.8.6	Use technology, including the Internet, to produce and publish writing and present the relationships between information and ideas efficiently as well as to interact and collaborate with others.
		W.8.10	Write routinely over extended time frames (time for research, reflection, and revision) and shorter time frames (a single sitting or a day or two) for a range of discipline-specific tasks, purposes, and audiences.

Common Core State Standards, continued

Project 4: Write as a Storyteller

Pages	Lesson	Code	Standards Text
100W–101W	**Modern Fairy Tale: Revise**		Write narratives to develop real or imagined experiences or events using effective technique, relevant descriptive details, and well-structured event sequences.
		W.8.3.a	Engage and orient the reader by establishing a context and point of view and introducing a narrator and/or characters; organize an event sequence that unfolds naturally and logically.
		W.8.3.c	Use a variety of transition words, phrases, and clauses to convey sequence, signal shifts from one time frame or setting to another, and show the relationships among experiences and events.
		W.8.3.d	Use precise words and phrases, relevant descriptive details, and sensory language to capture the action and convey experiences and events.
		W.8.4	Produce clear and coherent writing in which the development, organization, and style are appropriate to task, purpose, and audience.
		W.8.5	With some guidance and support from peers and adults, develop and strengthen writing as needed by planning, revising, editing, rewriting, or trying a new approach, focusing on how well purpose and audience have been addressed.
102W	**Modern Fairy Tale: Edit and Proofread**	W.8.5	With some guidance and support from peers and adults, develop and strengthen writing as needed by planning, revising, editing, rewriting, or trying a new approach, focusing on how well purpose and audience have been addressed.
		L.8.1	Demonstrate command of the conventions of standard English grammar and usage when writing or speaking.
		L.8.2	Demonstrate command of the conventions of standard English capitalization, punctuation, and spelling when writing.
		L.8.2.c	Spell correctly.
		L.8.3	Use knowledge of language and its conventions when writing, speaking, reading, or listening.
103W	**Grammar Workout: Check Subject-Verb Agreement**	L.8.1	Demonstrate command of the conventions of standard English grammar and usage when writing or speaking.
		L.8.3	Use knowledge of language and its conventions when writing, speaking, reading, or listening.

Common Core State Standards, continued

Common Core State Standards, continued

Project 5: Write to Solve a Problem

SE Pages	Lesson	Code	Standards Text
108W–113W	Problem-and-Solution Paragraph: Model Study and Prewrite	W.8.5	With some guidance and support from peers and adults, develop and strengthen writing as needed by planning, revising, editing, rewriting, or trying a new approach, focusing on how well purpose and audience have been addressed.
114W–115W	Problem-and-Solution Paragraph: Draft	W.8.1	Write arguments to support claims with clear reasons and relevant evidence.
		W.8.1.a	Introduce claim(s), acknowledge and distinguish the claim(s) from alternate or opposing claims, and organize the reasons and evidence logically.
		W.8.1.b	Support claim(s) with logical reasoning and relevant evidence, using accurate, credible sources and demonstrating an understanding of the topic or text.
		W.8.5	With some guidance and support from peers and adults, develop and strengthen writing as needed by planning, revising, editing, rewriting, or trying a new approach, focusing on how well purpose and audience have been addressed.
		W.8.10	Write routinely over extended time frames (time for research, reflection, and revision) and shorter time frames (a single sitting or a day or two) for a range of discipline-specific tasks, purposes, and audiences.
116W–117W	Problem-and-Solution Paragraph: Revise		Write arguments to support claims with clear reasons and relevant evidence.
		W.8.1.a	Introduce claim(s), acknowledge and distinguish the claim(s) from alternate or opposing claims, and organize the reasons and evidence logically.
		W.8.1.b	Support claim(s) with logical reasoning and relevant evidence, using accurate, credible sources and demonstrating an understanding of the topic or text.
		W.8.1.e	Provide a concluding statement or section that follows from and supports the argument presented.
		W.8.4	Produce clear and coherent writing in which the development, organization, and style are appropriate to task, purpose, and audience.
		W.8.5	With some guidance and support from peers and adults, develop and strengthen writing as needed by planning, revising, editing, rewriting, or trying a new approach, focusing on how well purpose and audience have been addressed.

Common Core State Standards, continued

Chapter 3   The Many Writers You Are, continued

Project 5: Write to Solve a Problem

SE Pages	Lesson	Code	Standards Text
118W	Problem-and-Solution Paragraph: Edit and Proofread	W.8.5	With some guidance and support from peers and adults, develop and strengthen writing as needed by planning, revising, editing, rewriting, or trying a new approach, focusing on how well purpose and audience have been addressed.
		L.8.1	Demonstrate command of the conventions of standard English grammar and usage when writing or speaking.
		L.8.2	Demonstrate command of the conventions of standard English capitalization, punctuation, and spelling when writing.
		L.8.2.c	Spell correctly.
		L.8.3	Use knowledge of language and its conventions when writing, speaking, reading, or listening.
119W	Grammar Workout: Check Verbs in the Past Tense	L.8.1	Demonstrate command of the conventions of standard English grammar and usage when writing or speaking.
		L.8.3	Use knowledge of language and its conventions when writing, speaking, reading, or listening.
120W	Spelling Workout: Check Verbs with -ed and -ing	L.8.2	Demonstrate command of the conventions of standard English capitalization, punctuation, and spelling when writing.
		L.8.2.c	Spell correctly.
121W	Mechanics Workout: Check Capitalization of Proper Nouns	L.8.2	Demonstrate command of the conventions of standard English capitalization, punctuation, and spelling when writing.

Project 6: Write as a Community Member

SE Pages	Lesson	Code	Standards Text
122W–131W	Problem-and-Solution Essay: Model Study and Writing Trait: Focus and Unity		Write arguments to support claims with clear reasons and relevant evidence.
		W.8.1.a	Introduce claim(s), acknowledge and distinguish the claim(s) from alternate or opposing claims, and organize the reasons and evidence logically.
		W.8.1.b	Support claim(s) with logical reasoning and relevant evidence, using accurate, credible sources and demonstrating an understanding of the topic or text.
		W.8.1.e	Provide a concluding statement or section that follows from and supports the argument presented.
		W.8.4	Produce clear and coherent writing in which the development, organization, and style are appropriate to task, purpose, and audience.

Common Core State Standards, continued

Project 6: Write as a Community Member

SE Pages	Lesson	Code	Standards Text
		W.8.5	With some guidance and support from peers and adults, develop and strengthen writing as needed by planning, revising, editing, rewriting, or trying a new approach, focusing on how well purpose and audience have been addressed.
		W.8.10	Write routinely over extended time frames (time for research, reflection, and revision) and shorter time frames (a single sitting or a day or two) for a range of discipline-specific tasks, purposes, and audiences.
132W–133W	Writing Strategy: State a Claim		Write arguments to support claims with clear reasons and relevant evidence.
		W.8.1.a	Introduce claim(s), acknowledge and distinguish the claim(s) from alternate or opposing claims, and organize the reasons and evidence logically.
		W.8.4	Produce clear and coherent writing in which the development, organization, and style are appropriate to task, purpose, and audience.
		W.8.10	Write routinely over extended time frames (time for research, reflection, and revision) and shorter time frames (a single sitting or a day or two) for a range of discipline-specific tasks, purposes, and audiences.
134W–135W	Writing Strategy: Stay in Control from Start to Finish		Write arguments to support claims with clear reasons and relevant evidence.
		W.8.1.a	Introduce claim(s), acknowledge and distinguish the claim(s) from alternate or opposing claims, and organize the reasons and evidence logically.
		W.8.1.c	Use words, phrases, and clauses to create cohesion and clarify the relationships among claim(s), counterclaims, reasons, and evidence.
		W.8.1.e	Provide a concluding statement or section that follows from and supports the argument presented.
		W.8.10	Write routinely over extended time frames (time for research, reflection, and revision) and shorter time frames (a single sitting or a day or two) for a range of discipline-specific tasks, purposes, and audiences.
136W–137W	Problem-and-Solution Essay: Prewrite		Write arguments to support claims with clear reasons and relevant evidence.
		W.8.1.a	Introduce claim(s), acknowledge and distinguish the claim(s) from alternate or opposing claims, and organize the reasons and evidence logically.

Common Core State Standards, continued

Project 6: Write as a Community Member

SE Pages	Lesson	Code	Standards Text
		W.8.1.b	Support claim(s) with logical reasoning and relevant evidence, using accurate, credible sources and demonstrating an understanding of the topic or text.
		W.8.5	With some guidance and support from peers and adults, develop and strengthen writing as needed by planning, revising, editing, rewriting, or trying a new approach, focusing on how well purpose and audience have been addressed.
138W–139W	Problem-and-Solution Essay: Draft	W.8.1	Write arguments to support claims with clear reasons and relevant evidence.
		W.8.1.a	Introduce claim(s), acknowledge and distinguish the claim(s) from alternate or opposing claims, and organize the reasons and evidence logically.
		W.8.1.b	Support claim(s) with logical reasoning and relevant evidence, using accurate, credible sources and demonstrating an understanding of the topic or text.
		W.8.1.c	Use words, phrases, and clauses to create cohesion and clarify the relationships among claim(s), counterclaims, reasons, and evidence.
		W.8.1.e	Provide a concluding statement or section that follows from and supports the argument presented.
		W.8.5	With some guidance and support from peers and adults, develop and strengthen writing as needed by planning, revising, editing, rewriting, or trying a new approach, focusing on how well purpose and audience have been addressed.
		W.8.10	Write routinely over extended time frames (time for research, reflection, and revision) and shorter time frames (a single sitting or a day or two) for a range of discipline-specific tasks, purposes, and audiences.

Common Core State Standards, continued

Project 6: Write as a Community Member

Pages	Lesson	Code	Standards Text
140W–141W	Problem-and-Solution Essay: Revise		Write arguments to support claims with clear reasons and relevant evidence.
		W.8.1.a	Introduce claim(s), acknowledge and distinguish the claim(s) from alternate or opposing claims, and organize the reasons and evidence logically.
		W.8.1.b	Support claim(s) with logical reasoning and relevant evidence, using accurate, credible sources and demonstrating an understanding of the topic or text.
		W.8.1.c	Use words, phrases, and clauses to create cohesion and clarify the relationships among claim(s), counterclaims, reasons, and evidence.
		W.8.1.e	Provide a concluding statement or section that follows from and supports the argument presented.
		W.8.4	Produce clear and coherent writing in which the development, organization, and style are appropriate to task, purpose, and audience.
		W.8.5	With some guidance and support from peers and adults, develop and strengthen writing as needed by planning, revising, editing, rewriting, or trying a new approach, focusing on how well purpose and audience have been addressed.
142W	Problem-and-Solution Essay: Edit and Proofread	W.8.5	With some guidance and support from peers and adults, develop and strengthen writing as needed by planning, revising, editing, rewriting, or trying a new approach, focusing on how well purpose and audience have been addressed.
		L.8.1	Demonstrate command of the conventions of standard English grammar and usage when writing or speaking.
		L.8.2	Demonstrate command of the conventions of standard English capitalization, punctuation, and spelling when writing.
		L.8.2.c	Spell correctly.
		L.8.3	Use knowledge of language and its conventions when writing, speaking, reading, or listening.
143W	Grammar Workout: Check Irregular Past Tense Verbs	L.8.1	Demonstrate command of the conventions of standard English grammar and usage when writing or speaking.
		L.8.3	Use knowledge of language and its conventions when writing, speaking, reading, or listening.
144W	Spelling Workout: Check Prefixes and Suffixes	L.8.2	Demonstrate command of the conventions of standard English capitalization, punctuation, and spelling when writing.

Common Core State Standards, continued

Project 6: Write as a Community Member

Pages	Lesson	Code	Standards Text
		L.8.2.c	Spell correctly.
145W	Mechanics Workout: Check Abbreviations	L.8.2	Demonstrate command of the conventions of standard English capitalization, punctuation, and spelling when writing.
146W	Problem-and-Solution Essay: Publish, Share, and Reflect	W.8.5	With some guidance and support from peers and adults, develop and strengthen writing as needed by planning, revising, editing, rewriting, or trying a new approach, focusing on how well purpose and audience have been addressed.
		W.8.6	Use technology, including the Internet, to produce and publish writing and present the relationships between information and ideas efficiently as well as to interact and collaborate with others.
147W	Presentation Manual: Emphasize Your Points		Engage effectively in a range of collaborative discussions (one-on-one, in groups, and teacher-led) with diverse partners on grade 8 topics, texts, and issues, building on others' ideas and expressing their own clearly.
		SL.8.1.c	Pose questions that connect the ideas of several speakers and respond to others' questions and comments with relevant evidence, observations, and ideas.
		SL.8.1.d	Acknowledge new information expressed by others, and, when warranted, qualify or justify their own views in light of the evidence presented.
		SL.8.4	Present claims and findings, emphasizing salient points in a focused, coherent manner with relevant evidence, sound valid reasoning, and well-chosen details; use appropriate eye contact, adequate volume, and clear pronunciation.

Project 7: Write as a Researcher

Pages	Lesson	Code	Standards Text
148W–157W	Research Report: Model Study and Research Strategy: Develop a Game Plan	W.8.4	Produce clear and coherent writing in which the development, organization, and style are appropriate to task, purpose, and audience.
		W.8.5	With some guidance and support from peers and adults, develop and strengthen writing as needed by planning, revising, editing, rewriting, or trying a new approach, focusing on how well purpose and audience have been addressed.
		W.8.7	Conduct short research projects to answer a question (including a self-generated question), drawing on several sources and generating additional related, focused questions that allow for multiple avenues of exploration.

Common Core State Standards, continued

Project 7: Write as a Researcher

Pages	Lesson	Code	Standards Text
158W–165W	Research Strategy: Locate Information Sources	W.8.5	With some guidance and support from peers and adults, develop and strengthen writing as needed by planning, revising, editing, rewriting, or trying a new approach, focusing on how well purpose and audience have been addressed.
		W.8.6	Use technology, including the Internet, to produce and publish writing and present the relationships between information and ideas efficiently as well as to interact and collaborate with others.
		W.8.7	Conduct short research projects to answer a question (including a self-generated question), drawing on several sources and generating additional related, focused questions that allow for multiple avenues of exploration.
		W.8.8	Gather relevant information from multiple print and digital sources, using search terms effectively; assess the credibility and accuracy of each source; and quote or paraphrase the data and conclusions of others while avoiding plagiarism and following a standard format for citation.
166W–169W	Research Strategy: Get Information from the Web	W.8.6	Use technology, including the Internet, to produce and publish writing and present the relationships between information and ideas efficiently as well as to interact and collaborate with others.
		W.8.7	Conduct short research projects to answer a question (including a self-generated question), drawing on several sources and generating additional related, focused questions that allow for multiple avenues of exploration.
		W.8.8	Gather relevant information from multiple print and digital sources, using search terms effectively; assess the credibility and accuracy of each source; and quote or paraphrase the data and conclusions of others while avoiding plagiarism and following a standard format for citation.
		W.8.9	Draw evidence from literary or informational texts to support analysis, reflection, and research.
		W.8.9.b	Apply grade 8 Reading standards to literary nonfiction (e.g., "Delineate and evaluate the argument and specific claims in a text, assessing whether the reasoning is sound and the evidence is relevant and sufficient; recognize when irrelevant evidence is introduced").

Common Core State Standards, continued

Project 7: Write as a Researcher

SE Pages	Lesson	Code	Standards Text
170W–173W	**Research Strategy: Sort through the Information**	W.8.7	Conduct short research projects to answer a question (including a self-generated question), drawing on several sources and generating additional related, focused questions that allow for multiple avenues of exploration.
		W.8.8	Gather relevant information from multiple print and digital sources, using search terms effectively; assess the credibility and accuracy of each source; and quote or paraphrase the data and conclusions of others while avoiding plagiarism and following a standard format for citation.
		W.8.9	Draw evidence from literary or informational texts to support analysis, reflection, and research.
		W.8.9.b	Apply grade 8 Reading standards to literary nonfiction (e.g., "Delineate and evaluate the argument and specific claims in a text, assessing whether the reasoning is sound and the evidence is relevant and sufficient; recognize when irrelevant evidence is introduced").
174W–177W	**Research Strategy: Take Good Notes**		Write informative/explanatory texts to examine a topic and convey ideas, concepts, and information through the selection, organization, and analysis of relevant content.
		W.8.2.a	Introduce a topic clearly, previewing what is to follow; organize ideas, concepts, and information into broader categories; include formatting (e.g., headings), graphics (e.g., charts, tables), and multimedia when useful to aiding comprehension.
		W.8.2.b	Develop the topic with relevant, well-chosen facts, definitions, concrete details, quotations, or other information and examples.
		W.8.7	Conduct short research projects to answer a question (including a self-generated question), drawing on several sources and generating additional related, focused questions that allow for multiple avenues of exploration.
		W.8.8	Gather relevant information from multiple print and digital sources, using search terms effectively; assess the credibility and accuracy of each source; and quote or paraphrase the data and conclusions of others while avoiding plagiarism and following a standard format for citation.

Common Core State Standards, continued

Project 7: Write as a Researcher

SE Pages	Lesson	Code	Standards Text
178W–181W	**Research Strategy: Avoid Plagiarism**	W.8.8	Gather relevant information from multiple print and digital sources, using search terms effectively; assess the credibility and accuracy of each source; and quote or paraphrase the data and conclusions of others while avoiding plagiarism and following a standard format for citation.
		L.8.2	Demonstrate command of the conventions of standard English capitalization, punctuation, and spelling when writing.
182W–187W	**Research Strategy: Organize Your Notes**	W.8.5	With some guidance and support from peers and adults, develop and strengthen writing as needed by planning, revising, editing, rewriting, or trying a new approach, focusing on how well purpose and audience have been addressed.
188W–189W	**Research Strategy: Develop an Outline**	W.8.2	Write informative/explanatory texts to examine a topic and convey ideas, concepts, and information through the selection, organization, and analysis of relevant content.
		W.8.2.a	Introduce a topic clearly, previewing what is to follow; organize ideas, concepts, and information into broader categories; include formatting (e.g., headings), graphics (e.g., charts, tables), and multimedia when useful to aiding comprehension.
		W.8.4	Produce clear and coherent writing in which the development, organization, and style are appropriate to task, purpose, and audience.
		W.8.5	With some guidance and support from peers and adults, develop and strengthen writing as needed by planning, revising, editing, rewriting, or trying a new approach, focusing on how well purpose and audience have been addressed.
		W.8.7	Conduct short research projects to answer a question (including a self-generated question), drawing on several sources and generating additional related, focused questions that allow for multiple avenues of exploration.
190W–193W	**Research Report: Draft**	W.8.2	Write informative/explanatory texts to examine a topic and convey ideas, concepts, and information through the selection, organization, and analysis of relevant content.
		W.8.2.a	Introduce a topic clearly, previewing what is to follow; organize ideas, concepts, and information into broader categories; include formatting (e.g., headings), graphics (e.g., charts, tables), and multimedia when useful to aiding comprehension.
		W.8.2.b	Develop the topic with relevant, well-chosen facts, definitions, concrete details, quotations, or other information and examples.

Common Core State Standards, continued

Chapter 3   The Many Writers You Are, continued

Project 7: Write as a Researcher

SE Pages	Lesson	Code	Standards Text
		W.8.2.c	Use appropriate and varied transitions to create cohesion and clarify the relationships among ideas and concepts.
		W.8.2.d	Use precise language and domain-specific vocabulary to inform about or explain the topic.
		W.8.2.e	Establish and maintain a formal style.
		W.8.2.f	Provide a concluding statement or section that follows from and supports the information or explanation presented.
		W.8.5	With some guidance and support from peers and adults, develop and strengthen writing as needed by planning, revising, editing, rewriting, or trying a new approach, focusing on how well purpose and audience have been addressed.
		W.8.7	Conduct short research projects to answer a question (including a self-generated question), drawing on several sources and generating additional related, focused questions that allow for multiple avenues of exploration.
		W.8.9	Draw evidence from literary or informational texts to support analysis, reflection, and research.
		W.8.9.b	Apply grade 8 Reading standards to literary nonfiction (e.g., "Delineate and evaluate the argument and specific claims in a text, assessing whether the reasoning is sound and the evidence is relevant and sufficient; recognize when irrelevant evidence is introduced").
		W.8.10	Write routinely over extended time frames (time for research, reflection, and revision) and shorter time frames (a single sitting or a day or two) for a range of discipline-specific tasks, purposes, and audiences.
194W–197W	Research Report: How to Cite Sources	W.8.8	Gather relevant information from multiple print and digital sources, using search terms effectively; assess the credibility and accuracy of each source; and quote or paraphrase the data and conclusions of others while avoiding plagiarism and following a standard format for citation.

Common Core State Standards, continued

Project 7: Write as a Researcher

Pages	Lesson	Code	Standards Text
198W–199W	Research Report: Revise		Write informative/explanatory texts to examine a topic and convey ideas, concepts, and information through the selection, organization, and analysis of relevant content.
		W.8.2.a	Introduce a topic clearly, previewing what is to follow; organize ideas, concepts, and information into broader categories; include formatting (e.g., headings), graphics (e.g., charts, tables), and multimedia when useful to aiding comprehension.
		W.8.2.b	Develop the topic with relevant, well-chosen facts, definitions, concrete details, quotations, or other information and examples.
		W.8.2.c	Use appropriate and varied transitions to create cohesion and clarify the relationships among ideas and concepts.
		W.8.4	Produce clear and coherent writing in which the development, organization, and style are appropriate to task, purpose, and audience.
		W.8.5	With some guidance and support from peers and adults, develop and strengthen writing as needed by planning, revising, editing, rewriting, or trying a new approach, focusing on how well purpose and audience have been addressed.
200W	Research Report: Edit and Proofread	W.8.5	With some guidance and support from peers and adults, develop and strengthen writing as needed by planning, revising, editing, rewriting, or trying a new approach, focusing on how well purpose and audience have been addressed.
		L.8.1	Demonstrate command of the conventions of standard English grammar and usage when writing or speaking.
		L.8.2	Demonstrate command of the conventions of standard English capitalization, punctuation, and spelling when writing.
		L.8.2.c	Spell correctly.
		L.8.3	Use knowledge of language and its conventions when writing, speaking, reading, or listening.
201W	Grammar Workout: Check Subject and Object Pronouns	L.8.1	Demonstrate command of the conventions of standard English grammar and usage when writing or speaking.
		L.8.3	Use knowledge of language and its conventions when writing, speaking, reading, or listening.

Common Core State Standards, continued

Project 7: Write as a Researcher

Pages	Lesson	Code	Standards Text
202W	**Spelling Workout:** **Check Words with** **Silent Consonants**	L.8.2	Demonstrate command of the conventions of standard English capitalization, punctuation, and spelling when writing.
		L.8.2.c	Spell correctly.
203W	**Mechanics Workout:** **Check Punctuation and** **Capitalization of Sources**	L.8.2	Demonstrate command of the conventions of standard English capitalization, punctuation, and spelling when writing.
204W	**Research Report:** **Publish, Share, and Reflect**	W.8.5	With some guidance and support from peers and adults, develop and strengthen writing as needed by planning, revising, editing, rewriting, or trying a new approach, focusing on how well purpose and audience have been addressed.
		W.8.6	Use technology, including the Internet, to produce and publish writing and present the relationships between information and ideas efficiently as well as to interact and collaborate with others.
205W	**Presentation Manual:** **Use Multimedia**	W.8.6	Use technology, including the Internet, to produce and publish writing and present the relationships between information and ideas efficiently as well as to interact and collaborate with others.
		SL.8.1	Engage effectively in a range of collaborative discussions (one-on-one, in groups, and teacher-led) with diverse partners on grade 8 topics, texts, and issues, building on others' ideas and expressing their own clearly.
		SL.8.1.a	Come to discussions prepared, having read or researched material under study; explicitly draw on that preparation by referring to evidence on the topic, text, or issue to probe and reflect on ideas under discussion.
		SL.8.1.c	Pose questions that connect the ideas of several speakers and respond to others' questions and comments with relevant evidence, observations, and ideas.
		SL.8.1.d	Acknowledge new information expressed by others, and, when warranted, qualify or justify their own views in light of the evidence presented.
		SL.8.2	Analyze the purpose of information presented in diverse media and formats (e.g., visually, quantitatively, orally) and evaluate the motives (e.g., social, commercial, political) behind its presentation.
		SL.8.5	Integrate multimedia and visual displays into presentations to clarify information, strengthen claims and evidence, and add interest.

Common Core State Standards, continued

Chapter 3 The Many Writers You Are, continued

Project 8: Write as a Poet

SE Pages	Lesson	Code	Standards Text
226W–229W	Narrative Poem: Model Study and Prewrite	W.8.5	With some guidance and support from peers and adults, develop and strengthen writing as needed by planning, revising, editing, rewriting, or trying a new approach, focusing on how well purpose and audience have been addressed.
230W–231W	Narrative Poem: Draft	W.8.3	Write narratives to develop real or imagined experiences or events using effective technique, relevant descriptive details, and well-structured event sequences.
		W.8.3.d	Use precise words and phrases, relevant descriptive details, and sensory language to capture the action and convey experiences and events.
		W.8.5	With some guidance and support from peers and adults, develop and strengthen writing as needed by planning, revising, editing, rewriting, or trying a new approach, focusing on how well purpose and audience have been addressed.
		W.8.10	Write routinely over extended time frames (time for research, reflection, and revision) and shorter time frames (a single sitting or a day or two) for a range of discipline-specific tasks, purposes, and audiences.
232W–233W	Narrative Poem: Revise	W.8.3	Write narratives to develop real or imagined experiences or events using effective technique, relevant descriptive details, and well-structured event sequences.
		W.8.3.d	Use precise words and phrases, relevant descriptive details, and sensory language to capture the action and convey experiences and events.
		W.8.4	Produce clear and coherent writing in which the development, organization, and style are appropriate to task, purpose, and audience.
		W.8.5	With some guidance and support from peers and adults, develop and strengthen writing as needed by planning, revising, editing, rewriting, or trying a new approach, focusing on how well purpose and audience have been addressed.
234W	Narrative Poem: Edit and Proofread	W.8.5	With some guidance and support from peers and adults, develop and strengthen writing as needed by planning, revising, editing, rewriting, or trying a new approach, focusing on how well purpose and audience have been addressed.
		L.8.1	Demonstrate command of the conventions of standard English grammar and usage when writing or speaking.

Common Core State Standards, continued

Project 8: Write as a Poet

SE Pages	Lesson	Code	Standards Text
		L.8.2	Demonstrate command of the conventions of standard English capitalization, punctuation, and spelling when writing.
		L.8.2.c	Spell correctly.
		L.8.3	Use knowledge of language and its conventions when writing, speaking, reading, or listening.
235W	**Grammar Workout: Check Descriptive Adjectives**	L.8.1	Demonstrate command of the conventions of standard English grammar and usage when writing or speaking.
		L.8.3	Use knowledge of language and its conventions when writing, speaking, reading, or listening.
236W	**Spelling Workout: Check Suffixes in Verbs Ending in y**	L.8.2	Demonstrate command of the conventions of standard English capitalization, punctuation, and spelling when writing.
		L.8.2.c	Spell correctly.
237W	**Mechanics Workout: Check Punctuation in Poems**	L.8.2	Demonstrate command of the conventions of standard English capitalization, punctuation, and spelling when writing.

Project 9: Write as a Consumer

SE Pages	Lesson	Code	Standards Text
238W–241W	**Business Letter: Model Study and Prewrite**	W.8.5	With some guidance and support from peers and adults, develop and strengthen writing as needed by planning, revising, editing, rewriting, or trying a new approach, focusing on how well purpose and audience have been addressed.
		W.8.6	Use technology, including the Internet, to produce and publish writing and present the relationships between information and ideas efficiently as well as to interact and collaborate with others.
		W.8.8	Gather relevant information from multiple print and digital sources, using search terms effectively; assess the credibility and accuracy of each source; and quote or paraphrase the data and conclusions of others while avoiding plagiarism and following a standard format for citation.

Common Core State Standards, continued

Project 9: Write as a Consumer

Pages	Lesson	Code	Standards Text
242W–243W	Business Letter: Draft	W.8.1	Write arguments to support claims with clear reasons and relevant evidence.
		W.8.1.a	Introduce claim(s), acknowledge and distinguish the claim(s) from alternate or opposing claims, and organize the reasons and evidence logically.
		W.8.1.b	Support claim(s) with logical reasoning and relevant evidence, using accurate, credible sources and demonstrating an understanding of the topic or text.
		W.8.1.d	Establish and maintain a formal style.
		W.8.1.e	Provide a concluding statement or section that follows from and supports the argument presented.
		W.8.5	With some guidance and support from peers and adults, develop and strengthen writing as needed by planning, revising, editing, rewriting, or trying a new approach, focusing on how well purpose and audience have been addressed.
		W.8.10	Write routinely over extended time frames (time for research, reflection, and revision) and shorter time frames (a single sitting or a day or two) for a range of discipline-specific tasks, purposes, and audiences.
244W–245W	Business Letter: Revise		Write arguments to support claims with clear reasons and relevant evidence.
		W.8.1.a	Introduce claim(s), acknowledge and distinguish the claim(s) from alternate or opposing claims, and organize the reasons and evidence logically.
		W.8.1.b	Support claim(s) with logical reasoning and relevant evidence, using accurate, credible sources and demonstrating an understanding of the topic or text.
		W.8.1.c	Use words, phrases, and clauses to create cohesion and clarify the relationships among claim(s), counterclaims, reasons, and evidence.
		W.8.1.d	Establish and maintain a formal style.
		W.8.1.e	Provide a concluding statement or section that follows from and supports the argument presented.
		W.8.4	Produce clear and coherent writing in which the development, organization, and style are appropriate to task, purpose, and audience.
		W.8.5	With some guidance and support from peers and adults, develop and strengthen writing as needed by planning, revising, editing, rewriting, or trying a new approach, focusing on how well purpose and audience have been addressed.

Common Core State Standards, continued

Project 9: Write as a Consumer

Pages	Lesson	Code	Standards Text
246W	**Business Letter: Edit and Proofread**	W.8.5	With some guidance and support from peers and adults, develop and strengthen writing as needed by planning, revising, editing, rewriting, or trying a new approach, focusing on how well purpose and audience have been addressed.
		L.8.1	Demonstrate command of the conventions of standard English grammar and usage when writing or speaking.
		L.8.2	Demonstrate command of the conventions of standard English capitalization, punctuation, and spelling when writing.
		L.8.2.c	Spell correctly.
		L.8.3	Use knowledge of language and its conventions when writing, speaking, reading, or listening.
247W	**Grammar Workout: Check Comparative Adjectives**	L.8.1	Demonstrate command of the conventions of standard English grammar and usage when writing or speaking.
		L.8.3	Use knowledge of language and its conventions when writing, speaking, reading, or listening.
248W	**Spelling Workout: Check Adjectives Ending in -er and -est**	L.8.2	Demonstrate command of the conventions of standard English capitalization, punctuation, and spelling when writing.
		L.8.2.c	Spell correctly.
249W	**Mechanics Workout: Check Capitalization and Punctuation in Letters**	L.8.2	Demonstrate command of the conventions of standard English capitalization, punctuation, and spelling when writing.

Common Core State Standards, continued

Project 10: Write as a Friend

Pages	Lesson	Code	Standards Text
250W–253W	Friendly Letter: Model Study and Prewrite	W.8.4	Produce clear and coherent writing in which the development, organization, and style are appropriate to task, purpose, and audience.
		W.8.5	With some guidance and support from peers and adults, develop and strengthen writing as needed by planning, revising, editing, rewriting, or trying a new approach, focusing on how well purpose and audience have been addressed.
254W–255W	Friendly Letter: Draft	W.8.3	Write narratives to develop real or imagined experiences or events using effective technique, relevant descriptive details, and well-structured event sequences.
		W.8.3.a	Engage and orient the reader by establishing a context and point of view and introducing a narrator and/or characters; organize an event sequence that unfolds naturally and logically.
		W.8.3.b	Use narrative techniques, such as dialogue, pacing, description, and reflection, to develop experiences, events, and/or characters.
		W.8.3.e	Provide a conclusion that follows from and reflects on the narrated experiences or events.
		W.8.5	With some guidance and support from peers and adults, develop and strengthen writing as needed by planning, revising, editing, rewriting, or trying a new approach, focusing on how well purpose and audience have been addressed.
		W.8.10	Write routinely over extended time frames (time for research, reflection, and revision) and shorter time frames (a single sitting or a day or two) for a range of discipline-specific tasks, purposes, and audiences.
256W–257W	Friendly Letter: Revise		Write narratives to develop real or imagined experiences or events using effective technique, relevant descriptive details, and well-structured event sequences.
		W.8.3.a	Engage and orient the reader by establishing a context and point of view and introducing a narrator and/or characters; organize an event sequence that unfolds naturally and logically.
		W.8.3.c	Use a variety of transition words, phrases, and clauses to convey sequence, signal shifts from one time frame or setting to another, and show the relationships among experiences and events.

Common Core State Standards, continued

Common Core

Chapter 3 The Many Writers You Are, continued			
Project 10: Write as a Friend			
Pages	**Lesson**	**Code**	**Standards Text**
		W.8.3.d	Use precise words and phrases, relevant descriptive details, and sensory language to capture the action and convey experiences and events.
		W.8.4	Produce clear and coherent writing in which the development, organization, and style are appropriate to task, purpose, and audience.
		W.8.5	With some guidance and support from peers and adults, develop and strengthen writing as needed by planning, revising, editing, rewriting, or trying a new approach, focusing on how well purpose and audience have been addressed.
258W	**Friendly Letter: Edit and Proofread**	W.8.5	With some guidance and support from peers and adults, develop and strengthen writing as needed by planning, revising, editing, rewriting, or trying a new approach, focusing on how well purpose and audience have been addressed.
		L.8.1	Demonstrate command of the conventions of standard English grammar and usage when writing or speaking.
		L.8.2	Demonstrate command of the conventions of standard English capitalization, punctuation, and spelling when writing.
		L.8.2.c	Spell correctly.
		L.8.3	Use knowledge of language and its conventions when writing, speaking, reading, or listening.
259W	**Grammar Workout: Check Adverbs**	L.8.1	Demonstrate command of the conventions of standard English grammar and usage when writing or speaking.
		L.8.3	Use knowledge of language and its conventions when writing, speaking, reading, or listening.
260W	**Spelling Workout: Check Adverbs Ending in -ly**	L.8.2	Demonstrate command of the conventions of standard English capitalization, punctuation, and spelling when writing.
		L.8.2.c	Spell correctly.
261W	**Mechanics Workout: Check Apostrophes in Contractions**	L.8.2	Demonstrate command of the conventions of standard English capitalization, punctuation, and spelling when writing.

Common Core State Standards, continued

Project 11: Write to Describe

Pages	Lesson	Code	Standards Text
262W–265W	Story Scene: Model Study and Prewrite		Write narratives to develop real or imagined experiences or events using effective technique, relevant descriptive details, and well-structured event sequences.
		W.8.3.d	Use precise words and phrases, relevant descriptive details, and sensory language to capture the action and convey experiences and events.
		W.8.5	With some guidance and support from peers and adults, develop and strengthen writing as needed by planning, revising, editing, rewriting, or trying a new approach, focusing on how well purpose and audience have been addressed.
266W–267W	Story Scene: Draft	W.8.3	Write narratives to develop real or imagined experiences or events using effective technique, relevant descriptive details, and well-structured event sequences.
		W.8.3.a	Engage and orient the reader by establishing a context and point of view and introducing a narrator and/or characters; organize an event sequence that unfolds naturally and logically.
		W.8.3.b	Use narrative techniques, such as dialogue, pacing, description, and reflection, to develop experiences, events, and/or characters.
		W.8.3.d	Use precise words and phrases, relevant descriptive details, and sensory language to capture the action and convey experiences and events.
		W.8.5	With some guidance and support from peers and adults, develop and strengthen writing as needed by planning, revising, editing, rewriting, or trying a new approach, focusing on how well purpose and audience have been addressed.
		W.8.10	Write routinely over extended time frames (time for research, reflection, and revision) and shorter time frames (a single sitting or a day or two) for a range of discipline-specific tasks, purposes, and audiences.
268W–269W	Story Scene: Revise	W.8.3	Write narratives to develop real or imagined experiences or events using effective technique, relevant descriptive details, and well-structured event sequences.
		W.8.3.c	Use a variety of transition words, phrases, and clauses to convey sequence, signal shifts from one time frame or setting to another, and show the relationships among experiences and events.

Common Core State Standards, continued

Project 11: Write to Describe

Pages	Lesson	Code	Standards Text
		W.8.3.d	Use precise words and phrases, relevant descriptive details, and sensory language to capture the action and convey experiences and events.
		W.8.4	Produce clear and coherent writing in which the development, organization, and style are appropriate to task, purpose, and audience.
		W.8.5	With some guidance and support from peers and adults, develop and strengthen writing as needed by planning, revising, editing, rewriting, or trying a new approach, focusing on how well purpose and audience have been addressed.
270W	Story Scene: Edit and Proofread	W.8.5	With some guidance and support from peers and adults, develop and strengthen writing as needed by planning, revising, editing, rewriting, or trying a new approach, focusing on how well purpose and audience have been addressed.
		L.8.2	Demonstrate command of the conventions of standard English capitalization, punctuation, and spelling when writing.
		L.8.2.c	Spell correctly.
		L.8.3	Use knowledge of language and its conventions when writing, speaking, reading, or listening.
271W	Grammar Workout: Check for Complete Sentences	L.8.1	Demonstrate command of the conventions of standard English grammar and usage when writing or speaking.
		L.8.3	Use knowledge of language and its conventions when writing, speaking, reading, or listening.
272W	Spelling Workout: Check Sound-Alike Words	L.8.2	Demonstrate command of the conventions of standard English capitalization, punctuation, and spelling when writing.
		L.8.2.c	Spell correctly.
273W	Mechanics Workout: Check Commas in Lists	L.8.2	Demonstrate command of the conventions of standard English capitalization, punctuation, and spelling when writing.

Common Core State Standards, continued

Project 12: Write as a Reader

Pages	Lesson	Code	Standards Text
274W–283W	Literary Analysis: Model Study and Writing Trait: Development of Ideas	W.8.4	Produce clear and coherent writing in which the development, organization, and style are appropriate to task, purpose, and audience.
		W.8.5	With some guidance and support from peers and adults, develop and strengthen writing as needed by planning, revising, editing, rewriting, or trying a new approach, focusing on how well purpose and audience have been addressed.
		W.8.9.a	Draw evidence from literary or informational texts to support analysis, reflection, and research. Apply grade 8 Reading standards to literature (e.g., "Analyze how a modern work of fiction draws on themes, patterns of events, or character types from myths, traditional stories, or religious works such as the Bible, including describing how the material is rendered new").
		W.8.10	Write routinely over extended time frames (time for research, reflection, and revision) and shorter time frames (a single sitting or a day or two) for a range of discipline-specific tasks, purposes, and audiences.
284W–287W	Writing Strategy: Good Beginnings and Good Endings		Write arguments to support claims with clear reasons and relevant evidence.
		W.8.1.a	Introduce claim(s), acknowledge and distinguish the claim(s) from alternate or opposing claims, and organize the reasons and evidence logically.
		W.8.1.e	Provide a concluding statement or section that follows from and supports the argument presented.
288W–291W	Writing Strategy: Explain and Support Your Ideas		Write arguments to support claims with clear reasons and relevant evidence.
		W.8.1.a	Introduce claim(s), acknowledge and distinguish the claim(s) from alternate or opposing claims, and organize the reasons and evidence logically.
		W.8.1.b	Support claim(s) with logical reasoning and relevant evidence, using accurate, credible sources and demonstrating an understanding of the topic or text.
		W.8.1.e	Provide a concluding statement or section that follows from and supports the argument presented.
		W.8.9	Draw evidence from literary or informational texts to support analysis, reflection, and research.

Common Core State Standards, continued

Project 12: Write as a Reader

Pages	Lesson	Code	Standards Text
		W.8.9.b	Apply grade 8 Reading standards to literary nonfiction (e.g., "Delineate and evaluate the argument and specific claims in a text, assessing whether the reasoning is sound and the evidence is relevant and sufficient; recognize when irrelevant evidence is introduced").
292W–293W	Literary Analysis: Prewrite	W.8.4	Produce clear and coherent writing in which the development, organization, and style are appropriate to task, purpose, and audience.
		W.8.5	With some guidance and support from peers and adults, develop and strengthen writing as needed by planning, revising, editing, rewriting, or trying a new approach, focusing on how well purpose and audience have been addressed.
		W.8.9	Draw evidence from literary or informational texts to support analysis, reflection, and research.
		W.8.9.a	Apply grade 8 Reading standards to literature (e.g., "Analyze how a modern work of fiction draws on themes, patterns of events, or character types from myths, traditional stories, or religious works such as the Bible, including describing how the material is rendered new").
294W–295W	Literary Analysis: Draft	W.8.1	Write arguments to support claims with clear reasons and relevant evidence.
		W.8.1.a	Introduce claim(s), acknowledge and distinguish the claim(s) from alternate or opposing claims, and organize the reasons and evidence logically.
		W.8.1.b	Support claim(s) with logical reasoning and relevant evidence, using accurate, credible sources and demonstrating an understanding of the topic or text.
		W.8.1.d	Establish and maintain a formal style.
		W.8.1.e	Provide a concluding statement or section that follows from and supports the argument presented.
		W.8.9	Draw evidence from literary or informational texts to support analysis, reflection, and research.
		W.8.9.a	Apply grade 8 Reading standards to literature (e.g., "Analyze how a modern work of fiction draws on themes, patterns of events, or character types from myths, traditional stories, or religious works such as the Bible, including describing how the material is rendered new").

Common Core State Standards, continued

Pages	Lesson	Code	Standards Text
		W.8.10	Write routinely over extended time frames (time for research, reflection, and revision) and shorter time frames (a single sitting or a day or two) for a range of discipline-specific tasks, purposes, and audiences.
296W–297W	Literary Analysis: Revise		Write arguments to support claims with clear reasons and relevant evidence.
		W.8.1.a	Introduce claim(s), acknowledge and distinguish the claim(s) from alternate or opposing claims, and organize the reasons and evidence logically.
		W.8.1.b	Support claim(s) with logical reasoning and relevant evidence, using accurate, credible sources and demonstrating an understanding of the topic or text.
		W.8.1.c	Use words, phrases, and clauses to create cohesion and clarify the relationships among claim(s), counterclaims, reasons, and evidence.
		W.8.4	Produce clear and coherent writing in which the development, organization, and style are appropriate to task, purpose, and audience.
		W.8.5	With some guidance and support from peers and adults, develop and strengthen writing as needed by planning, revising, editing, rewriting, or trying a new approach, focusing on how well purpose and audience have been addressed.
		W.8.9	Draw evidence from literary or informational texts to support analysis, reflection, and research.
298W	Literary Analysis: Edit and Proofread	W.8.5	With some guidance and support from peers and adults, develop and strengthen writing as needed by planning, revising, editing, rewriting, or trying a new approach, focusing on how well purpose and audience have been addressed.
		L.8.1	Demonstrate command of the conventions of standard English grammar and usage when writing or speaking.
		L.8.2	Demonstrate command of the conventions of standard English capitalization, punctuation, and spelling when writing.
		L.8.2.a	Use punctuation (comma, ellipsis, dash) to indicate a pause or break.
		L.8.2.c	Spell correctly.
		L.8.3	Use knowledge of language and its conventions when writing, speaking, reading, or listening.

Common Core State Standards, continued

Project 12: Write as a Reader

Pages	Lesson	Code	Standards Text
299W	**Grammar Workout: Check Compound and Complex Sentences**		Demonstrate command of the conventions of standard English capitalization, punctuation, and spelling when writing.
		L.8.2.a	Use punctuation (comma, ellipsis, dash) to indicate a pause or break.
		L.8.3	Use knowledge of language and its conventions when writing, speaking, reading, or listening.
300W	**Spelling Workout: Check Words You Have to Know or Look Up**	L.8.2	Demonstrate command of the conventions of standard English capitalization, punctuation, and spelling when writing.
		L.8.2.c	Spell correctly.
301W	**Mechanics Workout: Check Punctuation in Longer Sentences**	L.8.2	Demonstrate command of the conventions of standard English capitalization, punctuation, and spelling when writing.
		L.8.2.a	Use punctuation (comma, ellipsis, dash) to indicate a pause or break.
302W	**Literary Analysis: Publish, Share, and Reflect**	W.8.5	With some guidance and support from peers and adults, develop and strengthen writing as needed by planning, revising, editing, rewriting, or trying a new approach, focusing on how well purpose and audience have been addressed.
		W.8.6	Use technology, including the Internet, to produce and publish writing and present the relationships between information and ideas efficiently as well as to interact and collaborate with others.
303W	**Presentation Manual: How to Conduct a Book-Club Meeting**	SL.8.1	Engage effectively in a range of collaborative discussions (one-on-one, in groups, and teacher-led) with diverse partners on grade 8 topics, texts, and issues, building on others' ideas and expressing their own clearly.
		SL.8.1.a	Come to discussions prepared, having read or researched material under study; explicitly draw on that preparation by referring to evidence on the topic, text, or issue to probe and reflect on ideas under discussion.
		SL.8.1.b	Follow rules for collegial discussions and decision-making, track progress toward specific goals and deadlines, and define individual roles as needed.
		SL.8.1.c	Pose questions that connect the ideas of several speakers and respond to others' questions and comments with relevant evidence, observations, and ideas.
		SL.8.1.d	Acknowledge new information expressed by others, and, when warranted, qualify or justify their own views in light of the evidence presented.
		SL.8.4	Present claims and findings, emphasizing salient points in a focused, coherent manner with relevant evidence, sound valid reasoning, and well-chosen details; use appropriate eye contact, adequate volume, and clear pronunciation.

Common Core State Standards, continued

Project 13: Write to Explain

Pages	Lesson	Code	Standards Text
304W–307W	Cause-and-Effect Paragraph: Model Study and Prewrite	W.8.4	Produce clear and coherent writing in which the development, organization, and style are appropriate to task, purpose, and audience.
		W.8.5	With some guidance and support from peers and adults, develop and strengthen writing as needed by planning, revising, editing, rewriting, or trying a new approach, focusing on how well purpose and audience have been addressed.
308W–309W	Cause-and-Effect Paragraph: Draft	W.8.2	Write informative/explanatory texts to examine a topic and convey ideas, concepts, and information through the selection, organization, and analysis of relevant content.
		W.8.2.a	Introduce a topic clearly, previewing what is to follow; organize ideas, concepts, and information into broader categories; include formatting (e.g., headings), graphics (e.g., charts, tables), and multimedia when useful to aiding comprehension.
		W.8.2.b	Develop the topic with relevant, well-chosen facts, definitions, concrete details, quotations, or other information and examples.
		W.8.2.c	Use appropriate and varied transitions to create cohesion and clarify the relationships among ideas and concepts.
		W.8.2.d	Use precise language and domain-specific vocabulary to inform about or explain the topic.
		W.8.2.e	Establish and maintain a formal style.
310W–311W	Cause-and-Effect Paragraph: Revise	W.8.2	Write informative/explanatory texts to examine a topic and convey ideas, concepts, and information through the selection, organization, and analysis of relevant content.
		W.8.2.a	Introduce a topic clearly, previewing what is to follow; organize ideas, concepts, and information into broader categories; include formatting (e.g., headings), graphics (e.g., charts, tables), and multimedia when useful to aiding comprehension.
		W.8.2.b	Develop the topic with relevant, well-chosen facts, definitions, concrete details, quotations, or other information and examples.
		W.8.4	Produce clear and coherent writing in which the development, organization, and style are appropriate to task, purpose, and audience.
		W.8.5	With some guidance and support from peers and adults, develop and strengthen writing as needed by planning, revising, editing, rewriting, or trying a new approach, focusing on how well purpose and audience have been addressed.

Common Core State Standards, continued

Project 13: Write to Explain

SE Pages	Lesson	Code	Standards Text
312W	Cause-and-Effect Paragraph: Edit and Proofread	W.8.5	With some guidance and support from peers and adults, develop and strengthen writing as needed by planning, revising, editing, rewriting, or trying a new approach, focusing on how well purpose and audience have been addressed.
		L.8.1	Demonstrate command of the conventions of standard English grammar and usage when writing or speaking.
		L.8.2	Demonstrate command of the conventions of standard English capitalization, punctuation, and spelling when writing.
		L.8.2.a	Use punctuation (comma, ellipsis, dash) to indicate a pause or break.
		L.8.2.c	Spell correctly.
		L.8.3	Use knowledge of language and its conventions when writing, speaking, reading, or listening.
313W	Grammar Workout: Participles as Adjectives	L.8.1	Demonstrate command of the conventions of standard English grammar and usage when writing or speaking.
		L.8.2.a	Demonstrate command of the conventions of standard English capitalization, punctuation, and spelling when writing. Use punctuation (comma, ellipsis, dash) to indicate a pause or break.
		L.8.3	Use knowledge of language and its conventions when writing, speaking, reading, or listening.
314W	Spelling Workout: Check Sound-Alike Words	L.8.1	Demonstrate command of the conventions of standard English grammar and usage when writing or speaking.
		L.8.2	Demonstrate command of the conventions of standard English capitalization, punctuation, and spelling when writing.
		L.8.2.c	Spell correctly.
		L.8.3	Use knowledge of language and its conventions when writing, speaking, reading, or listening.
315W	Mechanics Workout: Check Apostrophes in Contractions	L.8.2	Demonstrate command of the conventions of standard English capitalization, punctuation, and spelling when writing.

Common Core State Standards, continued

Project 14: Write as a Reporter

Pages	Lesson	Code	Standards Text
316W–325W	Cause-and-Effect Essay: Model Study and Writing Trait: Voice and Style	W.8.4	Produce clear and coherent writing in which the development, organization, and style are appropriate to task, purpose, and audience.
		W.8.5	With some guidance and support from peers and adults, develop and strengthen writing as needed by planning, revising, editing, rewriting, or trying a new approach, focusing on how well purpose and audience have been addressed.
326W–329W	Writing Strategy: Choose the Right Voice		Write informative/explanatory texts to examine a topic and convey ideas, concepts, and information through the selection, organization, and analysis of relevant content.
		W.8.2.d	Use precise language and domain-specific vocabulary to inform about or explain the topic.
330W–333W	Writing Strategy: Use Figurative Language	W.8.6	Use technology, including the Internet, to produce and publish writing and present the relationships between information and ideas efficiently as well as to interact and collaborate with others.
		L.8.5	Demonstrate understanding of figurative language, word relationships, and nuances in word meanings.
		L.8.5.a	Interpret figures of speech (e.g. verbal irony, puns) in context.
334W–335W	Cause-and-Effect Essay: Prewrite	W.8.4	Produce clear and coherent writing in which the development, organization, and style are appropriate to task, purpose, and audience.
		W.8.5	With some guidance and support from peers and adults, develop and strengthen writing as needed by planning, revising, editing, rewriting, or trying a new approach, focusing on how well purpose and audience have been addressed.
336W–337W	Cause-and-Effect Essay: Draft	W.8.2	Write informative/explanatory texts to examine a topic and convey ideas, concepts, and information through the selection, organization, and analysis of relevant content.
		W.8.2.a	Introduce a topic clearly, previewing what is to follow; organize ideas, concepts, and information into broader categories; include formatting (e.g., headings), graphics (e.g., charts, tables), and multimedia when useful to aiding comprehension.
		W.8.2.b	Develop the topic with relevant, well-chosen facts, definitions, concrete details, quotations, or other information and examples.

Common Core State Standards, continued

Project 14: Write as a Reporter

Pages	Lesson	Code	Standards Text
		W.8.2.c	Use appropriate and varied transitions to create cohesion and clarify the relationships among ideas and concepts.
		W.8.2.d	Use precise language and domain-specific vocabulary to inform about or explain the topic.
		W.8.2.e	Establish and maintain a formal style.
338W–339W	Cause-and-Effect Essay: Revise	W.8.2	Write informative/explanatory texts to examine a topic and convey ideas, concepts, and information through the selection, organization, and analysis of relevant content.
		W.8.2.a	Introduce a topic clearly, previewing what is to follow; organize ideas, concepts, and information into broader categories; include formatting (e.g., headings), graphics (e.g., charts, tables), and multimedia when useful to aiding comprehension.
		W.8.2.b	Develop the topic with relevant, well-chosen facts, definitions, concrete details, quotations, or other information and examples.
		W.8.2.c	Use appropriate and varied transitions to create cohesion and clarify the relationships among ideas and concepts.
		W.8.2.d	Use precise language and domain-specific vocabulary to inform about or explain the topic.
		W.8.4	Produce clear and coherent writing in which the development, organization, and style are appropriate to task, purpose, and audience.
		W.8.5	With some guidance and support from peers and adults, develop and strengthen writing as needed by planning, revising, editing, rewriting, or trying a new approach, focusing on how well purpose and audience have been addressed.
340W	Cause-and-Effect Essay: Edit and Proofread	W.8.5	With some guidance and support from peers and adults, develop and strengthen writing as needed by planning, revising, editing, rewriting, or trying a new approach, focusing on how well purpose and audience have been addressed.
		L.8.1	Demonstrate command of the conventions of standard English grammar and usage when writing or speaking.
		L.8.2	Demonstrate command of the conventions of standard English capitalization, punctuation, and spelling when writing.
		L.8.2.a	Use punctuation (comma, ellipsis, dash) to indicate a pause or break.

Common Core State Standards, continued

Project 14: Write as a Reporter

Pages	Lesson	Code	Standards Text
		L.8.2.c	Spell correctly.
		L.8.3	Use knowledge of language and its conventions when writing, speaking, reading, or listening.
341W	Grammar Workout: Participial Phrases	L.8.1	Demonstrate command of the conventions of standard English grammar and usage when writing or speaking.
		L.8.1.a	Explain the function of verbals (gerunds, participles, infinitives) in general and their function in particular sentences.
			Demonstrate command of the conventions of standard English capitalization, punctuation, and spelling when writing.
		L.8.2.a	Use punctuation (comma, ellipsis, dash) to indicate a pause or break.
		L.8.3	Use knowledge of language and its conventions when writing, speaking, reading, or listening.
342W	Spelling Workout: Check Words with Greek and Latin Roots		Demonstrate command of the conventions of standard English capitalization, punctuation, and spelling when writing.
		L.8.2.c	Spell correctly.
		L.8.3	Use knowledge of language and its conventions when writing, speaking, reading, or listening.
			Determine or clarify the meaning of unknown and multiple-meaning words or phrases based on grade 8 reading and content, choosing flexibly from a range of strategies.
		L.8.4.b	Use common, grade-appropriate Greek or Latin affixes and roots as clues to the meaning of a word (e.g., precede, recede, secede).
343W	Mechanics Workout: Check Commas	L.8.2	Demonstrate command of the conventions of standard English capitalization, punctuation, and spelling when writing.
		L.8.2.a	Use punctuation (comma, ellipsis, dash) to indicate a pause or break.
344W	Cause-and-Effect Essay: Publish, Share, and Reflect	W.8.5	With some guidance and support from peers and adults, develop and strengthen writing as needed by planning, revising, editing, rewriting, or trying a new approach, focusing on how well purpose and audience have been addressed.

Common Core State Standards, continued

Project 14: Write as a Reporter

Pages	Lesson	Code	Standards Text
		W.8.6	Use technology, including the Internet, to produce and publish writing and present the relationships between information and ideas efficiently as well as to interact and collaborate with others.
		W.8.10	Write routinely over extended time frames (time for research, reflection, and revision) and shorter time frames (a single sitting or a day or two) for a range of discipline-specific tasks, purposes, and audiences.
345W	Presentation Manual: How to Stay Focused	SL.8.1	Engage effectively in a range of collaborative discussions (one-on-one, in groups, and teacher-led) with diverse partners on grade 8 topics, texts, and issues, building on others' ideas and expressing their own clearly.
		SL.8.1.c	Pose questions that connect the ideas of several speakers and respond to others' questions and comments with relevant evidence, observations, and ideas.
		SL.8.4	Present claims and findings, emphasizing salient points in a focused, coherent manner with relevant evidence, sound valid reasoning, and well-chosen details; use appropriate eye contact, adequate volume, and clear pronunciation.
		SL.8.6	Adapt speech to a variety of contexts and tasks, demonstrating command of formal English when indicated or appropriate.

Project 15: Write as an Advocate

Pages	Lesson	Code	Standards Text
346W–351W	Public Service Announcement: Model Study and Writing Strategy: Write Effective Sentences		Write arguments to support claims with clear reasons and relevant evidence.
		W.8.1.c	Use words, phrases, and clauses to create cohesion and clarify the relationships among claim(s), counterclaims, reasons, and evidence.
		W.8.5	With some guidance and support from peers and adults, develop and strengthen writing as needed by planning, revising, editing, rewriting, or trying a new approach, focusing on how well purpose and audience have been addressed.
		W.8.10	Write routinely over extended time frames (time for research, reflection, and revision) and shorter time frames (a single sitting or a day or two) for a range of discipline-specific tasks, purposes, and audiences.

Common Core State Standards, continued

Project 15: Write as an Advocate

Pages	Lesson	Code	Standards Text
352W–353W	**Public Service Announcement: Prewrite**		Write arguments to support claims with clear reasons and relevant evidence.
		W.8.1.a	Introduce claim(s), acknowledge and distinguish the claim(s) from alternate or opposing claims, and organize the reasons and evidence logically.
		W.8.1.b	Support claim(s) with logical reasoning and relevant evidence, using accurate, credible sources and demonstrating an understanding of the topic or text.
		W.8.4	Produce clear and coherent writing in which the development, organization, and style are appropriate to task, purpose, and audience.
		W.8.5	With some guidance and support from peers and adults, develop and strengthen writing as needed by planning, revising, editing, rewriting, or trying a new approach, focusing on how well purpose and audience have been addressed.
354W–355W	**Public Service Announcement: Draft**	W.8.1	Write arguments to support claims with clear reasons and relevant evidence.
		W.8.1.a	Introduce claim(s), acknowledge and distinguish the claim(s) from alternate or opposing claims, and organize the reasons and evidence logically.
		W.8.1.b	Support claim(s) with logical reasoning and relevant evidence, using accurate, credible sources and demonstrating an understanding of the topic or text.
		W.8.1.c	Use words, phrases, and clauses to create cohesion and clarify the relationships among claim(s), counterclaims, reasons, and evidence.
		W.8.1.d	Establish and maintain a formal style.
		W.8.1.e	Provide a concluding statement or section that follows from and supports the argument presented.
		W.8.5	With some guidance and support from peers and adults, develop and strengthen writing as needed by planning, revising, editing, rewriting, or trying a new approach, focusing on how well purpose and audience have been addressed.
356W–357W	**Public Service Announcement: Revise**	W.8.1	Write arguments to support claims with clear reasons and relevant evidence.

Common Core State Standards, continued

Chapter 3 The Many Writers You Are, continued

Project 15: Write as an Advocate

Pages	Lesson	Code	Standards Text
		W.8.1.a	Introduce claim(s), acknowledge and distinguish the claim(s) from alternate or opposing claims, and organize the reasons and evidence logically.
		W.8.1.b	Support claim(s) with logical reasoning and relevant evidence, using accurate, credible sources and demonstrating an understanding of the topic or text.
		W.8.1.e	Provide a concluding statement or section that follows from and supports the argument presented.
		W.8.4	Produce clear and coherent writing in which the development, organization, and style are appropriate to task, purpose, and audience.
		W.8.5	With some guidance and support from peers and adults, develop and strengthen writing as needed by planning, revising, editing, rewriting, or trying a new approach, focusing on how well purpose and audience have been addressed.
358W	Public Service Announcement: Edit and Proofread	W.8.5	With some guidance and support from peers and adults, develop and strengthen writing as needed by planning, revising, editing, rewriting, or trying a new approach, focusing on how well purpose and audience have been addressed.
		L.8.1	Demonstrate command of the conventions of standard English grammar and usage when writing or speaking.
			Demonstrate command of the conventions of standard English capitalization, punctuation, and spelling when writing.
		L.8.2.a	Use punctuation (comma, ellipsis, dash) to indicate a pause or break.
		L.8.2.c	Spell correctly.
		L.8.3	Use knowledge of language and its conventions when writing, speaking, reading, or listening.
359W	Grammar Workout: Check Present Perfect Tense	L.8.1	Demonstrate command of the conventions of standard English grammar and usage when writing or speaking.
		L.8.3	Use knowledge of language and its conventions when writing, speaking, reading, or listening.

Common Core State Standards, continued

Common Core State Standards, continued

Project 16: Write as a Citizen

Pages	Lesson	Code	Standards Text
		W.8.7	Conduct short research projects to answer a question (including a self-generated question), drawing on several sources and generating additional related, focused questions that allow for multiple avenues of exploration.
		W.8.8	Gather relevant information from multiple print and digital sources, using search terms effectively; assess the credibility and accuracy of each source; and quote or paraphrase the data and conclusions of others while avoiding plagiarism and following a standard format for citation.
		W.8.9	Draw evidence from literary or informational texts to support analysis, reflection, and research.
372W–373W	**Writing Strategy: Use Charts, Tables, and Pictures**		Write arguments to support claims with clear reasons and relevant evidence.
		W.8.1.a	Introduce claim(s), acknowledge and distinguish the claim(s) from alternate or opposing claims, and organize the reasons and evidence logically.
		W.8.4	Produce clear and coherent writing in which the development, organization, and style are appropriate to task, purpose, and audience.
374W–375W	**Persuasive Essay: Prewrite**		Write arguments to support claims with clear reasons and relevant evidence.
		W.8.1.a	Introduce claim(s), acknowledge and distinguish the claim(s) from alternate or opposing claims, and organize the reasons and evidence logically.
			Write informative/explanatory texts to examine a topic and convey ideas, concepts, and information through the selection, organization, and analysis of relevant content.
		W.8.2.b	Develop the topic with relevant, well-chosen facts, definitions, concrete details, quotations, or other information and examples.
		W.8.4	Produce clear and coherent writing in which the development, organization, and style are appropriate to task, purpose, and audience.
		W.8.5	With some guidance and support from peers and adults, develop and strengthen writing as needed by planning, revising, editing, rewriting, or trying a new approach, focusing on how well purpose and audience have been addressed.

Common Core State Standards, continued

Project 16: Write as a Citizen

Pages	Lesson	Code	Standards Text
		W.8.6	Use technology, including the Internet, to produce and publish writing and present the relationships between information and ideas efficiently as well as to interact and collaborate with others.
		W.8.7	Conduct short research projects to answer a question (including a self-generated question), drawing on several sources and generating additional related, focused questions that allow for multiple avenues of exploration.
		W.8.8	Gather relevant information from multiple print and digital sources, using search terms effectively; assess the credibility and accuracy of each source; and quote or paraphrase the data and conclusions of others while avoiding plagiarism and following a standard format for citation.
		W.8.9	Draw evidence from literary or informational texts to support analysis, reflection, and research.
376W–377W	Persuasive Essay: Draft	W.8.1	Write arguments to support claims with clear reasons and relevant evidence.
		W.8.1.a	Introduce claim(s), acknowledge and distinguish the claim(s) from alternate or opposing claims, and organize the reasons and evidence logically.
		W.8.1.b	Support claim(s) with logical reasoning and relevant evidence, using accurate, credible sources and demonstrating an understanding of the topic or text.
		W.8.1.c	Use words, phrases, and clauses to create cohesion and clarify the relationships among claim(s), counterclaims, reasons, and evidence.
		W.8.1.d	Establish and maintain a formal style.
		W.8.1.e	Provide a concluding statement or section that follows from and supports the argument presented.
		W.8.5	With some guidance and support from peers and adults, develop and strengthen writing as needed by planning, revising, editing, rewriting, or trying a new approach, focusing on how well purpose and audience have been addressed.
		W.8.10	Write routinely over extended time frames (time for research, reflection, and revision) and shorter time frames (a single sitting or a day or two) for a range of discipline-specific tasks, purposes, and audiences.

Common Core State Standards, continued

Project 16: Write as a Citizen

Pages	Lesson	Code	Standards Text
378W–379W	**Persuasive Essay: Revise**	W.8.1	Write arguments to support claims with clear reasons and relevant evidence.
		W.8.1.a	Introduce claim(s), acknowledge and distinguish the claim(s) from alternate or opposing claims, and organize the reasons and evidence logically.
		W.8.1.b	Support claim(s) with logical reasoning and relevant evidence, using accurate, credible sources and demonstrating an understanding of the topic or text.
		W.8.1.e	Provide a concluding statement or section that follows from and supports the argument presented.
		W.8.4	Produce clear and coherent writing in which the development, organization, and style are appropriate to task, purpose, and audience.
		W.8.5	With some guidance and support from peers and adults, develop and strengthen writing as needed by planning, revising, editing, rewriting, or trying a new approach, focusing on how well purpose and audience have been addressed.
380W	**Persuasive Essay: Edit and Proofread**	W.8.5	With some guidance and support from peers and adults, develop and strengthen writing as needed by planning, revising, editing, rewriting, or trying a new approach, focusing on how well purpose and audience have been addressed.
			Demonstrate command of the conventions of standard English grammar and usage when writing or speaking.
		L.8.1.d	Recognize and correct inappropriate shifts in verb voice and mood.*
		L.8.2	Demonstrate command of the conventions of standard English capitalization, punctuation, and spelling when writing.
		L.8.2.c	Spell correctly.
		L.8.3	Use knowledge of language and its conventions when writing, speaking, reading, or listening.
381W	**Grammar Workout: Check for Consistent Verb Voice and Mood**		Demonstrate command of the conventions of standard English grammar and usage when writing or speaking.
		L.8.1.b	Form and use verbs in the active and passive voice.
		L.8.1.c	Form and use verbs in the indicative, imperative, interrogative, conditional, and subjunctive mood.

Common Core State Standards, continued

Chapter 3	The Many Writers You Are, continued

Project 16: Write as a Citizen

Pages	Lesson	Code	Standards Text
382W	Spelling Workout: Check Words with *q*, *ie*, and *ei*	L.8.2	Demonstrate command of the conventions of standard English capitalization, punctuation, and spelling when writing.
		L.8.2.c	Spell correctly.
383W	Mechanics Workout: Check Capitalization of Proper Adjectives and Academic Courses	L.8.2	Demonstrate command of the conventions of standard English capitalization, punctuation, and spelling when writing.
384W	Persuasive Essay: Publish, Share, and Reflect	W.8.5	With some guidance and support from peers and adults, develop and strengthen writing as needed by planning, revising, editing, rewriting, or trying a new approach, focusing on how well purpose and audience have been addressed.
		W.8.6	Use technology, including the Internet, to produce and publish writing and present the relationships between information and ideas efficiently as well as to interact and collaborate with others.
385W	Presentation Manual: How to Present a Persuasive Essay		Engage effectively in a range of collaborative discussions (one-on-one, in groups, and teacher-led) with diverse partners on grade 8 topics, texts, and issues, building on others' ideas and expressing their own clearly.
		SL.8.1.c	Pose questions that connect the ideas of several speakers and respond to others' questions and comments with relevant evidence, observations, and ideas.
		SL.8.3	Delineate a speaker's argument and specific claims, evaluating the soundness of the reasoning and relevance and sufficiency of the evidence and identifying when irrelevant evidence is introduced.
		SL.8.4	Present claims and findings, emphasizing salient points in a focused, coherent manner with relevant evidence, sound valid reasoning, and well-chosen details; use appropriate eye contact, adequate volume, and clear pronunciation.
		SL.8.6	Adapt speech to a variety of contexts and tasks, demonstrating command of formal English when indicated or appropriate.